OpenCable™ Architecture

Michael Adams

Cisco Systems

Cisco Press

Cisco Press
201 West 103rd Street
Indianapolis, IN 46290 USA

Michael Adams

Published by:
Cisco Press
201 West 103rd Street
Indianapolis, IN 46290 USA

Printed in the United States of America 2 3 4 5 6 7 8 9 0

Library of Congress Cataloging-in-Publication Number: 99-61715

ISBN: 1-57870-135-X

Warning and Disclaimer

This book is designed to provide information about OpenCable™ architecture. Every effort has been made to make this book as complete and as accurate as possible, but no warranty or fitness is implied.

The information is provided on an "as is" basis. The author, Cisco Press, and Cisco Systems, Inc. shall have neither liability nor responsibility to any person or entity with respect to any loss or damages arising from the information contained in this book or from the use of the discs or programs that may accompany it.

The opinions expressed in this book belong to the author and are not necessarily those of Cisco Systems, Inc.

Feedback Information

At Cisco Press, our goal is to create in-depth technical books of the highest quality and value. Each book is crafted with care and precision, undergoing rigorous development that involves the unique expertise of members from the professional technical community.

Readers' feedback is a natural continuation of this process. If you have any comments regarding how we could improve the quality of this book, or otherwise alter it to better suit your needs, you can contact us through e-mail at ciscopress@mcp.com. Please make sure to include the book title and ISBN in your message.

We greatly appreciate your assistance.

Trademark Acknowledgments

All terms mentioned in this book that are known to be trademarks or service marks have been appropriately capitalized. Cisco Press or Cisco Systems, Inc. cannot attest to the accuracy of this information. Use of a term in this book should not be regarded as affecting the validity of any trademark or service mark. OpenCable is a registered trademark of Cable Labs.

Publisher	John Wait
Executive Editor	Alicia Buckley
Cisco Systems Program Manager	Jim LeValley
Managing Editor	Patrick Kanouse
Project Manager	Kathy Trace
Project Editor	Theresa Wehrle
Copy Editor	Nancy Albright
Team Coordinator	Amy Lewis
Book Designer	Gina Rexrode
Cover Designer	Aren Howell
Compositor	Steve Gifford
Indexer	Tim Wright

CISCO SYSTEMS

CISCO PRESS

Corporate Headquarters
Cisco Systems, Inc.
170 West Tasman Drive
San Jose, CA 95134-1706
USA
http://www.cisco.com
Tel: 408 526-4000
800 553-NETS (6387)
Fax: 408 526-4100

European Headquarters
Cisco Systems Europe s.a.r.l.
Parc Evolic, Batiment L1/L2
16 Avenue du Quebec
Villebon, BP 706
91961 Courtaboeuf Cedex
France
http://www europe.cisco.com
Tel: 33 1 69 18 61 00
Fax: 33 1 69 28 83 26

American Headquarters
Cisco Systems, Inc.
170 West Tasman Drive
San Jose, CA 95134-1706
USA
http://www.cisco.com
Tel: 408 526-7660
Fax: 408 527-0883

Asian Headquarters
Nihon Cisco Systems K.K.
Fuji Building, 9th Floor
3-2-3 Marunouchi
Chiyoda-ku, Tokyo 100
Japan
http://www.cisco.com
Tel: 81 3 5219 6250
Fax: 81 3 5219 6001

Cisco Systems has more than 200 offices in the following countries. Addresses, phone numbers, and fax numbers are listed on the Cisco Connection Online Web site at http://www.cisco.com/offices.

Argentina • Australia • Austria • Belgium • Brazil • Canada • Chile • China • Colombia • Costa Rica • Croatia • Czech Republic • Denmark • Dubai, UAE Finland • France • Germany • Greece • Hong Kong • Hungary • India • Indonesia • Ireland • Israel • Italy • Japan • Korea • Luxembourg • Malaysia Mexico • The Netherlands • New Zealand • Norway • Peru • Philippines • Poland • Portugal • Puerto Rico • Romania • Russia • Saudi Arabia • Singapore Slovakia • Slovenia • South Africa • Spain • Sweden • Switzerland • Taiwan • Thailand • Turkey • Ukraine • United Kingdom • United States • Venezuela

About the Author

Michael Adams is the principal network architect for Time Warner Cable, responsible for all aspects of networking in the Pegasus Digital Program. He has served as the co-chair of the JEC Digital Standards Sub-Committee, and as chair of the Working Group 3 for the SCTE Digital Video Standards Committee. He is one of the primary architects of the OpenCable initiative, as well as the co-author of the point-of-deployment module interface (OCI-C2) specification and the primary author of the network interface (OCI-N) specification. He is a founding member of the OpenCable Technical Team.

Technical Reviewers

The technical reviewers of OpenCable Architecture are

Yvette Gordon, Vice President of Interactive Services, SeaChange

Andy Scott, Director of Engineering, National Cable Television Association

George Abe, Palomer Ventures

Joe Buehl, Principal Software Architect, Time Warner Cable

Louis Williamson, Senior Project Engineer, Time Warner Cable

Tom Lookabaugh, President, DiviCom

Charlie Kennamer, Senior Director, Engineering Services, AT&T Broadband and Internet Services

Laurie Priddy, President, National Digital Television Center; Senior Vice President, AT&T Broadband and Internet Services

Mike Hayashi, Vice President of Advanced Engineering, Time Warner Cable

Mark Eyer, Principal Staff Engineer, Sony Electonics

John Carlucci, Principal Engineer, DiviCom

Ron Boyer, Senior Project Engineer, Time Warner Cable

Luc Vantalon, Director of Digital TV, SCM Microsystems

Jim Chiddix, Chief Technical Officer, Time Warner Cable

Paul Bosco, Vice President and General Manager, Cable Products and Solutions, Wireless Products and Solutions, Cisco Systems

Dedications

To my father, Roy W. Adams, who said I would write a book someday.

Acknowledgments

Heartfelt thanks to everyone who helped to make this book a reality:

George Abe, for starting the ball rolling

Andy Scott and **Yvette Gordon**, for their excellent comments and additions to every single chapter

Louis Williamson and **Mike Hayashi**, for being wonderful cable mentors and for chapter reviews

Jim Chiddix, for support, encouragement and overall review

John Carlucci and **Tom Lookabaugh**, for unparalleled MPEG expertise

Joe Buehl, for software guidance and reviewing Part 2

Ron Boyer, for advice on the mysteries of HFC

Charlie Kennamer, for *Headend In The Sky* expertise

Laurie Priddy, for OpenCable chapter reviews

Luc Vantalon, for the point of deployment module

Mark Eyer, for writing so many DVS specifications

Paul Bosco, for overall review

Lynette Quinn, for keeping me on schedule

Kathy Trace, for being a great writing coach

Alicia Buckley, for keeping it all on track

Theresa Wehrle, for super copy editnig(sic)

Shelagh, **David**, and **Jack Adams**, for all those weekends and evenings that I disappeared into the home office.

Leslie Ellis, for collaboration on Chapter 1.

Contents at a Glance

Contents

Foreword

by Jim Chiddix, Chief Technical Officer, Time Warner Cable

For sixty years, as the television-watching public we have considered television a passive form of sit back-and-relax entertainment. We've asked the question thousands of times: "What's on?" That question is about to become a meaningless phrase. Something very big is happening. It's a culmination of sorts: past lessons; hard work on broadband plant; and the revolutionary spread of a worldwide network that, for the most part, speaks in a unified language. Suddenly, millions of homes have digital set-top boxes. Initially, these boxes used proprietary technology. But OpenCable opens a door for meshing set-top boxes into television sets, DVD players, and tightly integrated consumer devices sold at retail.

The inevitable shift from analog to digital television is a matter of critical mass. In a sense, we're at a precipice, peering into the misty invisibility of software and resultant applications that will transform television into a medium that suits our times.

As we near the end of the century, it's notable to observe how much time is a continuum of constant connectivity. Our living rooms are our offices, and our offices are our living rooms; we work not 8–5, but in bursts from waking to resting, snaring half-hour respites for pockets of leisure. Our television experience will be an extension of that continuum. With video on demand, we'll watch the television shows we want to watch, when we want to watch them. In determining a way to link the Internet resource to television, we won't necessarily log onto URLs but maybe we'll take advantage of a personalized offering that meets—even surpasses—our expectations.

This isn't the first attempt to define and create a television platform that is in sync with the future. In 1993 in Orlando, Florida, we pulled out all the stops to create a first of its kind, truly advanced broadband network. It involved a great deal of unsustainable and expensive technology, but that wasn't the point. We were fortunate enough to afford that opportunity of experimentation, partly to see what worked and what it cost, but mostly to ascertain what customers would do if they could use their televisions to interact with programs, merchants, and communications.

From those tests, we have quantifiable conjectures about what television can be to a millennium society. We have another half-decade of work behind us on making cable plants capable of digital transmissions and expanded capacity. Computing technology costs have plummeted since our FSN, and performance continues to skyrocket; set-tops today are more powerful than the highest-end FSN boxes, at a fraction of the cost.

Another part of the precipice is software. Courtesy of the Internet, a pervasive set of software and networking standards exist. Those standards are the fabric of OpenCable; their ubiquity significantly widens the pool of potential television applications developers. In Orlando, one of the real challenges we faced was the need to pay enormous sums to attract applications developers to the platform, because software had to be done in proprietary languages against a limited customer base.

That's no longer true. With the pervasiveness of MPEG video combined with the largess of OpenCable, the simple truth is that we'll be getting a lot more television. That cries of interactive navigation systems—consistently the item that tops the satisfaction list among digital cable subscribers. A good navigation system also paves the way for VOD and personalized viewing options (e-commerce and individualized advertisements are within reach, too).

All of these concepts are scrutinized in Michael's book. In our swiftly changing environment, this book is the rare example of a single text that will stand the time test for survivability. That's because this book details the OpenCable foundation, its technical underpinnings, and its commercial potential. Certainly, events will occur that extend the discussions contained in these pages. But developments are nebulous without a foundation; this is the foundation.

My endorsement of Michael and this book rests on the simple fact that he is an expert. He's been in the thick of OpenCable since its earliest days, saw us through the "first" interactive television days, and owns an equally rich understanding of set-top architecture.

Thank you, Michael, for documenting this place in the development of television.

Introduction

The cable industry is currently in the midst of a revolution. Existing systems that were engineered for broadcast television are being called upon to support a host of new applications and services. The race is on to upgrade cable systems to high-speed, two-way communications networks while continuing to support plain old television services.

A lot of consumers, industry analysts, and policy observers are asking "Where is digital TV headed?", "Is it for real?", "Will I be able to get it on cable?", and "What new services will be offered?"

These questions are difficult to answer because they are dependent on so many factors—including market forces, technical realities, investment levels, and learning curves. Nevertheless, here are some safe bets:

- **Competition**—Competition is here to stay. Analog cable systems have to add digital services to compete with direct broadcast satellite, digital terrestrial broadcasting, and even the Internet.
- **Retail Availability**—Government regulation mandates the competitive retail availability of navigation devices. The first digital cable-ready devices will start to appear on the market toward the end of 2000, soon after the July 1st FCC deadline requiring cable operators to make separable security modules available.
- **Convergence**—Convergence, which is the fusion of digital television, data communications and personal computing technologies, will fundamentally change the way we watch television, surf the Internet, and communicate with each other.

OpenCable is the cable industry's response to these market forces. OpenCable is an initiative lead by Cable Television Laboratories (CableLabs) on behalf of the cable operators. OpenCable seeks to set a common set of requirements for set-top equipment so that new suppliers from the consumer electronics and computer industries can start to build equipment for connection to cable systems. This book takes a first attempt at discussing OpenCable issues and progress.

Purpose of this Book

The OpenCable initiative started with an effort by cable operators to find alternative, lower-cost sources for digital set-top converters. The computer and consumer electronics industries have demonstrated an impressive ability to reduce the cost of almost any type of electronic equipment (PCs, laptops, CD players, televisions, VCRs, satellite receivers, DVD players, and so on). Moreover, this reduction in cost has been combined with the rapid introduction of new features and increased levels of performance. However, it quickly became apparent that the computer and consumer electronics industries need a blueprint in order to build a digital cable set-top.

OpenCable is a set of functional requirements and interface specifications that provides this blueprint. This book examines in detail the new architectures being developed by the cable industry as part of the OpenCable initiative. It also reviews the development of digital cable television systems and interactive television services because OpenCable draws on these roots.

The goals of this book are:

- To provide a comprehensive and practical overview of digital cable television systems. This book describes the headend, optical transport, distribution hub, hybrid-fiber coax, and set-top terminal equipment and how these components are interconnected. These topics include some unique aspects of cable systems that are not generally known outside of the cable industry due to their limited publication and recent development.
- To summarize the important issues in digital cable television. This book addresses the competitive, regulatory and technical challenges associated with the introduction of digital cable television services.

- To review the recent developments in interactive television, including the Time Warner Full Service Network (FSN), and to show how the concepts have evolved, since FSN's introduction in 1994, through the development of Time Warner Cable's Pegasus digital program.
- To explain the OpenCable initiative. This book covers the market forces driving the OpenCable initiative and provides a detailed technical analysis of the OpenCable Architecture.

This book is not intended to be a comprehensive engineering reference, but it does offer a roadmap to, and some interpretation of, the myriad specifications for the serious researcher into cable systems architecture.

Nor is this a book on analog cable systems. Where appropriate, I have referred the reader to specific sections of the excellent text *Modern Cable Television Technology; Video, Voice, and Data Communications,* by Ciciora, Farmer, and Large, for answers to most questions on analog cable.

In stating both positive and negative issues surrounding digital cable television (in general) and OpenCable (in particular), it is not my intention to promote or criticize any industry. During my tenure at Time Warner Cable, I have come to know and admire representatives of many companies and organizations involved in all aspects of digital television. I have always been impressed with the effort, brainpower, and public spiritedness of these professionals in business and government, who will no doubt change the way we all receive and respond to information in our homes.

Audience

This book is for the following audiences:

- Anyone who would like to learn more about digital cable systems. If you need a broad-based familiarity with the recent developments in digital television, this book provides an accessible introductory text whether you are a business development manager, industry analyst, legal counsel, or regulator.
- Engineers and technical managers who are already involved in the cable industry and would like to learn more about the digital technology that is enhancing (and, in some cases, replacing) familiar analog techniques.
- Application developers who want to deploy their skills in developing new services for digital cable systems.
- Network developers who are being called upon to build broadband networks that seamlessly interleave video, audio, and data communications techniques.

My overall goal in writing this book is to provide a networking perspective on digital cable systems. I feel it is important to give the business development, marketing, and applications development teams a good background in the network architecture that is so fundamental to digital cable systems. This fact, more than any other, has prompted me to pick up my word processor and write. I hope this book will introduce these concepts to a wider audience and act as a valuable reference to my colleagues in the cable industry.

Structure

The body of this book is divided into three main parts:

- **Part I—Digital Cable Television.** Chapter 1 presents, in high-level terms, the nature of the digital revolution and its impact on television. Chapter 2 provides a brief overview of analog cable technology and the hybrid fiber coax (HFC) upgrade path. Chapter 3 introduces the advanced analog set-top converter. Chapter 4 explains some of the key digital technologies that will be referred to in the rest of the book. Chapter 5 explains how digital television services are added to existing analog cable systems. Chapter 6 describes the hardware and software characteristics of a digital set-top. Chapter 7 contains case studies of the two predominant choices for digital broadcast systems available to North American cable operators: General Instruments DigiCable system and Scientific Atlanta's Digital Broadband Delivery System (DBDS).

- **Part II—Interactive and On-Demand Services.** Chapter 8 discusses the development of interactive services for cable systems. Chapter 10 introduces on-demand services, which provide a dedicated multimedia stream to the customer. Chapter 9 and 11 provide case studies of interactive and on-demand services respectively from the Time Warner Full Service Network and the Time Warner Pegasus program.
- **Part III—OpenCable Architecture.** Chapter 12 introduces the market drivers for OpenCable. Chapter 13 describes the OpenCable Architectural model. Chapter 14 explains the functional requirements for an OpenCable device, for example a digital set-top or a digital cable ready receiver. Chapter 15 introduces the OpenCable headend interfaces (OCI-H1, OCI-H2, and OCI-H3). Chapter 16 describes the OpenCable Network Interface (OCI-N). Chapter 17 describes the Consumer Interface (OCI-C1), which connects the OpenCable device to the consumer devices in the home. Chapter 18 describes the interface to a replaceable security module (OCI-C2).

Features and Text Conventions

The following text design and content features used in this book are intended to help understanding of the subject matter:

- Key terms are italicized the first time they are used and defined. Similarly, all abbreviations are expanded the first time they are used.
- Bullet points are used to outline the key topic areas at the start of each major section. Section subheadings use consistent terminology to ease quick reference to specific information.
- Chapter summaries placed at the end of each chapter provide a brief recapitulation of the subject matter covered in that chapter.
- References to further information are included at the end of every chapter.

Timeliness

While writing this book, I made numerous changes and additions to reflect the most recent standards developments, FCC directives, and technical innovations. In this rapidly evolving field, some changes will no doubt have occurred by the time you read this book. Nevertheless, the material contained in this book will provide you with a solid foundation for understanding the complex issues surrounding this intriguing subject.

PART I

Digital Cable Television

CHAPTER 1

Why Digital Television?

Television pictures live in an analog world—with infinite possibilities of hue and color—which is exactly what the human eye requires for a realistic and satisfying viewing experience. What's more, television as we know it is now 60 years old and enjoys nearly 100% penetration in 100 million U.S. households.

Given that, does the "if it ain't broke, don't fix it" axiom apply? Not exactly. Although the shift to digital television will require serious engineering attention and capital expenditures, the resultant product will add greatly to quality and new service opportunities. How and why did digital television evolve and what is driving digital television into our homes?

Digital Technology Evolution

Digital technology has fascinated engineers since the first digital computers were developed. It wasn't just the fascination among engineers for the next new gadget. Well, there was some of that. But, at the same time, digital techniques represented a more efficient way of doing what had already been done with vacuum tubes (or "valves"). Ultimately, transistor technology replaced vacuum tubes because the high density and low-power dissipation characteristics of semiconductor junctions were ideal for fabricating the complex digital circuits needed to build computers.

In lockstep with the rapid evolution of digital technology, engineers continued to push the envelope in applying digital technology to every conceivable problem. Consequently, the digital push has become something of a Holy Grail in engineering. In fact, there is currently so little interest in analog electronics that it is sometimes necessary to tempt analog-savvy engineers out of retirement because so few younger engineers are entering the field with any interest or experience in analog techniques.

Silicon Integration and Moore's Law

The fuel-propelling digital technology clearly came from the computer industry, which has spent the last fifty years in a race to build faster computers. In practical application, this means reducing the physical dimensions of transistor junctions as a way to increase the clock frequency of a circuit—without increasing power dissipation. The semiconductor segment leapt to action, finding ways to shrink transistor sizes so that more of them could squeeze onto the silicon die of an integrated circuit.

For example, early transistor-transistor logic (TTL) chips contained between about 30 and 100 transistors—a huge technical breakthrough at the time. TTL was quickly replaced with complementary metal-oxide semiconductor (CMOS). With the reduced power dissipation of CMOS, larger integrated circuits were built. Soon, an entire computer processor could be placed on a single chip. Enter the microprocessor.

This phenomenon gave rise to one of the most frequently cited harbingers of technological change: Moore's Law. Hardly a technical presentation goes by—regardless of industry segment—without someone mentioning Moore's Law in the context of startlingly swift technological growth.

Moore's Law stems from Intel chairman emeritus Gordon Moore, who observed that the number of transistors on a chip was doubling every 18 months. When he confirmed this trend, it was dubbed Moore's Law, an axiom that continues with no end in sight until perhaps 2030. (For more information on Moore's Law, see http://www.intel.com/pressroom/kits/bios/moore.htm.) Millions of transistors are now routinely placed on a silicon die, and many chips are now I/O-limited, which means that the cost of the chip has more to do with the number of leads and the packaging cost than the number of transistors it contains.

Very large scale integration (VLSI) encourages the designer to place as many functions as possible on a single chip. The ultimate goal: a single chip that performs all the functions of a product (whether it is a television receiver, a set-top, or a personal computer). Because it is tricky to mix analog and digital functions on a chip, it makes sense to do all possible functions in the digital domain. For example, relatively complicated digital circuits are replacing even trivial analog functions, such as audio mixing.

Analog-to-Digital Conversion

When it was realized (in the 1970s) that almost all analog processing could be done with more precision and much greater flexibility in the digital domain, the race was on to shift more analog functions to digital.

The first step in this process is called *analog-to-digital (A/D) conversion*. The analog signal is sampled (measured in time close enough together to adequately represent the analog signal) and its instantaneous value is represented as a binary value. After A/D conversion, most analog signal processing can be done in the digital domain. This technique is known as *digital signal processing (DSP)*. After signal processing, a process known as *digital-to-analog (D/A) conversion* reconstructs the (modified) analog signal.

Early DSP applications had an analog input and an analog output, but soon the digital representation became the reference signal that was stored or transmitted. An early user of these techniques was the music industry, which embraced digital techniques so roundly, it is nearly impossible to purchase cassette tapes and vinyl records today. Their successor, the compact disc, was introduced in the 1980s and harnessed Moore's Law as a way to dramatically improve sound quality and the amount of music stored per CD (relative to analog predecessors).

By the 1990s, digital techniques had evolved (thanks in part to Moore's law) to tackle the hundredfold increase in bandwidth of video (compared to audio).

A/D conversion and DSP are now cost-effective tools for television services and have found their way into most of the technologies described in Chapter 4, "Digital Technologies." This trend shows no sign of slowing down and continues to drive the migration to digital television.

Convergence with the Personal Computer

Moore's Law also made the development of personal computers (PCs) practical. Early PCs were very limited in performance and memory—remember when 4 MB of RAM was a big deal? But reductions in price and quantum leaps in performance combined to create a multibillion dollar industry around the PC. Standalone PCs remain somewhat limited in what they can do; all applications must be loaded from stored media, and it is still somewhat slow and cumbersome to share data with other PC users. Still, PC networking is transforming the PC; it is now possible to pipe in applications and data from the Internet and to use the PC as a communications tool. The development of standard protocols to support World Wide Web services also introduced a new mode for research and entertainment.

PCs are now powerful enough to perform sophisticated multimedia processing (using digital signal processing). Suddenly, *convergence* has reemerged as a buzzword to describe the personal computer as the focus of entertainment, computing, and communications services in the home.

In the home, the notion of convergence will also create a *divergence* of in-home electronics, where the swift impact of Moore's Law creates customized, inexpensive chip-sets that can be installed in many communications and entertainment gadgets. The cable modem gained wide U.S. acceptance in 1999; industry analysis firm Paul Kagan Associates (PKA) anticipates that 1.6 million cable subscribers will use a cable modem, at $40 per month, to link to the Internet at high speed (27 Mbps shared over a node versus 56 Kbps via dial-up). That figure could leap to 20 million subscribers by 2005, according to PKA (including other broadband connectivity devices, such as DSL and wireless modems).

By the end of 2000, as many as three million advanced digital set-tops (that include a cable modem) will populate U.S. homes. Add to that DVD players, personal organizers, and boxes such as those made by TiVo and Replay that enable truly on-demand television viewing.

Convergence has many faces, but it is really just the parallel application of evolving digital technologies across different fields. The technology of the Internet and the World Wide Web are already finding their way into advanced analog set-top converters (see Chapter 3, "The

Analog Set-Top Converter"). This means that services previously experienced only with a PC can now be experienced on the family television (with a wireless keyboard). This trend will continue at a faster pace and is certainly helping to drive us into a digital world, although it has yet to be seen which platform will be dominant in the home.

Internet Convergence

Over a ten-month period—since I began the research for this book—the Internet gestated from a powerful communications tool looking for a way to grow up to a multibillion dollar industry. The Internet has become a useful means for such tools as e-mail and research/fact-finding, which is now an inexorable part of the lives of nearly 50 million users.

It also stands to lighten the wallets of U.S. consumers by billions of dollars over the coming years, through electronic commerce—a phenomenon that saw early adopter usage during the Christmas 1998 season, but will almost certainly attract the masses going forward. This is largely because the Internet uses a technological language, known as Internet Protocol (IP), that will undoubtedly be the fulcrum that pries open a cornucopia of advanced broadband services.

This isn't tomfoolery, and its impact on digital video applications is dramatic. The belief in heady revenues from providing Web-based entertainment services led to the concept of an Internet-based entertainment device, such as Microsoft's WebTV, which surpassed the one million–user mark in 1999. OpenCable boxes will be similarly outfitted to deliver Web-based information, interactivity, and e-commerce to cable subscribers. If the trend line toward a "free" Internet continues, service providers will be all the more inclined to seek revenue sources, such as e-commerce and advertising, outside of subscription fees.

Obviously the Internet and the World Wide Web are cool showcases for the potential for digital entertainment services, and it would be foolish to ignore them. Very foolish! Building television systems with digital technology is a smart investment decision considering this potential. Of course, building digital into television is just one piece of the puzzle. Service providers also need to link their digital products and services into existing—and new—back-office systems, such as provisioning and customer service. Again, many of these solutions exist for the PC-oriented Internet. Just as it was clever to repurpose existing digital techniques for use in television, another smart investment is to identify, repurpose, and use the many back-end Internet software management packages for content management, network management, and so on.

New Services

The gradual process of blending entertainment with communications has already started and will continue; Internet sites will continue folding in digital video clips, and broadcast and cable providers will continue folding in Internet content to their programs. When you click on an Internet site and browse from business news to people news to movie clips, you are experiencing this today. New services will take further steps in this direction and will use a combination of digital television technology with enhancements based on high-speed communications technologies that use the increased bandwidth of cable systems.

It is possible to enhance analog television services; a small handful of interactive television players has been pursuing the category since the mid-1990s. So far, the techniques have seen little endorsement, mostly because the services are somewhat awkward to use and limited in scope. The possibilities for enhancing digital television are much greater, and there is a cleaner integration path because everything is in the digital domain. Examples are interactive services (see Chapter 8, "Interactive Services") and on-demand services (see Chapter 10, "On-Demand Services").

New Business Models

New services enable new business models; there are many new business models that are currently being tested, such as

- Video-on-demand (VOD)—The first VOD business model was published last year (www.schange.com). The reduction in media server cost combined with the development of software to support VOD services has triggered the deployment of commercial VOD systems.
- Linked advertising—Linked advertising gives customers the ability to customize how they receive advertisements over television. For example, they can skip them altogether (perhaps for a fee—we'll see how that model evolves!), request more information (such as a coupon), or specify areas for which they would like to see ads (cars, household products, financial, and so on).
- Linked merchandising—This model lets customers buy products that are shown in a program (for example, the hero's leather jacket or the heroine's little black dress) and provides discounts for services with the purchase of entertainment services (for example, a discount pizza with a movie purchase).
- Linked communications—Examples include linking a chat session to a live television broadcast, allowing the customer to play along with a television game show, and so on.

Of course, nobody knows whether these or other business models will unlock new revenue streams. A persistent sociological argument exists throughout the category about whether people want to *lean back* and let television entertain them, or whether most people prefer to do heavy interactivity on their *lean-forward* PC. There are also issues around family viewing—will Mom and Dad sit by patiently while the kids click off to who-knows-where during a television broadcast? and vice versa?

Nonetheless, most of these models are enabled by the evolution to digital television. Moreover, a software-based approach can be flexible enough to support these and many other potential business models. In other words, software applications can be developed and deployed independently of the hardware infrastructure, allowing many incremental business opportunities.

Advantages of Digital Television

Digital technology brings a number of concrete advantages when applied to television services. The most important of these are

- Channel expansion—Digital compression allows the cable operator to expand the number of channel offerings by a factor of 10.
- On-demand services—Digital compression also provides bandwidth economies that make video-on-demand commercially viable.
- Quality—Although there is a carefully controlled *loss* of quality inherent in the digital compression process, further transmission losses in quality due to noise and distortion can be eliminated in a well-designed digital system.
- Security—Digital scrambling, or *encryption*, provides a very secure means to enforce conditional access (where only people who pay for the service get the service) with no loss of quality.
- Flexibility—Digital compression formats can be changed instantaneously to suit the program material, which means that multiple video and audio streams are supported.
- Data transmission—Digital transmission systems are agnostic about the nature of the payload they carry and, as such, contain a multiplex of video, audio, and data. This allows the transmission of any kind of data, which may be used for program enhancement, program downloading, Web-casting, and many other applications.

Channel Expansion

Channel expansion adds more programming choices to a service tier. Channel expansion is not a new concept, but cable operators, terrestrial broadcasters, and satellite operators were historically limited by spectrum availability. For many years, cable operators expanded their channel offerings by upgrading their systems to carry more and more analog channels. Meanwhile, terrestrial broadcasters were confined to channels allocated by the FCC. Satellite operators added more channel capacity by launching more satellites—at considerable expense.

Digital compression allows approximately a 10:1 expansion in the number of channels for a given amount of spectrum. In fact, it was the development of digital compression techniques that made direct satellite broadcasting an economically palatable proposition, giving rise to such companies as DirecTV and EchoStar.

On-Demand Services

Digital compression is an essential element of on-demand services because it reduces the bandwidth occupied by each channel by a factor of 10. On-demand services allocate a dedicated digital program stream (or channel) to each active user. Chapter 11, "On-Demand Cable System Case Studies," discusses on-demand services in detail.

Quality

It is difficult to maintain the quality of an analog television picture from its origination at the television camera until its final appearance at the television receiver. Each time it is amplified, copied, or transmitted, noise and distortion creep into the signal. In the studio, these effects can be minimized by the careful use of high-quality equipment. However, the path to the customer's home is more difficult to maintain. As a result, some noise and distortion mar most analog television pictures, in the form of *snowy* and *ghosted* images.

Analog-to-digital conversion transforms the analog signal from the television camera into a digital stream—before noise and distortion have a chance to impair the signal. After the signal is digitized, it can be copied perfectly as many times as required. Assuming the cable system is properly maintained, only noise and distortion between the D/A converter and the display itself can degrade the picture. As a result, digital television pictures are almost completely free of noise and distortion. (See Chapter 4 for a discussion of some of the potential drawbacks of digital compression.)

Security

To collect payment for premium television services—the most common examples are HBO and Showtime—it is necessary to prevent unauthorized viewers from watching the programs. In analog television, scrambling is used, but this analog transformation of the signal introduces distortion. It is also relatively easy to defeat analog scrambling (see Chapter 3). In 1999, the cable industry could lose more than $5 billion to unauthorized access of premium cable signals.

A digital stream, by contrast, is a string of ones and zeros. As such, the science of cryptography can be applied to encrypt the bit stream into literally trillions of different permutations. Without the correct *key*, deciphering the encrypted stream is like searching for a needle in a haystack the size of New York. With the correct key, however, the original bit stream can be recovered with perfect accuracy and no loss in quality is incurred.

Flexibility

Digital techniques are very flexible, in part because they decouple the encoding process from the transmission process. The encoding process can be changed to sample the picture with higher resolution or with a faster refresh rate, and the only impact is a change in the bit rate of the digital stream. The transmission process accepts any digital stream as long as the bit rate does not exceed the transmission rate. Thus, it is possible to send 4 video streams and 19 audio streams, if that is desired, as long as there is adequate transmission capacity. If a very high-quality video stream is required, it can be designed to fill almost the entire transmission payload. In fact, that is the basis for high definition television.

Data Transmission

The transmission process used for digital television is completely agnostic of the payload. The bits might be used to send video, audio, or data with equal ease. Thus, it is possible to add data to a television program. (This is also possible with analog television using the vertical blanking interval [VBI] lines, but the data is sent as a series of white or black dots and the payload is limited to about 19 Kbps on each VBI line.) Using digital transmission techniques, much higher data rates are possible, in the order of megabits per second.

Summary

This chapter presented a brief overview of some of the history and technical advantages that favor the transition of television from analog to digital. The concrete advantages of digital technology are

- Channel expansion
- On-demand services
- Quality
- Security
- Flexibility
- Data transmission

However, there are other, less measurable, aspects of digital television that include

- Industry trends toward a digital approach based on very large scale integration of silicon chips and digital signal processing
- Convergence with the computer and communications industries and the influence of the Internet and the World Wide Web
- Potential new service and revenue opportunities that are enabled by digital technology

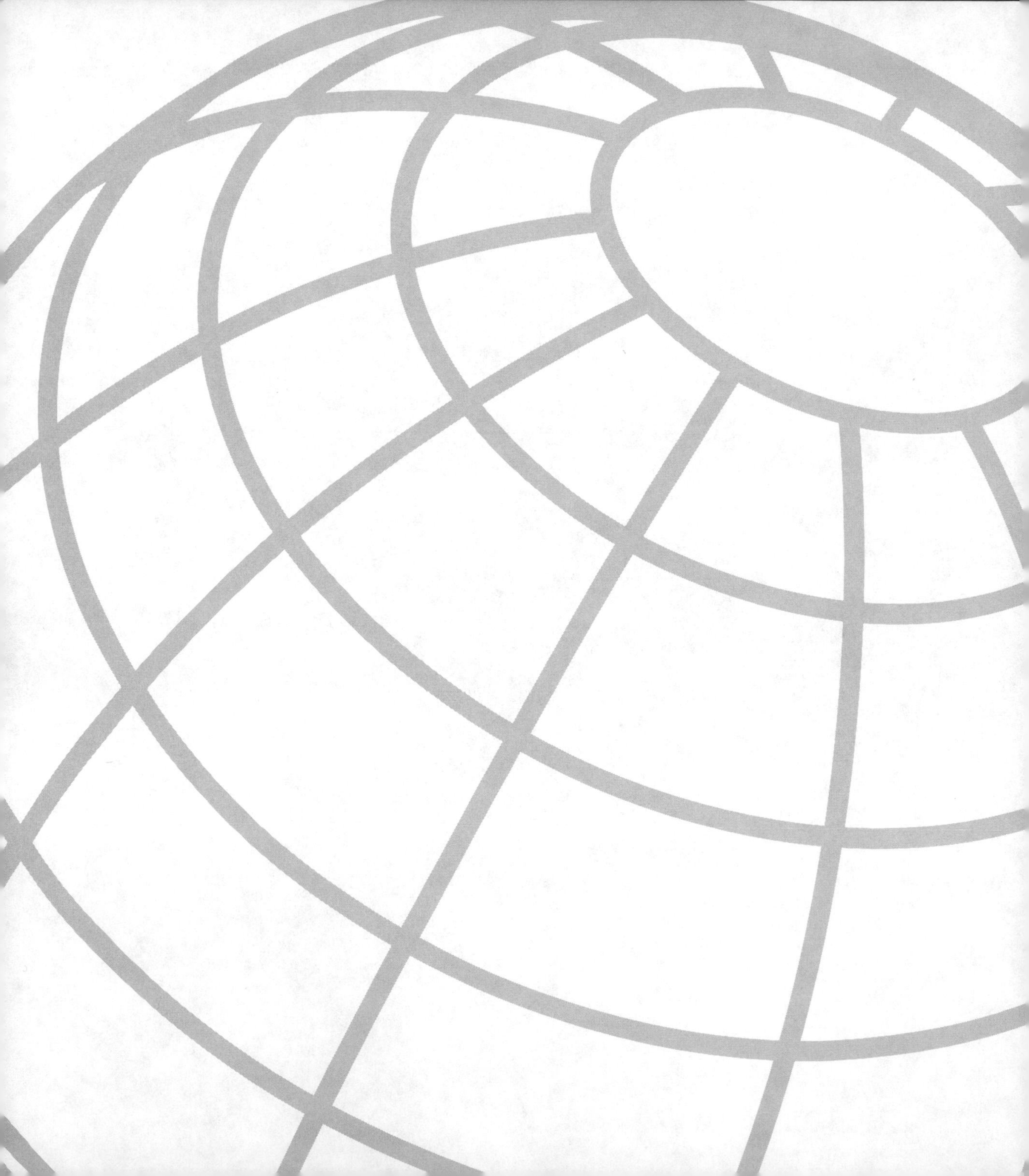

CHAPTER 2

Analog Cable Technologies

Cable systems have evolved rapidly since 1990 through the use of fiber-optic technology. Until this time, cable systems were designed to support broadcast of the same channel lineup throughout the cable system and suffered from limitations in frequency range and signal quality. With the introduction of fiber optics into cable distribution networks, the characteristics of the cable system are changed dramatically:

- The frequency range is increased to 870 MHz (or higher), expanding the analog channel lineup and creating an additional spectrum for digital channels.
- The signal quality is greatly improved by reducing RF amplifier cascades, minimizing noise and distortion.
- The cable system is effectively segmented into many parallel distribution networks. Although the broadcast signals are split and fed into every distribution network, the segmentation enables narrowcast services, such as multiple commercial insertion zones and video-on-demand.
- The cable system is much more reliable and easier to maintain because it incorporates physical link redundancy and because of the smaller serving area of the node.

There are many excellent references that describe the coaxial and fiber-optic technologies in detail (see *Modern Cable Television Technology; Video, Voice, and Data Communications* by Walter Ciciora and others); this chapter briefly addresses the implications for network architecture of these technologies.

Analog Channel Expansion

Fiber-optic distribution allows the cable operator to expand the analog channel lineup and to create an additional spectrum for digital channels, allowing a gradual migration from analog to digital services. This provides advantages to both the cable operator and the customer:

- Analog revenues continue to fund the core business of the cable television industry during the migration to digital services.
- Customers can still use their existing television receivers. Practically all television receivers available in the retail market support *only* the NTSC analog standard, and these receivers have a long projected life expectancy of 10 to 15 years.

- Multiple television receivers can be supported at no extra cost to the customer for unscrambled analog services. Additional televisions do not require a set-top converter to receive *basic* (or unscrambled) analog services.
- Cable operators can continue to provide analog cable services well into the twenty-first century, well beyond the proposed sunset date of 2007 for analog terrestrial broadcast.

The primary reason for a plant upgrade is to improve signal quality and to reduce system outages. However, an important requirement for any upgrade of the cable distribution network is to support and expand analog services. With this in mind, how can the upgrade also move the cable industry forward toward the deployment of advanced services, such as digital broadcast, interactive services, and on-demand services?

The Hybrid Fiber Coax Upgrade

The upgrade path for nearly all cable operators is based on hybrid fiber coax (HFC) architecture. The HFC architecture is attractive to the cable operator because it improves the analog performance of the cable plant, increases the number of channels, and provides a migration path toward the support of digital services. The HFC upgrade also makes the cable system easier to maintain and reduces system outages, improving overall service to the customer.

Figure 2-1 shows part of a cable distribution network before the fiber upgrade. The trunk amplifiers are optimized to compensate for the signal loss introduced by coaxial cable over the considerable distance from the headend to the furthest customers, with the lowest possible distortion and noise. Even so, the cascade of 24 or more trunk amplifiers required to reach the serving area introduces significant distortion and noise.

The trunk fans out at convenient geographical points in the network to form a tree-and-branch structure. Figure 2-1 shows one such branch point, where a passive device (such as a splitter or a directional coupler) directs the signal to feed additional trunks. In this way, the trunk fans out to feed many thousands of homes from the single cable that leaves the headend. However, the branching trunk cable makes up only about 12% of the total cable length in a typical cable system; the role of the trunk is to feed the *serving areas*, which contain the other 88% of the cable length.

Figure 2-1 *Coaxial Cable Distribution Network*

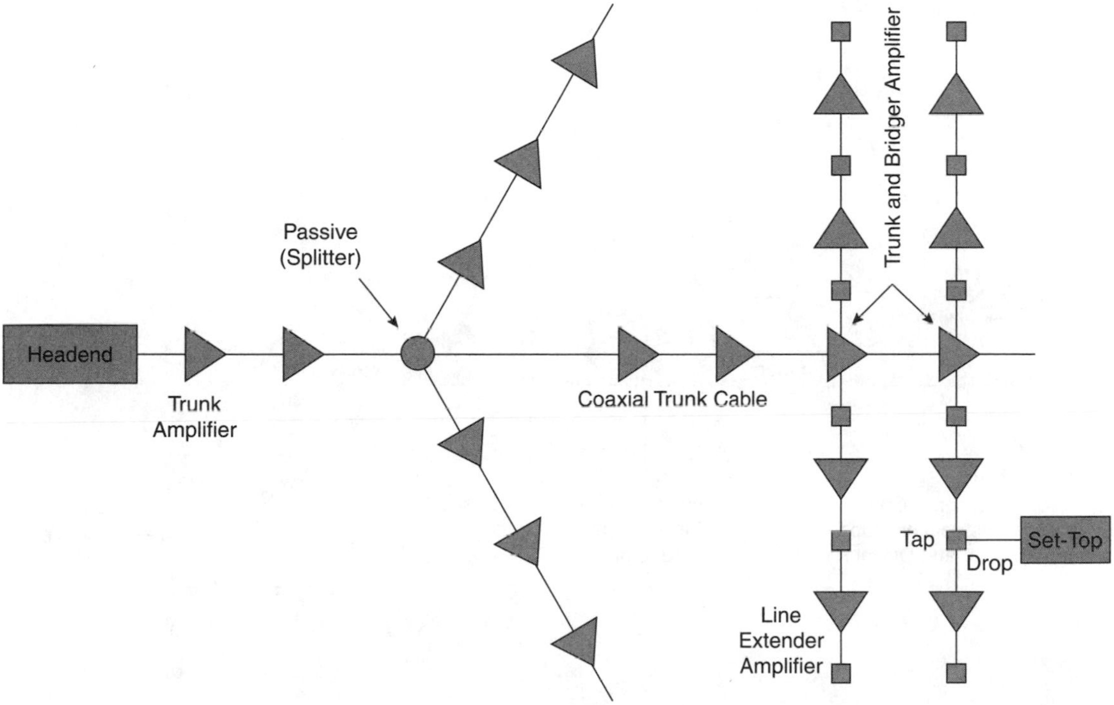

At the serving area, the distribution network fans out rapidly from the trunk by means of bridger amplifiers and line extender amplifiers to the customer homes. This final section of the distribution network is commonly known as the *last mile* because it is usually within one mile of the customer. Finally, a portion of the signal is coupled to a *drop cable* at the *tap*. The drop cable runs from the tap to the set-top in the customer's home.

In Figure 2-2, the cascade of trunk amplifiers is replaced by a fiber-optic link. The RF signal modulates the optical signal at the headend and is detected and converted back to RF at the fiber node. (In many systems, the signal is boosted at the distribution hub using optical amplification, or by conversion to an RF signal followed by conversion back to an optical signal.)

Figure 2-2 *HFC Distribution Network*

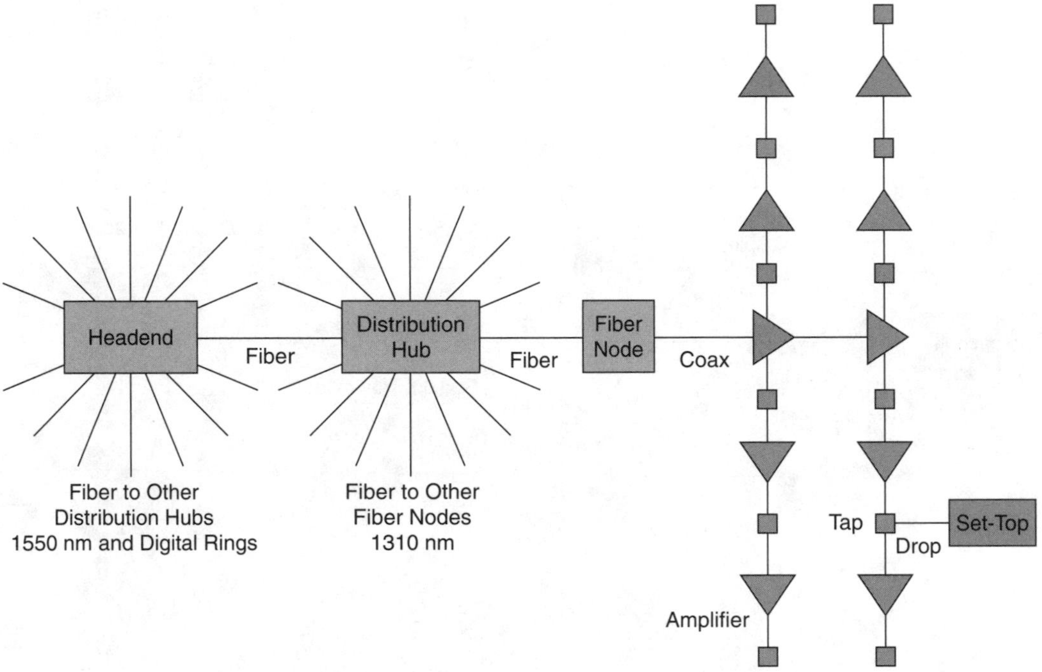

The performance of the optical link is superior to that of the coaxial link because of the reduction of amplifier actives and the isolation of system outages. The service and signal quality to the customer is improved. More importantly, the distribution network is segmented into a large number of parallel distribution networks, allowing the reuse of the RF spectrum (narrowcasting).

HFC Topology

Most hybrid fiber coaxial networks are based on the three-level hierarchy shown in Figure 2-3, which includes a headend (origination of content), a distribution hub (typically 20,000 homes passed), and a fiber node (typically 500 homes passed). The fiber node converts the optical signal into RF for the last mile distribution to the set-top. Fiber nodes are usually connected to a distribution hub in a star network to reduce cost. A star network is acceptable because a fiber cut affects only one fiber node and a very limited number of customers.

Figure 2-3 *HFC Topology*

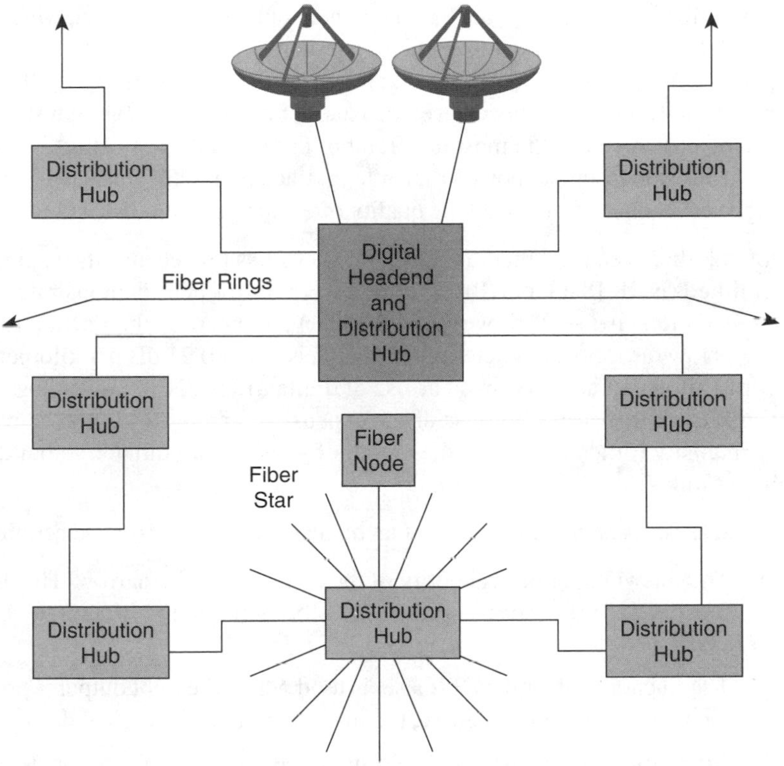

The distribution hub is a different matter entirely—it supplies a large number of fiber nodes, and the consequences of a loss of signal are far greater. Distribution hubs are usually fed by two fiber spans that are *diverse-routed*—that is, they take a different physical route. A convenient way to achieve diverse-routing is by means of a ring structure (see Figure 2-3). Typically, four to six distribution hubs are placed on a ring. A distribution hub might feed a very large number of fiber nodes, depending mainly on the customer density; 40 is an average number of fiber nodes per distribution hub.

At the top level of the hierarchy is the headend. Headend facilities are similar in many ways to distribution hubs, but the headend also is a satellite receiver site. In most cases, the headend site also serves as a distribution hub for the fiber nodes closest to the headend.

Linear Optical Transmission

Hybrid fiber coax networks are based on linear optical transmission, which uses *amplitude modulation* of an optical carrier. This is in contrast to digital (on-off) modulation of an optical carrier, as specified in the Synchronous Optical Network (SONET) standard. Linear optical transmission has been developed and refined by the cable industry to meet its specific requirements; the most important of these is reducing distortion and noise while increasing optical output power. Linear long-reach optics allow the cable industry to reduce amplifier cascades, improving the quality of existing analog distribution systems.

Optical fiber is an ideal medium for cable transmission because its bandwidth is virtually unlimited (NHK [the Japan Broadcasting Corporation] has demonstrated transmission at 3,000 *gigabits* per second over a single fiber) and because the attenuation of light in a fiber is low (at 1550 nanometers, attenuation is about 0.25 dB per kilometer and it is 0.34 dB per kilometer at 1310 nm). The use of digital transmission in analog cable systems is prohibitively expensive because of the expense of analog-to-digital conversion. Instead, the intensity (or amplitude) of the output of a laser is modulated to build an end-to-end analog link.

For successful analog modulation of an optical carrier, it must have certain characteristics:

- The linewidth, or optical purity of the carrier, must be narrow. The distributed feedback (DFB) laser incorporates a diffraction grating to limit the oscillation to a single wavelength.
- The linear region of the DFB laser is used where the light output is proportional to the modulation current. Likewise, the linear region of the optical detector must be used.
- Noise sources must be kept to a minimum at the laser and at the detector.

For these reasons, adjustment of analog-modulated optical links is more complicated than their digitally modulated counterparts. Furthermore, degradation of an analog link is more visible than that of a digital link. Nevertheless, the cable industry has deployed HFC upgrades widely with excellent results [Chiddix].

Return Path Activation

Two-way operation of the cable system plant is essential to support advanced services, such as impulse pay-per-view, interactive, on-demand, and cable modem. Although activation of the return path is possible in a coaxial-only cable system, the HFC upgrade makes it much more practical because it segments the system into small groups of homes passed.

In the coaxial portion of the network, the signal is amplified in both the forward (toward the customer) and reverse directions. This is achieved over a single cable by partitioning based on frequency spectrum. In the forward direction, frequencies from 54 to 870 MHz are amplified, and a high-pass filter attenuates frequencies below 54 MHz. In the reverse direction, frequencies from 5 to 40 MHz are amplified, and a low-pass filter attenuates frequencies above 40 MHz. The combination of a high-pass filter in the forward direction and a low-pass filter in the reverse direction is called a *diplex filter*.

In the reverse direction, the coaxial system is just like a giant antenna that aggregates the signal from every customer (see Figure 2-4). Unfortunately, this arrangement also aggregates *noise* and *ingress* signals—noise that is generated in the return amplifiers and ingress that is picked up due to problems, such as loose connectors or perhaps poorly shielded equipment connected to the cable in the home. If the return signals from too many homes are aggregated, the noise and ingress will swamp the desired signal from the set-top or cable modem. HFC divides the coaxial system into small groups of about 500 homes passed and limits the amount of noise and ingress aggregation.

Figure 2-4 *Noise Funneling*

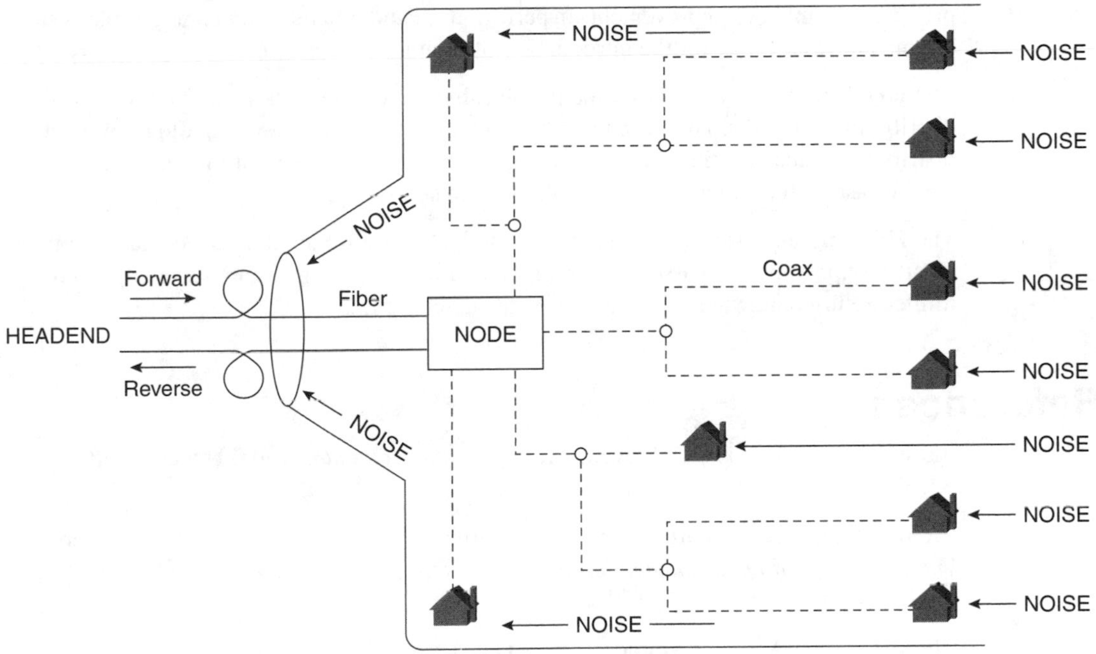

Another factor is the relatively small amount of usable bandwidth in the reverse direction. The frequency range is limited from between about 5 MHz to 40 MHz, which limits the number of return carriers that can be allocated. To make matters worse, certain portions of the spectrum might be unusable because of strong radio interference pickup from citizen's band radios and other EMI sources that operate and radiate in the return frequency band. Fortunately, the return bandwidth required by 500 homes passed is relatively small and can be accommodated in the remaining part of the return spectrum.

At the fiber node, the return signal modulates a return laser, and a separate fiber is used to carry the signal back to the distribution hub. At the distribution hub, the return signal is converted back into an RF signal and fed to a demodulator. The demodulator converts the signal back into the digital bit-stream that was transmitted by the set-top or cable modem. Often, a digital fiber-optic transmission system provides the final leg of the return system path from the distribution hub to the headend (see Chapter 5, "Adding Digital Television Services to Cable Systems").

Summary

This chapter provided a brief overview of analog cable technology and the hybrid fiber coax upgrade path that has been adopted by cable operators. The HFC architecture not only provides a number of improvements in performance and reliability for analog cable systems but also paves the way for the introduction of digital services.

The HFC upgrade effectively segments the cable system into a large number of parallel distribution networks. This architecture is supported by a three-level topology of headend, distribution hubs, and fiber nodes. The segmentation of the distribution network enables narrowcasting for on-demand and cable modem services.

The HFC upgrade also enables return path activation by subdividing the cable system into small groups of homes passed. The problems of noise and ingress are reduced, and the limited return bandwidth is reused by each subnetwork.

References

Baldwin, Thomas F. and D. Stevens McVoy. *Cable Communication*. Upper-Saddle River, NJ: Prentice-Hall, 1983.

Ciciora, Walter, James Farmer, and David Large. *Modern Cable Television Technology; Video, Voice, and Data Communications*. San Francisco, CA: Morgan Kaufmann Publishers, Inc., 1999.

Chiddix, James A. "Time Warner Cable's Development of Broadband Optical Fiber Technology for the Cable Television/Telecommunications Industry." Time Warner Cable. October 4, 1994 (see technical papers at http://www.pathfinder.com/corp/twcable/).

CHAPTER 3

The Analog Set-Top Converter

The set-top converter is probably the most talked-about element in the cable system, and it is where a great deal of the capital budget is spent. The set-top converter is variously hated, tolerated, and accepted by cable customers. It has been the focus of much cable legislation and regulation.

Initially, set-top converters were deployed to give access to more channels because early televisions couldn't tune most of the frequencies used by cable systems. The set-top converter also gave the subscriber desirable features, such as remote control, volume control, and channel number display. These were appreciated by customers until cable ready televisions made these features redundant and set-top converters began to get in the way of features on the cable ready television. The set-top converter continues to play a role in giving the subscriber new features and services; for example, the advanced analog set-top converter introduces program guides, digital music, and VCR commanders. These features increase customer acceptance of set-top converters even though they might interfere with some of the features of cable ready television (for example, picture-in-picture).

As the number of channels increased and pay channels appeared, access control became more important. Cable systems introduced *traps* (filters), or *interdiction* (jamming) to deny access to premium services. (For more information on program denial techniques in analog cable systems, see *Modern Cable Television Technology; Video, Voice, and Data Communications* by Walter Ciciora and others.) In cable systems that use traps or interdiction, customers do not require a set-top converter if they have a cable ready television. Other cable customers purchase only basic services and do not require a set-top converter.

Nonetheless, most cable customers in North America are familiar with a set-top converter that is leased to them by their cable operator. Analog scrambling has been widely deployed by cable systems because traps are too easy to defeat and interdiction is extremely expensive. In cable systems that use analog scrambling, a set-top converter provides the only alternative to access pay services.

Analog set-top converters have evolved considerably over the past 20 years and can be divided into four major categories:

- *Basic set-top converters* that perform only a tuning function—Basic set-tops are almost obsolete because nearly all television receivers are now *cable ready* (that is, they have an F-connector input and can tune according to the cable frequency plan).

- *De-scrambling set-top converters* that perform tuning and conditional access functions—The authorized services enabled for the set-top must be programmed into it before it is installed in the customer's home.
- *Addressable set-top converters* that perform tuning and conditional access functions—The authorized services enabled for a particular set-top are controlled remotely, from the headend, by sending messages that are addressed to the set-top (and that set-top alone).
- *Advanced analog set-top converters,* which are addressable set-tops that support additional features, such as an on-screen display (OSD), an electronic program guide (EPG), and impulse pay-per-view (IPPV).

Since 1995, advanced analog set-top converters have been replacing other set-top types in many cable systems. Therefore, this chapter focuses on the advanced analog set-top converter.

Figure 3-1 shows the block diagram of a typical advanced analog set-top. Although there are a number of different implementation approaches, this block diagram describes most advanced analog set-tops. Optional blocks are shown using broken lines.

Figure 3-1 *Block Diagram for a Typical Advanced Analog Set-Top*

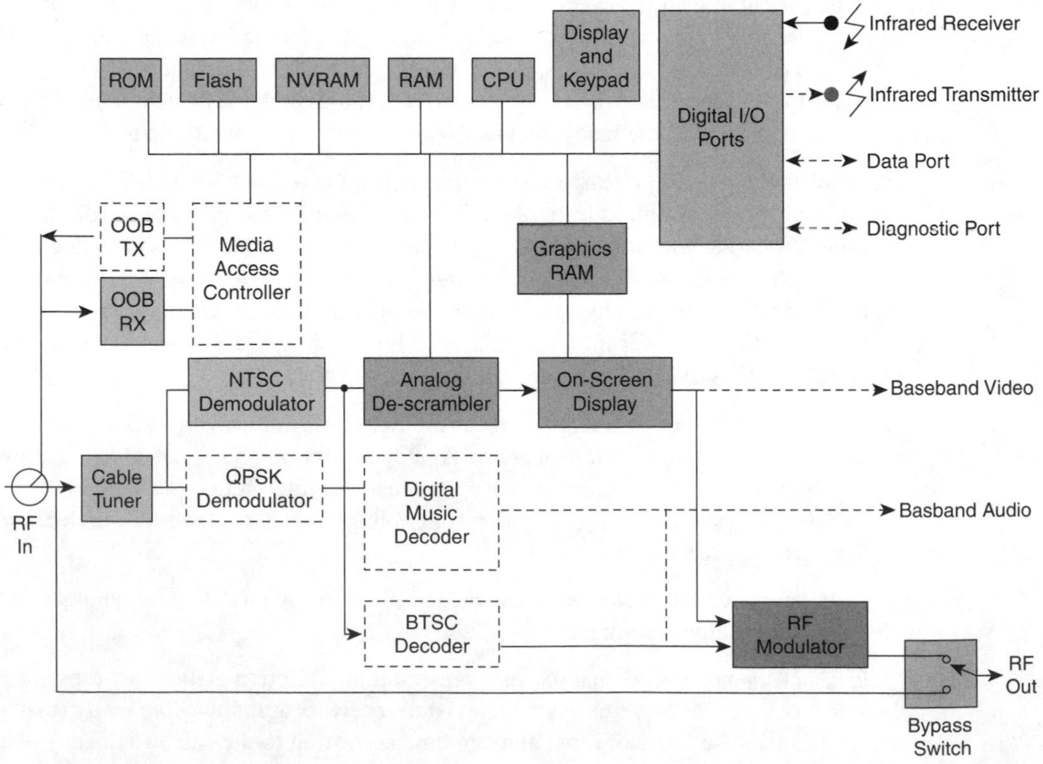

The next sections consider Figure 3-1 in detail after breaking it down into its major subsystems:

- Cable network interface—This subsystem is the interface between the cable system and the set-top. This interface includes the cable tuner and, optionally, an out-of-band (OOB) receiver, an OOB transmitter, a Media Access Controller (MAC), and a VBI decoder.
- Conditional access system—This subsystem provides the means by which access to specific services is granted to the user, based on payment for those services. In analog set-tops, a video de-scrambling circuit performs this function. (Some manufacturers also use some form of audio scrambling.)
- On-screen display (OSD)—Visual information is presented to the user by means of an OSD, which overlays text and graphics onto the video output.
- Audio processing—Most set-tops include a remote volume control and, occasionally, other audio processing options are offered to the customer, such as Broadcast Television System Committee (BTSC) stereo decoding or digital music decoding.
- Microprocessor subsystem—This subsystem is the brains of the set-top and includes a microprocessor with ROM, Flash, NVRAM, RAM, an LED display, and a keypad.
- Inputs—All set-tops have a coaxial F-connector input. In addition, user control signals are received via an infrared receiver from a remote control. Other inputs might include a data port and a diagnostic port.
- Outputs—All set-tops have an F-connector output for a National Television Systems Committee (NTSC) channel modulated at broadcast channel 3 or channel 4. (Other channels are available as well.) In addition, the set-top could have *baseband* (or *composite*) video and baseband audio outputs.
- Infrared transmitter—Set-tops can include an infrared transmitter to control a VCR.
- Remote control—Advanced analog set-tops are usually supplied with a remote control (not shown in Figure 3-1).

The Cable Network Interface

The cable network interface is shown in Figure 3-2. It is completely specified for clear (unscrambled) video, but most of the cable network interface is proprietary and varies from one set-top model to another.

Figure 3-2 *Cable Network Interface*

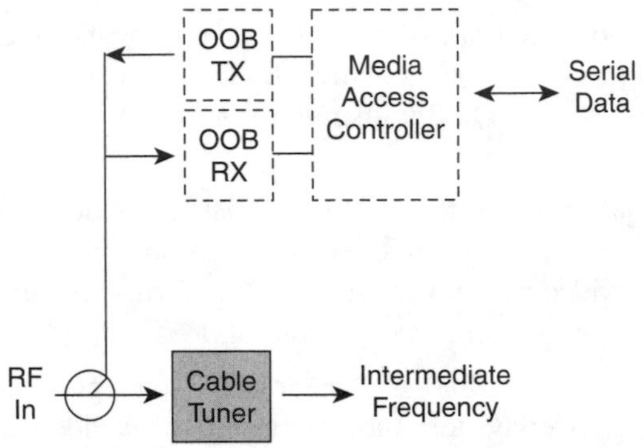

The standard aspects are

- The cable frequency plan, specified by the Electronic Industry Association (EIA) standard EIA-542 "Cable Television Channel Identification Plan" (see Chapter 8 of *Modern Cable Television Technology; Video, Voice, and Data Communications* by Walter Ciciora and others).
- The video and audio channel format, specified by the National Television Systems Committee (NTSC) specification, which includes extensions for color.
- Stereo and Secondary Audio Program (SAP) encoding, specified by the BTSC standard.

The proprietary aspects of the cable network interface are

- The video de-scrambling system—Not only is this different from one vendor's system to another, but a single vendor might have a number of different scrambling systems.
- The out-of-band signaling system—Each vendor's system is proprietary, and there is only limited compatibility across the different set-top models within a vendor's product range.

The proprietary aspects of the analog cable network interface present some difficult problems for the cable operator. After an operator has selected a set-top, that set-top effectively dictates the specification of the cable network interface. The operator is locked in to that set-top model and any compatible models (which are usually available only from the same vendor).

On the other hand, the existence of a number of proprietary scrambling systems discourages signal theft. As long as a scrambling system is not deployed too widely, it is not economic for the pirate to try to defeat it. Unfortunately, simple analog scrambling systems based on video sync-suppression and video inversion have become so widely deployed that they present an easy target for signal theft.

The cable network interface consists of the following components:

- A cable tuner
- An out-of-band receiver
- An optional out-of-band transmitter
- An optional media access control circuit

These components are described in more detail in the following sections.

Cable Tuner

The cable tuner selects a single 6 MHz channel between 50 and 860 MHz and rejects all other channels. The frequency is converted in two steps to an intermediate frequency (IF) that is suitable for demodulation by the NTSC demodulator. Tuning requirements for analog set-tops are fundamentally straightforward and have not changed for some time; the tuner performance is tightly specified to include image rejection, tuning range, sensitivity, and so on over the entire radio-frequency spectrum of the cable plant. Analog tuner performance is specified in EIA-23, and the cable frequency plan is specified by EIA-542.

NTSC Demodulator

The NTSC demodulator detects and recovers the video and audio signals from the tuned channel. Although designs vary, the requirements for NTSC demodulation are well known, and it is a standard component in the analog set-top.

Out-of-Band Receiver

The out-of-band receiver tunes and demodulates a narrow, digitally modulated carrier and feeds the recovered serial data to the media access controller. The out-of-band channel specification is proprietary and the channel is of quite limited capacity (in the order of kilobits per second).

Some addressable set-tops lack an out-of-band receiver and one or more VBI lines are used to send addressed messages to the set-top in lieu of the out-of-band channel. (The VBI lines are video scan lines that are not displayed by the television receiver, and that are used to send coded data, including closed captioning information.)

Out-of-Band Transmitter

The out-of-band transmitter modulates a serial data stream onto a narrow carrier for transmission upstream to the cable headend. The out-of-band channel specification is proprietary and typically uses a very robust modulation technique such as frequency shift keying (FSK). When analog set-tops with out-of-band transmitters were first deployed, the return system was not very sophisticated and the noise floor was typically high due to noise funneling (see the section Return Path Activation in Chapter 2, "Analog Cable Technologies"). Therefore, the out-of-band transmitter was designed to operate in that environment.

In addition, the impulse pay-per-view application uses a store-and-forward approach that retries each out-of-band channel transaction until it is successful. Even in the presence of errors, the transaction is eventually completed.

Media Access Control

The media access control (MAC) function ensures that only one set-top transmits at any given time on the cable return path (which is a shared medium). In analog set-tops, this function is typically accomplished by polling. In a polled system, the set-top is allowed to transmit only in response to a poll. This is a very simple MAC to implement, but it can take hours to poll every set-top in turn. Therefore, polled systems are impractical for any kind of interactive signaling.

Conditional Access System

The conditional access system provides the means by which access to specific services is granted to the user based on payment for those services. The conditional access system, depicted in Figure 3-3, uses embedded security components in the set-top. Most modern analog set-top converters use an Application Specific Integrated Circuit (ASIC) that contains the analog descrambler/demodulator, OOB data reader, microprocessor, and data decryptor. Many of the early set-top converters were defeated by monitoring various points in the unit to see how signals changed; embedding everything in a single ASIC prevents this.

Every aspect of the analog conditional access system is highly proprietary. It is common for set-top purchase contracts to include financial remedies in the case of a security breach that might include the cost of upgrading or replacing security elements. Thus, the set-top vendor has every incentive to make the conditional access system as obscure and complicated as possible in an effort to defeat signal theft. This approach has been nicknamed *security through obscurity.*

Figure 3-3 *Conditional Access System*

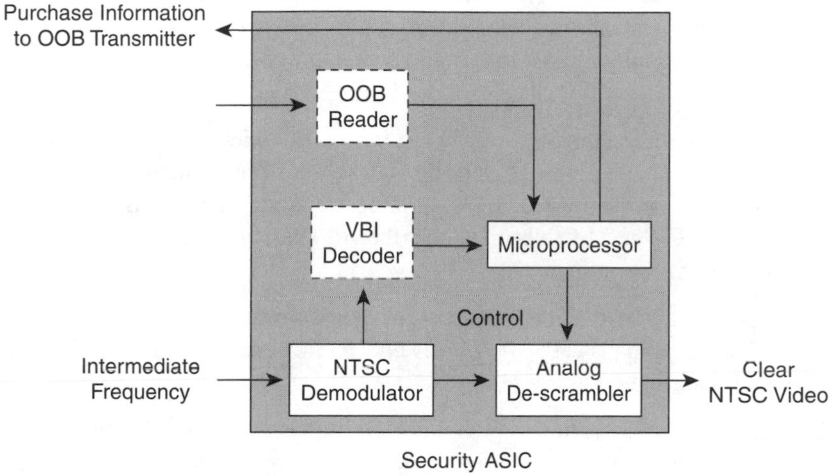

Analog De-scrambler

The analog de-scrambler is designed to restore a scrambled channel to its original form. There are a number of analog scrambling techniques, including video sync-suppression, video inversion, line dicing, line rotation, line shuffling, and time jitter. However, most scrambling systems in North America rely on video sync-suppression and video inversion. (See Chapter 18 of *Modern Cable Television Technology; Video, Voice, and Data Communications* by Walter Ciciora and others for an excellent tutorial on analog scrambling techniques.)

Analog scrambling has a number of limitations:

- There is a slight degradation in picture quality due to the analog scrambling and de-scrambling process.
- Cable ready televisions allow the customer to tune to scrambled channels and to occasionally display distorted, but recognizable, pictures for brief periods (usually when a vertical bar at the left edge of the picture provides the receiver with a substitute for the horizontal synchronization pulse).
- Some analog scrambling systems do not mask the audio channel of a scrambled channel. This has limited the transmission of adult programming to late at night (the so-called *safe-harbor times*) on systems without audio masking.
- Analog scrambling is far too easy to defeat. A quick survey of the World Wide Web (WWW) yields a list of many individuals and companies offering "retail" set-tops that will de-scramble all channels on a given cable system.

On-Screen Display

Figure 3-4 depicts the on-screen display (OSD), which generates a graphical overlay on the video output. In advanced analog set-tops, the OSD is quite primitive compared to digital set-tops. It is usually limited to text and simple graphics and supports only a small palette of colors.

The OSD is usually implemented by a single chip, which might be integrated with other functions in recent designs. Most designs use a dual-ported memory and allow the CPU to write a bitmap of the desired graphical image. The graphical image is typically combined with the NTSC signal by selecting either the video signal or the graphical image in memory, based on its x-y coordinate.

The combined signal is filtered to prevent illegal transitions in the NTSC signal. The best example of filtering is called *anti-alias filtering,* where adjacent field lines are filtered to prevent flickering.

Despite its limitations, the on-screen display supports a menu-driven user interface, an electronic program guide and, often, other applications. (See the section Applications later in this chapter.)

Figure 3-4 *On-Screen Display*

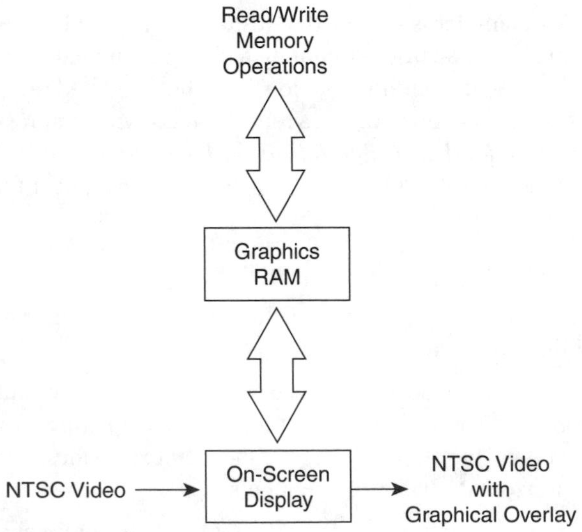

Audio Processing

The audio processing capabilities of analog set-tops are typically limited to a volume control function, though BTSC stereo decoding and digital music services have occasionally been offered. Figure 3-5 shows that the analog carrier is usually fed into the RF modulator without any modification. This arrangement has the advantage that BTSC stereo and the secondary audio program carriers are available for demodulation by circuitry in the television receiver.

Figure 3-5 *Audio Processing*

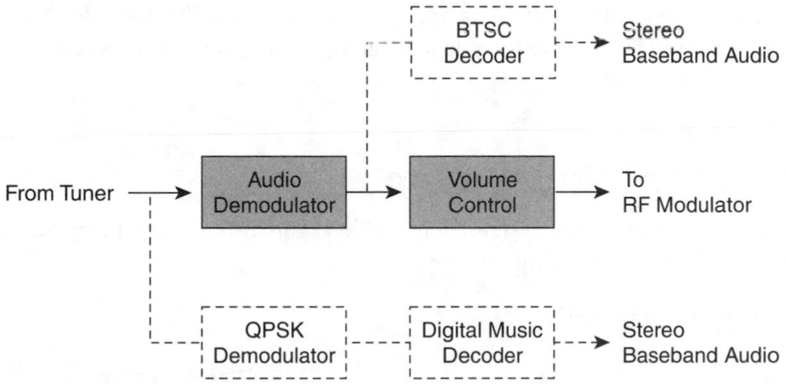

Volume Control

A volume control function is commonly included in analog set-tops (refer to Figure 3-5). This feature is very useful when the set-top is used with older televisions without a remote control, or if the customer wants to use the set-top remote control for all functions.

The volume control function works by adjusting the level of the audio signal that is fed into the RF modulator. Signal-to-noise ratio inevitably suffers, but many customers do not seem to notice. Because the BTSC decoder in the television receiver gives good stereo separation only if the audio deviation is set to its optimum value, the set-top has a *best-stereo* setting that sets the volume control to the optimum level.

Digital Music

Two proprietary digital music systems have been developed in North America:

- Digital Music Express (DMX)
- Music Choice

These systems use a narrowband quaternary phase shift keying (QPSK) modulated carrier to send digital stereo music signals through the cable system. Typically, a separate device is required to receive digital music, and this has slowed its acceptance. However, it is possible to combine the digital music receiver circuitry into the set-top box, as shown in Figure 3-5. (See the "CFT-2200" section, later in this chapter.)

BTSC Stereo and SAP Decoding

The BTSC/SAP feature is extremely rare on analog set-tops and, although it has been offered as an option (refer to Figure 3-5), few set-tops with this feature have been deployed. (See the "CFT-2200" section, later in this chapter.) A BTSC/SAP decoder provides the option of baseband audio outputs that can be used as input to a stereo system or the television receiver.

Microprocessor Subsystem

The microprocessor subsystem, depicted in Figure 3-6, differentiates the advanced analog set-top from earlier analog set-tops.

Figure 3-6 *Microprocessor Subsystem*

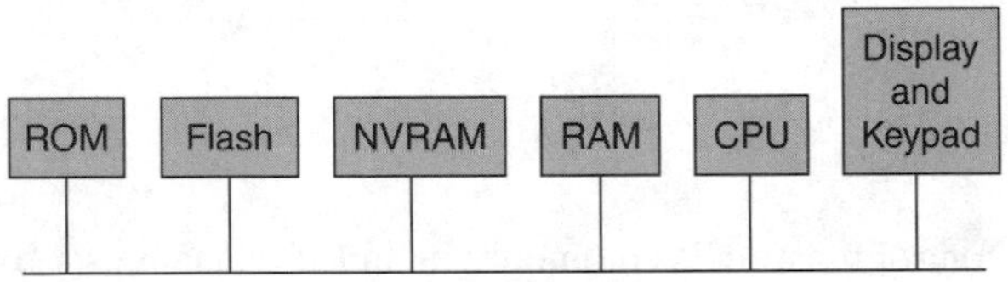

The microprocessor subsystem enables a new range of features for the cable operator and the cable customer:

- The advanced set-top contains firmware that supports a very flexible, menu-driven, user interface that, in combination with the OSD, allows greater ease-of-use and more complex features to be offered to the customer.
- The electronic program guide (EPG) allows the customer to scan the program offerings using the OSD, usually by means of a table of channels (the rows of the table) and times (the columns of the table). The EPG relies on program guide data that is usually sent to all set-tops periodically in the out-of-band channel or it might be embedded in the VBI.
- In some advanced analog set-tops, the firmware can be downloaded over the network so that additional features (or bug-fixes) can be distributed to set-tops that have been deployed. For example, a change in the EPG display could be made.

These features, particularly the EPG, have been well received by cable customers.

The microprocessor subsystem has a number of components, which are shown in Figure 3-6 and described in the following sections:

- The central processing unit
- The memory subsystem
- The display and keypad

Central Processing Unit

The central processing unit (CPU) is typically an 8- or 16-bit microprocessor. By trailing the microprocessor price-performance curve of the processors commonly used in personal computers, the analog set-top limits the cost of the CPU to just a few dollars.

CPU performance is low, typically between 1 and 3 million instructions per second (mips), but this is adequate for the limited set of embedded applications that a set-top has to perform if they are coded efficiently. The firmware is typically written in a mix of assembly language and C.

Memory Subsystem

The memory subsystem contains a number of different types of memory, each having a specific purpose. In more recent designs that use a microcontroller, part of the memory might be contained on the same chip as the microprocessor.

The different types of memory are

- Read-only memory
- Flash memory
- Nonvolatile random access memory
- Random access memory

Read-Only Memory

ROM contains the firmware for the set-top. ROM is the least expensive type of memory and is used for storing program instructions and data that are never changed. Because "never" is a long time, programs are usually not committed to ROM until they are thoroughly debugged, which requires exhaustive, thorough testing of the program. This testing takes time, so early versions of the set-top might use programmable read-only memory (PROM) to speed the development cycle. When the code is stable, it will typically be stored as masked-ROM because it is the cheapest type of ROM. (In the masked-ROM process, the program is lithographically etched into the chip as the final metal connection layer.)

Flash Memory

Flash memory is also referred to as electrically erasable programmable read-only memory (EEPROM). Flash memory can be erased and rewritten thousands of times, so it is ideal for storing program code and data that might need to be changed due to bug-fixes or other enhancements. Flash memory is typically two to three times more expensive than ROM.

Some advanced analog set-tops support field upgrade of their functions, and this is achieved by downloading new program code and data over the network. Such field upgrades can be very useful to the cable operator but are also fraught with peril! If the download mechanism is not well designed, the set-top might be left in an undefined state or might fall back to a basic set of functions.

One disadvantage of certain types of flash memory is that it might not support the access speed required by the microprocessor. In this case, the contents of the flash memory can be copied to RAM before execution, or the microprocessor can be programmed to insert wait cycles. The first solution requires additional RAM, whereas the second solution can seriously affect performance.

Nonvolatile Random Access Memory

NVRAM is used to store any program variables or user data that must survive when the set-top loses AC power. There are two common techniques for implementing NVRAM:

- The use of NVRAM chips—These chips are very reliable, but they are expensive and available only in limited sizes (2 KB is used in some advanced analog designs).
- The use of battery-backed RAM—This is standard RAM that is powered by a small on-chip battery. The RAM size can be many times larger than NVRAM chips, but if the battery fails it must be replaced.

Random Access Memory

RAM is read/write memory that retains its contents only while it is powered. RAM is used to store data and program code. You are probably familiar with the dramatic reduction in the price of RAM for personal computers. The same trends make analog set-tops with 1 or 2 MB of RAM economical.

One of the main uses for RAM in an analog set-top is the storage of program guide data. The program guide data is sent to the analog set-top at a rate of only 10 to 20 Kbps. This is adequate because the program schedule data is fairly static, that is, it does not change very much or very often. The program guide data is stored in RAM as it is received and is then available for instantaneous access by the electronic program guide.

Display and Keypad

In an advanced analog set-top, customers use the OSD and the remote control for most of their interaction with the set-top. However, remote controls have a way of slipping down the back of the couch or exhausting their batteries, so a keypad is usually included on the set-top itself for this eventuality.

For convenience, the OSD is supplemented by a 4-digit display that can be used to display the channel number or the time.

RF Modulator

The RF modulator (refer to Figure 3-1) takes the composite NTSC video and audio carriers and places them on channel 3 or channel 4 for output to the television receiver. Channel 3 or channel 4 selection might be by a switch on the set-top or by software control. Output channel options are given so that interference from local broadcast stations operating on the same channel can be avoided.

RF Bypass Switch

The RF bypass switch (refer to Figure 3-1) is actually a coaxial relay that returns to the bypass setting when the set-top is powered off. In this position, the RF bypass switch allows all cable channels to pass through the set-top unchanged to the television receiver. (This behavior is mandated by the 1992 Cable Act.)

When the set-top is powered, the RF bypass switch normally connects the output of the RF modulator to the set-top output (and to the television receiver connected to it).

However, some analog set-tops include a remote control button that toggles the bypass switch. This is intended to allow the customer to use the set-top for a watch-and-record function, as shown in Figure 3-7.

Figure 3-7 *Watch and Record Using the Bypass Switch*

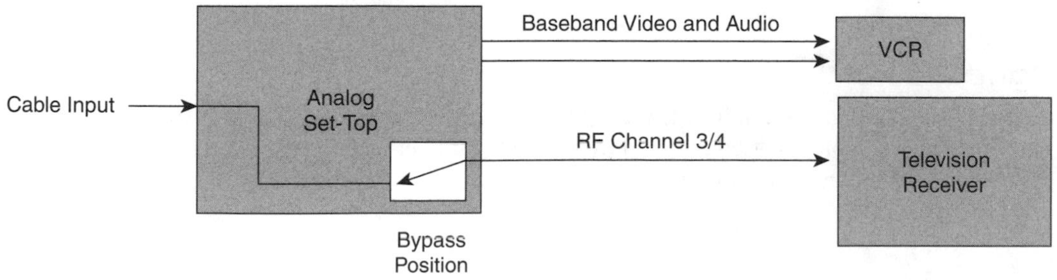

The VCR is connected to the baseband video and audio outputs of the set-top and records a program (which might be scrambled) while the RF signal is bypassed to the television receiver so that the customer can view any unscrambled service. (There are probably a few people in North America who regularly use this feature, but it causes great confusion to everyone else.) This feature might be combined with automatic control of the VCR and is discussed in more detail in the section "Infrared Transmitter," later in this chapter.

Inputs

The advanced analog set-top has the following inputs:

- The cable input
- An infrared receiver
- A diagnostic port
- A data port

The cable input is the familiar 75-ohm F-connector but the other inputs use proprietary connectors and standards. These four inputs are described in the following sections.

Cable Input

The cable input is a 75 ohm female F-connector. It is the only radio frequency input to the shielded set-top unit. Shielding is important to prevent off-air television broadcasts from interfering with the cable channels.

Infrared Receiver

An infrared receiver is mounted on the front of the set-top box to allow line-of-sight operation with an infrared remote control. Advanced analog set-tops are often supplied with a *universal* remote control, which can also control the television and the VCR but often causes considerable confusion to the average customer.

Diagnostic Port

It is quite common for the set-top to have a serial data port for diagnostic purposes. This port is typically used during development of the set-top firmware and might be completely disabled in a production unit.

Data Port

A data port on the set-top can be used for various expansion purposes. The most common of these is to satisfy the requirements stated in Section 17 of the 1992 Cable Act:

- To watch a program on one channel while simultaneously using a video cassette recorder to tape a program on another channel
- To use a video cassette recorder to tape two consecutive programs that appear on different channels
- To use advanced television picture generation and display features

These requirements are colloquially known as the watch-and-record and picture-in-picture (PIP) requirements and can be satisfied if the set-top contains multiple tuners and multiple de-scramblers. However, the customer demand for these features is low, and it is generally not economical to manufacture a special set-top for this purpose. Instead, the data ports of two standard (single-tuner, single de-scrambler) set-tops are connected with a serial data connection so that they behave as a dual-tuner, dual de-scrambler set-top, as shown in Figure 3-8. In this arrangement, all user interface functions are handled by one set-top (the master), and the second set-top (the slave) merely provides a second tuner and de-scrambler function for the master set-top.

Figure 3-8 *Dual Set-Top Arrangement*

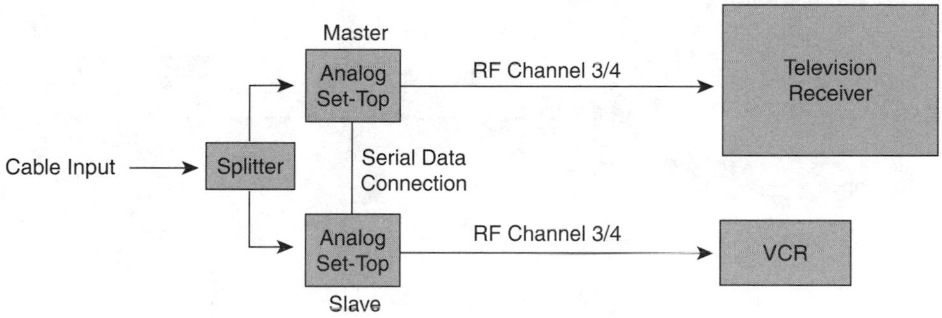

Outputs

The advanced analog set-top has the following outputs:

- RF channel 3/4 output
- Baseband video
- Baseband audio
- Infrared transmitter

The RF output is always present and uses the standard 75 ohm F-connector. All other outputs are optional. The outputs are discussed in the following sections.

RF Output

An RF output provides the simplest and most common method of connection to a television receiver or VCR. As discussed previously in this chapter, the RF output carries

- A clear NTSC signal modulated onto channel 3 or channel 4. This signal is present only when the set-top is active.
- The entire cable spectrum from the RF input. This signal is present when the set-top is powered off or when the bypass switch is activated.

Baseband Video

An optional baseband video output is provided for connection to the *video-in* input of a television or VCR. This signal is sometimes called a *composite signal* because it contains the baseband luminance information and the modulated chrominance information according to the NTSC standard. The RCA-style connector is the *de facto* standard for this signal.

One advantage of the baseband video signal is that it allows the customer to use the input selector on the television receiver to switch between the output of the set-top and the broadband cable signal, as shown in Figure 3-9.

Figure 3-9 *Baseband Video Output*

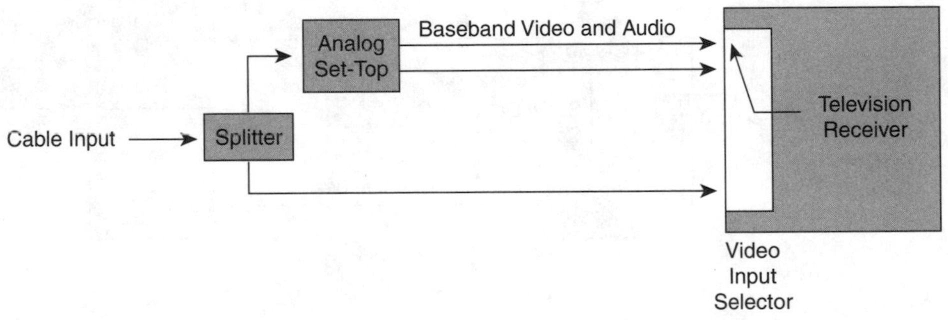

Baseband Audio

An optional baseband audio output is provided for connection to the *audio-in* input of a television or VCR. This signal is usually monaural because a BTSC decoder is rarely included in an analog set-top. Even when a stereo baseband audio output is available, most customers are disappointed to learn that a hi-fi stereo VCR cannot make stereo recordings from its baseband audio inputs because it does not have a BTSC stereo encoder.

Infrared Transmitter

An optional infrared transmitter is used to control a VCR. (This is sometimes called an *IR blaster.*) If correctly configured, as shown in Figure 3-10, this can simplify the VCR recording considerably. It allows the customer to select and record a program without programming the VCR.

Figure 3-10 *Watch and Record Operation*

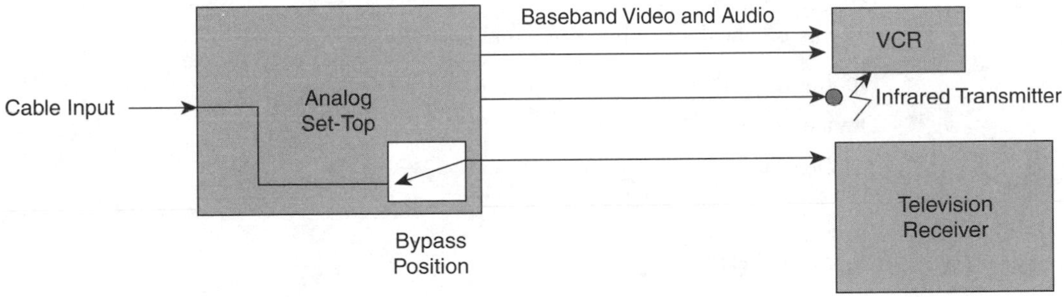

The operation is as follows:

- The customer selects a program to record using the EPG. This causes the set-top to set an internal timer that will wake up the set-top when the program starts.
- When the program starts, the set-top wakes up, tuned to the desired program. It then sends a control sequence to the infrared transmitter (which has been positioned to illuminate the VCR's infrared receiver). The control sequence turns on the VCR and starts recording the program.
- When the program finishes, the set-top sends a control sequence to the infrared transmitter that stops recording the program and turns off the VCR. The set-top then goes back to sleep.

What could be simpler? But did you remember to put a blank tape in the VCR? And did you remember to leave the VCR in its off state? (If you left it on, the infrared signal to turn it on will have turned it off!)

Software Architecture

The software architecture of an advanced analog set-top is designed to support a limited set of embedded applications. In this environment, the software architecture shown in Figure 3-11 is quite adequate.

Figure 3-11 *Set-Top Software Architecture*

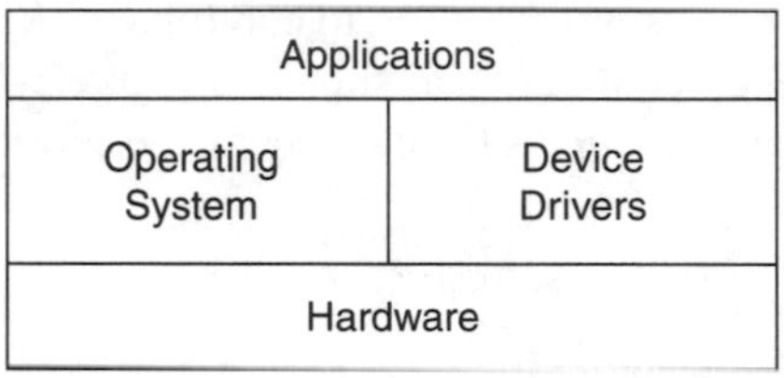

The software can be divided into three main categories:

- Operating system
- Device drivers
- Applications

Operating System Software

The set-top operating system is quite simple because only a few functions are required:

- Task scheduling—Task scheduling provides the basic mechanism for ensuring that applications are run in sequence so that each has a turn to use the processor.
- Timers—Timers are used to trigger task execution at some future time and are used by unattended recording and sleep timer applications.
- Interrupt handling—The operating system dispatches interrupts to the appropriate device driver.

A number of commercial operating systems have been developed that satisfy these requirements; examples are pSOS, VRTX, and VxWorks. It is also quite simple to develop an operating system with these functions in-house.

The operating system is simple because all other functions—for example, memory management—are done by the application.

Device Drivers

Device drivers are programs that work directly with the hardware devices and are often written in assembly language for optimum performance. The device driver hides the details of the hardware from the applications. However, in an embedded applications environment, the distinction between a driver and an application is sometimes blurred.

Applications

The set-top applications perform all the desired functions of the set-top and are typically coded in C language or assembly language. The applications developer is responsible for ensuring that the application does not corrupt its own or other applications data, because there is no memory management in the operating system or hardware. Therefore, the applications are *trusted* and must be tested thoroughly, because if an application fails, it causes the set-top to crash or hang up.

The set-top applications are not portable; that is, they cannot be readily moved to a different set-top platform because they rely too much on the specifics of the underlying hardware. Until recently, this was not a significant issue, because each set-top software development effort is typically done separately as a standalone project and the software development effort was relatively small.

Case Studies

Two advanced analog set-tops are being widely deployed in North America. They are the CFT-2200 from General Instrument and the 8600X from Scientific Atlanta.

This section provides a brief overview of the hardware and software features of these advanced analog converters. The limitations of advanced analog converters are discussed together with the lessons that have been learned from deploying them.

CFT-2200

The CFT-2200 is the latest in a series of advanced analog set-tops from General Instrument (GI), and several million units have been deployed.

The CFT-2200 has a single, 50 to 860 MHz tuner and supports GI analog scrambling formats. It uses a secure microprocessor smart card to provide for upgrade of the conditional access system.

The CFT-2200 has an out-of-band receiver that tunes a proprietary control channel in the FM band. A factory-installed module provides an RF transmitter for two-way operation.

The CFT-2200 supports an infrared transmitter and has an optional data port that uses the RS-232 standard.

The CFT-2200 uses a Motorola 68000 microprocessor with a performance of about 10 mips. GI calls this the Feature Expansion Module Processor, and it is powerful enough to run a number of different applications:

- EPG—GI gives the cable operator a choice of an EPG developed in-house or the Prevue Express EPG, which is licensed from Prevue Networks Incorporated.

- Impulse pay-per-view—The secure processor and return module allow the customer to buy an event (typically a movie) and collect the purchase information from the set-top. The event purchase price is added to the next monthly bill.
- Enhanced audio—An optional hardware module supports digital music services offered by Music Choice. A BTSC stereo decoder is optional.
- Internet browsing and e-mail—The WorldGate TV online application uses the VBI lines to send Web pages at up to 128 Kbps to the set-top. The software also supports email and chat services. An infrared keyboard is supplied to allow the customer to type.
- Enhanced programming—An application provided by Wink Communications uses the VBI lines to carry data to the set-top that is associated with the television programming. The Wink application enhances the programming with text and graphics. These enhancements are *authored* to the program before it is transmitted. Wink also allows the customer to interact with the program enhancements.
- Interactive services—The LocalWorks application developed by CableSoft allows local information to be provided to the customer.

8600X

The 8600X Home Communications Terminal (HCT) is the latest in a series of advanced analog set-tops from Scientific Atlanta (SA), and several million units have been deployed.

The 8600X HCT has a single, 50 to 860 MHz tuner and supports SA analog scrambling formats and GI-compatibility mode.

The 8600X HCT lacks an out-of-band receiver. Instead, it uses the VBI lines to insert control data into one or more channels at the headend. The 8600X HCT is programmed to tune to these channels whenever the set-top is switched off from the remote control or the keypad. The disadvantage of this approach is that while the set-top is left switched on and tuned to a channel that does not contain the control data, it does not receive any control updates and could eventually become deauthorized. This problem can also occur when the set-top is connected to a switched wall outlet and has no AC power when it is not being used.

The 8600X HCT has options for an RF transmitter for two-way operation. The 8600X HCT supports an infrared transmitter and has a data port. The 8600X HCT uses an 8-bit microprocessor with a performance of about 3 mips. This processor is used to support the following bundled applications:

- EPG—The EPG application is developed by SA.
- Impulse pay-per-view—The secure processor and return module allow the customer to buy an event (typically a movie) and collect the purchase information from the set-top. The event purchase price is added to the next monthly bill.

The 8600X also supports a plug-in module, known as the genius card, that contains additional memory. This card is required to run supported third-party applications:

- Enhanced programming—An application provided by Wink Communications uses the VBI lines to carry data to the set-top that is associated with the television programming. The Wink application enhances the programming with text and graphics. These enhancements are *authored* to the program before it is transmitted. Wink also allows the customer to interact with the program enhancements.
- Internet browsing and e-mail—The WorldGate TV online application uses the VBI lines to send Web pages at up to 128 Kbps to the set-top. The software also supports e-mail and chat services. An infrared keyboard is supplied to allow the customer to type.

Limitations

Advanced analog set-tops have a number of limitations that have slowed the deployment of advanced services:

- The advanced analog set-top has performance, memory, and graphics limitations that do not allow support of sophisticated applications.
- The advanced analog set-top has no application sharing support and is generally limited to running a single interactive application.
- Communication between the set-top and the headend are limited to a single, narrow channel that is shared by all set-tops. This limitation has been partially solved by Wink Communications and Worldgate by using multiple VBI lines, but it is still a fundamental issue that prevents scaling of the system.
- Any new applications must be ported to the proprietary hardware platform. This requires an agreement with the set-top provider and takes time. As the number of applications grow, and as third-party application developers develop more applications, the lack of application portability becomes a significant issue.

Lessons Learned

The advanced analog deployment experience has taught the cable industry a great many lessons that can be applied to digital cable deployment and which provide some of the foundations for the OpenCable architecture:

- The cable network interface must be consistent across set-tops from all vendors, and in practice this can be achieved only by establishing a cable network interface standard.
- The conditional access system must be upgradable on an ongoing basis to provide continued protection from signal theft.

- A scalable, two-way communications network is required for interactive applications support.
- As applications become more sophisticated, they require more processor and graphics performance and more memory.
- A standard applications environment is required to allow applications to be easily ported to new set-top platforms as they become available.
- The operating system must have the capability of supporting concurrent execution of more than one application.

Summary

This chapter has covered the hardware and software characteristics of the analog set-top converter. There are many aspects of analog set-tops that make the services that cable operators can provide to their customers less than ideal. The analog set-top fosters proprietary interfaces and provides a limited applications platform. It does not always interoperate well with other video equipment—such as television receivers, VCRs, and home-theater equipment—in the customer's home. There are many valuable lessons to be learned from the analog set-top in the transition to digital cable systems.

References

Book

Ciciora, Walter, James Farmer, and David Large. *Modern Cable Television Technology; Video, Voice, and Data Communications*. San Francisco, CA: Morgan Kaufmann Publishers, Inc., 1999.

Internet Resources

CableSoft Web site

www.cablesoft.com

Consumer Electronics Manufacturers Association Web site

www.cemacity.org

General Instrument Web site

www.gi.com

Music Choice Web site

www.musicchoice.com

PreVue Web site

www.prevue.com

Scientific Atlanta Web site

www.sciatl.com

Wink Web site

www.wink.com

Worldgate Web site

www.wgate.com

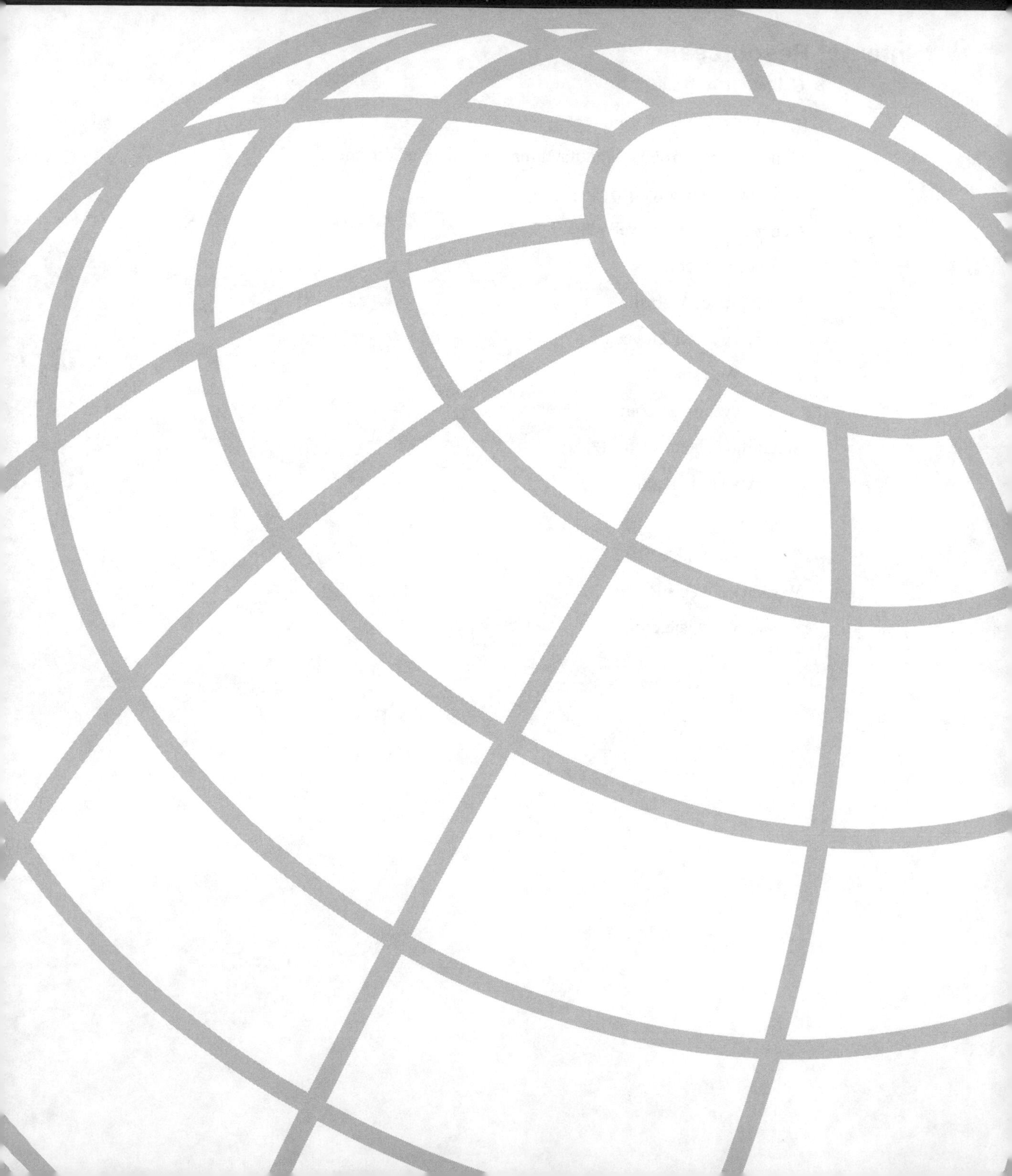

CHAPTER 4

Digital Technologies

Digital technology is becoming pervasive in all types of services. As computing power continues to increase according to Moore's Law (see Chapter 1, "Why Digital Television?"), more and more functions can be tackled in the digital domain. An excellent example is the transmission of television pictures.

Nevertheless, digital technology is not a panacea. The complexity of the techniques can introduce reliability and quality issues. In addition, only a few engineers thoroughly understand all these techniques, making us more reliant on a smaller number of *de facto* standard chip-sets.

This chapter introduces a number of key digital technologies. If you are familiar with these technologies, you might want to skim through or skip over this chapter. There are many excellent texts (see the list of references at the end of the chapter) that explain how these digital technologies work. This chapter does not attempt to repeat them, but instead provides a commentary on why these techniques are so important and what they mean in practical terms. This chapter discusses

- Video compression—The basic principles of the video compression algorithms commonly used for entertainment quality video, the importance of choosing the correct parameters for video encoding, and some alternative video compression algorithms.
- Audio compression—The basic principles of MPEG-2 audio compression and Dolby AC-3 audio compression.
- Data—Arbitrary *private* data can be carried by the underlying layers.
- System information—Tabular data format used by the digital receiver device to drive content navigation, tuning, and presentation.
- Timing and synchronization—A mechanism is required to recover the source timing at the decoder so that the presentation layer can synchronize the various components and display them at exactly the intended rate.
- Packetization—The segmentation and encapsulation of elementary data streams into transport packets.
- Multiplexing—The combining of transport streams containing audio, video, data, and system information.

- Baseband transmission—The various mechanisms for carrying digital transport streams: the Digital Video Broadcast (DVB) asynchronous serial interface (ASI), Synchronous Optical Networks (SONET), Asynchronous Transfer Mode (ATM), and Internet Protocol (IP).
- Broadband transmission—The digital transmission payload must be modulated before it can be delivered by an analog cable system. Quadrature Amplitude Modulation (QAM) has been selected as the best modulation for *downstream* transmission in cable systems. Other modulation techniques include quaternary phase shift keying (QPSK) and vestigial side band (VSB) modulation.

Figure 4-1 shows how each of these techniques are layered. This diagram illustrates the in-band communications stack for a digital cable set-top and is discussed in Chapter 6, "The Digital Set-Top Converter," in more detail.

Figure 4-1 *Layered Model for Digital Television*

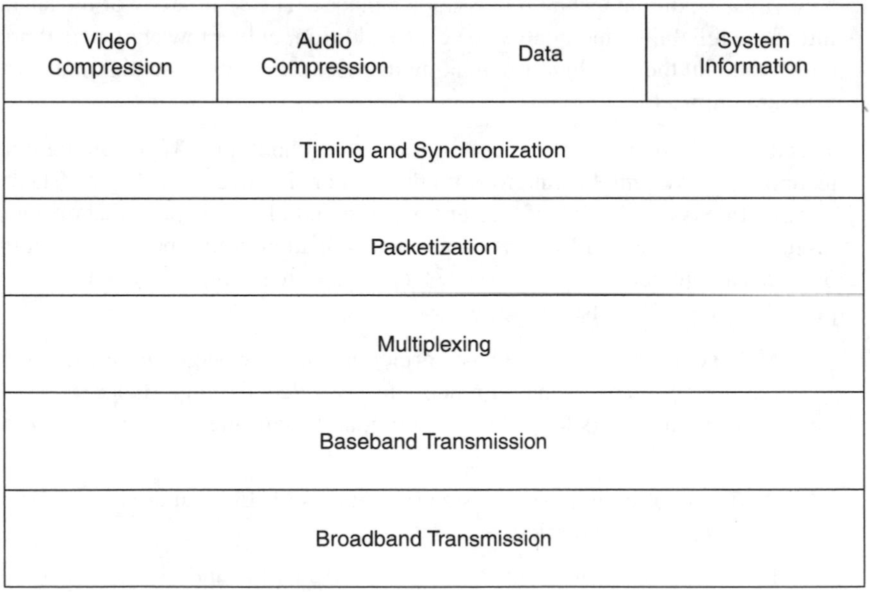

Video Compression

Image compression has been around for some time but video compression is relatively new. The processing requirements to compress even a single frame of video are large—to compress 30 frames (or 60 fields) per second of video requires massive processing power (delivered by rapid advances in semiconductor technology).

Nonetheless, digital video must be compressed before it can be transmitted over a cable system. Although other compression algorithms exist, the dominant standard for video compression is MPEG-2 (from Moving Picture Experts Group). Although MPEG-2 video compression was first introduced in 1993, it is now firmly established and provides excellent results in cable, satellite, terrestrial broadcast, and digital versatile disk (DVD) applications.

This section discusses

- MPEG-2 video compression—The basics of the MPEG-2 video compression algorithm and why it has become the dominant standard for entertainment-video compression
- Other video compression algorithms—Why other video compression algorithms have their applications and why they are unlikely to challenge MPEG-2 video compression in the entertainment world for some time
- Details on MPEG-2 video compression—Some more details on the use of MPEG-2 video compression and its parameters

MPEG-2 Compression

MPEG-2 video compression is the *de facto* standard for entertainment video. MPEG-2 video compression is popular for a number of reasons:

- It is an international standard [ISO/IEC IS 13818-2].
- MPEG-2 places no restrictions on the video encoder implementation. This allows each encoder designer to introduce new techniques to improve compression efficiency and picture quality. Since MPEG-2 video encoders were first introduced in 1993, compression efficiency has improved by 30 to 40%, despite predictions by many that MPEG-2's fundamental theoretical limitations would prevent this.
- MPEG-2 fully defines the video decoder's capability at particular levels and profiles. Many MPEG-2 chip-sets are available and will work with any *main level at main profile (MP@ML)*–compliant MPEG-2 bit-stream from any source. Nevertheless, quality can change significantly from one MPEG-2 video decoder to another, especially in error handling and video clip transitions.
- MPEG-2 video compression is part of a larger standard that includes support for transport and timing functions.

Moreover, MPEG-2 is likely to remain as the dominant standard for entertainment video because it has been so successful in establishing an inventory of standard decoders (both in existing consumer electronics products and in the chip libraries of most large semiconductor companies). Additional momentum comes from the quantity of real-time and stored content already compressed into MPEG-2 format. Even succeeding work by the MPEG committees has been abandoned (MPEG-3) or retargeted to solve different problems (MPEG-4 and MPEG-7).

MPEG-2 is a *lossy* video compression method based on motion vector estimation, discrete cosine transforms, quantization, and Huffman encoding. (*Lossy* means that data is lost, or thrown away, during compression, so quality after decoding is less than the original picture.) Taking these techniques in order:

- *Motion vector estimation* is used to capture much of the change between video frames, in the form of best approximations of each part of a frame as a translation (generally due to motion) of a similar-sized piece of another video frame. Essentially, there is a lot of *temporal redundancy* in video, which can be discarded. (The term *temporal redundancy* is applied to information that is repeated from one frame to another.)
- *Discrete cosine transform (DCT)* is used to convert spatial information into frequency information. This allows the encoder to discard information, corresponding to higher video frequencies, which are less visible to the human eye.
- *Quantization* is applied to the DCT coefficients of either original frames (in some cases) or the DCT of the residual (after motion estimation) to restrict the set of possible values transmitted by placing them into groups of values that are almost the same.
- *Huffman encoding* uses short codes to describe common values and longer codes to describe rarer values—this is a type of *entropy coding*.

The foregoing is a highly compressed summary of MPEG-2 video compression (with many details omitted). However, there are so many excellent descriptions of MPEG compression (see *DTV: The Revolution in Electronic Imaging*, by Jerry C. Whitaker; *Digital Compression for Multimedia: Principles and Standards*, by Jerry D. Gibson and others; *Testing Digital Video*, by Dragos Ruiu and others; and *Modern Cable Television Technology; Video, Voice, and Data Communications,* by Walter Ciciora and others) that more description is not justified here. Instead, the following sections concentrate on the most interesting aspects of MPEG:

- What are MPEG-2's limitations?
- What happens when MPEG-2 breaks?
- How can compression ratios be optimized to reduce transmission cost without compromising (too much) on quality?

MPEG Limitations

If MPEG-2 is so perfect, why is there any need for other compression schemes? (There are a great many alternative compression algorithms, such as wavelet, pyramid, fractal, and so on.) MPEG-2 is a good solution for coding relatively high-quality video when certain transmission requirements can be met. However, MPEG-2 coding is rarely used in Internet applications because the Internet cannot generally guarantee the quality of service (QoS) parameters required for MPEG-2–coded streams. These QoS parameters are summarized in Table 4-1.

Table 4-1 *MPEG-2 QoS Parameters for Entertainment Quality Video*

Bit Rate	**1.5–20 Mbps Constant or Variable Bit Rate (CBR or VBR)**
Bit error rate (BER)	Less than 1 in 10^{-10}
Packet/cell loss rate	Less than 1 in 10^{-8}
Packet/cell delay variation	Less than 500 nS

As you can see from the table, for entertainment-quality video, MPEG-2 typically requires a reasonably high bit rate, and this bit rate must be guaranteed. Video-coding will, in general, produce a variable information rate, but MPEG-2 allows for CBR transmission facilities (for example, satellite transponders, microwave links, and fiber transmission facilities). As such, MPEG-2 encoders attempt to take advantage of every bit in the transmission link by coding extra detail during less-challenging scenes. When the going gets tough—during a car chase, for example—MPEG-2 encoders use more bits for motion and transmit less detail. Another way to think of this is that MPEG-2 encoding varies its degree of loss according to the source material. Fortunately, the human visual system tends to work in a similar way, and we pay less attention to detail when a scene contains more motion. (This is true of a car chase whether you are watching it or you are in it!)

MPEG-2 coded material is extremely sensitive to errors and lost information because of the way in which MPEG-2 puts certain vital information into a single packet. If this packet is lost or corrupted, there can be a significant impact on the decoder, causing it to drop frames or to produce very noticeable blocking artifacts. If you think of an MPEG-2 stream as a list of instructions to the decoder, you can understand why the corruption of a single instruction can play havoc with the decoded picture.

Finally, MPEG-2 is extremely sensitive to variations in transmission delay. These are not usually measurable in synchronous transmission systems (for example, satellite links) because each bit propagates through the system according to the clock rate. In packet- or cell-based networks, however, it is possible for each packet-sized group of bits to experience a different delay. MPEG-2 was designed with synchronous transmission links in mind and embeds timing information into certain packets by means of timestamps. If the timestamps experience significant *jitter* (or cell delay variation), it causes distortions in audio and video fidelity due to timing variations in the sample clocks—for example, color shifts due to color subcarrier phase variations.

MPEG-2 Artifacts

What are MPEG artifacts? In practice, all lossy encoders generate *artifacts,* or areas of unfaithful visual reproduction, all the time; if the encoder is well designed, all these artifacts will be invisible to the human eye. However, the best laid plans sometimes fail; the following are some of the more common MPEG-2 artifacts:

- If the compression ratio is too high, there are sometimes simply not enough bits to encode the video signal without significant loss. The better encoders will progressively *soften* the picture (by discarding some picture detail); however, poorer encoders sometimes break down and overflow an internal buffer. When this happens, all kinds of visual symptoms—from bright green blocks to dropped frames—can result. After such a *breakdown*, the encoder will usually recover for a short period until once again the information rate gets too high to code into the available number of bits.
- Another common visible artifact is sometimes visible in dark scenes or in close-ups of the face and is sometimes called *contouring*. As the name suggests, the image looks a little like a contour map drawn with a limited set of shades rather than a continuously varying palette. This artifact sometimes reveals the macro-block boundaries (which is sometimes called *tiling*). When this happens, it is usually because the encoder allocates too few quantization levels to the scene.

NOTE Macro-blocks are areas of 16-by-16 pixels that are used by MPEG for DCT and motion-estimation purposes. See Chapter 3 of *Modern Cable Television Technology; Video, Voice, and Data Communications* by Walter Ciciora and others, for more details.

- High-frequency *mosquito* noise will sometimes be apparent in the background. Mosquito noise is often apparent in surfaces, such as wood, plaster, and wool, that contain an almost limitless amount of detail due to their natural texture. The encoder can be overtaxed by so much detail and creates a visual effect that looks as if the walls are crawling with ants.

There are many more artifacts associated with MPEG encoding and decoding; however, a well-designed system should rarely, if ever, produce annoying visible artifacts.

MPEG-2 Operating Guidelines

To avoid visible artifacts due to encoding, transmission errors, and decoding, the entire MPEG-2 system must be carefully designed to operate within certain guidelines:

- The compression ratio cannot be pushed too high. Just where the limit is on compression ratio for given material at a certain image resolution and frame rate is a subject of intense and interminable debate. Ultimately, the decision involves engineers and artists and will vary according to encoder performance (there is some expectation of improvements in rate with time, although also some expectation of a law of diminishing returns). Table 4-2 gives some guidance based on experience.

Table 4-2 *MPEG-2 Resolution Versus Minimum Bit Rate Guidelines*

Material	Resolution	Minimum Bit Rate (CBR)
Movies	360 x 240 (CIF)	1.5 Mbps
Movies	360 x 480 (half)	2 Mbps
Movies	540 x 480 (3/4)	3 Mbps
Movies	720 x 480 (full)	4 Mbps
Sports (video)	540 x 480 (3/4)	5 Mbps
Sports (video)	720 x 480 (full)	6 Mbps

- The transmission system must generate very few errors during the average viewing time of an event. For example, in a two-hour movie, the same viewers may tolerate very few significant artifacts (such as frame drop or green blocks). In practice, this means that the transmission system must employ forward error correction (FEC) techniques.

Other Video Compression Algorithms

There are a great many alternative video compression algorithms, such as wavelet, pyramid, fractal, and so on (see Chapter 7 of *Digital Compression for Multimedia: Principles and Standards* by Jerry D. Gibson and others). Many have special characteristics that make them suitable for very low bit rate facilities, for software decoding on a PC, and so on. However, it is unlikely that they will pose a significant threat to MPEG-2 encoding for entertainment video in the near future.

Compression Processing Requirements

Let's take a full-resolution video frame that contains 480 lines, each consisting of 720 pixels. The total frame, therefore, contains 345,600 pixels. Remember that a new frame arrives from the picture source every 33 milliseconds. Thus, the pixel rate is 10,368,000 per second. Imagine that the compression process requires about 100 operations per pixel. Obviously, a processor with a performance of 1,000 million instructions per second (mips) is required.

In practice, custom processing blocks are often built in hardware to handle common operations, such as motion estimation and DCT used by MPEG-2 video compression.

Details of MPEG-2 Video Compression

The following sections detail some of the more practical aspects of MPEG-2 video compression:

- Picture resolution—MPEG-2 is designed to handle the multiple picture resolutions that are commonly in use for broadcast television. This section defines what is meant by picture resolution and how it affects the compression process.
- Compression ratio—MPEG-2 can achieve excellent compression ratios when compared to analog transmission, but there is some confusion about the definition of compression ratios. This section discusses the difference between the MPEG compression ratio and the overall compression ratio.
- Real-time MPEG-2 compression—Most of the programs delivered over cable systems are compressed in real-time at the time of transmission. This section discusses the special requirements for real-time MPEG-2 encoders.
- Non–real-time MPEG-2 compression—Stored-media content does not require a real-time encoder, and there are certain advantages to non–real-time compression systems.
- Statistical multiplexing—This section explains how statistical multiplexing works in data communications systems and what special extensions have been invented to support the statistical multiplexing of MPEG-2 program streams.
- Re-multiplexing—Re-multiplexing, or grooming, of compressed program streams is discussed, including a recent technique that actually allows the program stream to be dynamically reencoded to reduce its bit rate.

Picture Resolution

MPEG-2 compression is a family of standards that defines many different profiles and levels. (For a complete description of all MPEG-2 profiles and levels, see Chapter 5 of *DTV: The Revolution in Electronic Imaging* by Jerry C. Whitaker.) MPEG-2 compression is most commonly used in its main profile at its main level (abbreviated to MP@ML). This MPEG-2 profile and level is designed for the compression of standard definition television pictures with a resolution of 480 vertical lines.

The resolution of a picture describes how many pixels are used to describe a single frame. The higher the resolution, the more pixels per frame. In many cases, the luminance information is coded with more pixels than the chrominance information.

NOTE The retina of the human eye perceives more detail with rod cells, which are sensitive only to the intensity of light—the *luminance*—and perceives less detail with cone cells, which are sensitive to the color of light—the *chrominance*.

Chroma subsampling takes advantage of the way the human eye works by sampling the chrominance with less detail than the luminance information. In the MPEG-2 main profile (MP), the chrominance information is subsampled at half the horizontal and vertical resolution compared to the luminance information. For example, if the luminance information is sampled at a resolution of 480 by 720, the chrominance information is sampled at a resolution of 240 by 360, requiring one-fourth the number of pixels. This arrangement is called 4:2:0 sampling. The effect of 4:2:0 sampling is to nearly halve the video bandwidth compared to sampling luminance and chrominance at the same resolution.

Compression Ratio

The *compression ratio* is a commonly misused term. It is used to compare the spectrum used by a compressed signal with the spectrum used by an equivalent NTSC (National Television Systems Committee) analog signal. Expressed this way, typical compression ratios achieved by MPEG-2 range from 6:1 to 14:1. Why is the term confusing?

If you take the same video signal and modulate it as an analog signal (uncompressed) and compress it using MPEG-2, you have two very different things. The analog signal is an analog waveform with certain bandwidth constraints so that it fits into 6 MHz, whereas the MPEG-2 elementary stream is just a string of bits that cannot be transmitted until further processing steps are taken. These steps include multiplexing, transport, and digital modulation, and they all affect how much bandwidth is required by the compressed signal.

To compare apples with apples, you must take the same video signal and convert it to an uncompressed digital signal (this is actually the first step in the compression process and is termed *analog-to-digital conversion* or simply *sampling*). You can now compare the uncompressed digital signal with the MPEG-2 compressed elementary stream for a true comparison of the input bit rate and the output bit rate of the compression process. A full-resolution uncompressed video signal sampled in 4:2:0 (see the previous section, "Picture Resolution") requires 124.416 Mbps. MPEG-2 can squeeze this down to about 4 Mbps with little or no loss in perceived quality; this is a true compression ratio of 124:4 or 31:1. This is very different than the commonly quoted range of 6:1 to 14:1.

To continue the math, take the 4 Mbps video elementary stream and add an audio stream at 192 Kbps to create a program stream at 4.192 Mbps. Add information to describe how the streams are synchronized and place the data into short transport packets for efficient multiplexing with other streams. You now have a payload of approximately 4.3 Mbps. Using 64-QAM modulation (see the section Broadband Transmission in this chapter), six 4.3 Mbps streams fit into its 27 Mbps payload. Thus, we could express this as a 6:1 compression ratio.

This is all very confusing! In this example, a video signal with a 31:1 *MPEG-2* video compression ratio is roughly equivalent to an *overall* compression ratio of 6:1. (If the example employs 256-QAM and statistical multiplexing, you might achieve an overall compression ratio of 12:1 although the MPEG-2 video compression ratio is still 31:1.)

In this book, the terms *MPEG-2 video compression ratio* and *overall compression ratio* will be used to distinguish these very different measures.

Real-Time MPEG-2 Compression

Real-time compression is commonly used at satellite up-links to compress a video signal into a digital program stream as part of the transmission (or retransmission) process. Very often, the encoder runs for long periods of time without manual intervention. There must be sufficient *headroom* in the allocated bit rate to allow the encoder to operate correctly for all kinds of material that it is likely to encode. (*Headroom* refers to available, but normally unused, bits that are allocated to allow for the video compression of difficult scenes.) Each channel requires a dedicated encoder, so price is a definite issue for multichannel systems. The encoder must also be highly reliable, and in many cases automatic switching to a backup encoder is required.

Non–Real-Time MPEG-2 Compression

Non–real-time encoders are technically similar to real-time encoders, but have very different requirements. In fact, they may encode in real-time but their application is to encode to a stored media (such as a tape or disc), and a highly-paid *compressionist* usually monitors the compression of each scene. (Compressionists are studio engineers who not only understand how to operate the encoding equipment but also apply their artistic judgment in selecting the best trade-off between compression ratio and picture quality.) Therefore, encoder price is less of an issue and performance is extremely important because the compressed material will be viewed over and over again. In the case of digital versatile disks (DVDs), no annoying visible artifacts, however subtle, can be tolerated, because the picture quality will be carefully evaluated by a magazine reviewer.

Statistical Multiplexing

Statistical multiplexing is a technique commonly used in data communications to extract the maximum efficiency from a CBR link. A number of uncorrelated, bursty traffic sources are multiplexed together so that the sum of their peak rates exceed the link capacity. Because the sources are uncorrelated, there is a low probability that the sum of their transmit rates will exceed the link capacity. However, although the multiplex can be engineered so that periods of link oversubscription are rare, they will occur. (See Murphy's law!) In data communications networks, periods of oversubscription are accommodated by packet buffering and, in extreme cases, packet discard. (The Internet is a prime example of an oversubscribed, statistically multiplexed network where packet delay and loss may be high during busy periods.)

Video material has a naturally varying information rate—when the scene suddenly changes from an actor sitting at a table to an explosion, the information rate skyrockets. Although MPEG-2 is designed to compensate by encoding more or less detail according to the amount of motion, the encoded bit rate may vary by a ratio of 5 to 1 during a program.

This makes MPEG-2 program streams excellent candidates for statistical multiplexing, except for the fact that MPEG-2 is extremely sensitive to delay and loss. As such, statistical multiplexing cannot be used for MPEG-2 if there is any probability of loss due to oversubscription.

Therefore, statistical multiplexing has been specially modified for use with MPEG by the addition of the following mechanisms:

- A series of real-time encoders are arranged so that their output can be combined by a multiplexer into a single multi-program transport stream (MPTS). Each encoder has a control signal that instructs it to set its target bit-rate to a certain rate.
- The multiplexer monitors the sum of the traffic from all the encoders as it combines them, and in real-time decides whether the bit rate is greater or lower than the transmission link capacity.
- When one encoder has a more challenging scene to compress, it requests that its output rate be allowed to rise. The hope is that one of the other encoders will have less-difficult material and will lower its output rate.

However, there is a significant probability that all the encoders could be called upon to encode a challenging scene at the same time. When this happens, the aggregate bit rate will exceed the link capacity. A conventional statistical multiplexer would discard some packets, but in the case of MPEG-2, this would be disastrous and almost guarantee poor-quality video at the output of the decoders.

Instead, the multiplexer buffers the additional packets and requests that the encoders lower their encoded bit rate. The buffered packets are delayed by only a few milliseconds, but MPEG-2 is extremely sensitive to delay variation. The multiplexer can fix this within limits; as long as the decoder pipeline does not underflow and the timestamps are adjusted to compensate for the additional time they are buffered, the decoder continues to function normally.

Some statistical multiplexers use a technique called *look ahead statistical multiplexing* (pioneered by DiviCom—see http://www.divi.com/). In this technique, the material is encoded or statistics are extracted in a first pass, the information is passed to the multiplexer (while the original input video is passing through a pipeline delay), and bit rates are assigned for each encoder; so when the real encoding happens, a reasonable bit rate is already assigned. This solves some of the nasty feedback issues that can happen in less sophisticated designs.

Reencoding

Until recently, it was impossible to modify an encoded MPEG-2-bit stream in real-time. It is now possible, however, to parse the MPEG-2 syntax and modify it to reduce the bit rate by discarding some of the encoded detail. This technique was pioneered by Imedia Corporation (http://www.imedia.com/) and allows the feedback loop between the MPEG encoders and the multiplexer to be removed. In a reencoding (or translation) system, the multiplexer is used to combine a number of variable bit rate MPEG-2 streams. If, at any instant in time, the aggregate bit rate of all of the streams exceeds the transmission link capacity, the multiplexer will *reencode* one or more of the streams to intelligently discard information to reduce their bit rate. Unlike statistical multiplexing, where the multiplexer could not discard any bits, the multiplexer reduces the bit rate by discarding some information—for example, fine detail.

Reencoding is a very useful technique to use whenever a number of multi-program transport streams are groomed—that is, a new output multiplex is formed from program streams taken from several input multiplexes. Without some means of adapting the coded rate, re-multiplexing would result in considerable inefficiency and the output multiplex would contain fewer channels.

A second application of reencoding is in Digital Program Insertion (DPI). DPI *splices* one single-program transport program stream into another so that the viewer is unaware of the transition. It can be used to insert local advertisements into a broadcast program. Reencoding allows the inserted segment to be rate-adapted to the segment that it replaces. DPI is discussed in more detail in Chapter 15, "OpenCable Headend Interfaces."

Although reencoding techniques are extremely useful, feedback-controlled statistical multiplexing is superior from a compression-efficiency perspective when it is possible to collocate encoders and multiplexers. Hence, feedback-controlled statistical multiplexing tends to dominate at original encoding sites that include statistical multiplexing, whereas reencoding is appropriate at nodes where grooming of statistically multiplexed signals needs to be performed.

Audio Compression

Audio compression is a companion to video compression, but the techniques are very different. First, the audio signal requires much less bandwidth than the video signal. For example, a stereo audio pair sampled at 48 KHz and using 16-bit samples requires 1.536 Mbps (compared to 124 Mbps for the video signal). It would be quite possible to send uncompressed audio. Moreover, audio compression cannot achieve the same compression ratio as video; a typical rate for the stereo audio pair is 192 Kbps, an 8:1 compression ratio.

Nevertheless, it is easy to make an economic argument for audio compression. For example, in a 40 Mbps transmission link, an additional two video channels can be carried if audio compression is used (assuming 4 Mbps video).

There are two leading contenders for audio compression for entertainment quality audio: MPEG audio compression and Dolby AC-3.

MPEG-1 Layer 2 (Musicam)

MPEG-1 Layer 2 audio compression, also known as Musicam, is specified in ISO/IEC IS 13818-3. MPEG audio compression delivers near–CD quality audio using a technique called *sub-band encoding*. MPEG audio compression is used mainly in Europe and is used by most direct-to-home satellite providers in the United States.

MPEG audio compression is a two-channel system, but it can encode a Dolby Pro-Logic signal, which includes two additional channels for rear and center speakers. (This is analogous to the way in which a Dolby Pro-Logic signal is carried by a BTSC [Broadcast Television System Committee] signal as part of an NTSC transmission).

Dolby AC-3

Dolby AC-3 is a more advanced system than MPEG audio compression. AC-3 was selected as the audio compression system for digital television in North America and is specified by ATSC Standard A/52. AC-3 encodes up to six discrete channels: left, right, center, left-rear, right-rear, and sub-woofer speakers. The sub-woofer channel carries only low frequencies and is commonly referred to as a 0.1 channel because it has such a limited frequency range. Thus, AC-3 5.1 gets its name from five full channels and a 0.1 channel. In addition, AC-3 has a two-channel mode that can be used to carry stereo and Dolby Pro-Logic encoded signals.

AC-3 also uses sub-band encoding but provides a number of advantages over MPEG audio compression:

- In AC-3 5.1, surround-sound effects are reproduced much more faithfully than is possible with Dolby Pro-Logic because of the additional channels.

- AC-3 5.1 distributes the available transmission link capacity between the 5.1 channels so that more bits are used for those channels containing more information at any particular time. This method effectively makes them statistically multiplexed discrete digital channels.
- AC-3 5.1 is a consumer-grade version of the theatrical Digital Theater Sound (DTS) system, so sound tracks may be directly transferred from the theatrical release.

AC-3 has been chosen as the audio system for digital terrestrial broadcasting and for DVD in the United States. It also has been selected by OpenCable.

Other Audio Compression Algorithms

As with video, many other audio compression algorithms exist. For example, RealAudio is commonly used for sending audio over the Internet, and MP3 has caused a stir in recordable audio. MP3 uses MPEG-1 Layer 3 audio compression, which is considerably more sophisticated than MPEG-1 Layer 2. Many audio compression algorithms have special characteristics that make them suitable for very low bit rate facilities, for software decoding on a PC, and so on. However, it is unlikely that they will pose a significant threat to Dolby AC-3 encoding for entertainment-quality audio in the near future.

Data

Many applications require a data communications path from the headend to the set-top. Part 6 of the MPEG-2 standard (ISO IEC 13818-6) describes how arbitrary data packets may be segmented into MPEG-2 transport packets at the headend and reassembled at the set-top. This mechanism is the basis for the broadcast carousel (see Chapter 8, "Interactive Services").

System Information

System information (SI) is a tabular data format used by the digital receiver device to drive content navigation, tuning, and presentation. See Figure 5-1, which shows that the system information can be sent as part of the in-band digital channel. Cable systems can also transmit system information in an out-of-band channel, as described in Chapter 5, "Adding Digital Television Services to Cable Systems."

There are several standards for system information:

- ATSC A/56—Also known as SI, A/56 was adopted by the cable industry before it was made obsolete by ATSC. DVS-011 and DVS-022 are SCTE standards based on A/56; they are used for basic navigation functions. (Program guide information is sent separately in a proprietary format.)

- DVS-234—Also known as SI, DVS-234 is an SCTE-proposed standard that seeks to establish a common service information standard for out-of-band cable channels. (See the section Out-of-Band Channels in Chapter 16, "OCI-N: the Network Interface.")
- ATSC A/65—Also known as *Program and System Information Protocol (PSIP)*, A/65 has been adopted for terrestrial digital broadcast. In addition to basic navigation functions (such as channel numbering), PSIP can carry content description information that can be used by the programmer to deliver information for electronic program guides. (See the section In-Band Channels in Chapter 16.)

MPEG-2 Systems Layer

The MPEG Systems Committee has defined a systems layer, specified by ISO-IEC 13818-1. (The MPEG-2 systems layer is commonly and confusingly known as MPEG-2 Transport because it defines a transport packet for transmission purposes.) The MPEG-2 systems layer combines the various components of a digital program into a multi-program transport stream. These components include

- Compressed video
- Compressed audio
- Data
- Timing information
- System information
- Conditional access information
- Program-related data

The MPEG-2 systems layer includes the following functions:

- Timing and synchronization—The transmission of timing information in transport packets to allow the receiver to synchronize its decoding rate with the encoder
- Packetization—The segmentation and encapsulation of elementary data streams into 188-byte transport packets.
- Multiplexing—The mechanisms used to combine compressed audio and video streams (elementary streams) into a transport stream.
- Conditional access—Provision for the transmission of conditional access information in the transport stream.

Timing and Synchronization

MPEG-2 transport includes timing and synchronization functions that assume a constant-delay network. The system timing information is transferred using program clock reference (PCR) timestamps, which are placed in the adaption header of certain packets. The PCR timestamps are used by the decoder to synchronize the decoder clock very accurately to the encoder. In many designs, the decoder clock is used to synthesize the NTSC color subcarrier, which must be controlled to an extremely fine tolerance (about 30 Hz).

In addition, the decoder uses the system timing as a reference for presentation and display timestamps, which are used to synchronize audio and video components of a single program transport stream.

Packetization

The MPEG-2 systems layer is packet-based and allows great flexibility in allocating bit rate between a number of program streams. The packets are of a fixed length, and each contains 184 bytes of payload and has a fixed–length, 4-byte link header, as depicted in Figure 4-2. Within each header is a 13-bit packet identifier (PID) that identifies the stream.

Figure 4-2 *MPEG-2 Transport Packet Format*

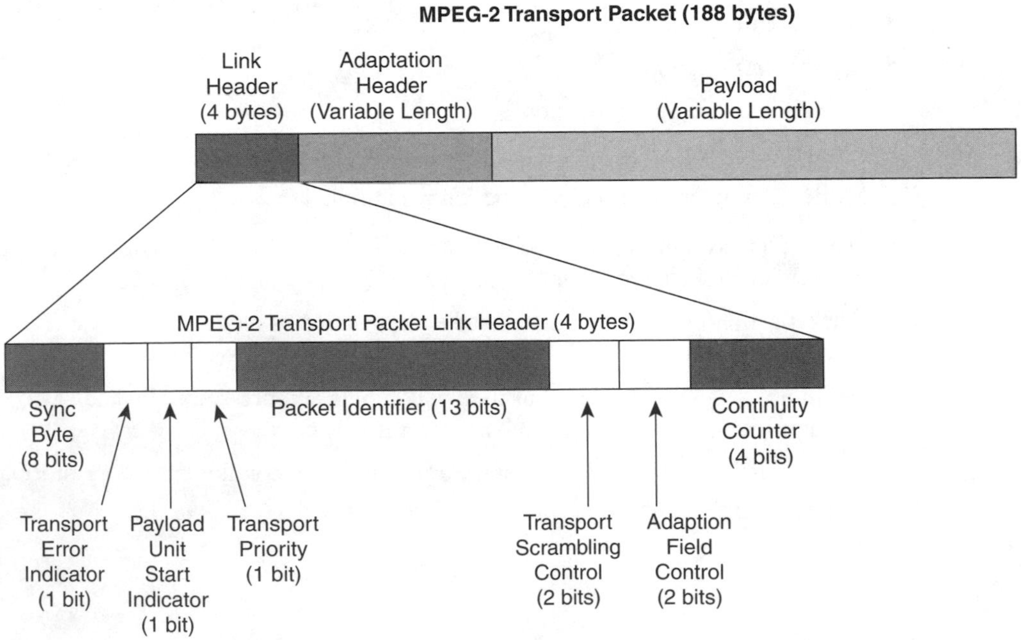

MPEG-2 transport packets use an *Asynchronous Transfer Mode*; that is, there is no direct relationship between the MPEG-2 system time and the clock used by the physical link. This approach supports great flexiblity in the choice of link layer (see the section "Broadband Transmission," later in this chapter), but it does make timing recovery more complicated.

Not surprisingly, MPEG-2 packets are very similar to ATM cells:

- MPEG-2 packets are fixed-length.
- The identifier has only local significance on the link.

However, MPEG-2 packets are very different from IP packets:

- IP packets are variable-length.
- The identifier (IP address) has global significance in the network.

Multiplexing

The MPEG-2 systems layer supports a two-level hierarchy of multiplexing: the single-program transport stream and the multi-program transport stream.

Individual program elementary streams (PESs) are packetized into MPEG-2 transport packets and multiplexed together to form a single program transport stream. An elementary stream map is included that describes the structure of the MPEG-2 multiplex; the program map table (PMT), as shown in Figure 4-3, tells the decoder which PID values to select for audio and video for that program. A program corresponds to what is traditionally called a channel—for example, HBO, CNN, and so on.

Figure 4-3 *Program Association and Program Map Tables*

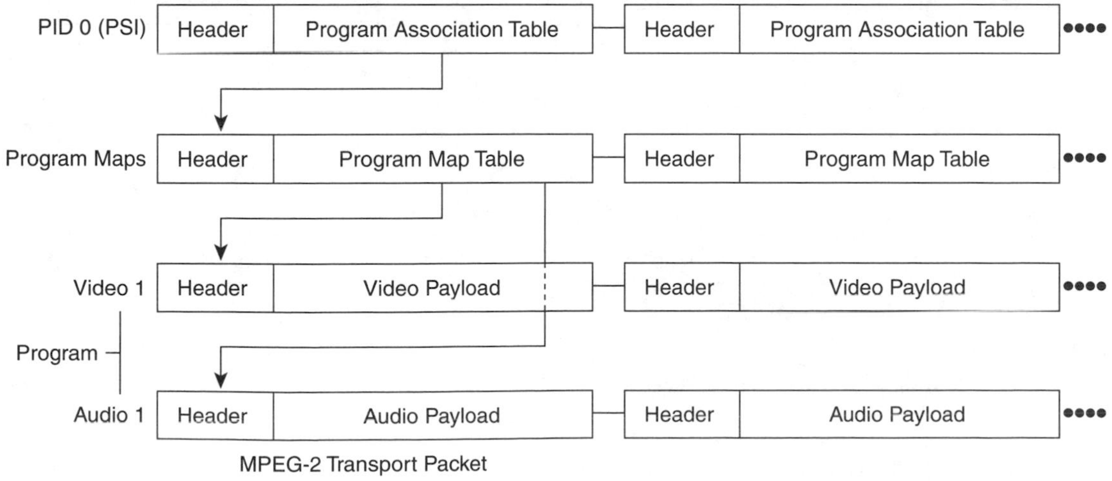

Multiple single-program transport streams are multiplexed together to form a multi-program transport stream (or system multiplex). A program stream map is included to describe the structure of multiplex; the program association table (PAT) has an entry for each program and contains a pointer to the PMT. The PAT is always transmitted using a PID of 0.

Multi-program transport streams can be combined or split into fragments by extracting the PAT from each stream and reconstructing a new PAT. This re-multiplexing operation is called *grooming*. See Chapter 15, "OpenCable Headend Interfaces," for more details.

Conditional Access

Part of the MPEG-2 transport stream is used to carry conditional access information. Conditional access is used for security, allowing only authorized decoders to access a video stream. The MPEG-2 systems committee was careful not to specify the conditional access system; instead, it standardized a mechanism that could be used by any conditional access system.

Transport packets with a PID equal to 1 (PID 1) are used to carry the conditional access table (CAT), shown in Figure 4-4. The CAT and the PMT can support multiple conditional access messages, and this mechanism is used for simulcrypt systems in Europe and for the Harmony agreement in North America that allows for dual conditional access (see the article "Multiple Conditional Access Systems," by Michael Adams and Tony Wasilewski, in *Communications Technology*).

Figure 4-4 *Conditional Access Table*

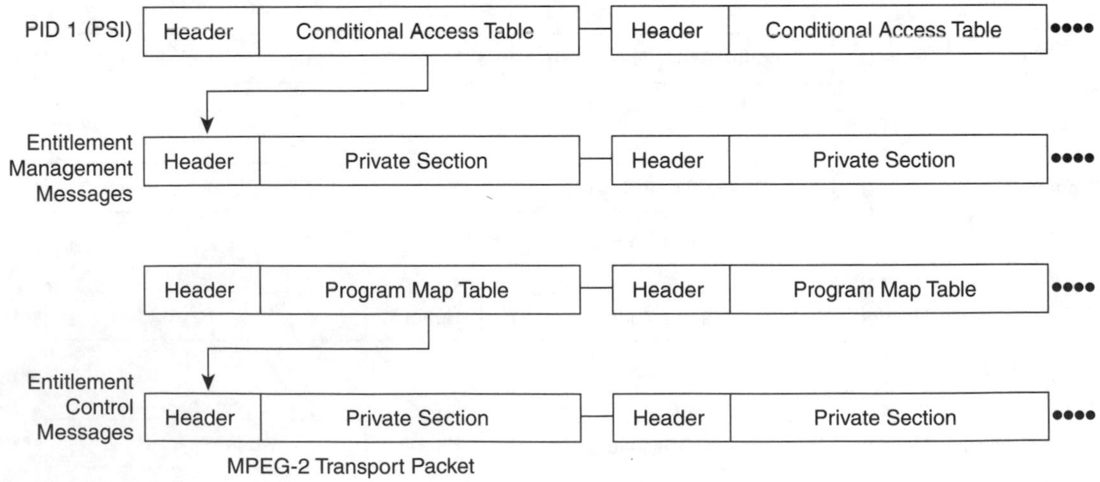

Limitations of MPEG-2 Systems Layer

The MPEG-2 systems layer was designed to support constant-delay broadcast networks. MPEG-2 transport packets can be adapted to travel over a communications network (as distinct from a communications link), but the QoS must be tightly controlled. The QoS required by MPEG can be provided by connection-oriented networks (for example, SONET or ATM networks). Connectionless, IP networks are evolving to adopt QoS and traffic engineering capabilities, driven initially by a very strong desire to make practical voice-over-IP; the net result is likely to be reasonable ways to engineer MPEG-over-IP (see *Quality of Service—Delivering QoS on the Internet and in Corporate Networks* by Paul Ferguson and Geoff Huston).

Transmission Mechanisms

There are a number of ways to transmit a multiplexed MPEG-2 transport stream. In some cases, where a dedicated synchronous transmission facility is available (such as SONET), the digital payload can simply be transmitted over a physical channel. In other cases, where it is necessary to transfer the payload over a shared network, higher-level network functions, such as routing and re-multiplexing, are supported by the network.

There are also two main categories of transmission networks: baseband and broadband. In baseband transmission, the entire physical media (twisted-pair, coaxial, laser-link, and so on) is dedicated to the transmission of a bit-stream. This makes transmission very robust but limits overall transmission rates to the maximum speed of a single transmitter or receiver. In broadband networks, each channel is modulated onto a carrier frequency in such a way as not to interfere with any of the other channels. Although broadband networks are not as inherently robust as baseband networks, they achieve a higher transmission capacity at lower cost than baseband networks.

This section covers baseband and broadband transmission as follows:

- Baseband transmission—ATM, SONET, SDH, IP, and DVB ASI provide a baseband transmission facility that can be used to carry MPEG transport streams. This section discusses each of them in turn and compares their suitability.
- Broadband transmission—QPSK, QAM, and VSB are alternative broadband modulation schemes that are commonly used to carry MPEG transport streams. This section discusses their application in cable systems.

Although baseband and broadband transmission are discussed separately, it is possible to layer multiple baseband channels onto a broadband system, and these techniques are by no means exclusive. For example, in the Orlando Full Service Network (see Chapter 11, "On-Demand Cable System Case Studies"), multiple ATM links were modulated and combined into a broadband cable system for delivery to the set-top.

Baseband Transmission

In baseband networks, the MPEG-2 transport packets must be adapted so they can be carried by the network. It was understood by the architects of the Grand Alliance system that it would be necessary to distribute MPEG-2 transport streams over a number of different network types, and considerable effort was spent in choosing an efficient mapping of MPEG-2 packets into ATM.

Asynchronous Transfer Mode

Asynchronous transfer mode (ATM) is a connection-oriented network protocol that can be used to build wide-area network (WAN) switched networks. ATM can provide guaranteed QoS metrics, which are sufficient to support MPEG transport streams. However, ATM adds an additional 12% overhead over native MPEG-2 transmission.

The following are characteristics of ATM:

- Multiplexing structure—ATM is a data-link protocol that can carry video, audio, or data in fixed-length cells that carry a 48-byte payload. Each cell has a 5-byte header that is used to identify the connection. ATM supports bandwidth-on-demand—by varying the cell rate, connections of any required bandwidth may be created.
- MPEG-into-ATM mapping—The mapping of MPEG-2 packets into ATM packets was studied by the Grand Alliance (GA), and the MPEG-2 packet size was set at 188 bytes to facilitate mapping into ATM adaptation layer type 1 or 2, as shown in Figure 4-5.

Figure 4-5 *Grand Alliance Mapping for AAL Type 1 or 2*

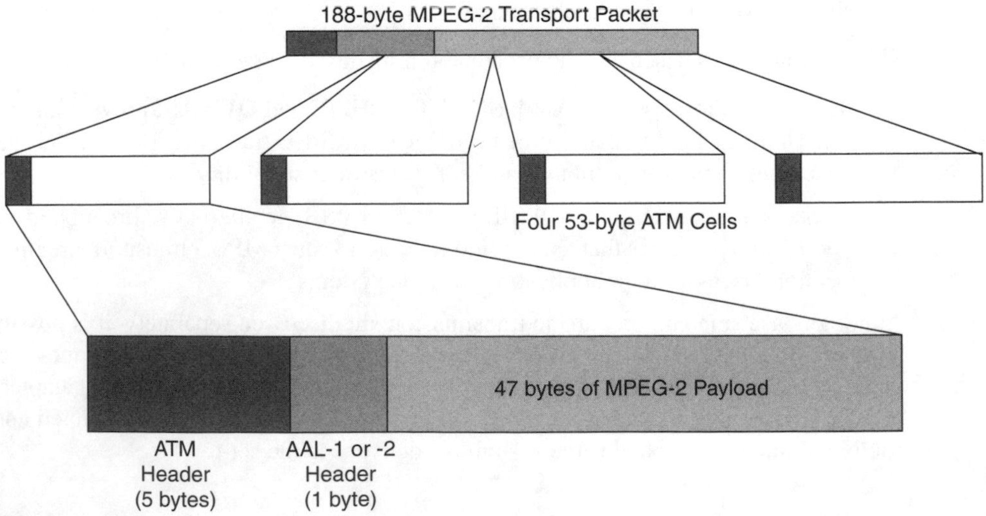

Since that time, an alternative adaptation layer, AAL type 5, has become popular in ATM applications, as illustrated in Figure 4-6. AAL type 5 mapping has been nicknamed *straight-8* mapping because it packs two transport packets into eight ATM cells.

Figure 4-6 *Straight-8 Mapping for AAL type 5*

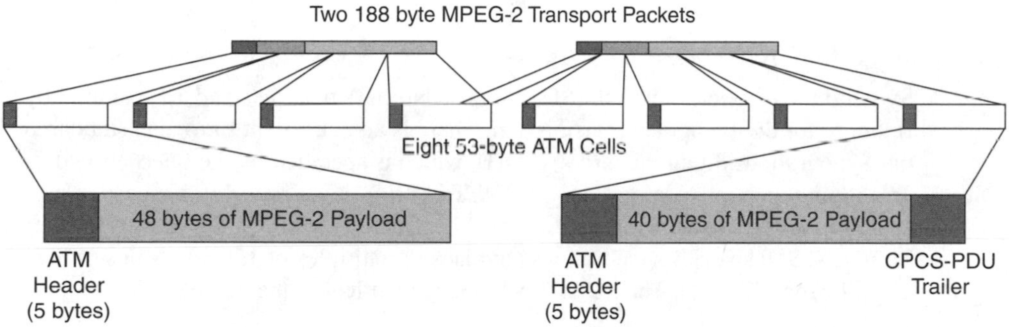

- Error detection and recovery—The header of each ATM cell is protected by a header error check sequence to protect the connection identifier from becoming corrupted. However, error detection of the payload is the responsibility of the ATM adaptation layer. AAL type 1 and 2 do not support error detection, whereas AAL type 5 computes a 32-bit cyclic redundancy check (CRC) across the payload. This provides a valuable error detection mechanism for data, but it is not much use for streaming (that is, video or audio) applications because there is no time to retransmit a corrupted packet.
- Timing—ATM specifies a timing mechanism for synchronous payloads called Synchronous Residual Time Stamp (SRTS). However, this mechanism is designed for telephone carrier emulation (for example, T1 or E1 emulation) and is not applicable to MPEG-2 transmission. Studies have shown that it is possible to transmit MPEG-2 across ATM networks without the need for system timestamp correction if the ATM cell delay variation is tightly controlled (see *Testing Digital Video,* by Dragos Ruiu and others). In addition, it is possible to use timing recovery mechanisms to "de-jitter" an MPEG-2 transport stream carried over ATM before delivering it back to a constant delay transmission system (such as QAM).
- Switching—The ATM cell structure was designed so that switches can be implemented entirely in hardware making multigigabit switches possible. ATM switches are extremely cost-effective for this reason. In video-on-demand applications, a switching function is required to deliver a program stream from a server to a particular set-top. Because MPEG-2 switches are not commercially available, ATM switches are often used to build video-on-demand networks (see the section Time Warner Full Service Network in Chapter 11).

- Limitations—ATM adaptation requires additional hardware to map MPEG-2 transport packets into cells at source and then to reassemble the cells into packets at the destination. This adaptation overhead is justified only if a true wide-area switching service is required. Few distribution applications have been deployed that require a switching function, and for broadcast systems the cost of ATM is not justified [Adams].

Synchronous Optical Networks

Synchronous Optical Network (SONET) is a North American standard specified by Bellcore for digital optical transmission. There is an equivalent European standard called the Synchronous digital hierarchy (SDH), which is specified by the International Telecommunications Union (ITU). SONET is a link-layer protocol that carries synchronous payloads in multiples of 50.112 Mbps (within a 51.84 Mbps STS-1). Similarly, SDH carries synchronous payloads in multiples of 150.336 Mbps (within a 155.52 Mbps STM-1). The SONET STS-3c is identical to the SDH STM-1.

The following are characteristics of SONET/SDH:

- Mapping—SONET and SDH are ideal candidates for the carriage of MPEG-2 transport streams, but no direct mapping exists for MPEG-2 into SONET or SDH payloads. An alternative approach is to map a multi-program transport stream (for example, the entire payload of a DVB ASI link) into a single ATM Virtual Channel. The ATM Virtual Channel is then mapped into a SONET payload. This approach has the advantage that only a single ATM segmentation and reassembly (SAR) process is required.
- Error detection and recovery—Optical networks run error-free if properly maintained, and failures are usually catestrophic due to equipment failure of a fiber cut. For this reason, SONET includes mechanisms for error monitoring and protection switching. A block check is used to monitor the error rate on each SONET link (which is usually zero). If the error rate exceeds a set threshold, a protection switch will be made to a spare link (assuming it is available and its error rate is below threshold). SONET protection switches take less than 50 milliseconds to complete but, despite this, are quite noticeable to a customer watching MPEG-2 compressed video.

Internet Protocol

IP is widely used as a data communications protocol. Recently, there has been considerable interest in using IP to carry telephony, audio, and video services. Although IP was not designed with QoS in mind, there has been considerable effort to provide QoS over IP networks (see *Quality of Service—Delivering QoS on the Internet and in Corporate Networks* by Paul Ferguson and Geoff Huston).

The following provides a brief description of IP:

- Multiplexing structure—IP is a network protocol that can carry arbitrary data in variable-length packets. IP supports bandwidth-on-demand—by varying the packet rate, flows of any required bandwidth may be created.

  IP's variable-length packet is a disadvantage in delay-sensitive applications, because larger packets can delay shorter packets by taking considerable time to traverse a link. However, as link speed increases, this effect is less noticeable. By using a technique called packet over SONET (PoS) to map IP packets directly into high-bandwidth SONET payloads, delays due to large packets are greatly reduced. (For example, at OC-12 rates of 622 Mbps, a 4 KB packet occupies the link for only 51 microseconds.)

- Error detection and recovery—Like ATM, IP's approach to error detection and recovery is datacentric. That is, errors may be detected by computing a CRC-32 across the packet, and if an error is detected the Transmission Control Protocol (TCP) is used to retransmit the packet.

  For streaming applications, retransmission is not useful, so user datagram protocol (UDP) is used because it has no payload error checking and requires less overhead than TCP.

- Routing—IP routers were first constructed from general purpose minicomputers. However, router design has evolved to the point that routers can be implemented almost entirely in hardware. By placing the packet-forwarding function in hardware, the forwarding delay can be reduced by orders of magnitude, and high-performance routers can approach ATM switches in delay performance.

  However, IP routing is fundamentally very different from ATM switching in architectural terms. Classical IP routing is completely connectionless, which means that there is no state knowledge in the IP routers about the packet flow. This makes IP routing very flexible and obviates any need for connection management; however, it also means that by nature it is impossible to predict the load on any particular link or router. Thus, there is a statistical probability that a particular route may become congested, and this can interfere with a particular IP flow. The effect to the user is that video may freeze, or voice may become garbled for some period of time until the congestion clears.

- Limitations—IP's ability to support connectionless networks is its Achilles' heel for any application requiring QoS guarantees. Connectionless networks support dynamic reconfiguration by rerouting around congested or failed links in the network. This makes packet delay variation very difficult to control and, as we have seen, MPEG-2 is extremely sensitive to variations in delay. Moreover, IP networks currently do not provide admission control mechanisms, so the only way to obtain bandwidth guarantees is by overprovisioning.

DVB Asynchronous Serial Interface

DVB asynchronous serial interface (ASI) was developed for the interconnection of professional MPEG-2 equipment and is a native baseband transmission facility for MPEG-2 transport streams. DVB ASI uses 8b/10b coding at a line rate of 270 Mbps yielding a maximum payload of 216 Mbps. DVB ASI is designed to use two physical media:

- Coaxial cable—Coaxial cable is less expensive than optical fiber and ideal for interconnecting racks of equipment in the headend. However, coaxial cable attenuation limits the reach to about 100 meters.
- Optical fiber—Optical fiber is more expensive than coaxial cable but supports considerably greater reach. Multimode fiber, which has a reach of several kilometers, is typically used, but there is no physical reason why single-mode fiber transceivers (with a reach of up to 100 kilometers) could not be used.

A brief description of DVB ASI's characteristics follows:

- Transmission format—The DVB ASI transmission format is shown in Figure 4-7. Each byte is encoded as 10 bits using 8b/10b coding, and each MPEG transport packet is preceded and trailed by at least 2 synchronization bytes. A packet may be interspersed with an arbitrary number of stuff bytes.
- Error detection and recovery—DVB ASI has no mechanisms for error detection or recovery because it is designed to be for interconnection of equipment over short distances.

Figure 4-7 *DVB ASI Transmission Format*

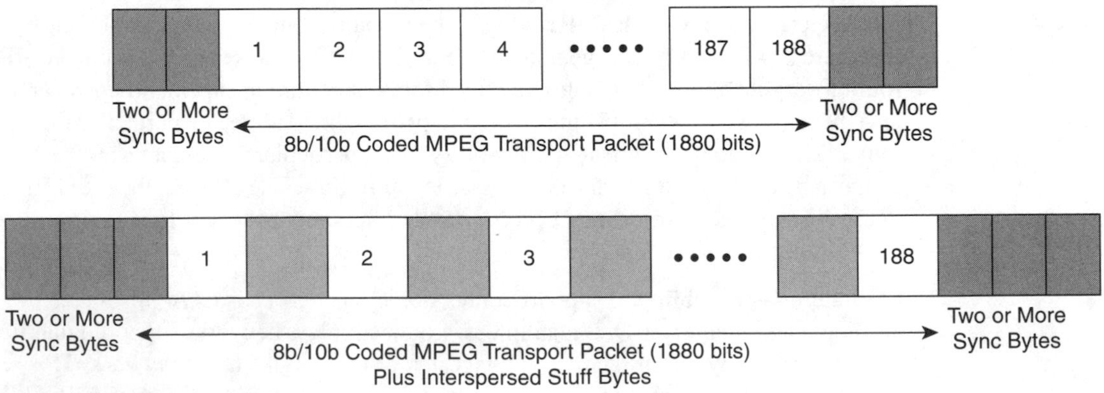

- Timing—DVB ASI, as its name suggests, is asynchronous. That is, there is no relationship between the line clock and the MPEG system timing. Therefore, each piece of equipment using a DVB ASI input performs timestamping using a high-fidelity local 27 MHz counter. (see the section MPEG-2 Systems Layer, later in this chapter). When MPEG-2 transport packets are output onto the ASI link, they are timestamped again to compensate for any jitter introduced by re-multiplexing.
- Limitations—DVB ASI is limited to the interconnection of equipment over short distances because of its lack of physical reach and error protection mechanisms.

Comparison of Baseband Transmission Alternatives

Table 4-3 compares ATM, SONET/SDH, IP, and DVB ASI for the baseband transmission of MPEG-2 transport streams. Although it is unfair, strictly speaking, to compare data link protocols with network protocols, this distinction is lost on the engineer who needs to decide how to move an MPEG-2 transport stream from one location to another.

Table 4-3 *Comparison of Baseband Transmission Alternatives for MPEG-2 Transport*

	ATM	**SONET/SDH**	**IP**	**DVB ASI**
Overhead	12% (5-byte cell header)	3.3%	14% (1 MPEG-2 transport packet per UDP packet)	1% (2 sync bytes per MPEG-2 transport packet)
QoS	Admission control and connection management guarantees	Constant bit rate link	Differentiated class of service	Constant bit rate link
Advantages	Supports switching and integrates voice, video, and data	Supports long-haul optical networks; may also be used to carry ATM, IP, and DVB ASI traffic	Supports routing, ubiquitous network layer for data communi-cations networks	Cost-effective interconnection of headend components
Disadvantages	ATM adaptation cost	Expensive Telco-class service, payloads only in multiples of 52 Mbps	Lack of proven QoS mechanisms for streaming services	Limited reach and lack of switching function

Baseband Transmission Interworking

As discussed in the previous sections on baseband transmission, it is quite common to layer one or more protocols on top of another. Figure 4-8 summarizes the protocol layerings that are, or are in the process of being, standardized.

Figure 4-8 *Standard Protocol Layering*

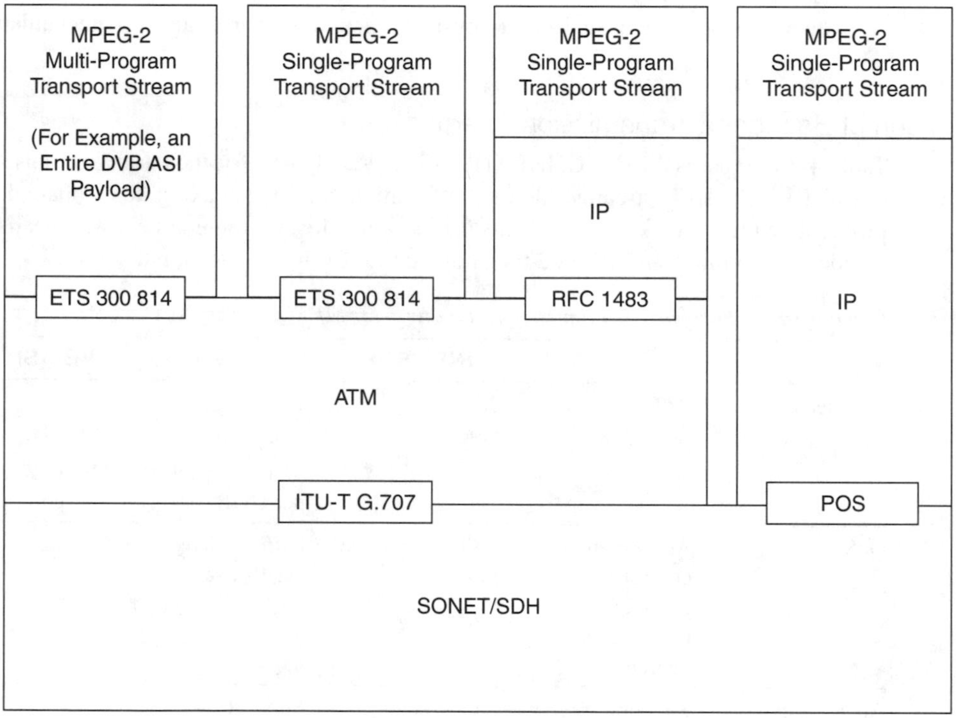

From left to right, Figure 4-8 illustrates the following mappings:

- An MPEG-2 multi-program transport stream is mapped into a single ATM Virtual Channel, providing transport of an entire DVB ASI payload over an ATM/SONET network.
- An MPEG-2 single-program transport stream is mapped into a single ATM Virtual Channel for transport over an ATM/SONET network.
- An MPEG-2 single-program transport stream is mapped into IP packets. The IP connection is supported by a single ATM Virtual Channel for transport over an ATM/ SONET network.
- An MPEG-2 single-program transport stream is mapped into IP packets. The IP connection is supported by a direct packet over an SONET (POS) adaptation layer to provide transport over an SONET network.

In networks, simplicity is usually most cost-effective, and DVB ASI is the simplest and least expensive approach for local interconnection of equipment. The mapping of an MPEG-2 MPTS into a single ATM virtual channel is also gaining favor with cable companies that need to deliver MPEG-2 transport streams over some distance.

Broadband Transmission

Transmission in a broadband system uses modulation to separate each channel into a given frequency band. This technique is often called frequency-division multiplexing (FDM). This section discusses the three common modulation techniques used for MPEG-2 transport in North America: QPSK, QAM, and VSB.

Error correction and protection techniques are typically employed in broadband transmission systems to reduce the number of errors introduced by analog transmission; these are also discussed in this section.

Quaternary Phase Shift Keying

Quaternary phase shift keying (QPSK) modulation is very robust in the presence of noise, so QPSK is used for satellite transmission links and for control channel modulation in cable systems (see the section Out-of-Band Communications in Chapter 5).

Figure 4-9 shows how QPSK modulation is applied to a baseband signal. Two bits are encoded per baud. The 2-bit *symbol* is divided into one in-phase (I) bit and one quadrature-phase (Q) bit, which are each converted to an analog level. These levels are used to modulate the amplitude and phase of a carrier.

Figure 4-9 *QPSK Modulator Block Diagram*

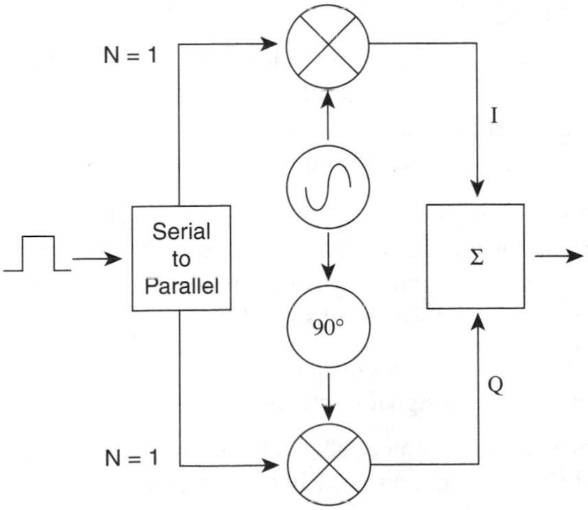

Figure 4-10 shows the constellation diagram for QPSK and the symbol mapping for each phase angle and amplitude vector. QPSK is very robust because the detector needs to detect only two levels and two phase angles to determine the symbol. (QPSK is equivalent to 4-QAM.)

Figure 4-10 *QPSK Constellation Diagram*

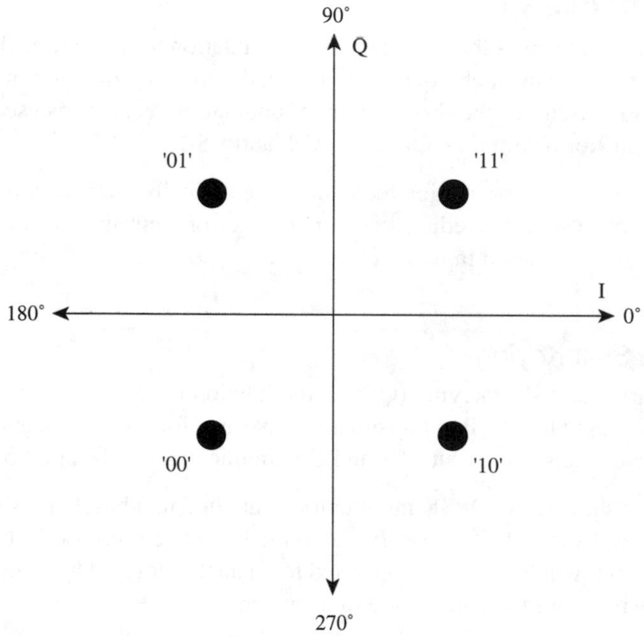

Quadrature Amplitude Modulation

Figure 4-11 shows how 64-QAM modulation is applied to a baseband signal. Six bits are encoded per baud, which is three times as efficient as QPSK. The 6-bit *symbol* is divided into three in-phase (I) bits and three quadrature-phase (Q) bits, which are each converted to an analog level. These levels are used to modulate the amplitude and phase of a carrier.

Using the North American standard for 64-QAM modulation (ITU J.83 Annex B), a payload of approximately 27 Mbps is achieved within a 6 MHz channel. This is an efficiency of 4.5 bits per baud—considerably less than the theoretical maximum of 6 bits per baud. There are two main reasons for this:

- The entire 6 MHz bandwidth cannot be used, and guard-bands need to be introduced on either side of the signal to prevent interference between adjacent channels.
- Error correction and protection mechanisms introduce some overhead (see the section Forward Error Correction, later in this chapter).

Figure 4-11 *64-QAM Modulator Block Diagram*

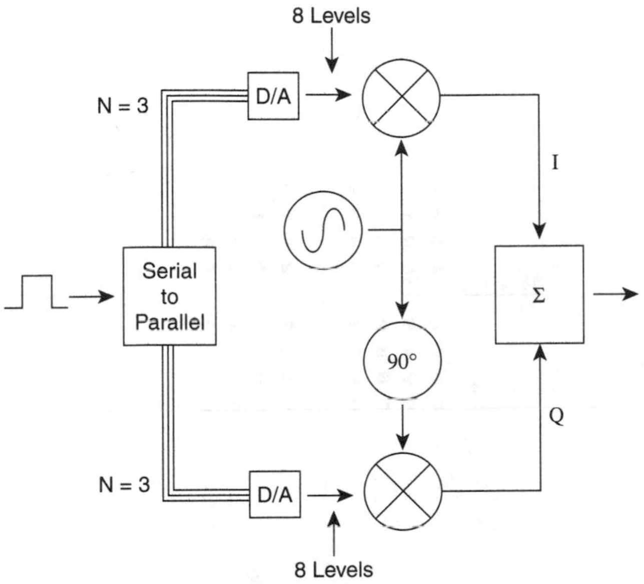

Figure 4-12 shows the constellation diagram for 64-QAM. There are 64 different phase angle and amplitude vectors and, for this reason, 64-QAM is less robust because the detector needs to differentiate between these to determine the symbol. In practice, 64-QAM requires a carrier-to-noise ratio in excess of 22 dB to work (see Chapter 4 of *Modern Cable Television Technology; Video, Voice, and Data Communications* by Walter Ciciora and others, for more details).

Figure 4-13 shows how 256-QAM modulation is applied to a baseband signal. Eight bits are encoded per baud, and this is 33% more efficient than 64-QAM. The 8-bit *symbol* is divided into four in-phase (I) bits and four quadrature-phase (Q) bits, which are each converted to an analog level. These levels are used to modulate the amplitude and phase of a carrier.

Using the North American standard for 256-QAM modulation (ITU J.83 Annex B), a payload of approximately 38.8 Mbps is achieved within a 6 MHz channel. This is an efficiency of 6.47 bits per baud—considerably less than the theoretical maximum of 8 bits per baud. A payload of 38.8 Mbps was chosen because it is sufficient to carry two HDTV channels.

Figure 4-12 *64-QAM Constellation Diagram*

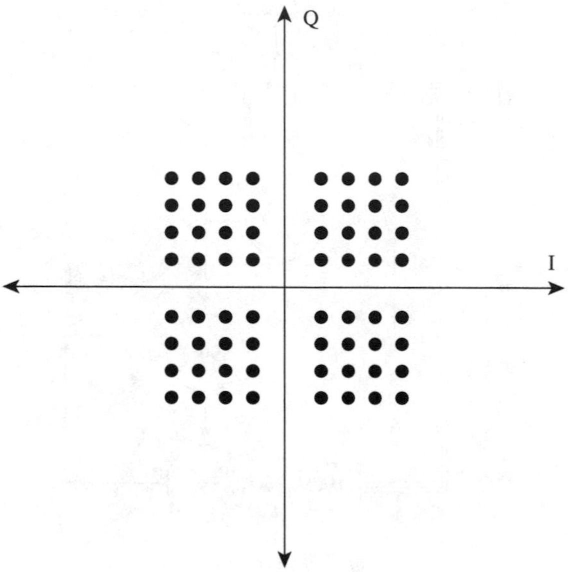

Figure 4-13 *256-QAM Modulator Block Diagram*

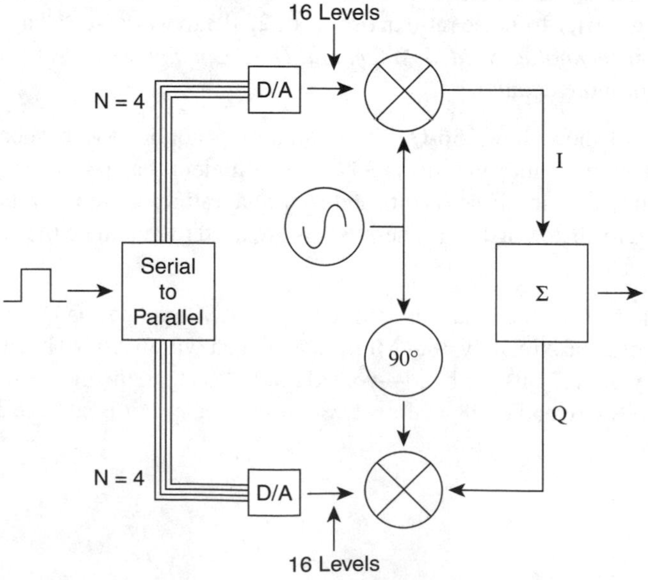

Figure 4-14 shows the constellation diagram for 256-QAM. There are 256 different phase angle and amplitude vectors, making the points on the constellation closer together; for this reason, 256-QAM is less robust than 64-QAM. In practice, 256-QAM requires a carrier-to-noise ratio in excess of 28 dB to work in practice (6 dB more than 64-QAM).

Figure 4-14 *256-QAM Constellation Diagram*

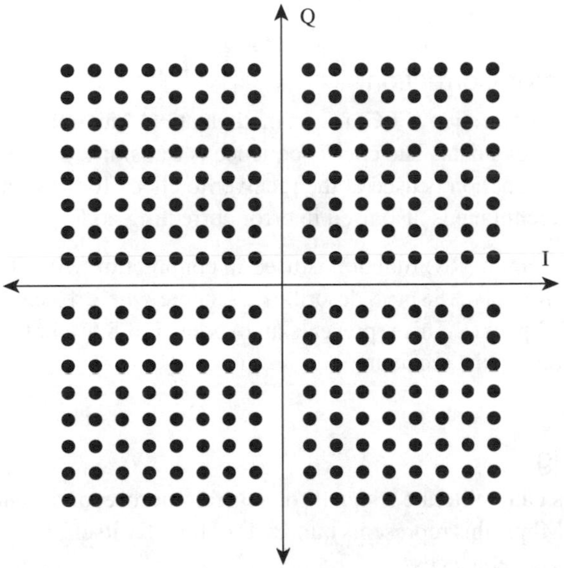

There has been some discussion of still higher orders of QAM modulation—512-QAM, 768-QAM, or even 1024-QAM. However, there are diminishing returns—1024-QAM increases the payload by only 25% over 256-QAM—and it is unlikely that these will be used in the near future.

Vestigial Side Band

VSB-8 modulation has been adopted for use in terrestrial digital broadcasting (see A.53 Annex D). VSB-8 has a payload of approximately 19.4 Mbps and was designed to carry a single HDTV channel. VSB-8 is a one-dimensional modulation scheme because it uses only amplitude modulation of the carrier (in contrast, QAM is two-dimensional modulation technique because it uses both I and Q components). In VSB-8 modulation, the baseband signal is coded as an 8-level value, so 3 bits are encoded per baud.

Error Correction and Protection

Analog transmission systems arc subjcct to noisc, distortion, and interference from other carriers. Therefore, error correction and protection techniques are used to maintain an acceptable error rate.

Three commonly used techniques are discussed in this section: forward error correction, interleaving, and trellis coding.

Forward Error Correction

Forward error correction (FEC) uses a mathematical function to generate a check sequence across the payload data. The check sequence is transmitted with the data, and the same mathematical function is used at the receiver to check for payload errors and to correct errors. This technique is also used in error correcting code (ECC) memory.

The Reed Solomon (RS) function is used in conjunction with QPSK, QAM, and VSB modulation. RS (204,188) t=8 describes a scheme where 16 check bytes are generated for each MPEG-2 packet. This represents an overhead of 8.5% but allows 1- and 2-byte errors to be corrected by the receiver.

Interleaving

Noise pulses can obliterate a signal for several microseconds, and at a 256-QAM payload rate of 38.8 Mbps, this represents hundreds of bits. By itself, FEC is incapable of correcting such long error sequences.

Interleaving effectively spreads the payload data over time. Figure 4-15 shows an example of a block interleaver developed by Scientific Atlanta for the Time Warner Full Service Network (see Chapter 11).

Figure 4-15 *Block Interleaver Used in the Time Warner Full Service Network*

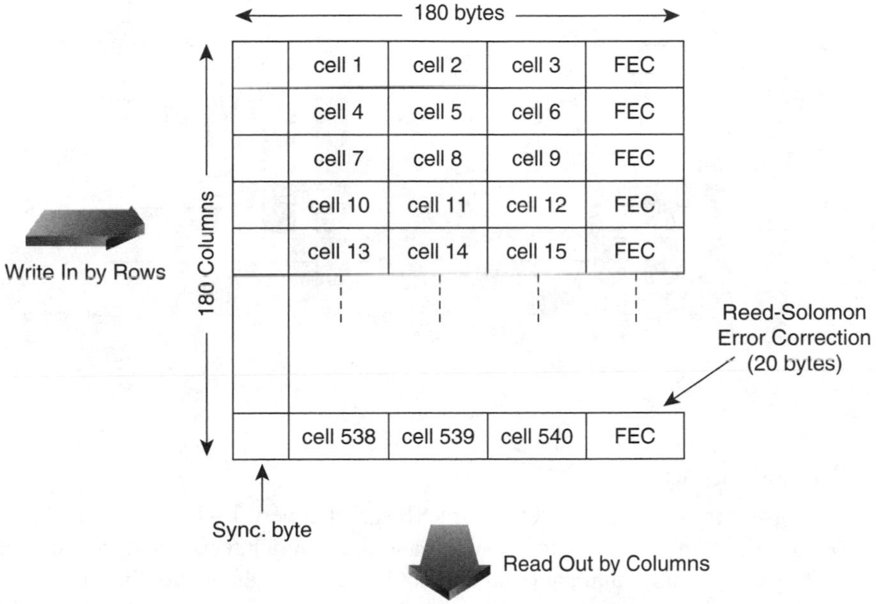

In this implementation, a noise pulse affects only 1 byte in each row, a situation that can be rectified by the RS correction. The main disadvantage of interleaving is buffer memory and delay, which are 32 KB and 11.5 milliseconds, respectively, in this implementation.

Convolutional interleavers require only half the memory and introduce only half the delay of block interleavers. For this reason, both ITU J.83 Annex B (QAM) and ATSC A/53 Annex D (VSB) use convolutional interleaving. Figure 4-16 shows an example of a convolutional interleaver with an interleave depth of six. The blocks (labeled J) buffer the payload and operate as a shift register. The interleaver (at the modulator) and the deinterleaver (at the demodulator) are synchronized so that the payload is reassembled in its original form.

The effect of interleaving is to distribute the errors due to a noise burst over a period of time so that the errored bits are no longer adjacent, which makes FEC more effective.

Figure 4-16 *Example of a Convolutional Interleaver*

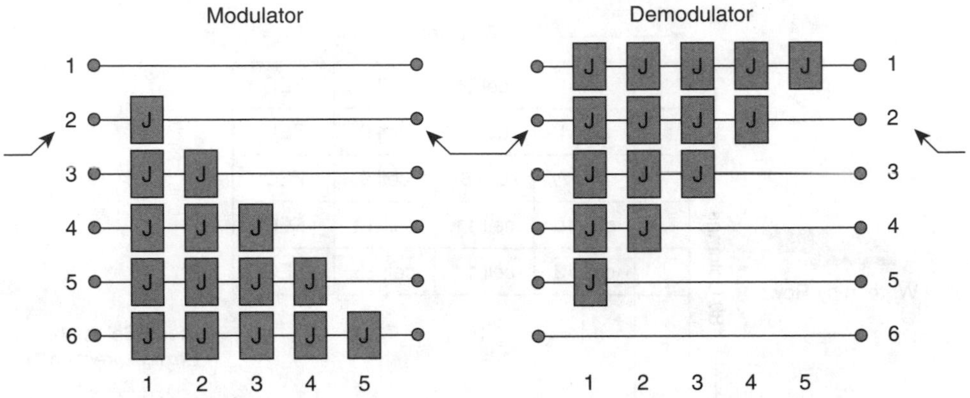

Trellis Coding

As noise is introduced into a QAM or VSB signal, it perturbs the points on the constellation diagram so that ultimately they overlap and the decoder sees the wrong symbol. Trellis coding adds some redundancy and uses sophistical mathematics at the receiver to determine the best fit of the constellation to a symbol. The trellis coding specified by ITU J.83 Annex B QAM uses a 14/15 coding rate to improve noise immunity by approximately 2 dB. VSB-8, which is designed for more challenging broadcast applications, specifies a 2/3 trellis coding rate, improving noise immunity but reducing payload rate by 33%.

Summary

This chapter introduced a number of important techniques and concepts:

- Video and audio compression algorithms and how they are used to increase the channel capacity of a cable system
- The MPEG-2 systems layer and the multiplexing of multiple program elementary streams into a single physical channel
- Baseband transmission mechanisms for compressed audio and video streams, including ATM, SONET, IP, and DVB ASI
- Broadband transmission mechanisms for compressed audio and video streams, including QPSK, QAM, and VSB modulation

References

Books

Ciciora, Walter, James Farmer, and David Large. *Modern Cable Television Technology; Video, Voice, and Data Communications*. San Francisco, CA: Morgan Kaufmann Publishers Inc., 1999.

Evans, Brian. *Understanding Digital TV—The Route to HDTV.* New York, NY: IEEE Press, 1995.

Ferguson, Paul, and Geoff Huston. *Quality of Service—Delivering QoS on the Internet and in Corporate Networks*. New York, NY: John Wiley and Sons, 1998.

Gibson, Jerry D., Toby Berger, Tom Lookabaugh, Dave Lindberg, and Richard L. Baker. *Digital Compression for Multimedia: Principles and Standards.* San Francisco, CA: Morgan Kaufmann Publishers, Inc., 1998.

Hodge, Winston William. *Interactive Television—A Comprehensive Guide to Multimedia Technologies.* New York, NY: McGraw-Hill, 1994.

Ruiu, Dragos *et al. Testing Digital Video*. Hewlett-Packard, 1997.

Whitaker, Jerry C. *DTV: The Revolution in Electronic Imaging*. New York, NY: McGraw-Hill, 1998.

Periodicals

Adams, Michael. "ATM and MPEG-2 in Cable TV Networks, Parts 1 and 2." *Communications Technology*, December 1995 and February 1996.

Adams, Michael, and Tony Wasilewski. "Multiple Conditional Access Systems." *Communications Technology,* April 1997.

Standards

ATSC Standard A/52, *Digital Audio Compression (AC-3)*, 1995.

ATSC Standard A/53, *Digital Television Standard*, 1995.

ATSC Document A/54, *Guide to the Use of the ATSC Digital Television Standard*, 1995.

NOTE The ATSC was formed to establish voluntary technical standards for advanced television systems, including digital high definition television (HDTV). The ATSC is supported by its members, who are subject to certain qualification requirements. ATSC documents are available at the ATSC Web site (see the section "Internet Resources").

Bellcore GR-253-Core Issue 2. *Synchronous Optical Network Standard.* 1995.

ISO/IEC IS 13818-1, International Standard. *MPEG-2 Systems*. 1994.

ISO/IEC IS 13818-2, International Standard. *MPEG-2 Video*. 1994.

ISO/IEC IS 13818-3, International Standard. *MPEG-2 Audio*. 1994.

ITU G-series, *Synchronous Digital Hierarchy Standard.*

Internet Resources

The Advanced Television Systems Committee (ATSC)

http://www.atsc.org/

Digital TV: A Cringely Crash Course

http://www.pbs.org/opb/crashcourse/

Dolby Web site of technical information on audio compression and related matters

http://www.dolby.com/tech/

DVB Web reference

http://www.dvb.org/

The Grand Alliance HDTV Specification 2.0

http://www.sarnoff.com/Papers/hdtv.html

CHAPTER 5

Adding Digital Television Services to Cable Systems

Cable operators are adding many types of digital services to their systems, including digital television, cable modem services, and telephony. This chapter focuses on digital services delivered through the television receiver. Such services might include broadcast, interactive, and on-demand services, but they have some important characteristics in common:

- The service fits into existing television viewing habits. This is sometimes called the *lean-back* model to contrast it with the *lean-forward* model of personal computer use. For example, the audience expects to be entertained, educated, and informed—viewing often coexists with other social activities, such as conversation, drinking, and eating.
- Video and audio quality are important to the service, to captivate the viewer despite other demands on his or her attention. (In the entertainment world, these are called *production values* and actually extend far beyond technical measures of quality, such as signal-to-noise ratio and video bandwidth.)

For convenience, I will refer to all these services generically as *digital television* to suggest a much broader category than digital picture and sound.

The first part of this chapter discusses the technical and market drivers for digital television. The second part of the chapter concentrates on the necessary enhancements to the cable network to support digital television services, which can be summarized as

- Hybrid fiber coaxial (HFC) upgrade (see Chapter 2, "Analog Cable Technologies")—Strictly speaking, it is not necessary to upgrade the cable system to carry digital television services. However, the additional spectrum required to carry both analog and digital television is a welcome *side effect* of an HFC upgrade.
- Broadband transmission (see Chapter 4, "Digital Technologies")—All cable systems are broadband analog networks, which means that any digital signals must be modulated onto a radio-frequency (RF) carrier before they can be carried by the cable system.

- Out-of-band communications—Cable systems were originally conceived as one-way broadcast networks. Adding a forward out-of-band channel, which is routed (to the distribution hub or fiber node), provides significant operational advantages. Adding a reverse out-of-band channel completes the two-way signaling path, effectively placing each digital set-top on a local area network (LAN).
- Data communications overlay—Interconnecting all the distribution hub LANs to the headend equipment with a data communications overlay network completes the infrastructure required for digital television and also enables interactive and on-demand services (see Part II, "Interactive and On-Demand Services").

Drivers for Digital Television

Digital channels have some major technical advantages over analog channels:

- Each additional digital channel can carry from 10 to 14 services in the same bandwidth that is occupied by a single analog channel (see the section Video Compression in Chapter 4).
- Digital channels are less sensitive to noise and distortion compared to analog channels, allowing the cable operator to run the digital channels at lower power levels than the analog channels to reduce laser loading and overall distortion (see the section Broadband Transmission in Chapter 4).
- Digital channels can carry data as easily as they carry video and audio. This means that new services can be added relatively easily to the payload (see Chapter 8, "Interactive Services").
- Premium digital channels are secured using digital cryptographic techniques that are much harder to break than analog scrambling (see Chapter 6, "The Digital Set-Top Converter").

However, the customer requires a relatively expensive digital set-top to receive digital channels (a capital outlay by the cable operator of about two to three times the cost of an analog set-top converter). Moreover, the customer cannot receive digital channels with an analog cable ready receiver. (See Chapter 18, "OCI-C2: the Security Interface," for a discussion of cable ready *digital* television.)

This section addresses the drivers for digital television by addressing the following:

- Channel expansion—Digital television squeezes many more channels into a given amount of cable spectrum than analog.
- DBS competition—Matching DBS channel line-ups and providing the all-important "digital picture and sound" sticker.
- High definition television (HDTV)—Compressed digital formats that provide the only way to send HDTV in North America.

- Consolidation with other digital services—Sharing the network infrastructure necessary for digital television with cable modem and telephony services.
- RF return traffic—The aggregation of reverse traffic.
- Business communications—Opportunities to reduce existing data communications costs by using a shared exterprise network.
- Network management—The increased need for network management to provide a highly reliable cable system.

Channel Expansion

It is a fundamental truth that no cable operator can ever have too much bandwidth or too many channels. New channels appear each year (for example, the Radio City Music Hall channel, BBC America, Food Network, Lifetime, OVATION, International Channel, Nick-At-Nite TV Land, Outdoor Channel, Discovery Kids, and Game Show Network, to name just a few), and this trend shows no sign of slowing down. Because each additional analog channel requires an additional 6 MHz of valuable spectrum, cable operators spend significant time and energy considering which channels to carry. (If you visit the Web site of a new channel, you will probably be asked to help lobby for carriage on your local cable system.) In New York, Manhattan Cable already carries more than 100 analog channels.

By using digital channels to carry new services, the pressure on cable system spectrum is reduced. At some future time, it will be possible to collapse existing analog channels into digital channels.

Direct Broadcast Satellite Competition

DirecTV, EchoStar, and others use "*digital* picture and sound quality" to market their services. In fact, poorly compressed digital video can be markedly inferior to analog (see the section Video Compression in Chapter 4). Digital video compression allows the operator to precisely control the amount of quality granted to each video channel without regard to the intervening transmission. This gives a digital operator the flexibility to offer some channels at higher quality than analog and some at lower quality—a flexibility that is quite valuable in terms of maximizing revenue. Because marketing is often a game of "spec"-manship, it is important for cable operators to match the specifications claimed by digital broadcast from satellite (DBS) operators.

High Definition Television

High definition television (HDTV) offers a resolution of up to 1,920 horizontal pixels by 1,080 vertical lines. Multiplying these numbers gives a pixel count of 2,073,600 pixels per frame. This is exactly six times as many pixels as a standard-definition (or full-resolution) picture with 720 horizontal pixels and 480 vertical lines.

HDTV offers a stunning increase in picture quality, and at normal viewing distances is almost as good as the human eye; for this reason, an HDTV picture has been described as "like looking through a window."

Because of its high bandwidth requirements, digital compression provides the only practical way to deliver HDTV.

HDTV Bandwidth Requirements

Without compression, an HDTV picture would require a bit rate of about 746 Mbps (assuming 8-bit, 4:2:0 sampling—see the section Picture Resolution in Chapter 4). If this signal was analog-modulated with the same efficiency as NTSC, it would require six times the 4.2 MHz video bandwidth of NTSC, or 25.2 MHz. In practice, the European HDMAC-60 system requires 24 MHz and the Japanese Multiple Sub-Nyquist Sampling Encoding (MUSE) system requires 9 or 12 MHz. Each of these systems is designed to use the entire bandwidth of a satellite transponder.

There is insufficient radio frequency spectrum to carry many analog HDTV channels, even on upgraded cable systems. In fact, HDTV is so bandwidth-hungry that no North American standard exists for analog HDTV transmission, and digital television provides the only form of HDTV carriage.

Using MPEG-2 main profile at high level (MP@HL) compression, the bit rate of an HDTV signal can be reduced to 18.8 Mbps, an MPEG compression ratio of nearly 40:1. (This is similar to a typical 31:1 compression ratio for SDTV—see the section Video Compression in Chapter 4.)

The North American standard (ITU J.83 Annex B) for QAM-256 modulation is designed with HDTV in mind. The QAM-256 transport payload is 38.48 Mbps, enough to carry two HDTV channels. Similarly, the VSB-8 (which is the North American terrestrial broadcast modulation standard defined by ATSC A/53) has a transport payload of 19.24 Mbps, enough to carry a single HDTV channel. (See the section Broadband Transmission in Chapter 4.)

Consolidation with Other Digital Services

Cable operators have offered many new service offerings based on digital technology—for example, local-area network (LAN) interconnection, telephony, cable modem services, meter reading, and power management. Some of these services cannot justify their own network infrastructure but generate significant revenue if they ride on a network infrastructure deployed for digital television.

Radio Frequency Return Traffic

Many cable operators have deployed advanced analog converters and are already struggling with an efficient way to aggregate radio-frequency (RF) return traffic and transport it back to the headend controller. Terminating the RF return at the hub and using a digital network to transport the return traffic to the headend is an attractive solution.

Business Communications

Nearly all cable operators have some existing leased or dial-up lines that are used to connect to billing providers and other services. The connection charges on these lines are an ongoing expense, and the ability to run *legacy* data communications, such as IBM's Systems Network Architecture (SNA), over a shared network infrastructure is an important consideration. Like any other business, cable operators are adopting enterprise network approaches to consolidate their internal communications needs to interconnect computers systems, LANs, and PBXs. Some of the larger cable systems span multiple area codes, and operators can save long-distance charges by using their own network infrastructure to carry voice calls.

Network Management

As digital services develop, cable operators have to address a new area: network management. New services being offered require higher availability (for example, telephony), and it is no longer sufficient to react to outages by truck rolls and to maintain headend equipment by responding to customer phone calls. A more proactive approach to network management often requires real-time monitoring of hub equipment, power supplies, and, in some cases, amplifiers. The network management traffic is digital in nature and often uses the Simple Network Management Protocol (SNMP) and requires a digital network overlay on top of the existing analog network.

Transmission of Digital Television

Chapter 2 describes how hybrid fiber coaxial (HFC) upgrades are used to expand the number of analog channels in a cable system. There are two techniques that can be used to transmit a digital television payload to the home:

- The digital payload can be carried all the way to the home in baseband digital form. This technique has been used experimentally (see *Residential Broadband* by George Abe, Chapter 5, which describes Heathrow fiber-to-the-home, NHK fiber-to-the-curb systems). Telcos are forced to deploy fiber closer to the home than cable companies because of the limited transmission distance that is achievable, and over the existing twisted-pair wiring to the home. Some telcos are still considering fiber-to-the-home, but it will remain uneconomical for some time because it is so expensive to deploy fiber to each home and then to illuminate each fiber with a separate laser.

- Broadband transmission can be used to convert the digital payload into analog form so that an existing analog network can carry it. However, the original digital payload must be recovered (demodulated) by a digital set-top before it can be used.

Not surprisingly, cable operators have chosen to use broadband transmission over their existing analog networks instead of building a separate digital overlay network. This allows the cable operator to maximize the benefits of an HFC upgrade. (See "Digital and Analog Can and Will Coexist," by Walter Ciciora.) Alternatively, some cable operators are using digital transmission to extend their channel lineups in un-upgraded systems (for example, AT&T BIS HITS).

Meanwhile some regional bell operating companies are still experimenting with digital overlay networks, and others are adopting a similar approach to cable (for example, Ameritech) or have deployed MMDS (for example, Bell South).

In practice, a digital set-top is necessary (see Chapter 6) for other purposes than demodulation. Even so, broadband transmission brings its own set of challenges (see the section Broadband Transmission, in Chapter 4).

Figure 5-1 illustrates a hybrid analog/digital channel lineup. The set-top converter tunes to any *one* 6 MHz channel at a time with an *in-band* tuner, effectively performing a switching function (more on this in the section QAM Matrix, in Chapter 10, "On-Demand Services"). Although it is possible to build a set-top converter with multiple tuners, most set-tops are single-tuner designs to minimize cost. Using a single tuner to select either an analog or a digital channel causes the set-top to have two distinct operational modes:

- Tuned to analog—The set-top receives a single analog channel and associated VBI data.
- Tuned to digital—The set-top receives a digital program multiplex that includes multiple video and audio and data channels.

Although a single-tuner set-top has access to many in-band digital channels, each with significant data capacity, in-band digital channels cannot be used for reliable data communications because

- The customer can tune the set-top to an analog channel at any time for an arbitrary period, reducing the in-band payload to a trickle (about 9,600 bps per VBI line).
- The customer can rapidly tune the set-top between digital channels, interrupting the data flow and causing the set-top to miss messages.

What is needed is a *dedicated* channel that is always available to support data communications with the set-top; this is the rationale for an *out-of-band* channel.

Figure 5-1 *Set-Top Tuning Model*

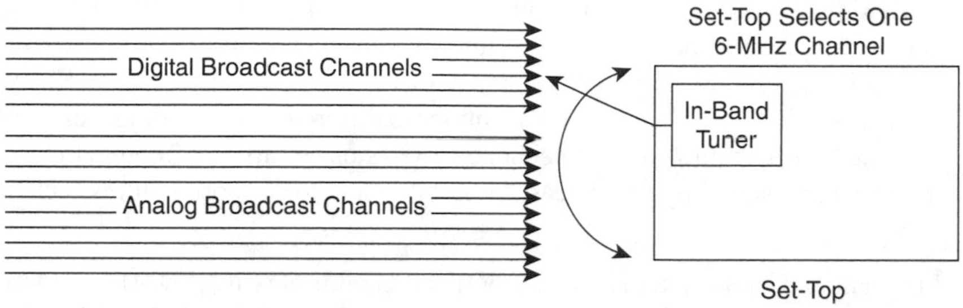

Out-of-Band Data Communications

The out-of-band (OOB) channel provides the foundation for a reliable data communications service between the headend and the set-top. This section describes

- Drivers—The motivation for a dedicated OOB channel
- Out-of-band architectures—A summary of the alternatives for the OOB channel
- Forward OOB channel—The forward path (from headend to set-top)
- Reverse OOB channel—The reverse path (from set-top to headend)
- SCTE DVS-178—A description of the OOB channel format developed by General Instrument
- SCTE DVS-167—A description of the OOB channel format adopted by Scientific Atlanta from the DAVIC OOB specification
- DOCSIS cable modem—Applying the DOCSIS standard for in-band data communication to provide an OOB channel for digital television services
- Out-of-band evolution—How the OOB channel evolves to provide a two-way, connectionless datagram service

Drivers

The "one-way" system described so far is sufficient for broadcast services. However, increased digital television revenues can be generated by offering the following:

- Impulse pay-per-view (IPPV)
- Video-on-demand (VOD)
- Interactive enhancements to television
- Standalone interactive services

All these services require reliable data communications to the digital set-top.

Out-of-Band Architectures

OOB signaling is by no means unique to the cable industry. The ISDN "D" channel is a good example of an out-of-band communications channel that is separated from the *bearer* channels by time-division multiplexing. Other examples include Frame Relay and ATM networks, which use a special link identifier to differentiate signaling from payload traffic. In Signaling System 7 (SS7), telephone systems use entirely different circuits to enable disassociated signaling for increased reliability and to support features such as toll-free services.

In broadband cable systems, frequency-division multiplexing (FDM) is used to separate the out-of-band channels from in-band channels. In Figure 5-2, a dedicated out-of-band receiver (OOB RX) allows the set-top to receive data at any time, independent of which analog or digital channel is selected by the in-band tuner. The *forward OOB channel* supports the flow of data from the headend to the set-top. A cable system with only a forward OOB channel allows one-way, addressed messages to be delivered to the set-top.

Figure 5-2 *Forward OOB Channel*

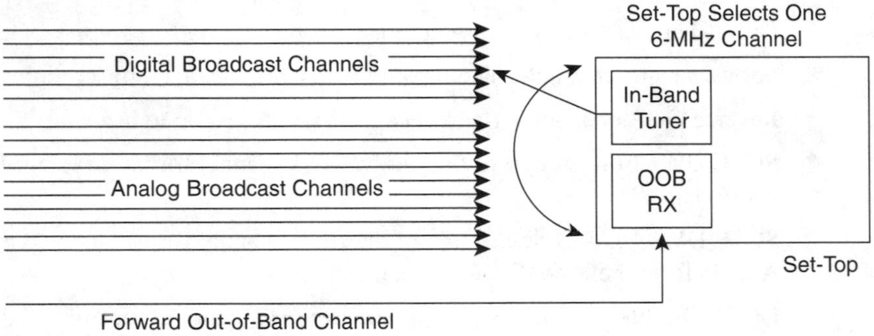

In upgraded cable systems, it is common to activate the return path (see the section Return Path Activation in Chapter 2), and these systems can support two-way out-of-band data communications. Advanced analog converters have established the viability of a reverse signaling path for IPPV. Figure 5-3 illustrates the addition of a dedicated out-of-band transmitter (OOB TX) to the digital set-top, allowing it to transmit data on a shared out-of-band carrier frequency.

Figure 5-3 *Reverse OOB Channel*

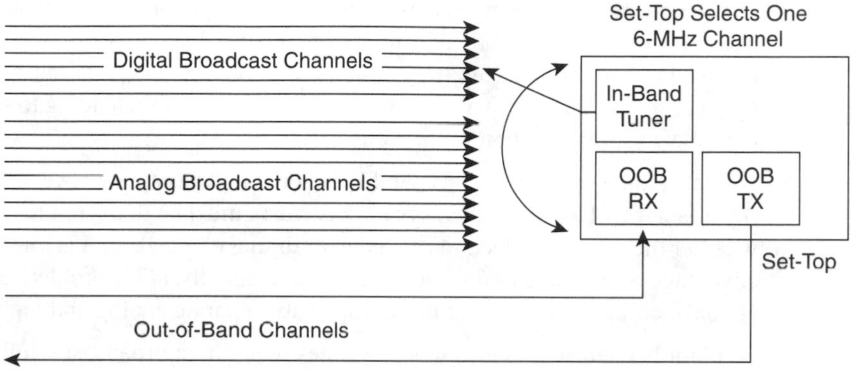

Because the *reverse OOB channel* is shared by a number of set-tops, a media access control (MAC) protocol is required. The MAC protocol is similar to that used by shared-media Ethernet networks. (One of the first shared-media networks in the world was the Aloha network built in Hawaii. The Aloha network introduced a contention resolution mechanism to allow a number of radio transmitters to share the same radio frequency channel.)

The forward and return out-of-band channels are discussed separately in the following sections, but it is important to think of these channels as a single bidirectional data communications channel.

Forward OOB Channel

The forward OOB channel delivers system messages to the set-top. System messages convey conditional access entitlement information, system information, program-guide information, emergency alert system information, and management commands to the set-top.

System messages can also be delivered in-band, as part of a 6 MHz channel, and this method is still used by some cable systems. However, in-band delivery has some significant disadvantages:

- To guarantee delivery, system messages must be simulcast in every 6 MHz channel because the set-top can be tuned to any channel. Simulcasting consumes a considerable amount of system bandwidth and requires message insertion equipment for every channel. (See the section 8600X in Chapter 3, "The Analog Set-Top Converter," for an example of the operational impacts when system messages are *not* simulcast).
- An analog NTSC channel has only a very limited capacity (about 9,600 bps per line) to carry data in the vertical blanking interval.

- Broadcast channels, whether they are in-band or out-of-band, repeatedly transmit a circular queue of system messages intended for every set-top in the cable system. (The queue is circular because there is no way to acknowledge that a message has been received by a set-top in a one-way system.) In large systems, this causes considerable queuing delay due to the volume of system messages, often leading to an operational nightmare (see the section Limitations in Chapter 3).
- Digital channels provide a considerable increase in data capacity over analog channels (by a factor of 100). However, system messages must be delivered regardless of whether the set-top is tuned to an analog or digital channel, so it is impossible to take advantage of the increased payload of digital channels. (This problem can be solved, at considerable cost, by building set-tops with separate analog and digital tuners.)

The last point is interesting, because it illustrates why direct broadcast satellite systems have no OOB channel. In DBS systems, all channels are digital, and each one can carry 6 to 12 services. System messages are simulcast on each digital channel at a rate of several hundred kilobits per second, an overhead of approximately 1%.

Not only do cable system designers perceive considerable value in the OOB channel, but they also extend its use in digital systems. Early OOB channel rates were quite limited by the cost and availability of high-speed modulation techniques, but inexpensive silicon is now available that supports multimegabit modulation rates. With higher-rate OOB channels, the system messages occupy only about 10% of the OOB channel capacity. The remaining 90% is earmarked for additional services, including extended program guides, email, and network games (see Chapter 8 for more information on these services).

Reverse OOB Channel

Like the forward OOB channel, the reverse OOB channel was first developed for advanced analog set-tops to support impulse pay-per-view (IPPV) services. These implementations (see the sections 8600X and CFT-2200, in Chapter 3) use very robust modulation, and each set-top can transmit only when polled by the headend controller. For this reason, their use is limited to the periodic collection of IPPV purchases (stored in the set-top until it is polled by the headend controller).

The Orlando Full Service Network (see Chapter 11, "On-Demand Cable System Case Studies") pioneered the use of a high-speed bidirectional OOB channel with a MAC function to allow the set-top to transmit spontaneously without waiting for a poll.

There are at least three digital out-of-band channel options available to the cable system designer: DVS-178, DVS-167, and DOCSIS cable modem.

SCTE DVS-178

DVS-178 was developed by General Instrument and is published as a contribution to the Society of Cable Telecommunications Engineers (SCTE) Digital Video Standards (DVS) subcommittee. DVS-178 was the first OOB channel format deployed and supports millions of first generation DCT-1000 digital set-tops. DVS-178 is designed for polled operation to support IPPV services.

DVS-178 uses a 2.048 Mbps forward channel and a 256 Kbps return channel. The forward and reverse channels employ QPSK modulation for a good balance of robustness and efficiency. The forward channel has a pass-band of 1.8 MHz and is centered at 72.75, 75.25, or 104.2 MHz. The return channel frequency range is from 8.096 to 40.160 MHz in 192 KHz steps. The forward channel uses the MPEG-2 transport stream format to carry system messages, and the return channel uses the ATM cell format. Media access control uses polling and Aloha. (See Table 5-1.)

SCTE DVS-167

The Digital Audio Visual Council (DAVIC) developed an out-of-band communications mechanism as part of the DAVIC systems specification. DVS-167 is extracted verbatim from the DAVIC 1.2, Part 8, "Lower Layer Protocols and Physical Interfaces," Section 7.8, "Passband Bi-directional PHY on Coax." DVS-167 was submitted by Scientific Atlanta as a contribution to the SCTE Digital Video Standards subcommittee. DVS-167 is used by DAVIC-compliant cable set-tops, including the Scientific Atlanta Explorer series, the Pioneer Voyager, and the Philips MediaOne set-top. An advantage of DVS-167 is that it was the first OOB channel standard, allowing multiple vendors to work toward common data communications, and has an efficient MAC layer that can support interactive services.

NOTE The European Digital Video Broadcast (DVB) standard has also adopted DAVIC OOB signaling.

DVS-167 specifies a 1.544 Mbps or 3.088 Mbps forward OOB channel and a 256 Kbps, 1.544 Mbps, or 3.088 Mbps reverse OOB channel. The forward and reverse channels employ QPSK modulation for a good balance of robustness and efficiency. The forward channel has a pass-band of 1 or 2 MHz and is tunable from 70 to 130 MHz in 250 KHz steps. The return channel is tunable from 8 to 26.5 MHz in 50 KHz steps. (See Table 5-1.)

Table 5-1 *Comparison of DVS-178 and DVS-167*

	DVS-178	**DVS-167**
Forward OOB Channel	2.048 Mbps	1.544 or 3.088 Mbps
Modulation	QPSK, differential coding for 90° phase invariance	Differentially encoded QPSK
Pass-band	1.8 MHz	1 MHz or 2 MHz
Frequency range	72.75, 75.25, or 104.2 MHz	70–130 MHz
Frequency step size	N/A	250 KHz
Forward error correction	96,94 Reed-Solomon block code, T=1, 8-bit symbols	55,53 Read Solomon block code, T=1, 8-bit symbols
Framing	Locked to MPEG-TS, two FEC blocks per MPEG packet	Signaling Link Extended Superframe (SL-ESF)
Interleaving	Convolutional (96,8)	Convolutional (55,5)
Reverse OOB Channel	256 Kbps	256 Kbps, 1.544, or 3.088 Mbps
Modulation	Differentially encoded QPSK	Differentially encoded QPSK
Pass-band	192 KHz	200 KHz, 1 MHz, or 2 MHz
Frequency range	8.096–40.160 MHz	8–26.5 MHz
Frequency step size	192 KHz	50 KHz
RF output power range	+24 dBmV–+60 dBmV	+25 dBmV–+53 dBmV

dBmV = decibels with respect to 1 millivolt in a 75-ohm system

The forward channel and reverse channel use a standard ATM cell format. The reverse channel is time-division multiplexed into fixed-length *slots* used by the Media Access Control layer. The DAVIC OOB MAC has three modes:

- *Contention mode* uses slotted-Aloha to opportunistically transmit in a similar way to Ethernet. Collision detection notification, carried by dedicated bits in the forward channel, provides the set-top with an indication of a reverse channel collision with another set-top. A reverse channel collision occurs when two or more set-tops attempt to transmit into the same time slot. Collision detection allows the set-tops to back off and retransmit after a random delay. Contention mode works well for short messages and in low traffic conditions because the probability of collisions is low. Additional modes are included for efficent operation for larger messages and higher traffic conditions.

- *Reservation mode* allows a set-top to request a guaranteed transmit opportunity for larger messages (longer than about 100 bytes). A request is sent in a single slot and a grant message is returned, which enumerates slots that can be used to transmit the message. Thus, there is no possibility of collision in reservation mode, because only one set-top is allocated any given slot—but the slot payload is wasted if the set-top does not use it.
- *Contentionless mode* guarantees a certain number of slots to a connection and is designed for delay-sensitive applications, such as telephony, video, and network games. The contentionless bandwidth must be established at connection set-up time, and any bandwidth that is not used by the set-top is wasted (that is, it cannot be used by another set-top). There is no possibility of collision in this mode.

DOCSIS Cable Modem

The DOCSIS cable modem standard was designed as an in-band mechanism for data transport. (See Chapter 4 of *Modern Cable Television Technology; Video, Voice, and Data Communications* by Walter Ciciora and others.) However, with the addition of a second tuner, the DOCSIS standard can be used to perform all the functions (and more) of DVS-167 and DVS-178. DOCSIS supports 64- or 256-QAM modulation for the forward (downstream) channel and QPSK or 16-QAM modulation for the reverse (upstream) channel, providing better spectral efficiency than DVS-167 or DVS-178. DOCSIS also supports much higher data rates that DVS-167 or DVS-178; the forward data rates are 30.343 or 42.884 Mbps, and the reverse data rates are 0.32, 0.64, 1.28, 2.56, 5.12, or 10.24 Mbps. There are a number of advantages and disadvantages to using DOCSIS as an out-of-band standard, which are summarized in Table 5-2.

Table 5-2 *The Pros and Cons of DOCSIS*

Advantages	Disadvantages
The DOCSIS standard is well established for use in cable modems.	The addition of the 6 MHz tuner and DOCSIS silicon increases the cost of a digital set-top.
Many cable systems are adding support in the hubs to terminate DOCSIS channels.	Some operators have chosen to treat television and cable modem services as separate businesses.
The DOCSIS forward channel offers considerably higher data rates than DVS-167 and DVS-178.	The DOCSIS forward channel consumes an entire 6 MHz channel (this is not a problem if the DOCSIS channel can be shared with cable modems).

Out-of-Band Evolution

OOB signaling has evolved to provide a real-time, two-way data-link between the set-top and termination equipment in the cable system. As with any data communications network, higher-layer protocols are required to support network functions, such as address management, message routing, network management, and the like.

The OOB data channel can use the TCP/IP protocol suite to avoid reinventing new protocols. TCP/IP provides connectionless services to the digital set-top over the OOB channels. Using an IP-based, connectionless network model has a number of advantages:

- System messages can be sent to individual set-tops without the overhead of establishing a connection. This is very important, because there might be thousands of digital set-tops, making connection management difficult.
- Data communications equipment, such as Ethernet hubs and IP routers, are available from multiple vendors. This equipment also provides a convenient way to aggregate return traffic from many hubs.
- Interactive applications (see Chapter 10) are frequently developed on LAN-based systems and then adapted to cable systems. TCP/IP provides a unifying software layer that supports this approach. In fact, interactive cable systems have been compared to giant LANs (see *Digital Cable Systems Really Are Giant LANs* by Hal Benner and Bill Wall).

Out-of-Band Channel Termination

RF modulators and demodulators terminate the OOB channels in the network. These RF modulators and demodulators do not have a generic name, so I will refer to them as the out-of-band termination system (OOBTS). The OOBTS provides functions equivalent to those implemented by the DOCSIS cable modem termination system (CMTS). In fact, the OOBTS *is* a DOCSIS CMTS, where DOCSIS is used for OOB signaling.

In early implementations, the OOBTS was located at the headend. However, this arrangement has some limitations:

- Large systems are difficult to support because the forward OOB channel becomes congested with system messages for tens, or hundreds, of thousands of set-tops.
- The return traffic must be brought back to the headend as an RF signal, making it difficult to maintain correct input levels to the OOBTS (see Chapter 14 of *Modern Cable Television Technology; Video, Voice, and Data Communications* by Walter Ciciora and others).

It is becoming common to place the OOBTS at the distribution hub. This approach provides better mechanisms for

- Hub-level addressing
- Return traffic aggregation
- Media access control (MAC)

Hub-Level Addressing

Any OOB channel has only limited traffic capacity, so it will eventually suffer message congestion as the cable system increases in size. However, the system can be divided into smaller subscriber groups, each served by its own out-of-band channel. Distribution hubs provide this scalability in the hybrid fiber coax architecture (see Chapter 2). Placing the OOBTS at the distribution hub allows the creation of a routed architecture in which only messages addressed to a set-top in a particular hub are inserted into the out-of-band channel for that hub. Moreover, if additional capacity is required, the distribution hub can be subdivided into still smaller subscriber groups, each with its own out-of-band channel.

At some level of scaling, physical limitations constrain the minimum size of the subscriber group, because the output of the laser transmitter is optically split to serve several fiber nodes. Adding more laser transmitters would solve the problem. Alternatively, additional out-of-band carrier frequencies can be allocated.

Return Traffic Aggregation

Combining return paths in a cable system also combines any noise and ingress from the cable drops. In practice, this funneling effect limits the number of fiber nodes that can be combined to somewhere between 8 and 40, depending on the modulation scheme. For QPSK modulation (as used by DVS-167, DVS-178, and DOCSIS), the return from between 8 and 16 nodes can be combined (depending on how well noise and ingress from the plant is managed). This means that more reverse OOB channels are needed than forward OOB channels. For this reason, DVS-167, DVS-178, and DOCSIS are all designed to support multiple reverse channels per forward channel.

After the return channels are terminated at the hub, they can be multiplexed into a single data channel for transport to the headend using off-the-shelf data communications technologies (for example, SONET, ATM, or IP networking).

Shared Media Access Control

Shared media access control (MAC) is the science of sharing a single channel between a number of traffic sources so that

- Each source (in this case the set-top transmitter) has a fair chance to access the shared media channel.
- Each source obtains a fair share of the available shared media capacity.
- The shared media channel can be used at close to its maximum capacity under all offered loads.

This set of requirements is difficult to achieve because each traffic source acts independently. Shared MAC protocols rely heavily on negative feedback—each source is designed to back off when another source is active. In Ethernet networks, *carrier-sense* is used to detect whether any other source is currently transmitting. However, this technique cannot be used in cable systems because of the return amplifier configuration. Therefore, the source needs feedback from the OOBTS to tell it when another source is transmitting. To provide this feedback signal, the OOBTS continuously sends feedback messages in the forward OOB channel to all sources.

Control theory states that too much delay can cause instability in any feedback loop. In practice, this means that the round-trip delay from the source to the OOBTS must be constrained. Placing the OOBTS at the distribution hub keeps round-trip delay down to an acceptable level.

Headend–to–Distribution Hub Interconnection

When the OOBTS is placed at the distribution hub, a mechanism is required to transport the OOB channel traffic between the headend and the distribution hubs. Figure 5-4 illustrates a typical cable system topology. A digital headend is connected to the distribution hubs by fiber rings in most cases (except for the distribution hub at the upper-left of Figure 5-4, which is connected by a fiber spur). The headend controller (located in the digital headend) requires a data communications service to each distribution hub.

Figure 5-4 *Typical Cable System Topology*

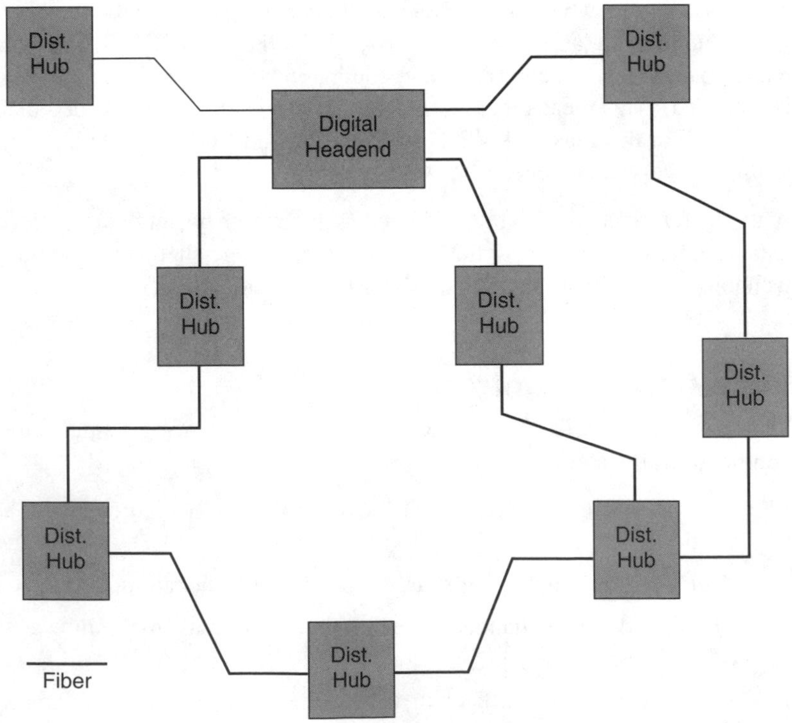

A number of off-the-shelf data communications solutions are available, which can provide cost-effective headend-to-hub interconnection using the fiber facilities:

- LAN extension products—Point-to-point Ethernet bridge extenders that use fiber facilities.
- SONET—Synchronous Optical Networks were originally developed for high-capacity telephone trunking applications using fiber facilities.
- ATM networks—Asynchronous transfer mode uses SONET facilities to build a connection-oriented network that supports data, video, and voice traffic.
- IP networks—Internet Protocol uses a ATM or SONET facilities to build a connectionless data communications network.

LAN Extension Products

A number of companies build products that can bridge LAN segments over a single fiber strand. These products are relatively inexpensive and provide a plug-and-play solution for connecting 10/100BASE-T devices over distances of up to about 60 fiber miles.

The major drawback of these products is that they provide only point-to-point connections, and this can consume a lot of fiber in cable systems with many hubs. At the headend, a fiber from each hub must be terminated.

SONETs

A SONET ring architecture matches typical cable system topologies quite well. However, SONET has a number of disadvantages for this application:

- The bit rates involved do not justify the cost of a SONET infrastructure in most cases.
- SONET does not perform a traffic aggregation function—it merely *back-hauls* traffic to a central location where a switch or router can perform that function.

In large cable systems, especially those that cover a considerable goegraphical area, SONET is sometimes justified as a foundation for ATM or IP Networks.

ATM Networks

ATM switches are available with SONET interfaces that support up to 29 dB of optical loss budget. Assuming a figure of 0.35 dB loss per fiber kilometer, these provide a reach of up to 80 kilometers (or 50 miles). Each SONET connection requires a fiber-pair (one fiber per direction).

An ATM network has a number of advantages over point-to-point solutions:

- Ring topologies can be supported that are *self-healing* so that a single fiber cut does not cause an outage.
- ATM provides several traffic classes with different *quality of service* parameters. This allows the ATM network to be shared between the out-of-band communications system and many other traffic types (for example cable modem, telephone, video transport, and so on).
- ATM provides traffic management tools, including rate control and admission control, that can be used to police traffic and prevent oversubscription of network bandwidth.

ATM solutions, however, require a greater capital investment than point-to-point solutions and also require more planning and provisioning.

IP Networks

IP routers are also available with SONET interfaces that support up to 29 dB of optical loss budget. Assuming a figure of 0.35 dB loss per fiber kilometer, these provide a reach of up to 80 kilometers (or 50 miles). Each SONET interface requires a fiber-pair (one fiber per direction).

An IP network provides certain advantages over point-to-point solutions:

- IP networks support arbitrary topologies by means of self-learning routing algorithms. They can discover and use alternative routes so that a single fiber cut does not cause an outage.
- IP provides several traffic classes with different *class of service* parameters. This allows the IP network to be shared between the out-of-band communications system and many other traffic types, for example cable modem, network management, and so on.
- IP provides traffic management tools in the Transport Control Protocol (TCP) that are designed to react to network loss and reduce offered load. Considerable work is also being done on *differentiated classes of service,* which shows considerable promise (see *Quality of Service* by Paul Ferguson and Geoff Huston).

However, IP solutions typically require a greater capital investment than point-to-point solutions and also require more planning and provisioning.

Summary

This chapter discussed how digital television services are added to analog cable systems and introduced the following concepts:

- The drivers for digital television—Including DBS competition, high-definition television, and consolidation with other digital services
- Transmission of digital television—The rationale for broadband transmission of digital payloads over cable systems

- Out-of-band architectures—The need for a reliable data communications network to support advanced digital television services and its implementation, using the forward and reverse out-of-band channels
- Out-of-band channel termination—The advantages of terminating and aggregating the data communication channels (including OOB and DOCSIS cable modem channels) at the distribution hub
- Headend-to-hub interconnection—The various data networking alternatives for interconnecting the headend and hub, including LAN extension, SONET, ATM, and IP

References

Books

Abe, George. *Residential Broadband.* Indianapolis, IN: Cisco Press, 1997.

Ciciora, Walter, James Farmer, and David Large. *Modern Cable Television Technology; Video, Voice, and Data Communications.* San Francisco, CA: Morgan Kaufmann Publishers, Inc., 1999.

Ferguson, Paul, and Geoff Huston. *Quality of Service: Delivering QoS on the Internet and in Corporate Networks.* New York, NY: John Wiley and Sons, 1998.

Periodicals

Benner, Hal, and Bill Wall. "Digital Cable Systems Really Are Giant LANs." *Communications Technology,* October 1998.

Ciciora, Walter. "Digital and Analog Can and Will Coexist." *Communications Technology,* January 1999.

Internet Resources

ASTC standards Web site

http://www.atsc.org/stan&rps.html.

Hi-Vision overview available at the NHK Web site

http://www.nhk.or.jp/hi-vision/hivi-e.html.

CHAPTER 6

The Digital Set-Top Converter

Digital set-top converters are evolving rapidly, and it is impossible to predict what capabilities they will possess in a few years' time. However, they can be divided into two major categories:

- Basic digital set-tops perform tuning, demodulation, conditional access, and decoding functions. This class of set-top provides a digital equivalent of the advanced analog set-top converter, providing similar electronic program guide and impulse pay-per-view functions for broadcast digital services.
- Advanced digital set-top converters perform all the functions of a basic digital set-top, and provide support for two-way, real-time data communications over the cable plant and support for more advanced applications.

Although this chapter focuses on the *basic* digital set-top, it also introduces some of the functional extensions of advanced digital set-tops. Cable operators are deploying digital set-tops for two main reasons:

- Channel expansion—Digital compression can greatly expand the number of channels in a cable system by delivering 6 to 10 programs in a single 6 MHz channel. For example, TCI (now AT&T BIS) has pursued a digital channel expansion strategy known as Head-End in The Sky (HITS) to avoid the cost of HFC upgrades.
- Competitive response to direct broadcast satellite (DBS)—DBS providers chose a digital system because it provides more channels than analog. They have aggressively marketed the "digital picture and sound quality" of their service. Although an upgraded hybrid fiber coax (HFC) system can rival the quality of a digital system, analog is beginning to sound old-fashioned to many customers. Thus, cable operators are forced to offer digital television to keep up with DBS competition.

There are many reasons to deploy more advanced digital set-tops, and these are described in Part II, "Interactive and On-Demand Services," but the basic digital set-top provides similar broadcast services to the advanced analog set-top—only digital.

Cable Environment

In contrast to analog cable, where fewer than 50% of cable customers have a set-top, a digital set-top is essential to provide digital services. In fact, a digital set-top converts the digital television picture into an analog NTSC picture to allow customers to use their existing analog television receivers and VCRs.

NOTE This situation will start to change in July 2000 with the availability of digital navigation devices. Customers will be able to buy digital set-tops or cable ready digital televisions that are capable of receiving premium services. See Chapter 18, "OCI-C2: the Security Interface."

The digital set-top has evolved directly from the advanced analog set-top (see Chapter 2, "Analog Cable Technologies"). In fact, to be successfully deployed in cable systems, the digital set-top is actually a hybrid analog/digital set-top. That is, the set-top must be able to support all existing analog services, as well as the new digital services. There are a number of reasons for this:

- The digital set-top is deployed side-by-side with existing analog set-tops (often in the same house), so cable customers naturally expect the digital set-top to provide all the familiar (analog) services as well as new (digital) services.
- This perception is reinforced by most service tier structures that bundle all analog services into the new digital tier. In other words, the customer is never offered a *digital-only* package.
- The digital set-top is considerably more expensive than an analog set-top, so the cable operator naturally expects it to perform all the functions of an analog set-top in addition to its new digital functions.

Although it is true that a digital-only set-top costs less to build than a hybrid analog/digital set-top, deploying a digital-only set-top requires that all existing analog services are *simulcast* in digital form. This approach not only requires more bandwidth but also involves significant capital investment at the headend for MPEG-2 encoders and multiplexers (see the section Headend Equipment in Chapter 7, "Digital Broadcast Case Studies," for more details).

For these reasons, this chapter focuses on the hybrid analog/digital set-top, which will be referred to as the *digital set-top*. (Please refer to Chapter 3, "The Analog Set-Top Converter," for information on the analog functions of a hybrid analog/digital set-top.)

Overview

Figure 6-1 shows the block diagram of the digital set-top. Although there are a number of different implementation approaches, this block diagram describes most digital set-tops. Optional blocks are shown using broken lines.

Figure 6-1 *Block Diagram for a Typical Digital Set-Top*

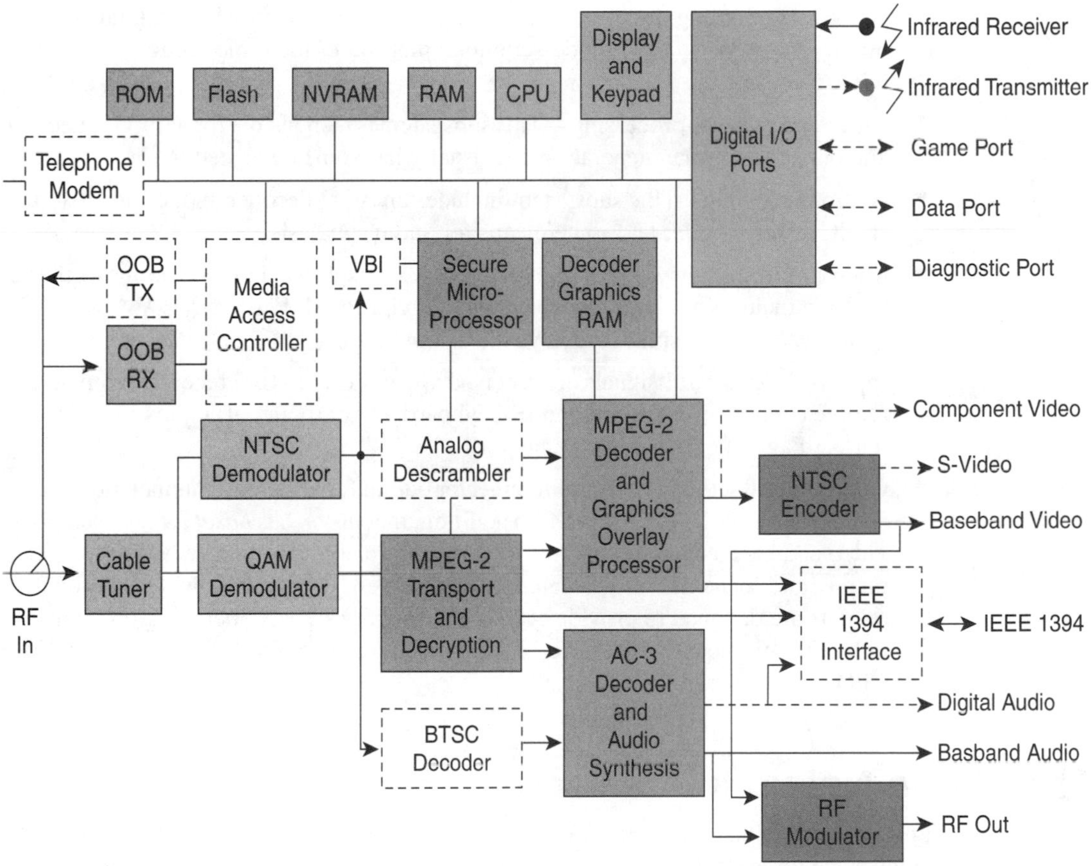

The next sections consider Figure 6-1 in detail after breaking it down into its major subsystems:

- The cable network interface (CNI)—All set-tops have a 75 ohm, F-connector, which is the interface between the cable system and the set-top (see Chapter 16, "OCI-N: The Network Interface"). The cable network interface circuitry in the set-top includes the cable tuner, NTSC demodulator, QAM demodulator, and an out-of-band (OOB) receiver. Optionally, an OOB transmitter, a media access controller, and a VBI decoder might also be included. When the cable system does not support an RF return path, a telephone modem is an option (in place of the OOB transmitter).

- Conditional access—Conditional access is the means by which access to specific services is granted to the customer, based on payment for those services. A digital decryption circuit, in conjunction with a secure microprocessor, performs the equivalent of analog de-scrambling for digital services. Optionally, digital set-tops might also include an analog de-scrambler that shares the same secure microprocessor.
- Video and graphics processing—This subsystem is responsible for MPEG-2 decoding and on-screen display generation and usually has some dedicated RAM.
- Audio processing—This subsystem includes an AC-3 decoder and, optionally, a BTSC stereo decoder and some means for audio synthesis.
- Microprocessor subsystem—The microprocessor subsystem is the brains of the set-top, and includes a microprocessor together with ROM, Flash, NVRAM, RAM memory, an LED display, and keypad.
- Inputs—User control signals are received via an infrared (IR) receiver from an IR remote control or (optionally) an IR keyboard. Other (optional) inputs include a data port, a diagnostic port, and a game port.
- Outputs—All set-tops have an F-connector output for an NTSC channel modulated at broadcast channel 3 or channel 4. In addition, the set-top has *baseband* (or *composite*) video and baseband audio outputs to allow the customer to realize higher-quality picture and sound than is possible via the channel 3/4 output. A host of optional outputs are designed to provide even higher-quality signals, including component video (for example, YPrPb or RGB), S-Video, digital audio (S/PDIF) and the IEEE-1394 digital interface.

The Cable Network Interface

Figure 6-2 shows the *cable network interface (CNI)* for a digital set-top. It is a superset of the interface for an analog set-top (see Chapter 3). Whereas in the analog world there are standards (NTSC, BTSC and EIA 542) that have been established over many years of practice, in the digital world most standards have been developed by standards committees.

Figure 6-2 *Cable Network Interface*

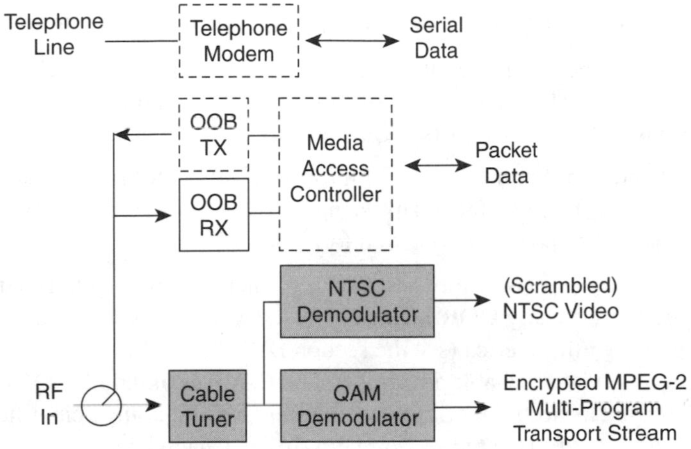

The digital modulation scheme is chosen to fit into the same 6 MHz frequency slots as specified by EIA 542, originally for analog channels. This approach has two major advantages:

- Digital and analog channels can be mixed within the same system without any loss in spectrum efficiency.
- A single 6 MHz tuner is used to tune both types of channel, thereby reducing set-top cost.

The standard aspects of the cable network interface are

- ATSC Digital Television Standard (A/53)—This standard describes the overall system characteristics of the U.S. Advanced Television System.
- RF Interface Specification for Television Receiving Devices and Cable Television Systems (EIA 23)—This standard provides RF performance recommendations for all receiving devices that might be directly connected to a cable television system, including the digital set-top.
- Cable Television Channel Identification Plan (EIA 542)—This standard specifies the frequencies of all cable channels. (See Chapter 8 of *Modern Cable Television Technology; Video, Voice, and Data Communications* by Walter Ciciora and others.)
- Digital Transmission Standard for Cable Television (SCTE DVS-031)—This standard specifies the modulation (64-QAM or 256-QAM), forward error correction, and framing of the digital payload (see Chapter 4, "Digital Technologies").
- Draft Digital Video Service Multiplex and Transport System Standard for Cable Television (originally DVS-093, now updated as DVS-241)—This standard references the MPEG-2 systems layer (see Chapter 4).

Another aspect of the cable network interface is called system (or service) information (SI). This provides information on channel numbering and allows basic navigation of the cable channels. There are currently two leading proposals for system information:

- Out-of-band—Service Information for Out-of-Band Digital Cable Television (SCTE DVS-234). This standard is based on ATSC A/56 and is used by both DCT series and Pegasus digital set-tops (see Chapter 7).
- In-band—Program and System Information Protocol for Terrestrial Broadcast and Cable (SCTE DVS-097). This standard is based on ATSC A/65 and is the terrestrial broadcast standard for system information.

The proprietary aspects of the cable network interface are the OOB data communication channels. A proprietary OOB channel format developed by General Instrument has been deployed in North America (see the section DVS-178 in Chapter 5, "Adding Digital Television Services to Cable Systems"). The DAVIC standard for OOB channels has also been deployed in North America by several vendors, including Scientific Atlanta, DiviCom, Pioneer, and Philips (see the section DVS-167 in Chapter 5).

The set-top components that terminate the cable network interface are described in the next sections. When compared to the analog design, the major addition is the QAM demodulator.

Cable Input

The cable input is a 75 ohm female F-connector. It is the only radio frequency input to the shielded set-top unit. Shielding is important to prevent off-air television broadcasts from interfering with the cable channels.

Tuner

Tuning requirements for digital set-tops are fundamentally the same as for analog, except that a 860-MHz tuner is usually specified because digital channels are commonly placed in the 550 to 860 MHz range above the highest analog channels. Digital tuner performance is similar to analog tuner performance, with the exception that phase noise must be tightly controlled to support the higher symbol rate used by 256-QAM modulation.

QAM Demodulator

The block labeled QAM Demodulator in Figure 6-2 is actually responsible for a number of related transmission functions:

- Adaptive equalization of the received signal to compensate for reflections introduced by the cable plant

- 64-QAM or 256-QAM demodulation according to the modulation type of the channel tuned
- Trellis code interpolation
- De-interleaving
- Forward error correction (FEC)

The output of the demodulator is a baseband digital stream at 26.97035 or 38.81070 Mbps for 64-QAM or 256-QAM modulation, respectively. (See the section Broadband Transmission in Chapter 4.)

NTSC Demodulator

The NTSC demodulator is a standard component from the analog set-top. In addition, many digital set-tops include an analog-to-digital (A/D) converter to digitize the demodulated video so that it can be manipulated by the graphics engine (see the section Analog Video Digitization later in this chapter).

Out-of-Band Channel Termination

There are two alternative out-of-band channel specifications currently being used in North America:

- SCTE DVS 167, as specified by General Instrument
- SCTE DVS 178, as specified by Scientific Atlanta and based on the DAVIC OOB

Please refer to the section Out-of-Band Data Communications in Chapter 5 for a detailed description of the out-of-band channel.

Out-of-Band Receiver

The out-of-band channel can be one-way or two-way. An out-of-band receiver is required in either case, and all digital set-tops include an out-of-band receiver. The out-of-band channel is of greatly increased capacity—in the order of megabits per second—compared to analog systems.

Out-of-Band Transmitter

An out-of-band transmitter is required for two-way operation of the out-of-band channel. Two-way signaling supports services such as impulse pay-per-view, video-on-demand, and interactive applications.

An out-of-band transmitter is optional for set-tops deployed in a one-way cable plant, although if an upgrade to two-way is planned it makes good sense to deploy a set-top with an OOB transmitter.

Media Access Control

The *Media Access Control (MAC)* function supports the out-of-band transmitter and allows a number of set-tops to share a common return path. The shared media access control can be quite sophisticated (see the section SCTE DVS-167 in Chapter 5).

Telephone Modem

The telephone modem provides an alternative to the out-of-band transmitter in a one-way plant. The modem is a standard data modem and usually supports a data rate from 300 to 9600 bps. The telephone modem is used to periodically call the headend modem bank to report purchase information. The call time is usually set to 2 or 3 a.m., so a separate phone line is not required. Unfortunately, this means that no interactive services can be supported, due to the lack of two-way, real-time data communications.

Transport Processing

Transport processing is required to break the MPEG-2 system multiplex into the specific packetized elementary streams (PES) that are required for the selected service (see the section MPEG-2 Systems Layer in Chapter 4). Transport processing is linked into the conditional access system because different services in a multiplex are typically encrypted using different working keys.

Transport processing can be broken down into a number of steps:

- Filter packet identifier (PID) 0 and process the MPEG-2 program association table (PAT) contained in it to discover what program transport streams are contained in the system multiplex.
- Obtain the program map PID for the desired program transport stream. Filter the program map PID and process the program map table (PMT) contained in it.
- Filter the packetized elementary stream PIDs for the selected program transport stream and route them to the appropriate video or audio decoders via the payload decryption engines (see Figure 6-3).
- Filter the entitlement control message (ECM) PID for the selected program stream and pass the ECMs to the secure microprocessor. (The PAT and PMT are described in the section Multiplexing in Chapter 4.)

Conditional Access System

The conditional access system provides the means by which access to specific services is granted to the customer based on payment for those services. The conditional access system uses embedded security components in the set-top—the MPEG-2 transport and decryption block and the secure microprocessor, shown in Figure 6-1. An optional analog de-scrambler provides backward-compatibility for scrambled analog channels.

Every aspect of the digital conditional access system is highly proprietary. It is common for set-top purchase contracts to include remedies in the case of security breach, which might include upgrading or replacing security elements. Thus, the set-top vendor has every incentive to make the conditional access system as obscure and complicated as possible in an effort to defeat signal theft.

Conditional access systems from General Instrument (Digicipher II), Scientific Atlanta (PowerKEY), and SECA (MediaGuard) have been deployed by the cable industry in North America. Nevertheless, all these digital conditional access systems have common design strategies that originate in the work done by the MPEG Systems Committee. The MPEG-2 transport stream is used to carry conditional access information, and the MPEG-2 systems layer is designed to support any conditional access system.

Figure 6-3 illustrates the basic principles of operation of the digital conditional access system.

Figure 6-3 *Conditional Access System*

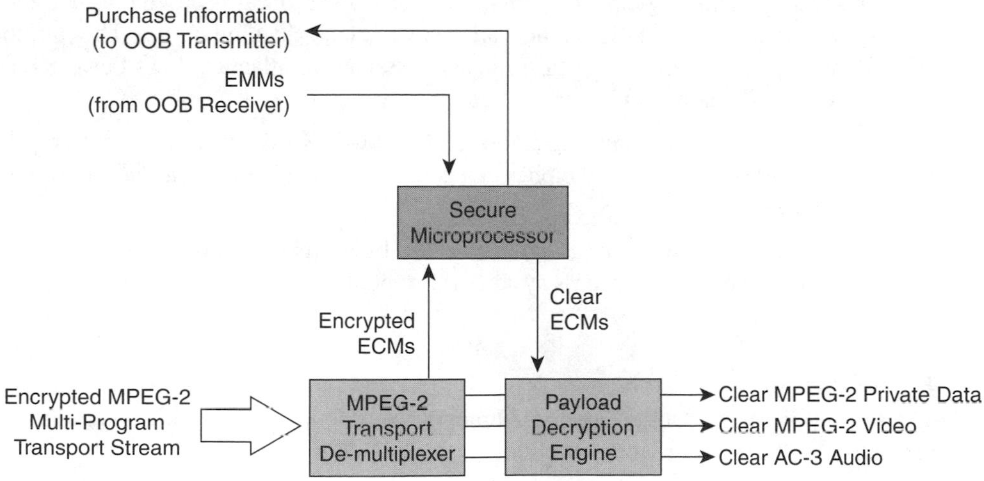

The following describes the operation of the digital condition access system:

- The MPEG transport de-multiplexer separates the transport stream into separate streams based on the packet identifier (PID), and selects the video, audio, and data packetized elementary streams for the selected service.
- The entitlement control messages (ECMs), which carry the encryption keys for the service are sent to the secure microprocessor. The ECMs also are encrypted; they are deciphered by the secure microprocessor before being sent to the payload decryption engine.
- The payload decryption engine deciphers the packetized elementary streams using the encryption keys supplied by the secure microprocessor.

The encryption keys are changed frequently (every few seconds) to reduce the chance that they can be discovered. The secure microprocessor can decipher only encryption keys for authorized services.

Digital Decryption

In a digital set-top, conditional access is achieved by using digital encryption to *scramble* the MPEG-2 transport stream. The payload decryption engine (refer to Figure 6-3) is responsible for deciphering the MPEG payload. Three digital encryption ciphers are commonly used by different systems:

- The *Harmony* Cipher—The Harmony Cipher was developed by General Instrument and is used in the Digicipher II conditional access system. It is based on the Data Encryption Standard (DES) cipher called cipher block chaining (CBC). The Harmony Agreement between General Instrument and Scientific Atlanta, allows PowerKEY to use the same Harmony Cipher as Digicipher II.
- The DVB common scrambling algorithm (CSA)—CSA is part of the simulcrypt system and is a closely held cipher that is licensed by ETSI to *bona fide* conditional access vendors.
- DES electronic code book (ECB)—The DES ECB cipher is supported by the PowerKEY conditional access system. It is a published ANSI standard.

Secure Microprocessor

The secure microprocessor provides the brains of the conditional access system and provides a number of important conditional access system functions:

- The secure microprocessor allows selective access to premium services under the control of the headend controller.
- The secure microprocessor receives entitlement management messages (EMM) from the out-of-band channel, as shown in Figure 6-3. The EMMs are encrypted and the secure microprocessor decrypts them to recover a *session* key.

- The secure microprocessor decrypts each ECM using the session key to recover a *working* key. The working key is sent to the payload decryption engine.
- The secure microprocessor stores purchase information until the headend controller collects it (via the out-of-band channel or telephone modem).

The secure microprocessor is actually a single-chip, secure microcontroller. The secure microprocessor is fabricated using a semiconductor process that makes it difficult to analyze the program and data contained in it. This physical security is essential because the secure microprocessor contains the secrets that secure the conditional access system. If a pirate can copy (or *clone*) the secure microprocessor, the condition access system is compromised.

Security Upgrade

All digital set-tops contain some means of upgrading the conditional access system without the need for a visit to the customer's home. The most common method of security upgrade is achieved by inserting a smart card. The smart card contains a secure microprocessor and is mailed to the customer. When the smart card is inserted into a slot in the set-top, it replaces the embedded secure microprocessor. When all customers have received and installed the smart card, the conditional access system is upgraded so that only set-tops with the smart card continue to work.

Security Replacement

Replacing the secure microprocessor by means of a smart card is effective in most security breaches, but if the means of payload encryption is compromised, smart card replacement will not close the breach.

Security replacement also supports portability—the ability to move the set-top from one system to another. This is the basis for retail set-top portability and is discussed in more detail in Chapter 18.

Analog De-scrambling

In a digital set-top, analog de-scrambling is an option. Two approaches are currently being considered by the cable industry:

- Include an analog de-scrambler in the digital set-top. The disadvantage with this approach is that analog scrambling is not that effective (see Chapter 3) and that each analog scrambling system is highly proprietary, effectively preventing new vendors from building an analog de-scrambling portion of the hybrid analog/digital set-top.

- Remove the need for an analog de-scrambler by simulcasting all analog-scrambled channels in digital form. This approach requires additional investment at the headend and consumes more cable spectrum. However, it reduces set-top cost and provides a migration path away from analog scrambling. (There also is some early indication from the FCC that this obviates the requirement for a separate analog de-scrambling module—see Chapter 18.)

Video and Graphics Processing

The video and graphics processing system is shown in Figure 6-4. This system processes both analog and digital video inputs, which are described in the following sections.

Figure 6-4 *Video and Graphics Processing System*

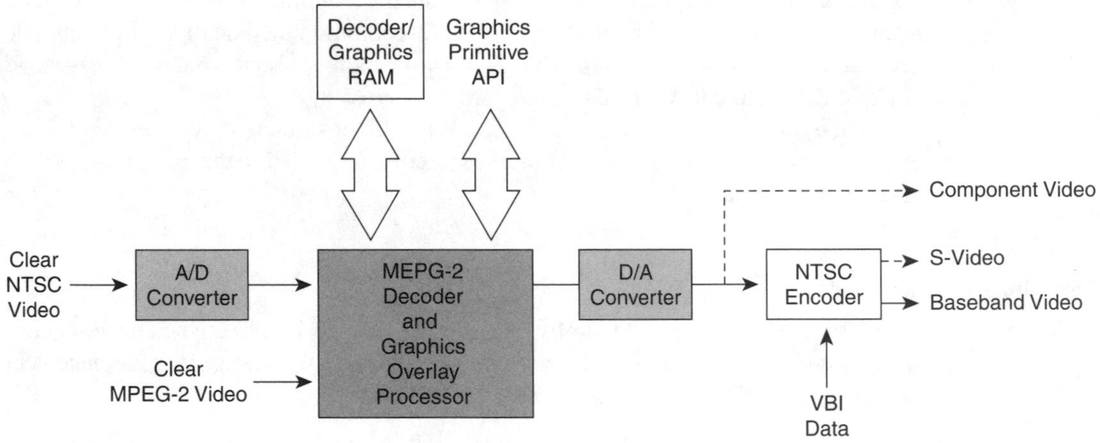

MPEG-2 Video Decoding

The video decoder is compliant to MPEG-2 main profile at main level (MP@ML), which supports all standard definition digital television programs. It is common to reduce the horizontal resolution to three-quarters or one-half of the full resolution supported by MP@ML to increase the compression ratio (see the section Picture Resolution in Chapter 4).

As high definition television signals become more common, and as main profile at high level (MP@HL) decoders become more affordable, digital set-tops will include the option of a high-definition decoder. However, the only output that currently supports an uncompressed high-definition video is the component video output. This is specified by EIA 770.3 (see the section Component Video in Chapter 17, "OCI-C2: the Consumer Interface").

Analog Video Processing

Two alternative approaches to analog video processing are commonly used in digital set-tops:

- Pass the analog video through to the set-top output in exactly the same way as an analog set-top (see Chapter 3).
- Convert the analog video into digital video and process it in the same way as the output of the MPEG-2 decoder.

Each approach has its advantages and disadvantages and will be described in the following sections.

Analog Video Pass-Through

The analog video pass-through approach uses the same video compositing approach as the advanced analog set-top (described in Chapter 3). This approach has significant disadvantages in a digital set-top:

- The on-screen-display does not support *alpha-blending*, making the on-screen display more intrusive because it completely obscures the video. (Alpha-blending is a technique that makes the graphics overlay transparent so that the video is visible through the overlay).
- Transformations of the analog video are not supported—for example video scaling and frame capture. These features are commonly used in advanced guides to maintain context in the program guide, using, for example, quarter-screen video.
- If the set-top offers S-Video or component video outputs, only digital channels will be present on these outputs because analog channels are not converted to these formats. This forces the customer to manually switch the television receiver input back to the baseband composite video or the RF input to watch analog channels.

These limitations cause the user interface designer to make a difficult choice: either to limit the digital user interface to the same level as the analog user interface, or to design the digital and analog user interface with a different look and feel.

Analog Video Digitization

Figure 6-4 illustrates the approach typical in second-generation digital set-top designs. The analog video is digitized, and each field is captured in the graphics memory. This approach allows digital transformations of the video (such as video scaling) with an appropriate graphics engine. The advantages of analog video digitization are that the user interface can be *seamless* across analog and digital programs. Moreover, the analog output is present on S-Video and component video outputs.

However, there are some disadvantages to this approach:

- It is more costly (although use of VLSI can mitigate this).
- If the analog video is of poor quality when captured, frame synchronization can be a problem.
- The process of A/D conversion and subsequent D/A conversion will inevitably cause some degradation in analog video quality due to sampling errors.

Nevertheless, these issues can be properly managed, and all advanced digital set-top designs perform analog video digitization.

On-Screen Display

The *on-screen display (OSD)* generates a graphical overlay on the video output. In digital set-tops, the on-screen display is generally more sophisticated than its analog forbears; it can support scalable fonts, graphics acceleration, and more colors. In addition *alpha-blending* is usually supported. (Alpha-blending is a technique that makes the graphics overlay transparent so that the video is visible through the overlay.)

The on-screen display is usually implemented into the same chip as the MPEG-2 decoder. The on-screen display usually includes a graphics processor, or accelerator, that offloads some of the graphics processing from the main processor. Graphics operations are described by means of a graphics application programming interface (API) that describes graphical operations as a series of *graphics primitives*. For example, a graphics primitive might instruct the graphics processor to draw a circle or a line or to display some text with a certain font, color, and transparency.

The resulting graphical image is combined with the video signal using alpha-blending. This allows the pixel value in each video line to be composed from the video input signal and the graphics image in memory, based on its x-y coordinate.

The combined signal is digitally filtered to prevent illegal transitions of the video signal. The best example of filtering is called *anti-alias filtering,* where adjacent field lines are filtered to prevent flickering.

The graphics processor can also support digital transformations of the video. This requires special hardware support or an extremely powerful processor because the chosen transformation must be applied to each field of video in less than one-sixtieth of a second. Common video transformations include

- Video scaling—The video is enlarged or scaled down in size. This can be used for picture-in-graphics or picture-in-picture composition.

- Field/frame capture—The video is captured in freeze-frame. This might be used in a multiprogram guide where multiple panels are used to show images captured from a series of available programs.
- Video warping—The video is spacially distorted according to a mathematical formula. For example, the video might be wrapped around the surface of a cylinder.

As in the advanced analog set-top, the main purpose of the on-screen display is to support a menu-driven user interface and an electronic program guide. However, the addition of video transformations and graphics acceleration in the advanced digital set-top mean that the look and feel of these applications can be much higher in quality. In addition, all these features can be useful for interactive applications, such as interactive advertising (see Chapter 8, "Interactive Services").

Digital-to-Analog Conversion

The output of the standard definition MPEG decoder is in CCIR-601 digital format. A digital-to-analog (D/A) converter transforms the digital video into a component analog signal, which has three components, as specified by EIA 770.1:

- Luminance (Y)—This component is the sum of all colors (R,G,B) and represents the brightness of the picture according to this equation:

  $Y = 0.299R + 0.587G + 0.114B$
- Color difference (Pb)—This component is a color difference signal formed by subtracting the luminance signal from the blue signal according to this equation:

  $Pb = B - Y = -0.299R - 0.587G + 0.886B$
- Color difference (Pr)—This component is a color difference signal formed by subtracting the luminance signal from the blue signal.

  $Pr = R - Y = 0.701R - 0.587G - 0.114B$

Some high-end television receivers accept a component video signal according to EIA 770.1, and this is an optional output from the set-top. However, most television receivers accept only an NTSC input.

NTSC Encoding

All television receivers accept an NTSC input, and the component video signal must be encoded according to the NTSC standard.

The NTSC encoder also accepts a data input to modulate onto the VBI lines. The most important VBI line is line 21 field 1, which is used to carry closed-captioning. It is an FCC regulation that closed-captioning must be present at the output of the set-top box if closed-captioning was transmitted with the program. There are two ways in which closed-captioning can be received by the set-top:

- An analog video signal can contain closed-captioning in line 21, field 1. Only the active video lines are digitized, so line 21 is lost during this process. The solution is that the set-top decodes line 21 and reinserts it at the NTSC encoder.
- A digital video signal can contain closed-captioning in the video user data (VUD), which is embedded in the video program elementary stream (PES). The set-top decodes the VUD to recover closed-captioning and inserts it in line 21 using the NTSC encoder.

As shown in Figure 6-4, the NTSC encoder generates two outputs: an S-Video and a composite output. The S-Video output uses two wires to carry luminance and chrominance signals separately. The composite (or baseband) signal is formed by modulating the chrominance information onto the luminance signal.

Audio Processing

Figure 6-5 shows the audio processing path for the digital set-top. This subsystem has to deal with both analog and digital audio inputs.

Figure 6-5 *Audio Processing Subsystem*

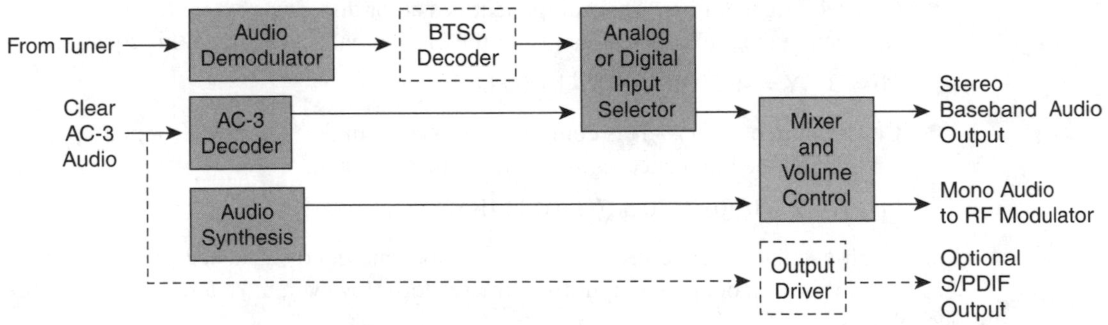

There are three sources of audio:

- Analog audio—The analog audio signal can be encoded in stereo using the BTSC standard and can include a secondary audio program.
- Digital audio—The digital audio signal can be encoded in 2 or 5.1 channel Dolby AC-3.
- Digitally synthesized audio—This audio signal provides the application programmer with the ability to generate sounds locally on the set-top.

The audio processing subsystem is responsible for decoding the audio inputs and selecting or mixing them appropriately.

Dolby AC-3 Audio Decoding

The Dolby AC-3 (also known as *Dolby Digital*) decoder provides multichannel digital audio from mono through 5.1 channels. Dolby AC-3 has been adopted by North American cable operators as the audio format of choice. (An alternative audio standard, MPEG-1 audio, is losing favor but is still supported by many set-tops; see the section Audio Compression in Chapter 4.)

Most digital set-tops provide only a 2-channel baseband audio output (stereo left and right channels), and the Dolby AC-3 decoder is designed to convert a 5.1 channel input signal into a 2-channel Dolby Pro-Logic encoded output.

BTSC Stereo Decoding

BTSC decoding is optional in some digital set-tops, but there are a number of reasons why BTSC decoding is a candidate for serious consideration:

- Seamless audio output—It is very expensive to BTSC *encode* the multichannel audio contained in digital channels, and BTSC encoding would cause a significant quality loss. Therefore, the customer is generally encouraged to use a baseband audio connection to the television receiver (or a separate audio amplifier). In this environment, a BTSC decoder is required to provide *seamless* stereo support for analog channels.
- High-end audio support—Including a BTSC decoder provides the customer with a convenient source of stereo baseband audio to supply home theater equipment. (Currently, the hi-fi VCR provides this function for many customers, but only for unscrambled analog channels.)

Audio Synthesis

The digital set-top usually includes some mechanisms for generating sounds. These sounds must be mixed with the audio signal at an appropriate volume level. Some of the common audio synthesis techniques include wave-files (a common PC format) and MIDI synthesis, which can be used to generate simple musical effects.

Audio synthesis is inexpensive to include in a large ASIC and is usually included for game support. Focus studies show that many customers disable clicks or beeps associated with the user interface if they are given the option of doing so.

Microprocessor Subsystem

The microprocessor subsystem in a digital set-top is similar to the one in an advanced analog set-top (see Chapter 3). (See Figure 6-6.) However, in a digital set-top, the microprocessor usually has considerably higher performance to support the additional processing requirements of a digital set-top:

- Each of the new digital components (QAM demodulator, MPEG-2 decoder, AC-3 decoder, and so on) requires a device driver that executes on the microprocessor.
- Higher CPU performance is needed to take advantage of additional graphics features.
- More applications are envisioned to justify the additional cost of a digital set-top.

Figure 6-6 *Microprocessor Subsystem*

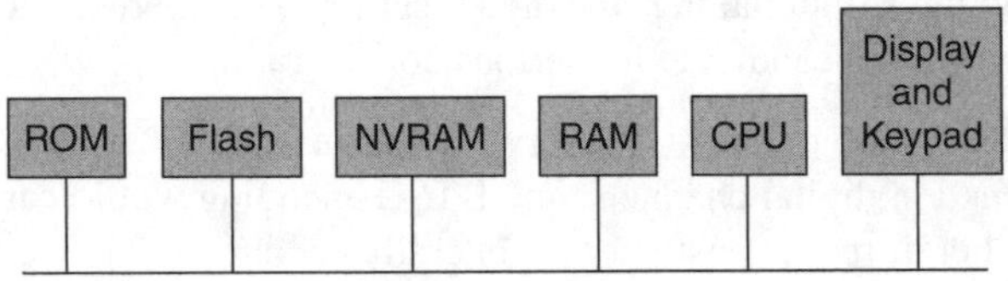

The microprocessor subsystem supports the same features as an advanced analog set-top:

- Menu-driven interface—The set-top contains software that supports a very flexible user interface that, in combination with the on-screen display, allows greater ease-of-use and more complex features to be offered to the customer.
- Electronic program guide (EPG)—The EPG allows the customer to scan the program offerings using the on-screen display, usually by means of a table of channels (the rows of the table) and times (the columns of the table).
- Software download—In most digital set-tops, the software can be downloaded over the network so that additional features (or bug-fixes) can be distributed to set-tops that have been deployed.

In advanced digital set-tops, *application sharing* must be supported to either download applications on request or to maintain multiple applications in set-top memory. Operating system support for application sharing becomes very important (see Chapter 8).

The microprocessor subsystem has a number of components:

- The central processing unit
- The memory subsystem
- The display and keypad

Central Processing Unit

The CPU is typically a 32-bit microprocessor. By trailing the microprocessor price-performance curve of the processors commonly used in personal computers, the digital set-top limits the cost of the CPU to just a few dollars. Another approach is to license a microprocessor core and to include it on the same chip used for other set-top functions. For example, a microprocessor core is commonly included in the transport ASIC.

The CPU performance of a basic, first-generation digital set-top is similar to an advanced analog set-top at 3 to 10 million instructions per second (mips). This is adequate for a limited set of embedded applications as long as they are coded efficiently (for example, in C or C++).

The CPU performance of advanced digital set-tops must be considerably higher than that of a basic digital set-top. A minimum performance of about 50 mips is required, although processors of 100 to 200 mips will soon be available at reasonable cost. Improved CPU performance is required by more sophisticated applications and by interpreted environments (such as JAVA) to enable application portability.

Memory Subsystem

The memory subsystem contains a number of different types of memory, each having a specific purpose. In more recent designs that use a microcontroller, part of the memory might be contained on the same chip as the microprocessor.

The different types of memory are

- Read-only memory ROM
- Flash memory
- Nonvolatile random access memory (NVRAM)
- Random access memory (RAM)

Read-Only Memory

Read-Only Memory (ROM) contains the firmware for the set-top. ROM is the least expensive type of memory, and it is used for storing program instructions and data that are never changed. Because "never" is a long time, programs are usually not committed to ROM until they are thoroughly debugged, which requires exhaustively thorough testing of the program. This testing takes time, so early versions of the set-top might use programmable read-only memory (PROM) to speed the development cycle. When the code is stable, it will typically be stored as masked-ROM because it is the cheapest type of ROM. (In the masked-ROM process, the program is lithographically etched into the chip as the final metal connection layer.)

As the software complexity of a digital set-top design increases, ROM is used less and less because it limits flexibility. ROM is now relegated to basic set-top bootstrap functions that are very unlikely to change.

Flash Memory

Flash memory is also referred to as electrically erasable programmable read-only memory (EEPROM). Flash memory can be erased and rewritten thousands of times, so it is ideal for storing program code and data that might need to be changed due to bug-fixes or other enhancements. Flash memory is typically two to three times more expensive than ROM.

Most digital set-tops support field upgrade of their functions, and this is achieved by downloading new program code and data over the network. Such field upgrades can be very useful to the cable operator but are also fraught with peril! If the download fails, the set-top might be left in an undefined state or might fall back to a basic set of functions. In addition, sometimes customer preferences, which are stored in the set-top, are lost.

One disadvantage of certain types of flash memory is that it cannot support the access speed required by the microprocessor. In this case, the contents of the flash can be copied to RAM before execution, or the microprocessor can be programmed to insert wait cycles. The first solution requires additional RAM, whereas the second solution can seriously affect performance.

Nonvolatile Random-Access Memory

Nonvolatile Random-Access Memory (NVRAM) is used to store any program variables or user data that must survive when the set-top loses AC power. There are two common techniques for implementing NVRAM:

- The use of NVRAM chips—These chips are very reliable, but they are expensive and available only in limited sizes (2 KB is used in some digital set-top designs).
- The use of battery-backed RAM—This is standard RAM that is powered by a small on-chip battery. The RAM size can be many times larger than NVRAM chips, but if the battery fails it must be replaced.

Random Access Memory

Random Access Memory (RAM) is read/write memory that retains its contents only while it is powered. RAM is used to store data and program code. You are probably familiar with the dramatic reduction in the price of RAM for personal computers. The same trends make digital set-tops with 4 to 8 MB of RAM economical.

The main uses for RAM in a digital set-top are

- MPEG-2 decode—Main profile at main level (MP@ML) MPEG decoding requires 2 MB of RAM. A high-definition, main profile at high level (MP@HL) decoder requires approximately 10 MB of RAM; however, some decoders use memory compression techniques to reduce this to 8 MB or less.)
- Graphics processing—A basic rule of thumb is that the more sophisticated the graphics processing, the more memory it requires. Graphics systems are often run in lower resolution and reduced color depth (less bits are allocated to describe the color of each pixel) to reduce memory requirements.
- Operating system—The operating system requires a relatively small amount of memory for its internal data structures and I/O buffers.
- Applications—Each application requires a certain amount of memory, which is dependent on the type of application and its design. If multiple applications are active simultaneously, the digital set-top must have sufficient RAM for their total memory requirements. (This is different from a PC, where applications can be swapped out of memory and onto disk if necessary.)

Display and Keypad

In a digital set-top, customers use the on-screen display and the remote control for most of their interaction with the set-top. However, remote controls have a way of slipping down the back of the couch or exhausting their batteries, so a keypad is usually included on the set-top itself for this eventuality.

For convenience, the on-screen display is supplemented by a 4-digit display that can be used to display the channel number or the time.

RF Modulator

The RF modulator takes the composite NTSC video and audio carriers and places them on channel 3 or channel 4 (although another channel might be available as an option) for output to the television receiver. Channel 3 or 4 selection might be by a switch on the set-top or by software control. Channel 3 or 4 is selected according to which is the *weakest* broadcast signal—that is, which will cause least interference at the television receiver input.

RF Bypass Switch

The RF bypass switch is actually a coaxial relay that returns to the bypass setting when the set-top is in standby. In this position, the RF bypass switch allows all cable channels to pass through the set-top unchanged to the television receiver. (This behavior was mandated by the 1992 Cable Act and later included in the Code of Federal Regulations by the FCC.)

An RF bypass option (see Figure 6-7) allows the customer to connect a VCR to the digital set-top in such a way as to provide recording of all channels.

Figure 6-7 *RF Bypass Option*

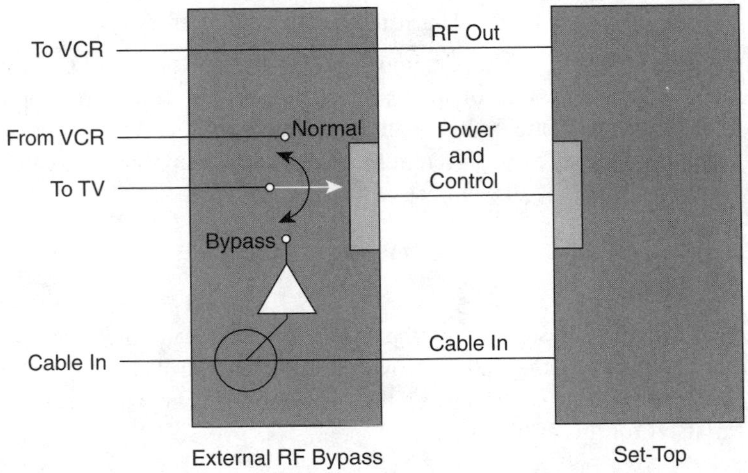

The bypass switch has two positions:

- Normal—The television receives the RF output of the set-top (via the optional VCR loop-through). The customer can view television programs and is able to record and play back using the VCR.
- Bypass—The television receives the entire cable spectrum from the RF input. The customer can tune unscrambled analog television programs with the television receiver.

Inputs

The digital set-top has the following inputs:

- Infrared receiver—An infrared receiver is mounted on the front of the set-top box to allow line-of-sight operation with an infrared remote control. All digital set-tops are supplied with a *universal* remote control, which can also control the television and VCR.

- Diagnostic port—It is quite common for the set-top to have a serial data port for diagnostic purposes. This port is typically used during development of the set-top firmware and can be completely disabled in a production unit for security reasons.
- Data port—A data port on the set-top can be used for various expansion purposes. The most common of these is to connect two digital set-tops to make them function as a dual-tuner set-top for watch-and-record applications (see the section Data Port in Chapter 3).
- Game port—The optional game port provides a way to connect a joystick or game controller to the set-top.

Outputs

The digital set-top has the following outputs:

- RF channel 3/4 output
- Baseband video
- Baseband audio
- Infrared transmitter
- Component video
- IEEE-1394

The RF output is always present and uses the standard 75 ohm F-connector. Baseband audio and video outputs are almost always provided because they provide a significant increase in quality over the RF channel 3/4 output.

All other outputs are optional.

RF Output

An RF output provides the simplest and the most common method of connection to a television receiver or VCR. The RF output carries a clear NTSC signal modulated onto channel 3 or channel 4.

Baseband Video

A baseband video output is provided for connection to the *video-in* input of a television receiver or VCR. This signal is sometimes called a *composite signal* because it contains the baseband luminance information and the modulated chrominance information according to the NTSC standard. The RCA-style connector is the *de facto* standard for this signal.

Baseband Audio

A baseband audio output is provided for connection to the *audio-in* input of a television, VCR, or home-theater. This is a stereo output when an optional BTSC decoder is included in the set-top.

S-Video

An optional S-Video (or Super-Video) output provides superior video bandwidth when compared with baseband NTSC. The S-Video output uses two wires to carry luminance and chrominance signals separately. The physical connection is provided by a 4-pin DIN connector.

Component Video

An optional component video output provides the highest-quality analog signal. Component video is now becoming more common on high-end television receivers, and the Electronic Industries Association (EIA) has published a standard, EIA 770.1, for component video interconnection. The physical connection is made using 3 RCA connectors. (Refer to the section Digital-to-Analog Conversion earlier in this chapter.)

However, there is no agreed-upon standard for copy protection of a component video output (although MacroVision Corporation has proposed a proprietary mechanism for copy protection).

IEEE 1394

IEEE-1394 or FireWire is a recent addition to PCs and will soon be available as an input to high-end television receivers. IEEE-1394 is a high-performance serial interface that supports isochronous and asynchronous transfer modes. It is intended as the de facto standard for digital interconnection of multimedia devices in the home (refer to Figure 6-1).

IEEE-1394 was originally introduced without any means for copy protection, and this has effectively limited its usefulness for anything but connecting video camcorders to display devices. The movie studios are very concerned about copy protection for a couple of reasons:

- The signal is transferred over the IEEE-1394 interface as an MPEG-2 transport stream carrying video and audio in compressed digital form. This makes it simple to store, to replicate, and to transmit the information, essentially providing anyone with his or her own pirate video store.

- The IEEE-1394 is becoming widely available on PCs. The PC is a flexible tool that can be made to perform almost any operation with the appropriate (or inappropriate) software. Thus, when a movie is available in digital form at a PC interface, it is simple to store it, manipulate it, and transmit it to other PC users (via the Internet).

To address these concerns, a Copy Protection Technical Working Group was formed to find copy protection mechanisms that could be adopted by the consumer electronics and computer industries. (See Chapter 17.)

Digital Audio

Most digital set-top designs include only a stereo, baseband output, which does not support the full capabilities of Dolby AC-3. S/PDIF is a *de facto* digital serial interface that was developed for digital transmission of the compressed AC-3 audio. Many DVD players support this output. S/PDIF (pronounced *spidiff*) stands for Sony/Philips digital interface.

S/PDIF is used to connect the digital audio signal to an external Dolby AC-3 decoder, which is usually packaged with a high-quality, 6-channel power amplifier. This arrangement provides the audiophile with the full capabilities of the Dolby AC-3 system.

Infrared Transmitter

An optional infrared transmitter is used to control a VCR. (This is sometimes called an *IR blaster*.) If correctly configured, this can simplify the watch-and-record function considerably (see Chapter 3).

Software

The software architecture of a basic digital set-top is designed to support a small number of embedded applications. In this environment, the software architecture shown in Figure 6-8 is quite adequate.

Figure 6-8 *Software Architecture*

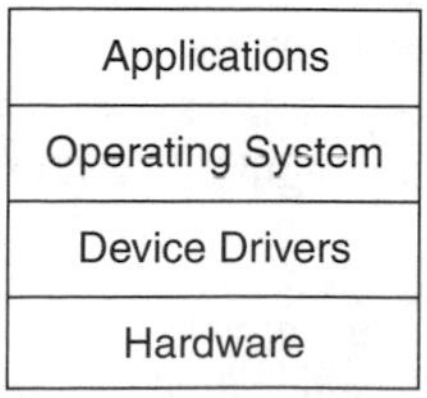

The software can be divided into three main categories:

- Device drivers
- Operating system
- Applications

Device Drivers

Device drivers are programs that work directly with the hardware devices and are often written in assembly language for optimum performance. The device drivers provide a hardware abstraction layer to the operating system.

Operating System

The set-top operating system is quite simple because only a few functions are required:

- Task scheduling—This provides the basic mechanism for ensuring that applications are run in sequence so that each has a turn to use the processor.
- Timers—Timers are used to trigger task execution at some future time and are used by unattended recording and sleep timer applications.
- Interrupt handling—The operating system dispatches interrupts to the appropriate device driver.

A number of commercial operating systems have been developed that satisfy these requirements, including pSOS, VRTX, and VxWorks. It is also quite simple to develop an operating system with these functions in-house.

The operating system is simple because all other functions—for example, memory management—are done by the application.

Applications

The set-top applications perform all the desired functions of the set-top and are typically coded in C or assembly language. The applications developer is responsible for ensuring that the application does not corrupt its own or other applications data, because there is no memory management in the operating system or hardware. Therefore, the applications are *trusted* and must be tested thoroughly; if an application fails, it will cause the set-top to crash or hang up.

Many digital set-top applications are not portable; that is, they cannot be readily moved to a different set-top platform because they rely too much on the specifics of the underlying operating system and hardware.

Limitations

A basic digital set-top has some of the same limitations as an advanced analog set-top: Any new applications must be ported to the proprietary operating system and hardware platform. This requires an agreement between the applications developer and the set-top provider. As the number of applications grow, and as third-party application developers develop more applications, the lack of application portability becomes a significant issue.

Summary

This chapter covered the hardware and software characteristics of a basic digital set-top and some of the extended features of the advanced digital set-top.

The basic digital set-top solves few of the problems associated with analog set-tops. The basic digital set-top has fewer proprietary interfaces, but still supports only a limited number of embedded applications. It cannot always interoperate well with other video equipment, such as television receivers, VCRs, and home-theater equipment, in the customer's home.

The advanced digital set-top can include hardware support for IEEE 1394, high definition television and digital audio (S/PDIF). Its additional CPU performance, graphics functions, and memory footprint allow it to function as an applications platform for interactive and on-demand services (see Part II).

References

Books

Ciciora, Walter, James Farmer, and David Large. *Modern Cable Television Technology; Video, Voice, and Data Communications*. San Francisco, CA: Morgan Kaufmann Publishers Inc., 1999.

Standards

EIA-770.1, "Analog 525 Line Component Video Interface—3 Channels." CEMA R.4 Video Systems Committee.

EIA-770.2, "Standard Definition TV Analog Component Video Interface." CEMA R.4 Video Systems Committee.

EIA-770.3, "High Definition TV Analog Component Video Interface." CEMA R.4 Video Systems Committee.

SCTE DVS-031, "Digital Transmission Standard for Cable Television." Society of Cable Telecommunication Engineers Digital Video Subcommittee.

SCTE DVS-093, "DVS-241 Draft Digital Video Service Multiplex and Transport System Standard for Cable Television." Society of Cable Telecommunication Engineers Digital Video Subcommittee.

SCTE DVS-234, "Service Information for Out-of-Band Digital Cable Television." Society of Cable Telecommunication Engineers Digital Video Subcommittee.

Internet Resource

Apple's FireWire Web site

http://www.developer.apple.com/hardware/FireWire

CHAPTER 7

Digital Broadcast Case Studies

This chapter considers the implementation of digital broadcast cable systems. The two predominant systems in North Amcrica are

- DigiCable—General Instrument developed the DigiCable system to meet TCI's requirements. DigiCablc has been deployed by multiple cable operators in North America, including TCI (now AT&T BIS), Comcast, and Shaw.
- Pegasus—Scientific Atlanta developed its Digital Broadband Delivery System (DBDS) in response to Time Warner Cable's Pegasus system requirements. Multiple cable operators in North America, including Time Warner Cable, Comcast, Cox, Marcus, and Rogers Cable, have adopted it.

This chapter is organized into three main sections:

- Architectural comparison—This section compares and contrasts the two system architectures and describes the different cable operator requirements for digital broadcast.
- DigiCable—This section describes the DigiCable system and its components in detail.
- Pegasus—This section describes the Pegasus system and its components in detail.

Architectural Comparison

DigiCable and Pegasus systems are very different in their implementation but share many common architectural features:

- Satellite distribution to headends—Digital programming is compressed at an uplink and delivered in compressed digital form to the headend location via satellite.
- Headend to subscriber distribution—QAM modulation is used for broadband transmission of the digital programming over an analog cable network.

- A *split* security model—The conditional access system used to secure the satellite link operates independently from the conditional access system used to secure the cable system.
- An out-of-band data channel—A separate QPSK carrier is used to deliver common system information associated with all in-band channels.

Satellite Distribution to Headends

In both systems, a satellite link distributes MPEG-2 compressed digital channels to cable headends, as shown in Figure 7-1. The up-link equipment generates an MPEG-2 multi-program transport stream (MPTS) for each satellite transponder. The processing for each transponder is as follows:

- A real-time encoder compresses the video and audio content, generating an MPEG-2 single program transport stream (SPTS) for each program. (The content may be received from an analog or digital satellite feed, or played back from a video tape or digital file server.)
- Each SPTS is secured using a conditional access system (CA_1). General Instrument's Digicipher II is by far the most common system in use in North America, and Scientific Atlanta's PowerVu is also used.
- Multiplexing equipment combines a number of SPTSs to generate an MPEG-2 multi-program transport stream (MPTS). The MPTS bit rate is chosen to fill the entire payload of a satellite transponder, which varies from between about 27 and 44 Mbps, depending on transponder bandwidth and forward error correction coding.
- The modulation equipment applies forward error correction to the MPTS and is responsible for QPSK modulation. The output is at L-band.
- The transmission equipment up-converts each L-band carrier to the satellite transmission band (C-band or Ku-band). Typically, 24 carriers are amplified, combined, and fed to the dish via a wave-guide.

Figure 7-1 *Satellite Distribution to Headends*

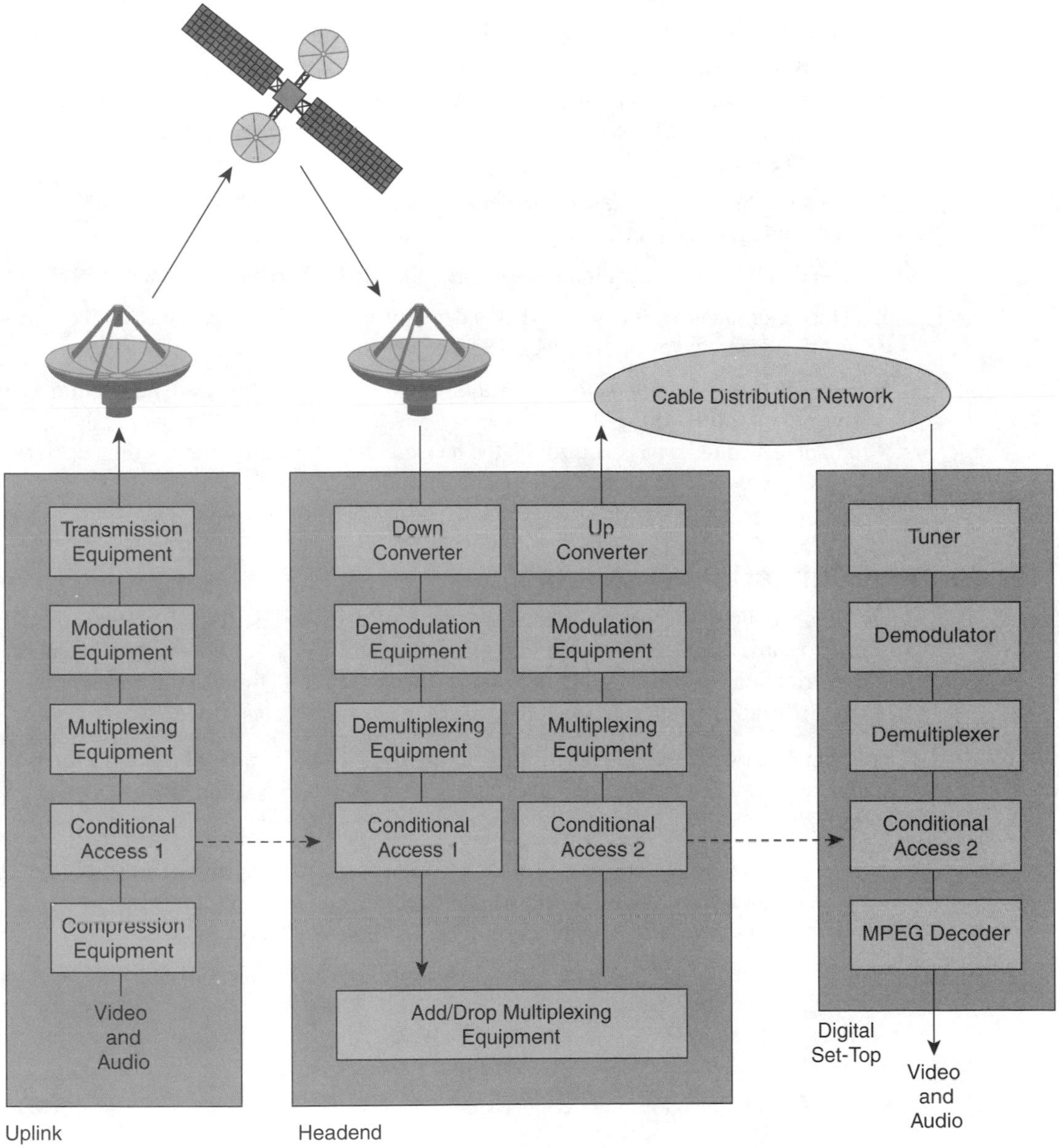

At each headend, the processing of the digital payload is fundamentally the same in DigiCable and Pegasus systems:

- The satellite signal is received and down-converted to L-band by a low-noise block (LNB) converter. (See Chapter 6 of *Modern Cable Television Technology; Video, Voice, and Data Communications* by Walter Ciciora and others.) The satellite modulation is QPSK (see the section Broadband Transmission section in Chapter 4, "Digital Technologies").
- Each L-band carrier is tuned and demodulated to recover the MPEG-2 MPTS by the demodulation equipment.
- The de-multiplexing equipment separates the MPTS into its component SPTS.
- The conditional access system (CA_1) decrypts each SPTS. Each SPTS is secured using a different key so that each SPTS can be authorized separately.
- The SPTS may be *groomed* by an Add/Drop Multiplexer at the headend to build a new system multiplex (or MPTS). In many systems, the MPTSs constructed at the up-link are designed to be passed through the headend intact, so grooming is unnecessary, thereby reducing headend equipment costs.

Headend-to-Subscriber Distribution

DigiCable and Pegasus systems use the same mechanisms to distribute broadcast digital services to subscribers, using QAM modulation to carry MPEG-2 MPTS over the analog cable distribution network to a digital set-top (see the section Digital Transmission in Chapter 5, "Adding Digital Television Services to Cable Systems").

The North American cable industry agreed to use the ITU J.83 Annex B standard for QAM modulation developed by General Instrument. The headend–to–set-top processing is shown in Figure 7-1:

- Each SPTS is secured using a conditional access system (CA_2). The DigiCable system uses General Instrument's Digicipher II conditional access system. The Pegasus system uses Scientific Atlanta's PowerKEY conditional access system.
- Multiplexing equipment combines a number of SPTSs to generate an MPEG-2 multi-program transport stream (MPTS). The MPTS bit rate is chosen to fill the entire payload of a QAM channel, which is 26.97035 Mbps for a 64-QAM channel or 38.81070 Mbps for a 256-QAM channel.
- The modulation equipment converts the MPEG-2 MPTS into a 6 MHz 64-QAM or 256-QAM channel.
- The up-converter places the QAM channel on the desired frequency.

The QAM channels are combined with existing analog NTSC channels and sent over the cable distribution network. In the customer's home, a hybrid digital/analog set-top is responsible for the final processing steps in the signal path (see Chapter 6, "The Digital Set-Top Converter," for more details):

- The chosen cable channel is selected by a tuner, which feeds an intermediate frequency to a QAM demodulator.
- The demodulator recovers the MPEG-2 MPTS.
- The de-multiplexer selects a single SPTS from the MPTS.
- The conditional access system (CA_2) decrypts the SPTS.
- The audio and video elementary streams in the SPTS are decoded and fed to the television receiver.

The signal path from the up-link to the customer has a great many processing elements, but the original SPTS encoded at the up-link is unchanged when it arrives at the set-top decoder. The great advantage of a digital system is that so many processing steps are possible while maintaining the integrity of every bit in the SPTS. Thus, the picture quality from a decoder placed at the up-link is identical to the picture quality from a set-top in the customer's home (assuming that the transmission system is properly maintained).

Split Security Model

The split security model separates the conditional access system for the satellite link from the conditional access for the cable system:

The digital channels are secured over the satellite delivery system by CA_1.

The digital channels are secured over the cable system by CA_2.The DigiCable system uses Digicipher II conditional access for the satellite link (CA_1) *and* for the cable system (CA_2). The Pegasus system uses Digicipher II *or* PowerVu conditional access for the satellite link (CA_1) and PowerKEY conditional access for the cable system (CA_2).

The split security model maintains complete independence between CA_1 and CA_2. This approach has significant operational benefits for the content provider and the cable operator:

- The content provider need only authorize equipment at the cable headend. This enables the content provider to manage *its* customer, the cable operator.
- Cable operators can choose their cable conditional access system independently of the satellite conditional access system.

- The cable operator can insert locally encoded channels into the channel lineup and secure them with the cable conditional access system. (This is particularly important for video-on-demand services. See the section Conditional Access in Chapter 10, "On-Demand Services").
- A security breach of either the CA_1 or CA_2 conditional access systems does not affect the integrity of the other conditional access system.

Out-of-Band Channel

Both the DigiCable and Pegasus systems rely on an out-of-band data channel. The out-of-band channel delivers common system information associated with all in-band channels to the digital set-tops:

- Entitlement management messages (EMM)—These messages are addressed to individual set-tops and carry secure authorization instructions from the conditional access system in the headend to the set-top.
- Service information (SI)—These messages provide the set-top with information to support channel navigation.
- Program guide information—These messages provide the program guide information to the EPG application in the set-top.
- Emergency alert system (EAS) messages—In response to an EAS message, the set-top displays a text message, plays an audio message, or force-tunes to an alert channel.

Central Versus Local Subscriber Management

The DigiCable system is designed to provide either central or local subscriber management. The Pegasus system is designed to provide only local subscriber management.

In central subscriber management, the satellite distribution system is used to control each cable headend by using part of a satellite transponder as a data communications link to carry authorization and control messages. In local subscriber management, a local headend controller provides all the management function for the cable system.

In both cases, the satellite distribution also provides a way of obtaining digital programming services from the content provider. However, in the centrally managed system, the programming and the management functions may be provided as a *bundled* package. In a locally managed system, multiple sources of digital programming may be combined, or *groomed*, as desired by the cable system operator.

DigiCable

The DigiCable system is supplied by General Instrument. It provides an end-to-end solution for the satellite and cable system distribution networks, including

- Up-link equipment, including MPEG-2 encoding, conditional access, and multiplexing equipment. (This equipment is not described in detail in this chapter.)
- Headend equipment, including satellite receiver, conditional access, and cable transmission equipment.
- Subscriber equipment, a range of digital set-top converters provided by GI, from the DCT-1000 to the DCT-5000 series Digital Communications Terminal (DCT).

Figure 7-2 illustrates how the headend processing functions are packaged in the DigiCable implementation:

- Integrated Receiver Transcoder (IRT)—The IRT efficiently packages the demodulation, conditional access, and modulation functions into a single rack-mounted chassis.
- Add-Drop Multiplexer (ADM)—The ADM can be used to groom the baseband outputs of several IRTs into a new MPEG-2 multi-program transport stream (MPTS). The output of the ADM is fed into an IRT, which applies conditional access and modulation to the MPTS. (Note: The ADM is not widely deployed due to incompatibilities with statistical multiplexing widely used by programmer providers.)
- C6U up-converter—The C6U is required to up-convert the output of the IRT, which is at a 44 MHz intermediate frequency, to the desired QAM channel frequency. The C6U is a dual-channel up-converter.

Figure 7-2 *DigiCable Headend Processing Functions*

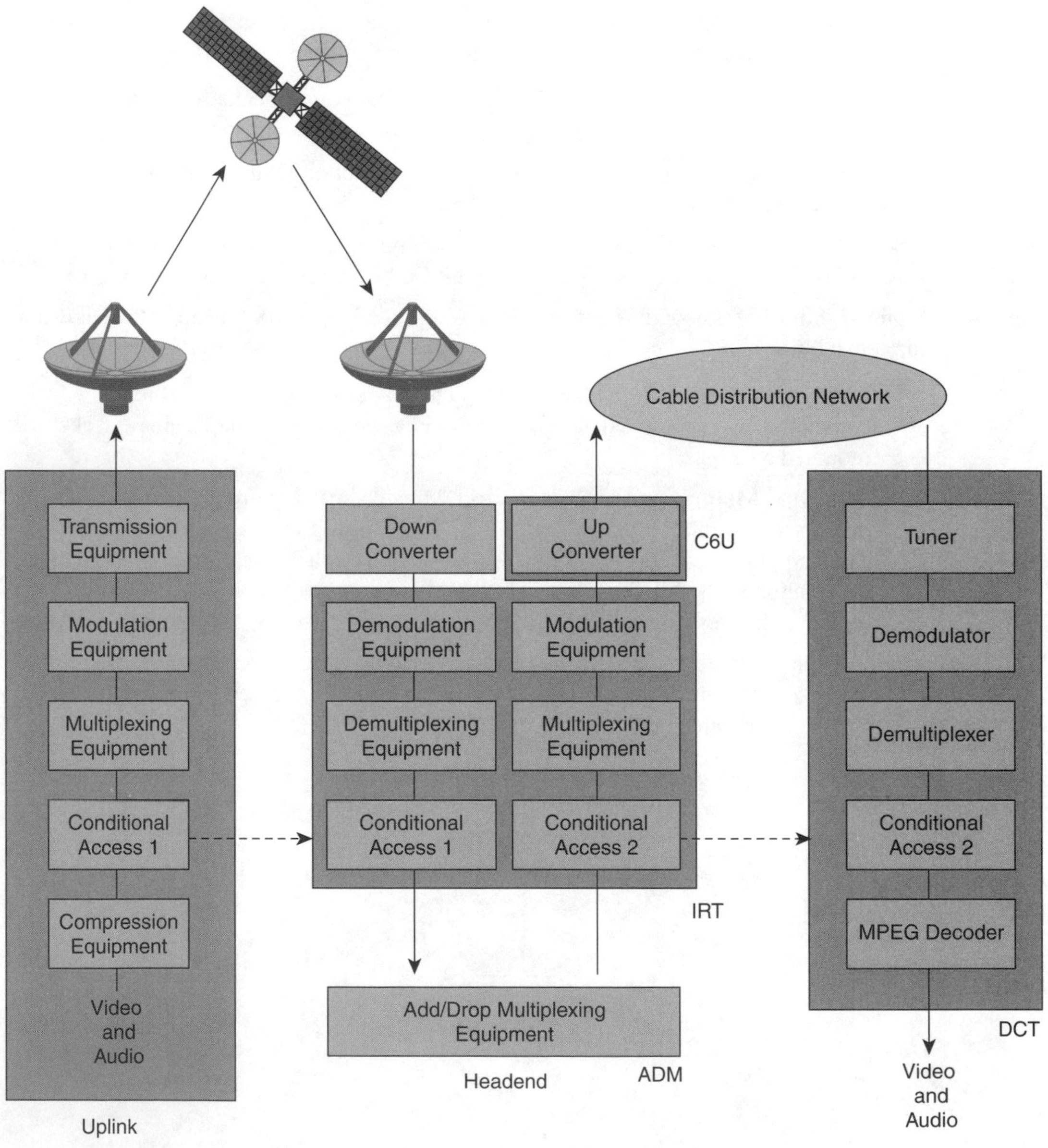

Head-End In The Sky Model

The DigiCable system was designed to meet TCI's (now AT&T BIS) requirement for centralized subscriber management. The Head-End In The Sky (HITS) model uses the satellite distribution system to control each cable headend from the National Authorization Service (NAS) in Littleton, Colorado. The NAS controller supports interfaces to the various NAS customer billing systems. It also supports multiple digital service providers, including HBO, Showtime, and Music Choice.

NOTE TCI transferred ownership of the National Authorization Service from HITS to General Instrument in June of 1998, though TCI (now AT&T BIS) continues to use the service as before.

Figure 7-3 shows a typical, *three-pack*, HITS configuration. In this configuration, the satellite feed is received by three IRTs, and each IRT is tuned to a different transponder frequency. The IRT provides demodulation, satellite conditional access, cable conditional access, and QAM modulation for an MPTS containing up to 12 programs. The IRT outputs are fed to C6U up-converters and combined in the main cable system feed.

Figure 7-3 shows the other headend components:

- The OM-1000 is an out-of-band modulator that generates a 2.048 Mbps, out-of-band control channel that is received by all digital set-tops.
- The Headend Management System (HMS) is an unattended workstation computer connected by an ethernet to the other components in the headend. Its main function is to collect IPPV purchase records from the digital set-tops (DCTs). It also provides remote management of the headend components.
- The dial-up modems provide a return path from the digital set-tops to the controller, and also provide a mechanism for connection back to the NAS.

Figure 7-3 *HITS Architecture*

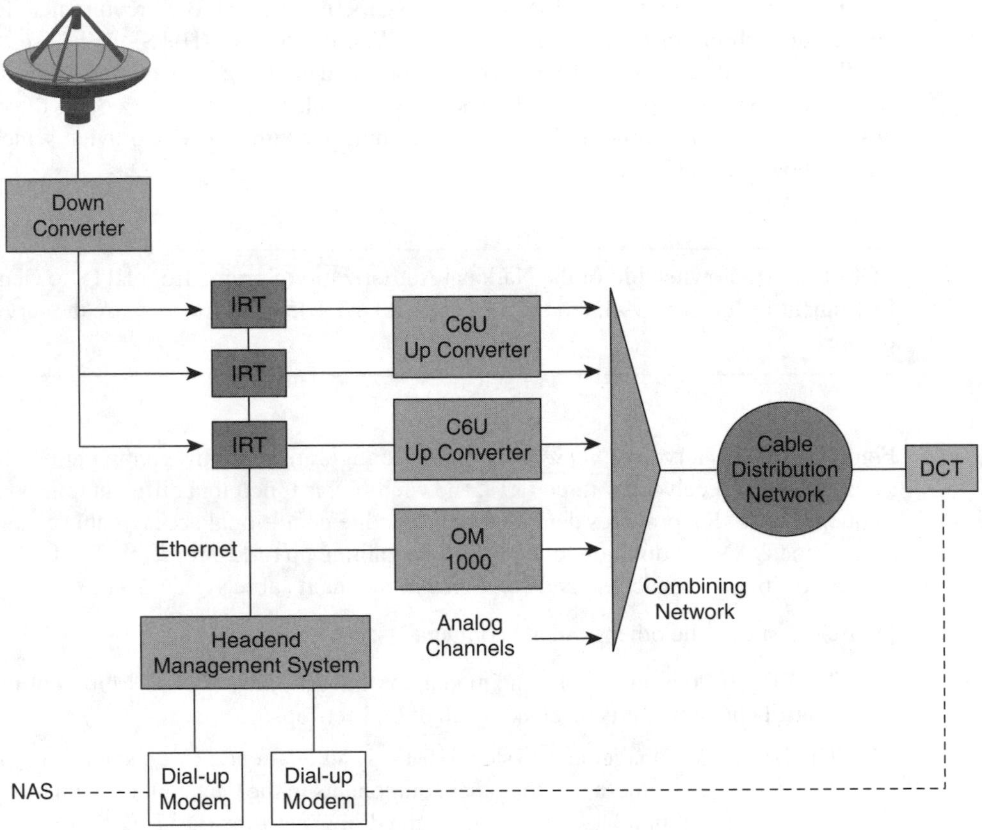

One IRT receives the control channel from the NAS. This 1.5 Mbps data stream is carried as MPEG-2 private data within the MPTS. The IRT recognizes the data stream and outputs it as user data protocol (UDP) packets over an ethernet connection. The NAS control channel carries information to manage both the headend and the subscribers. In each case, these messages arrive over the Ethernet connection from the IRT receiving the NAS control channel:

- The IRTs are managed by control messages addressed to them from the NAS. These messages include satellite conditional access (CA_1) authorization messages to the IRT decryption section as well as cable system conditional access (CA_2) messages to the encryption section of the IRT.
- The OM-1000 is managed by control messages addressed to it from the NAS.

- The Headend Management System (HMS) is managed by control messages addressed to it from the NAS.
- The digital set-tops receive control messages forwarded by the OM-1000 over the out-of-band data channel. These messages include conditional access (CA_2) authorization messages, system information tables, and program guide data messages.

Channel Expansion

The system described in Figure 7-3 shows how the HITS architecture expands the channel lineup of a small, un-upgraded cable system. The three IRTs add about 30 digital channels and 20 music channels to the channel lineup at a cost of only 18 MHz of spectrum. The system is cost-effective for small systems with only a few thousand subscribers because of the small number of highly integrated headend components.

Multiple Channel Lineups

The HITS system provides a single, satellite feed to a large number of cable systems. The program guide data provides information about the analog and digital channels. Each cable system may potentially have a different analog channel lineup, and a mechanism is required to support this environment. The solution is a feature in the service information protocol (SCTE DVS-147, since updated to DVS-234) called multiple Virtual Channel Tables (VCT).

DVS-147 supports up to 4,000 different VCTs, and each VCT is sent in the NAS control channel with a different multicast address. Every digital set-top is provisioned with a multicast address according to its geographical location, and uses this address to filter the proper VCT from all of the VCTs carried in the out-of-band control channel.

The *superset* program guide data is repeatedly broadcast in carousel fashion to all HITS systems. Each set-top recognizes its *own* VCT and uses the pointers contained in it to construct its own program guide from the superset program guide data.

Remote Purchase Record Collection and Forwarding

The National Authorization Service provides a store-and-forward approach to purchase record collection that manages the limited return bandwidth in a telephone return environment. In addition, the NAS now supports purchase collection via the cable upstream path, with upstream signals terminating at an RPD in the headend. The RPD is interfaced to the Headend Management System (HMS).

Each cable headend has an HMS (refer to Figure 7-3). The HMS is programmed to collect and forward purchase records from the digital set-tops:

- The purchase record collection system sends an addressed *poll* message to each set-top in turn over the out-of-band data channel at a scheduled time.
- The digital set-top responds to the poll by retrieving the IPPV purchase records from its secure microprocessor and sends them to the purchase record collection system using a dial-up telephone modem (or via the cable upstream path where the return has been activated).
- Periodically, the HMS dials up the NAS system and uploads the aggregate purchase records to it.
- The HMS sends an addressed message to each set-top in turn to clear the collected purchase records from the secure microprocessor after the purchase records are safely received and acknowledged by the NAS.

Split Security Model

In the HITS and NAS system, Digicipher II provides both the satellite conditional access system (CA_1) and the cable system conditional access system (CA_2), and the Digicipher II controllers are located at the NAS. Nevertheless, CA_1 and CA_2 are managed as completely independent security systems so that if a pirate discovers a session key for CA_2, it would be useless for CA_1.

Local Subscriber Management

The DigiCable architecture also supports a local subscriber management model. Figure 7-4 shows a diagram of an upgraded cable system that is locally managed.

A locally managed system requires a number of additional components in the headend to provide the functions that were centralized in the HITS model:

- The headend controller, which is called a Digital Access Controller (DAC)-6000 (previously called the ACC-4000D)—This controller is responsible for management and provisioning of all the headend components and digital set-tops. The DAC-6000 also provides the interface to the billing system for service provisioning and IPPV purchase reporting.
- The KLS-1000 key server—This device provides encryption services to the headend controller to support the Digicipher II conditional access system (CA_2).
- MPEG-2 encoding—Local analog channels may be encoded and multiplexed together for transmission over a QAM channel.

- The ADM-1000G add/drop multiplexer—The ADM-1000 is used to groom MPTSs received from multiple sources into a single MPTS for transmission over a QAM channel.

Figure 7-4 *Local Subscriber Management Model*

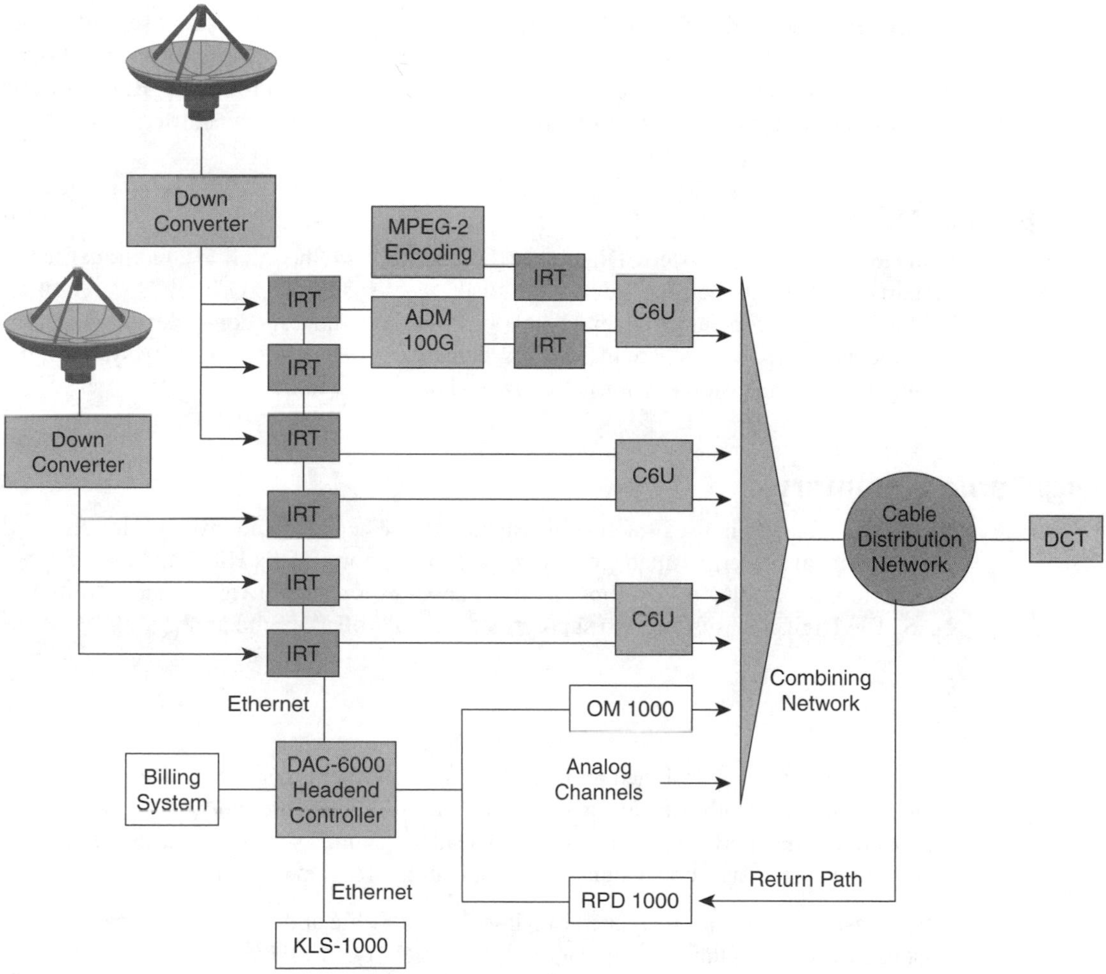

In Figure 7-4, the upgraded system provides an RF return path, and the digital set-tops may use it for return signaling. The DCT set-top has an optional RF return module called the StarVue RF module. The RPD-1000 receives a 256 Kbps QPSK return signal from the DCT set-top (as specified by DVS-178, see the section SCTE DVS-178 in Chapter 5). The RPD-1000 terminates and aggregates up to six return paths into a single ethernet output.

Finally, the billing system may be located on-premise. Alternatively, if a billing service bureau is used, a wide-area network (WAN) link is used to connect the headend controller to the billing system.

Channel Expansion

The system described in Figure 7-4 shows how a locally managed system uses DigiCable to expand the channel lineup of a larger, upgraded cable system. The number of IRTs is limited only by the available spectrum for digital. The locally controlled DigiCable system is cost-effective for larger systems with more than about 50 thousand subscribers.

Split Security Model

In the locally managed system, Digicipher II is used for both the satellite conditional access system (CA_1) and the cable system conditional access system (CA_1). The CA_1 controllers are located at the content provider up-link locations, and the CA_2 controller is located in the headend. CA_1 and CA_2 are managed as completely independent security systems; if a pirate discovers a session key for CA_2, it would be useless for CA_1.

DigiCable Summary

The DigiCable system uses satellite distribution to the headend and provides for either central or local subscriber management. Its design supports TCI's HITS and the NAS architecture by sending a 1.5 Mbps control channel over a satellite transponder from the NAS. The DigiCable system also supports a local controller architecture.

Pegasus

The Pegasus system is designed to meet TWC's requirements for local subscriber management. Headends are clustered into cable *divisions* that are independently managed and operated. Each division requires a local headend control system and uses the satellite distribution system as a convenient way of obtaining program content.

The Pegasus architecture is defined by Time Warner Cable and incorporates many of the lessons learned from the Time Warner Full Service Network. Pegasus is a phased system with two major phases:

- Phase 1.0 Digital Broadcast
- Phase 2.0 On-Demand Services

This chapter focuses on Pegasus Phase 1.0. On-demand services are discussed in Chapter 10. Pegasus also has minor phases, including Phase 1.1, which introduces interactive services to a broadcast system; these services are discussed in Chapter 9, "Interactive Cable System Case Studies."

Pegasus Phase 1.0 Goals

The Pegasus architecture introduces a number of important technical and business concepts. These are articulated in the Pegasus Phase 1.0 goals:

- Support interactive and broadcast digital services in an integrated manner—Pegasus is conceived as a broadcast digital system that grows to support interactive and on-demand services. (These services are examined in detail in Part II, "Ineractive and On-Demand Services.")
- Multiple access control based on robust digital cryptography—In analog conditional access systems, the actual scrambling method is proprietary. In a digital conditional access system, the payload encryption algorithm can be standardized without reducing the overall security of the system. (See "Multiple Conditional Access Systems," by Michael Adams and Tony Wasilewski.)
- Support many different content providers—Competition between content providers is essential to a cable operator to ensure that the cost of programming remains reasonable. Pegasus was designed to use digital programming services from all available content providers.
- Efficient use of forward and reverse bandwidth—Bandwidth (or spectrum) in a cable system is a limited resource, and much of a cable operator's decision-making revolves around making the best use of cable spectrum. This includes the choice of modulation, topology, channel allocation, system design, and many other factors. The Pegasus architecture formalizes many of the *rule-of-thumb* design rules that have evolved for a hybrid fiber coax (HFC) cable plant.
- Critical-mass, third-party applications platform—One of the most important concepts in the Pegasus architecture is the creation of an applications platform. The set-top hardware and operating system supports the development of *third-party* applications. The set-top becomes an attractive platform to applications developers only when it is deployed in sufficient numbers—that is, when it reaches *critical mass*. Lessons from other industries, namely the game console and personal computer industry, suggest that this critical mass is about one million units.

This last goal is worth examining in more detail. Historically, the set-top has been single-sourced from the same vendor that is responsible for building the headend components. This inevitably leads to closed, proprietary interfaces, as engineers within the same company iterate their way through the network interface design process. To ensure that the Pegasus initiative achieved its goal of a critical-mass applications platform, Time Warner Cable issued a set of requirements as the Pegasus RFP.

Pegasus Request for Proposal

Time Warner Cable issued the Pegasus Request for Proposal (RFP) in March 1996. The introduction included the following passage about the applications platform:

> A major goal of the Pegasus strategy has been to provide an application platform that lowers the barrier to entry for applications into the market for interactive services delivered over cable. As such the Pegasus set-top terminal needs to offer a level of platform independence to leverage the software tools, developer experience, and content that exists in the market today. The first step in achieving this platform independence was achieved at the hardware level by introducing multiple vendors for the set-top terminal hardware.

In fact, persuading multiple set-top vendors to build digital set-tops to a set of open standards is probably the most difficult part of the Pegasus program. There are many reasons why set-top vendors are reluctant to build to open standards:

- It is more difficult than building a proprietary set-top—There are many standards to choose from and each has to be interpreted carefully so that all implementations are interoperable.
- Standards are constructed by a committee and are often complicated due to compromise agreements—As someone once said, "A camel is a horse designed by a committee."
- Standards can limit the innovation of a company by spelling out too clearly how to do something.
- Standards are never quite finished—DirecTV learned this when it launched its service with a different transport packet length than the one that was ultimately agreed upon by the MPEG-2 Systems Committee.

Nevertheless, by 1996 there were many established standards for the transmission and coding of digital television (see the section The Cable Network Interface in Chapter 6). The Pegasus RFP leverages these standards to define the Pegasus network interface, which supports a family of digital set-tops from multiple vendors.

The Pegasus RFP is available on the Web at http://timewarner.com/rfp.

Pegasus Architecture

Figure 7-5 illustrates the Pegasus architecture.

Figure 7-5 *Pegasus Architecture*

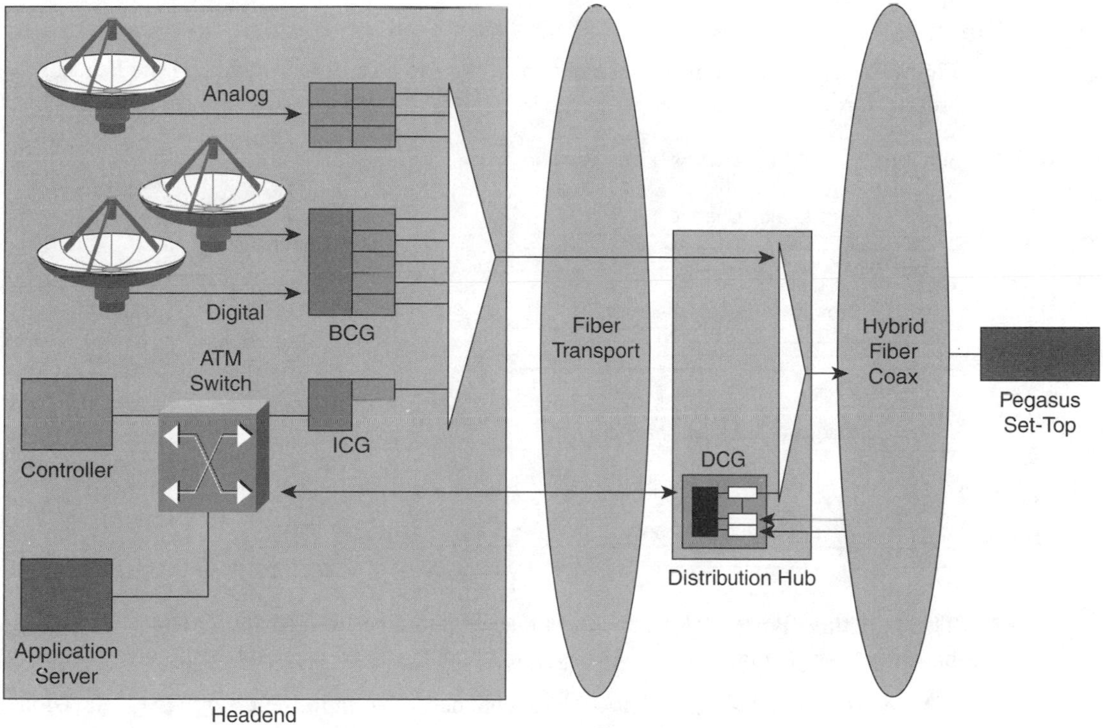

The major components are defined as *gateways* (the networking terminology that describes a communications device that connects two dissimilar networks):

- Broadcast cable gateway (BCG)—The BCG takes digital programming from the satellite distribution network and converts it into a form suitable for transmission over a cable distribution network.
- Interactive cable gateway (ICG)—The ICG takes data from an asynchronous transfer mode (ATM) network, reassembles the ATM cells, and converts it into MPEG-2 private data format. This allows data communications to the set-top using standard internet protocols, without the need for an ATM adaptation function in every set-top.

- Data channel gateway (DCG)—The DCG takes data from an ATM network and converts it into the DAVIC out-of-band channel format. The DCG function is distributed to the distribution hub locations of the cable system to allow traffic growth to be accommodated.

Digital Channels

Figure 7-6 shows the logical channel connections to a set-top provided by the Pegasus architecture.

Figure 7-6 *Set-Top Channel Connections Within Pegasus Architecture*

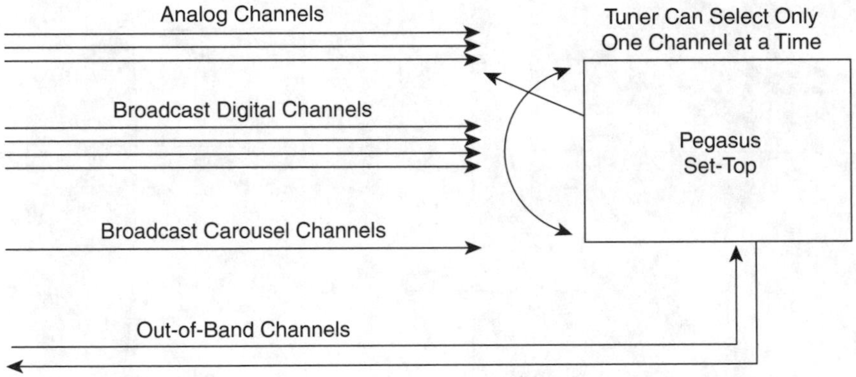

There are three types of in-band channel, each modulated as a 6 MHz channel. The set-top has only a single tuner, so only one type of channel can be received at any given time:

- Analog broadcast channels—These channels contain in-the-clear NTSC television channels.
- Digital broadcast channels—These channels are QAM-modulated channels, and each contains an MPTS.
- Broadcast carousel channels—These channels are also QAM-modulated, but they contain a data carousel that is used to provide application data and code to the set-top.

There are two types of out-of-band channel. In contrast to the in-band channels, the out-of-band channel is received by all Pegasus set-tops all of the time:

- Forward Data Channel (FDC)
- Reverse Data Channel (RDC)

The Pegasus architecture specifies a standard TCP-IP network to connect the digital set-tops to the headend. This network is owned and managed by the cable operator, not by the cable vendor.

Hub Interconnection

Figure 7-7 shows an example of an upgraded cable system. The system is organized into a single digital headend and a number of distribution hubs. The distribution hubs are interconnected into rings using bundles of fiber. Some fibers are used for analog distribution of the broadband signal out to the fiber node (see Chapter 2, "Analog Cable Technologies"); other fibers may be used to support a SONET connection between the headend ATM network and the data channel gateways in the hubs. (The DCG component is located at the hub for reasons explained in the section Out-of-Band Termination in Chapter 5.)

Figure 7-7 *Upgraded Cable System*

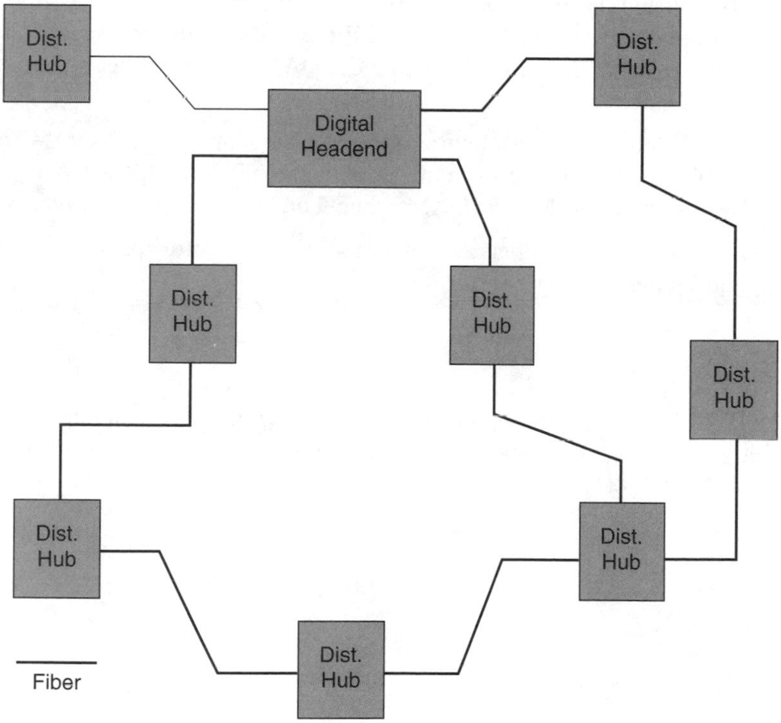

Network Management

The Pegasus RFP specified requirements for remote network management of all components in the system, whether they are located in the headend, the distribution hub, or the customer's home.

Digital Broadband Delivery System

The Digital Broadband Delivery System (DBDS) is Scientific Atlanta's implementation of the Pegasus system.

Figure 7-8 illustrates how the headend processing functions are packaged in the DBDS implementation:

- Integrated Receiver Decoder (IRD)—The IRD packages the satellite demodulation and conditional access functions into a single rack-mounted chassis.
- Broadband Integrated Gateway (BIG)—The BIG can be used to groom the baseband outputs of several IRDs into a new MPEG-2 multi-program transport stream (MPTS). The output of the BIG is fed into a CA QAM, which applies conditional access and modulation to the MPTS.
- Condition Access Quadrature Amplitude Modulator (CA QAM)—The CA QAM applies conditional access and modulation to the MPTS. The CA-QAM has a built in up-converter to place the QAM channel on the desired cable frequency.

So far, there are two suppliers of Pegasus set-tops: Scientific Atlanta (Explorer-series set-top) and Pioneer (Voyager-series set-top).

Headend Equipment

The DBDS is designed to support a local subscriber management model. Figure 7-9 shows a diagram of a locally managed cable system with an HFC upgrade.

Figure 7-8 *DBDS Headend Processing*

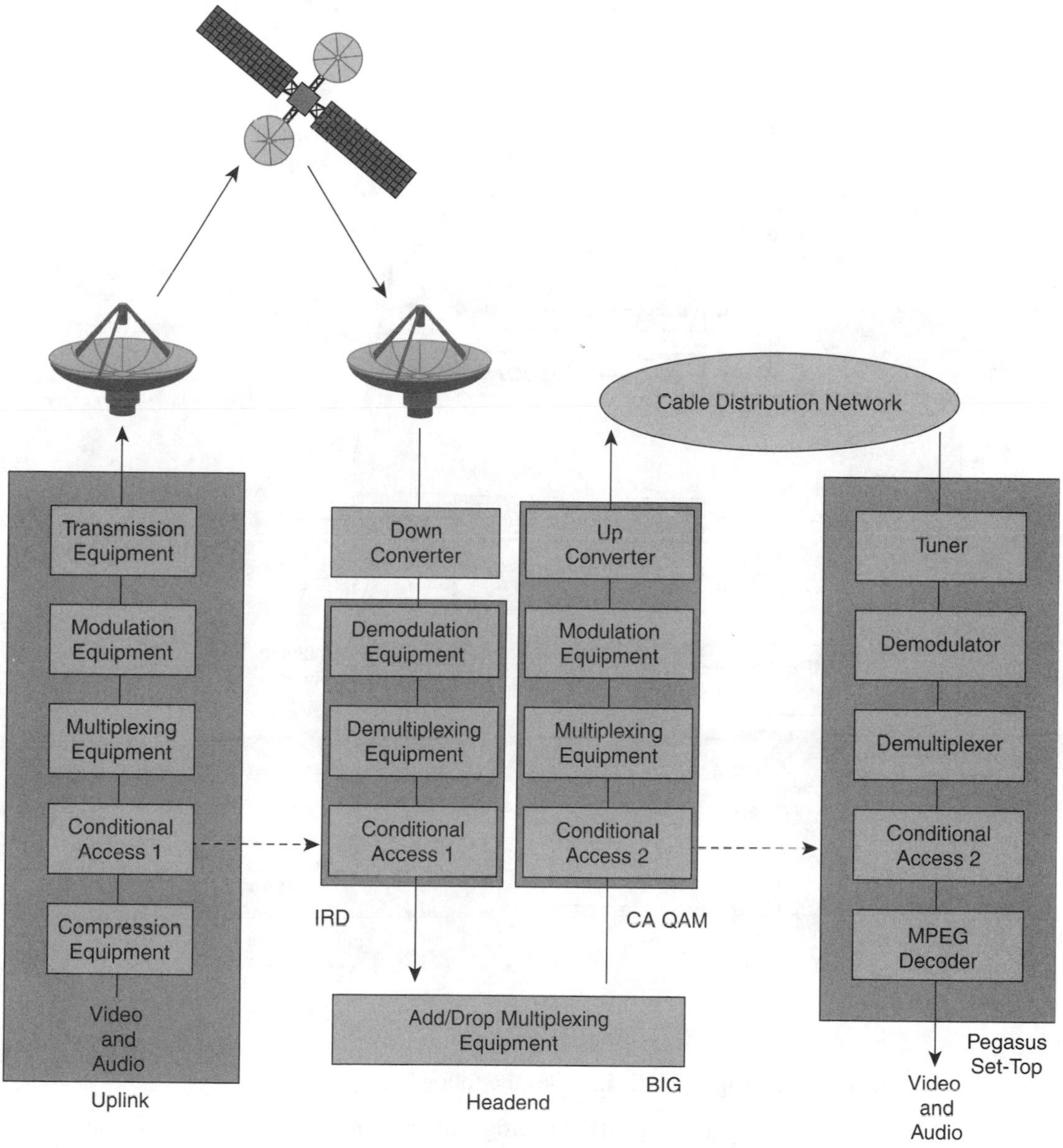

Figure 7-9 *HFC Upgrade on a Locally Managed Cable System*

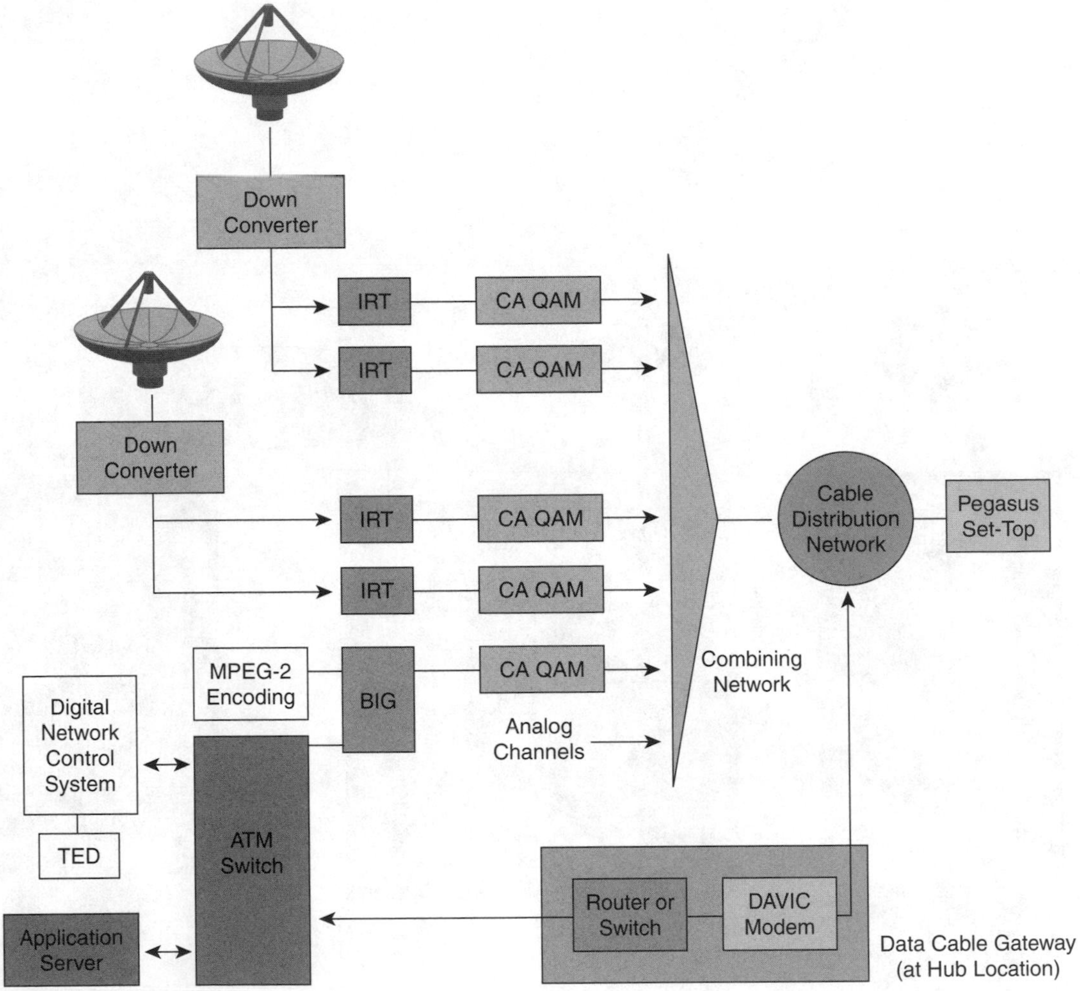

The locally managed model includes the following:

- Digital programming—Digital programming is received from satellite using either an Integrated Receiver Transcoder (IRT) for Digicipher II secured channels or an Integrated Receiver Decoder (IRD) for PowerVu secured channels.
- CA-QAM—If no grooming is required, the output of the IRT or IRD is fed directly into the CA QAM. The CA QAM applies PowerKEY conditional access and QAM modulation to the MPTS.

- The headend controller, or Digital Network Control System (DNCS)—The DNCS is responsible for management and provisioning of all the headend components and the Pegasus set-tops. The DNCS also provides the interface to the billing system for service provisioning and IPPV purchase reporting. The DNCS also supports an integrated network management system that is based on the Cabletron Spectrum tool-set.
- The Transaction Encryption Device (TED)—This device provides encryption services to the DNCS to support the PowerKEY conditional access system.
- MPEG-2 encoding—Local analog channels may be encoded and multiplexed together for transmission over a QAM channel.
- The Broadband Integrated Gateway (BIG) add/drop multiplexer—The BIG is used to groom MPTSs received from multiple sources into a single MPTS for transmission over a QAM channel and may also be used to multiplex local encoded channels into an MPTS. The BIG also provides an ATM-to-MPEG-2 adaptation function, which allows private data to be injected into the MPEG-2 MPTS from the application server or DNCS.
- Application server—The application server is a workstation class system that is used to support the server part of applications that are deployed in the DBDS. For example, an applications server supports the delivery of program guide data to client applications in the digital set-top.
- ATM switch—An ATM switch is used to interconnect the headend components and the hub components of the DBDS. ATM was chosen because it is a cost-effective networking technology that is available from multiple vendors. It also provides the quality of service guarantees required to deliver MPEG-2 transport streams.

The billing system may be located on-premise. Alternatively, if a billing service bureau is used, a WAN link is used to connect the headend controller to the billing system.

Hub Equipment

Figure 7-9 shows the DBDS equipment that is located at the hub locations in the cable system.

A router or switch provides a SONET optical interface for interconnection to the ATM switch at the headend. This equipment supports multiple DAVIC modems at the hub as the out-of-band communications traffic increases over time.

The DAVIC modem supports a 1.5 Mbps full-duplex communication to many thousands of Pegasus set-tops.

DBDS Summary

Scientific Atlanta's digital broadband delivery system uses satellite distribution to the headend and provides local subscriber management. Its design supports Time Warner Cable's Pegasus architecture.

Summary

This chapter described the two predominant choices available to a North American cable operator.

The DigiCable system was designed as a solution to the TCI HITS architecture and defines only proprietary interfaces. However, a number of these interfaces have now been published by General Instrument as part of the SCTE Digital Video Standards (DVS) subcommittee work. (Part of the SCTE DVS charter is to publish standards that reflect existing practice in the cable industry.)

The Pegasus architecture was designed as an open system and makes use of many international standards (predominantly from MPEG and DAVIC). Scientific Atlanta publishes any new standards that are developed in SCTE DVS.

References

Book

Ciciora, Walter, James Farmer, and David Large. *Modern Cable Television Technology; Video, Voice, and Data Communications.* San Francisco, CA: Morgan Kaufmann Publishers, Inc., 1999.

Periodical

Adams, Michael and Tony Wasilewski. "Multiple Conditional Access Systems." *Communications Technology*, April 1997.

PART II

Interactive and On-Demand Services

CHAPTER 8

Interactive Services

Interactive services provide extensions to the cable system to provide a new class of services. There are almost an infinite number of possible interactive services. Some examples are

- Home shopping
- Home banking
- E-mail
- Web access
- Electronic games
- Stock tickers

Interactive service uses local processing in the set-top combined with data communications services provided by the cable network to deliver new services via the television receiver. Moreover, interactive services can be integrated with broadcast television to provide *enhanced* television services, such as interactive advertising. With this promise, why are interactive services not already widely deployed on cable systems?

There are a number of reasons:

- Although cable operators have experimented with interactive services in trials and limited deployments for many years (see "The Trials and Travails of Interactive TV," in *IEEE Spectrum,* by Tekla Perry), cable operators have yet to deploy, in volume, an application platform that supports interactive services. (See the section Limitations in Chapter 3, "The Analog Set-Top Converter," for a discussion of the limitations of analog set-tops.)
- Interactive services have yet to prove their capability of generating real revenues in large-scale deployment. There is no single *killer* application, so a suite of interactive services is required.
- Television viewing is fundamentally a passive mode of interaction for most television viewers. In addition, many advertisers that support television channels might be reluctant to change the current relationship they have with their audience.

Nevertheless, this situation is ripe for change with the introduction of digital services. A digital cable system already has many of the necessary resources to support interactive applications, and the emergence and acceptance of the Internet are educating customers to expect more from their television sets.

Internet Convergence

Web browsing has increased phenomenally in popularity over recent years and most companies now host a Web site to promote their services or products. The ubiquitous connectivity provided by the Internet enables the Web, but the Internet was not built to support any particular application. The Internet has its origins in ARPANET, which was funded by the Advanced Research Projects Agency (ARPA) (see Chapter 1 of *Internetworking with TCP/IP, Third Edition, Volume 1,* by Douglas E. Comer). In fact, it was 25 years after ARPANET first went online (in 1969) before Web browsing was developed.

The Web originated in universities to facilitate the exchange of information, and these sites still provide the opportunity for serious research. However, the Web has become a tangle of pornographic, commercial, special interest, and vanity publishing sites. The noise of the Web often drowns out the valuable information that is buried in there, somewhere, like a needle in a haystack.

The emergence of the Web has provided a major impetus to interactive services on cable by providing a software toolbox for the applications developer. The challenge is to transfer the Internet-centric technology to a television environment. At first sight, it seems easy to emulate the success of the Internet by offering a Web-browsing service, but this approach is not as simple as it seems:

- Basic digital set-tops simply do not have the memory or performance to run a standard Web browser application written for the PC.
- Most Web sites are designed for presentation on a high-resolution computer monitor display. NTSC was not designed to handle these kinds of images and, in general, Web sites transfer poorly to a television environment.
- The Internet is a totally uncontrolled environment; applications and applets are downloaded at the customers' risk. In a cable system, the cable operator is responsible for the availability of the service and for repairing, or replacing, failed set-tops. Problems due to uncontrolled, untested applications and computer viruses could seriously damage a cable operator, financially and operationally.
- Internet applications are generally provided free of charge. An Internet service provider (ISP) bills the customer for the cost of Internet access. This has been called the "all you can eat" billing model. In contrast, cable operators resell content from a programmer on a service-by-service basis.

Goals of Interactive Services

There are a number of common goals for interactive services, regardless of the specific services offered. These goals must be satisfied for a service to be successful.

Interactive services must add value in some way for the programmer, cable operator, and customer. This added value can come from a number of sources:

- Customer-generated revenue—If an interactive service is useful or compelling, the customer will be prepared to pay for it. For example, advanced analog experience shows that customers are prepared to pay several dollars per month for an interactive program guide.
- Advertiser-generated revenue—If an interactive service can increase the effectiveness of existing commercials or allow the customer to access a companies product and service information, the advertiser will be prepared to pay the cable operator for that service.
- Enhanced customer perception and retention—Increased competition from DBS, MMDS, and others make it even more important to cable operators that their customers are happy with their cable service. Informational services have proven to be useful in terms of enhancing the customer's perception of the overall cable service.

Interactive services must also provide a satisfying experience for the customer. A poorly developed interactive service is worse than no interactive service at all. There are a number of areas where care must be taken:

- Interactive services must be friendly and intuitive to use. The service needs to be easily accessible from the remote control with little or no customer training.
- Interactive services must present an attractive, graphically rich interface. The customer is accustomed to the high production values of most television programming and will not tolerate an uninteresting or static user interface.
- Interactive services must be reliable and highly available. If an interactive service becomes popular with customers, they will be frustrated if it is unreliable or unavailable.

Interactive Versus On-Demand Services

Until recently, interactive television services were considered to be almost synonymous with on-demand services, specifically video-on-demand (see *Interactive Television* by Winston William Hodge). However, video-on-demand is a technology that supports a special class of interactive services and presents its own set of functions and limitations. To distinguish video-on-demand (and all related on-demand services) from interactive services, I will refer to them as on-demand services. On-demand services are described in Chapter 10, "On-Demand Services."

The following definitions serve to differentiate interactive services from on-demand services:

- Interactive services provide a wide-range of services to the customer, including e-mail, home shopping, home banking, network games, and many other services. Many of these services use the cable system as a two-way data communications medium.
- On-demand services also provide an interactive service to the customer but are differentiated by their control of a streaming media service. An on-demand service provides a dedicated video and audio stream to the customer via the cable system *in addition to* using the cable system as a two-way data communications medium.

Interactive Services

Most interactive services that have been developed to date can be grouped into one of the following categories:

- Navigation—Navigation services are actually a set of related services developed originally for the advanced analog set-top.
- Information—Informational services provide some kind of news or information service to the customer—for example, news, weather, sports, stocks, or calendar-of-events information.
- Communication—Communications services support some form of communication between customers—for example, e-mail, chat, telephony, or video conferencing.
- Electronic commerce services—Electronic commerce (e-commerce) provides the customer with a secure monetary transaction of some kind—for example, home shopping, home banking, or the ability to withdraw electronic cash.
- Video games—There are a wide variety of video games that fit into two major categories: single-player games where the user plays against the computer, and networked games where the user plays against another user over the network.
- Enhanced television services—Enhanced television is a term used for any service that takes an existing streaming media service and enhances it with a related interactive service. For example, enhanced commercials, play-along game shows, opinion polls, and surveys.

The next sections consider the interactive services in each of these categories in more detail.

Navigation

Traditionally, navigation services in a cable system include a number of services that are bundled together. These services include

- Analog and digital tuning—This service allows the customer to select the desired channel by using the up-and down channel button or by direct entry of the channel number.
- Interactive program guide—The electronic program guide (EPG) provides the majority of the navigation functions for a typical customer. The EPG provides rapid access to program schedules and descriptions.
- Impulse pay-per-view (IPPV) interface—The IPPV interface allows the customer to select and purchase IPPV events using the remote control.
- VCR remote control—The VCR remote control functions allow one-touch recording of a selected event and are linked into the IPG and IPPV services.
- Parental control—Parental control allows the customer to block programs based on rating or channel.
- Subscriber preferences and configuration—This part of the navigation service allows the customer to customize the configuration of the set-top.
- Digital music service—The navigation service allows the customer to select music channels and to view a description of each track as it is playing.
- Emergency alert system (EAS) support—EAS messages warn of extreme weather conditions and other hazards. (Although this is more of an informational service than a navigation service, EAS support is usually included in the navigation application.)

As new services are introduced to a cable system, each needs support from the navigation service to allow the customer to select it. New services can be advertised using the EPG, by allocating them to channel numbers, activating them with dedicated keys on the remote, or by means of on-screen menus.

Information Services

Information services naturally fit into the interactive mold when customers know what information they want and they want to access it immediately. The information can be news, weather, sports, stock reports, or any other information. In any case, an interactive service on a cable system can offer significant benefits to the customer:

- An interactive service can display the latest information using text and graphics. The information can be instantly available at any time the customer is watching television.
- The service can be tailored to the area served by the cable system. This kind of local service can provide information that is not readily available elsewhere.
- The service can be tailored to the individual customer according to preferences that he or she has expressed.

Communications Services

Communications services can be provided as interactive services. Most of these services require some kind of additional hardware—for example, a wireless keyboard. There are a number of candidate services from the Internet:

- E-mail—An e-mail service is attractive to customers who don't own a PC, or who don't have access to the Internet.
- Chat—Chat is a very popular application and has already been linked to television programming. Chat allows an online, multiperson conversation using short typed messages that are delivered in real-time.
- IP telephony—IP telephony uses packet-mode transmission and reception of voice conversation. This service holds a great deal of potential, but it is more likely to be successful if it is linked into television programming in some way.
- Video-conferencing—Video-conferencing from the television could become a new mode of social interaction. It is probably a bit further away because of the bandwidth requirements to do effective conferencing.

Electronic Commerce Services

Interactive services that provide for electronic commerce (e-commerce) are a very attractive target for the cable operator. Services could include home shopping, home banking, and even the ability to withdraw electronic cash from your bank account using the set-top. E-commerce has the following attractive properties:

- The amount of data that is required to support a transaction is relatively small.
- The set-top box contains an extremely sophisticated digital security system. This can be used to ensure that electronic transactions cannot be forged or altered.
- The billing model is simple; as in an ATM machine, a per-transaction fee could be charged either to the customer or to the service provider.

Video Games

Video games come in many different shapes and sizes. The dedicated video game console is a highly competitive business, with each supplier leapfrogging the others to give superior graphics, better realism, and more action. The digital set-top cannot match a dedicated game console with its highly optimized architecture for dedicated game playing. Nevertheless, a digital set-top can provide sufficient graphics and CPU performance to run some of the older, *classic*, video games. In addition, most games in the educational game category can be supported by a digital set-top.

There are two main categories of video games:

- Single-player—Single-player games match the player against the computer. A single-player game requires no communication with the outside world after it has been successfully downloaded into the set-top.
- Networked games—A networked game allows the player to play against other players in a shared *game-space*. Two-way, real-time communications are required to support networked games.

Both kinds of video games can be supported as an interactive service on a digital set-top, with some limitations:

- It is not economically feasible to keep pace with the performance of the latest generation of video game consoles. However, most classic and educational video games can be supported by a digital set-top.
- Some games require more memory than is available in a digital set-top. A solution is to break them into *levels* that are downloaded as the player progresses through the game.

An alternative approach is to use the set-top to provide a video game console with a data communications link into a network game space. In this model, the set-top provides communications resources to the game console via a standard network link—for example, Ethernet. The communications resource is used to download game software and to link game players over the network. Because the video game console is connected to a television, it is physically close to the set-top.

Enhanced Television Services

One of the most exciting interactive services is enhanced television. Enhanced television provides a bridge between the television model, where the viewer is completely passive, and the PC model, where the user is always active. This is achieved by giving the television viewer the option of jumping into an interactive session at certain predefined points in the television program. These predefined entry points are authored into the television content so that they become an intuitive and natural part of the television program.

Enhanced television programming is still in its infancy, mainly because there are few customers with the necessary platform to support it. Nevertheless, enhanced television services show a great deal of promise, and there is a range of potential services:

- Enhanced commercials—Enhanced commercials allow the customer to express interest in a broadcast commercial as it is playing. An icon appears during the commercial that tells the customer that this is an interactive commercial. If the customer expresses interest (by pressing a button on the remote control), he is directed to more information about the product or service being advertised and can arrange for a follow-up contact from the advertiser.

- Play-along game shows—In a play-along game show, the customer can match his wits against the contestants and the set-top automatically keeps track of the score. The highest-scoring customers could be invited to participate in future shows (in person!).
- Opinion polls and surveys—This service would allow the programmer to get nearly instantaneous feedback on various issues.

Applications Model

All interactive services are delivered by means of some application software or *application*. The application can provide a single interactive service (for example, an electronic game) or a general-purpose mechanism for delivering services (for example, a Web browser).

The application can run in the set-top or in a server (located at the headend or distribution hub), or it can be distributed between the set-top and the server. An application that runs in the set-top is called the *client* application, whereas an application that runs in the server is called the *server* application. A distributed application has both server and client components.

Client Applications

A client application is entirely contained in the set-top. Client applications are limited by a number of factors:

- Set-top physical resources—These include memory, processor bandwidth, graphics processing, and so on.
- Locality of information—A client application can provide a useful interactive service only if the information is local to the set-top. Information can be broadcast, such as program guide information, but the set-top has a limited capacity to store information.
- Communications—Although it is technically possible for two client applications to communicate, this approach raises so many synchronization, addressing, and security problems that it is essentially useless.

Nevertheless, many useful interactive services can be implemented by a client application. Examples are

- Navigation—Navigation services can be provided for any programming that can be described by means of broadcast guide information. Schedules for television programming, premium, and pay-per-view programming change relatively slowly and can be described by a finite amount of data.
- Games—Single-player video games are implemented as client applications.
- Information services—If the information data-set can be contained on the set-top or broadcast to it, informational services can be implemented as client applications.

- Enhanced television—If the client application code and data is delivered with the television programming, enhanced television services can be implemented as client applications.

Any interactive service that requires two-way communications with the network cannot be implemented as a client-only application. Although client applications are limited, they do have some significant advantages:

- Ease of implementation—Client applications are easy to code and easy to debug.
- No communication resources—A client application consumes no network bandwidth.
- No transactional resources—A client application requires no transactional support from a server. Therefore, client applications are inherently *scalable*—that is, the number of client instances can be increased without limit.

For these reasons, a client application is generally the best solution if it can provide the desired interactive service.

Server Applications

A server-based or *server* application runs on a server (typically located in the cable headend). Server applications are sometime called screen-server applications because the server generates all the information that is displayed on the television screen.

Server applications have been used for many years in traditional computing. The first computer terminals (visual display units or VDUs) provide only display and keyboard input functions. When a set-top is decoding an MPEG-2 stream, it provides a (sophisticated) display function.

A server application does all application processing and graphics rendering in the server and then ships the result to the set-top for display. (Typically, the screen image is compressed as an MPEG I-frame).

Server applications can be used for almost any application except those that require a very low delay between the user input and a screen update—for example, video games. In addition, server applications are easy to implement and can easily be updated with no impact on the set-top. Despite these qualities, they are very limited for mass deployment:

- Communication resources—A server application consumes significant network bandwidth. Regardless of how small the change, each update completely refreshes the screen contents. (Some applications use MPEG P-frames to reduce bandwidth, but the information density is still low.)
- Transactional resources—A server application requires a thread of execution for every set-top that is concurrently accessing the service. Therefore, server applications are inherently difficult to scale.

Server-based applications are generally inferior to client or distributed applications. However, server-based applications can be useful in some circumstances:

- If a set-top cannot support a client application, it is sometimes possible to use a server application instead. This approach can be used to extend the lifetime of digital set-tops that have limited memory space, graphics, or CPU performance. For example, suppose that an interior decoration service becomes popular and that it employs three-dimensional modeling techniques that require 32 MB of DRAM and a 300 mips CPU. Older set-tops can still support the service if it is implemented as a server application and the results transmitted as MPEG-2 frames.
- If the interactive service requires access to a large database, placing the application on the same server as the database can simplify implementation and optimize performance.

Most server-based applications can be better implemented as distributed applications, with both client and server parts.

Distributed Applications

A distributed application model provides the most flexible way to implement interactive services. This model allows the application processing to be shared between the client (set-top) and the server. Typically, the client application provides functions related to input and output (for example, graphics rendering, audio processing, keyboard input, and so on), and the server application provides computational functions. The distributed applications model provides the combined advantages of client and server applications:

- The client part of the distributed application is inherently scalable—Careful design of the client allows the distributed application to be scaled up without placing excessive transactional loads on the server.
- The server part of the distributed application can provide extended resources to the client—For example, the server part can be used to manage a shared database, to provide persistent storage, or to provide fast computation.

If an interactive service cannot be implemented as a client application, a distributed application is usually the best choice. However, distributed applications bring certain challenges:

- Implementation—Distributed applications can be difficult to code and difficult to debug. The programmer has to consider not only the client code and the server code but also the interactions between them.

- Communication resources—A distributed application consumes network bandwidth, which must be carefully managed.
- Fault tolerance—A distributed application operates correctly only when the server, and the communications link to it, are in service. Therefore, redundancy in the network and the server are necessary to make the service highly available.
- Transactional resources—A distributed application consumes server bandwidth. The server usually maintains a thread of execution for every client instance. Therefore, the server part of the application must be carefully designed so that it can support the required number of users.

Application Requirements

There are an infinite variety of interactive applications, each with its own unique presentation, features, and functions. It is helpful to divide interactive applications into a number of categories based on the resources that they require from the cable system:

- Software download—Interactive services are often provided by a client application program that executes in the set-top. Downloading the client application program when it is needed allows many applications to share the set-top memory. For example, a particular electronic game might be played by only 10 percent of customers and can be downloaded from a data carousel only when a customer selects it.
- Activation—The activation of an interactive service is achieved by executing a client application on the set-top. There are a number of different *triggers* for application execution: The user can explicitly request the service, it might be activated in response to in-band data, or it might be activated in response to an out-of-band message. For example, the EAS application is triggered when the set-top receives an emergency alert message.
- Communications—Many interactive services require a communications resource from the network. Different applications require connections with varying bit rates and quality-of-service parameters. For example, an e-mail application might establish a TCP/IP connection to check the customer's mailbox on the mail server.
- Streaming media—Enhanced television services often manipulate broadcast streaming media. For example, an interactive advertising application might generate overlay graphics and check for a remote control button-press.

Software Download

The application client software must be loaded on the set-top before the interactive service can be launched. There are many ways of loading the application, and the loading method is often used to categorize the application:

- Resident application—A *resident application* is normally resident all the time on the set-top. A resident application is usually fundamental to the operation of the set-top, so it makes sense to always have it loaded in memory. For example, the navigation application is usually resident.
- Broadcast application—A *broadcast application* is broadcast in-band as part of a streaming media service. This allows the application to be received simultaneously by all set-tops tuned to the streaming media service and has the advantage of placing no transactional load on the cable system.
- Solicited application—A *download request* is made to the cable system to load a solicited application. A resident or broadcast application usually requests a solicited application as a result of some action by the customer. For example, the customer selects channel 97 and causes the navigation application to download the home-shopping application.

Activation

Interactive services can be initiated in a number of different ways, and the set-top application can be executed in response to a number of different events:

- Synchronous applications—*Synchronous applications* are activated in response to in-band data that is carried as part of a streaming media service. For example, a synchronous application is invoked during a commercial to present some interactive options.
- Asynchronous applications—*Asynchronous applications* are activated in response to an out-of-band message. An example is the delivery of a new mail notification. A notification message is received on the out-of-band channel that activates the e-mail application. The e-mail application fields the message and illuminates the message-waiting light on the set-top.
- Menu applications—*Menu applications* are activated in response to a customer input. The input is usually received from the remote control or keypad, but other input devices, such as a keyboard or joystick, can also trigger application activation.
- Timer applications—*Timer applications* are activated in response to a timer expiration. For example, the unattended recording function supported by the navigator application sets a timer event. When the timer expires, it activates the unattended recording application.

Communications

Applications have a wide range of communications requirements, depending on the offered service and the application design. A well-designed application will always attempt to minimize its use of communications resources; such an application is sometimes called a *green* application:

- One-way applications—A *one-way application* uses only one-way communication resources. Nevertheless, such an application can provide *local* interactivity. An example is the interactive program guide application. The guide data is broadcast to the set-top and saved in memory. The customer interacts with the guide application locally, to find and display the program listing, without using further communications resources

All other interactive applications use two-way communications, but there are many different ways of providing two-way communications services in cable systems (see Chapter 5, "Adding Digital Television Services to Cable Systems"). Two-way applications can be subdivided into several categories based on the quality of service of the return channel (see "Residential Broadband Internet Services and Applications Requirements," by Timothy Kwok, in *IEEE Communications*):

- Store-and-forward—A *store-and-forward* communications resource is provided by advanced analog set-tops and by some first-generation digital set-tops. These set-tops are able to transmit data only when polled by the headend controller. A good example of a store-and-forward application is impulse pay-per-view (IPPV). The customer uses the IPPV application to order a movie and, as a result, access is granted to an encrypted channel for a period of time. A record of the purchase is stored in the secure microprocessor until it can be retrieved by a poll from the headend controller. Store-and-forward applications place a minimal transactional load on the headend controller and require minimal data transmission capacity in the network.
- Telephone-return—*Telephone-return applications* are very similar in their limitations to store-and-forward applications. They are typically used only to support IPPV services, but recently some providers have experimented with using them for applications that generate a real-time transaction. For example, an enhanced commercial that is designed to stimulate an impulse purchase. During the commercial, the customer is given the option of requesting more information by pressing a button on the remote control. If the customer decides to buy the advertised item (concert tickets, a compact disk, and so on), the application dials a toll-free number using the telephone modem in the set-top.
- Best-effort QoS—A two-way communications resource with a *best-effort* quality of service (QoS) can be used to support a wide range of services. These include home-shopping, home-banking, e-mail, Web browsing, and so on. These applications can provide an acceptable service even if the two-way communications resource supports only a best-effort QoS—that is, the data rate and the delivery of the data packets are not guaranteed. For example, a home-banking application that establishes a secure

TCP-IP session with the service provider via the cable system can tolerate best-effort QoS. If data packets are lost, the TCP-IP protocol will retransmit the packets. If the data rate is low, the customer will experience some delay in the service. Nevertheless, the customer will be satisfied as long as the network is engineered to provide sufficient capacity even during busy periods.

- Guaranteed QoS—Some services require QoS *guarantees* from the cable network. QoS guarantees specify a number of parameters, including packet delay, jitter, error rate, and loss rate. For example, a network game application might be designed to tolerate delays of up to 500 milliseconds, whereas a video-conferencing application might tolerate a delay of only 100 milliseconds.

Streaming Media

Interactive services are often linked to streaming media services. Interactive services that are ported from the Internet and provide a static visual display (text and graphics) to the television environment often look uninteresting. However, generating a streaming media session and allocating network resources for each customer is in the domain of on-demand services (see Chapter 10). Therefore, considerable effort has been put into linking applications to a broadcast stream to link interactive services into the viewing of regular broadcast television services (see "Interactive Multimedia Services to Residential Users" by Thodore Zahariadis and others in *IEEE Communications)*:

- Media-linked applications—*Media-linked applications* are linked to a streaming media service and are *authored* to work in conjunction with the content of the streaming media. Most enhanced television services fall into this category—for example, a commercial that is enhanced with a media-linked application. The application uses data in the streaming media to allow the customer to interact with the commercial to get more information or to request follow-up from a retailer.
- Media-related applications—*Media-related applications* are not linked with the content of a streaming media service but are somehow related to streaming media services. An example of a media-related application is the interactive program guide—it is not linked to the content of any of the streaming media services, but it does allow the customer to select the desired service.
- Media-independent applications—*Media-independent applications* are completely independent of streaming media services. Native Internet applications, such as e-mail, chat, and Web browsing, are media-independent. However, it is easy to conceive of a media-linked or media-related version of a Web browser. A media-linked browser might allow the customer to surf directly to the home page of an advertiser by pressing a remote control button during a commercial. A media-related Web browser might enhance a Web page with streaming media services; for example, the HBO Web page could include a small panel to show what is currently playing on HBO.

Application Resources

Each interactive application requires its own set of resources in the set-top, the network, and the server. An interactive cable system provides a set of mechanisms to provide resources to the application. These mechanisms must be supported by the hardware components and by networking protocols. Fortunately, many of the mechanisms have already been developed by the computer industry in the field of distributed computing (see *Internetworking with TCP/IP,* Third Edition, Volume 1, by Douglas E. Comer).

The Time Warner Full Service Network (see Chapter 9, "Interactive Cable System Case Studies") was developed using distributed computing techniques and pushed the applications envelope for a cable system. However, many issues in large distributed computer networks do not yet have good solutions. Therefore, using a broadcast model to support application resources is the best approach where it is feasible. For example, software download is generally accomplished using a point-to-point file transfer protocol in a distributed computing environment. In a broadcast cable system, software download uses a data carousel channel to continuously broadcast the file.

The following sections describe

- Set-top resources—These include CPU performance, graphics acceleration, memory, applications environment, and communication resources.
- Software download mechanisms—Data carousels, MPEG-2 Private Data, and the out-of-band channel can be used to support software download.
- Activation and synchronization mechanisms—These include resources required in a multimedia operating system to support applications.
- Communication mechanisms—These include one-way and two-way communications resources.

Set-Top Resources

A digital set-top that is designed to support interactive services must provide more resources than a basic broadcast digital set-top in the following areas:

- CPU performance
- Graphics acceleration
- Memory
- Applications environment
- Communications

CPU Performance

Digital set-tops designed to support interactivity incorporate a faster CPU than a broadcast digital set-top—offering an instruction rate of between 50 and 200 mips. The faster CPU offers a number of advantages to the cable operator:

- There is adequate performance to support a wide range of applications, including fast-action video games.
- Application efficiency is not so critical, and this enables portable applications environments, such as HTML, JavaScript, and Java.
- An interpreted language environment (such as Java) allows real-time bounds checking of all instructions. This provides an effective way of limiting the damage inflicted by a poorly tested application.

Graphics Acceleration

Many interactive applications need graphics acceleration to produce fast, rich, smooth graphics. Graphics acceleration is often required to support video games and can be used to enhance navigation services with animation effects. Graphics acceleration is particularly important in a television environment, because television is a highly visual medium with excellent production values—poor graphics look especially bad in this environment.

Memory

Most interactive services are implemented as client or distributed applications. In either case, the client code requires memory space to load and execute. A broadcast digital set-top might have as little as 1 MB of application memory, whereas an interactive set-top requires at least 4 MB.

Applications Environment

A developer-friendly applications environment is needed to allow third-party applications developers to add their applications to a digital set-top. The applications environment must support resource management so that multiple applications can share the set-top resources, including window management, memory management, and input-device management.

Communications

An interactive set-top must support communications resources to allow software download of applications. In addition, real-time, two-way communications resources are essential to support many interactive services.

Software Download Mechanisms

Placing an application in a set-top using software download over the cable network has significant advantages for the cable operator:

- New applications can be added at the headend and propagated to any set-top over the cable network.
- Applications can be stored at the headend and downloaded to the set-top only when required. This saves memory in the set-top.
- Applications can be updated and any bugs fixed. The new version can be downloaded to the set-top when required.

However, downloading applications each time they are needed has some serious disadvantages:

- It takes time to download an application. If the application is small, it can be downloaded over a high-speed channel in a fraction of a second. However, downloading a large application introduces delays and consumes large amounts of network capacity.
- If the download server or download channel is unavailable, the customer will see a loss of service. Making certain applications resident—for example, the navigator—increases the availability of the services provided by those applications.

Several download mechanisms are commonly used in interactive cable systems:

- Data carousel—The *data carousel* provides a mechanism to download applications software or data by continuously transmitting a set of files over a QAM channel. A standard mechanism is provided by the DSM-CC data carousel (see the standard DSM-CC, Digital Stored Media—Command and Control).
- MPEG-2 private data—An MPEG-2 transport stream can be used to download applications software or data by placing the data in a separate program elementary stream (PES).
- Out of band channel—The out of band channel provides a point to point datagram service between the set-top and a headend server.

Data Carousel

DSM-CC specifies a data carousel mechanism that allows information to be broadcast to a population of digital set-tops (see DSM-CC, Digital Stored Media—Command and Control). All, or part, of a QAM channel can be used to transmit a set of files in a continuous cycle. When a set-top requires a file, it tunes to the carousel and listens to the carousel until it retrieves the file it needs. Typically, several data carousels are used, each for a specific application—for example, program guide data, application download, and so on.

MPEG-2 Private Data

MPEG-2 transport supports the carriage of arbitrary binary data with MPEG-2 private data sections. MPEG-2 private data is used to carry application code and data as part of the MPEG-2 program to support enhanced television applications. When a set-top selects the MPEG-2 program, it activates a loader application, which listens to the MPEG-2 private data. As the enhanced television applications are received, the loader application places them in memory and activates them.

Out-of-Band Channel

The out-of-band channel provides a two-way communications path between the set-top and the headend. This path can be used to support standard download protocols, such as Boot Protocol (BOOTP) or Trivial File Transfer Protocol (TFTP). However, the out-of-band channel could easily become saturated with download traffic if it were used to load all interactive applications. For this reason, use of the out-of-band channel for download should be discouraged as a policy decision by the cable operator.

Activation and Synchronization Mechanisms

All applications need to be activated after they have been successfully downloaded. The activation might be immediate or synchronized to some event, such as a message or a timer expiration. In any case, the operating system is responsible for activation.

Synchronous applications need to synchronize their execution to streaming media. The application is authored with the streaming media and synchronized to it using the MPEG-2 display timestamps. Even so, the timing of the application download must be carefully planned by the application developer—the application must be loaded into memory before it can be activated. However, it must not be downloaded too early; that way, a previously loaded application has time to release memory and exit.

A multimedia operating system provides facilities for the actual synchronization of the application to the MPEG-2 display timestamp. (An application cannot be granted access to the MPEG-2 display hardware.) The operating system dispatches an event to the application at the appropriate display time. Examples of operating systems with synchronization facilities are PowerTV and OpenTV (see the section Internet Resources, later in this chapter, and see Chapter 9).

Communication Mechanisms

Many interactive applications require a communications resource. There are two main types of communications resource in an interactive cable system:

- One-way communications—In this case, the information required by the application must flow over a known channel so that the application can locate it.
- Two-way communications—In this case, some kind of session must be established by the application with a server.

Each type of communications has its own set of problems and solutions.

One-Way

In one-way communications, there are several modes of communication: broadcast, multicast, and unicast. Each has its uses according to the type of application:

- Broadcast—In this case, information that is useful to all applications is simply broadcast over the entire network. An example is program guide data or embedded MPEG-2 private data associated with a broadcast program.
- Multicast—Multicast communications are useful when the information is useful only to a group of set-tops. In a one-way network, the cable hub provides a convenient multicast group, which is used by SI and EAS messages.
- Unicast—Unicast communications are used for CAS messages in a one-way environment, but although the message is destined for only one set-top, it must be broadcast to all parts of the network where that set-top might be located.

Two-Way

In two-way communications, the same modes of communication exist in the forward direction (from the network to the set-top) as in one-way communications. However, the communications in the reverse direction are always unicast to a particular address in the network:

- Broadcast—In this case, the information is useful to all applications and can be simply broadcast over the network. An example is the broadcast carousel or embedded MPEG-2 private data in a broadcast program. The broadcast mode is used in two-way networks but must be designed never to elicit a response from the set-top, because this could trigger a *broadcast storm* of responses.
- Multicast—Multicast communications are useful when the information is sent to a group of set-tops. Communications protocols have been developed to support the general definition of multicast groups, and these can be applied to two-way networks. Thus, an application can signal on the reverse channel to add itself to a multicast group while it is active. Pointcast is an example of such an application.

- Unicast—Most two-way communications are point-to-point—that is, they use a unicast mode in the forward and return direction. This mode is used to establish a session between the client and server parts of a distributed application and requires some mechanism for them to discover each other.

Chapter 9 provides some practical examples of the implementation of these various types of communications resources.

Summary

This chapter considered the development of interactive services for cable systems. To be useful, interactive services must satisfy some basic goals and usability criteria that are significantly different than those for PC applications. They must be designed to fit into the television services so that they support, enhance, and extend them in a natural, intuitive, and friendly way.

An almost infinite variety of interactive services can be conceived, but they can be grouped into navigation, information, communication, electronic commerce, video games, and enhanced television applications. Some applications span categories—for example, an enhanced television application can also provide a communications service.

Interactive services are created for applications that can run in the set-top (client applications), the server (server applications), or both (distributed applications). Each type of application has its own advantages and disadvantages, but a rule of thumb is that client applications are easiest to implement. Distributed applications provide the most general model and are most suitable for use in a two-way environment.

Each application requires a different set of resources from the set-top, network, and server components. Application resources are divided into set-top, software download, activation and synchronization, and communications resources. An interactive cable system must provide resources to the application in all these areas to support interactive services.

References

Books

Comer, Douglas E. *Internetworking with TCP/IP, Third Edition, Volume 1.* Upper Saddle River, NJ: Prentice Hall, 1995.

Hodge, Winston William. *Interactive Television.* New York, NY: McGraw-Hill, 1995.

Periodicals

Kwok, Timothy, "Residential Broadband Internet Services and Applications Requirements." *IEEE Communications,* June 1997.

Milenkovic, Milan. "Delivering Interactive Services via a Digital TV Infrastructure." *IEEE Multimedia,* October–December 1998.

Perry, Tekla. "The trials and travails of Interactive TV." *IEEE Spectrum,* April 1996.

Zahariadis, Thodore, Corrado Rosa, Marco Pellegrinato, Anita Byork Lund, and George Stassinopoulos. "Interactive Multimedia Services to Residential Users." *IEEE Communications,* June 1997.

Standards

ISO/IEC 13818-6. "DSM-CC—Digital Stored Media—Command and Control."

Internet Resources

OpenTV

http://www.opentv.com

PowerTV

http://www.powertv.com

CHAPTER 9

Interactive Cable System Case Studies

This chapter discusses two interactive cable systems—the Time Warner Full Service Network and the Time Warner Pegasus program. These case studies are closely related; the same core team of engineers is responsible for both programs, and the Pegasus program has many of the same goals as the Full Service Network.

Time Warner Full Service Network

The Full Service Network (FSN) was conceived primarily as a vehicle for video-on-demand (VOD) services. In fact, in the early 1990s, interactive and on-demand services were considered to be much the same thing. VOD was the major goal of the FSN for a number of reasons. First, VOD has been the Holy Grail of engineers for many years. The idea that video can be captured, stored, and manipulated using digital techniques is fascinating, if only because it is such a wonderful engineering challenge. Second, the limitations of pay-per-view programming can be frustrating, and evidence suggests that customers really want a VOD service and are prepared to pay for it. This evidence is backed up by the success of the video rental business. In a short time, the (once-laughable) idea of renting videotapes of movies to customers for a fee has become a multibillion-dollar-a-year business.

Although the FSN was conceived as a VOD service, many other services were added to the rapidly evolving specifications in early 1993. These included other on-demand services, such as *sports-on-demand*, *news-on-demand*, and even *HBO-on-demand* (internally, these became known affectionately as SOD, NOD, and HOD). In addition, many interactive services were included in the FSN umbrella, including video games, home shopping, and later, even Web browsing. The framework for interactive services is an important FSN contribution and is discussed in detail in this chapter, but the development of on-demand services is examined separately in Chapter 10, "On-Demand Services."

FSN Network Architecture Goals

Time Warner Cable issued "a request for assistance in building a full service telecommunications network," in February 1993. At that stage in the FSN project, the service definition was broadly stated as "traditional CATV services, full video-on-demand with instant access, interactive television, interactive gaming, long distance access, voice, video telephone and personal communication services."

In contrast, the network architecture definition was precise and described the infrastructure to support the services in considerable detail:

"Our current vision for this project involves:

- a server at the headend,
- a switching system capable of performing all the necessary routing functions from the server to any of the full service customers,
- assembling of the data on a node by node basis using add drop multiplexing or equivalent technologies,
- digital modulation devices using QAM modulation or equivalent techniques,
- optical links from the headend to the node locations fed by single or multiple laser configurations,
- coaxial plant to the customers homes, and
- appropriate customer terminal equipment to translate the bit streams into usable services."

From its inception, the FSN was envisioned to provide a broad range of services, most of which were not fully defined at the beginning of the project. The FSN designers understood that to achieve this kind of flexibility, a *service-independent* approach was required. Traditionally, telephone, computer, and cable networks are all designed for a particular service, and, as a result, they can carry only a single traffic type. Carrying video, voice, and data over a single network became the fundamental goal of the FSN, because achieving that goal enabled the broad service flexibility that was required to meet the FSN's (deliberately) open-ended vision.

The FSN was also intended to prove that interactive services were feasible in a real cable system with a significant number of subscribers. Many trials of interactive services with only 50 or 100 subscribers have failed to discover any of the problems of system scaling. As a complex system increases in size, second- and third-order effects come into play—the problems of scaling. The FSN subscriber population was chosen to be 4,000 subscribers because this number is sufficiently large that scaling problems could be discovered (and hopefully resolved) during the design process.

To support interactive services, the FSN also specified a high-speed reverse data path from the set-top to the headend. The reverse data path transformed the cable system into a two-way system—it could be used to provide low-latency signaling for interactive games, for telephone conversations, or for video conferencing.

Network Overview

Figure 9-1 provides an overview of the FSN network. The description is divided into forward and reverse paths for clarity.

Figure 9-1 *Full Service Network*

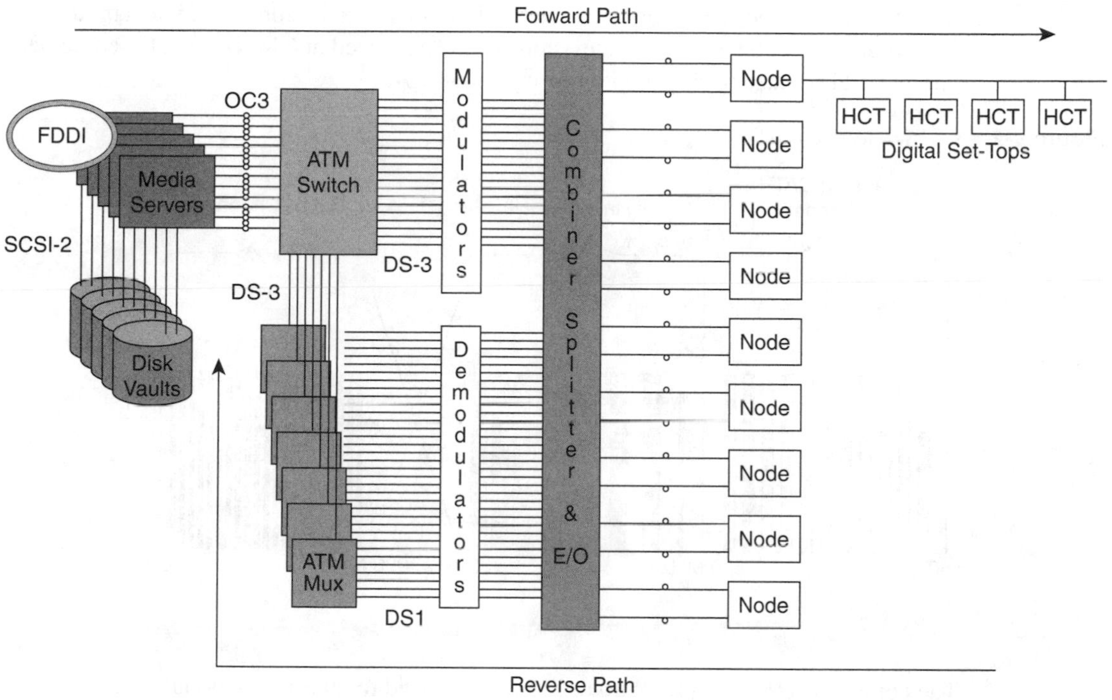

Forward Path

Eight media servers (SGI Challenge XL) are connected to disk vaults using fast and wide SCSI-2 interfaces. The disk vaults can be configured to provide a total of 3,000 gigabytes of media storage capacity, enough for about 500 movies.

The media servers are connected to an AT&T GCNS-2000 ATM switch. Each server is connected to the switch with six SONET OC3 connections. A total of 48 OC3s provide a total of 5,184 Mbps of usable payload bandwidth (after accounting for SONET and ATM overhead).

The media servers are also interconnected with an FDDI ring, which is used to transfer media content to the disk vaults and to collect billing records from the servers at 100 Mbps. (A separate FDDI ring was used to expedite development with the understanding that in the future ATM switching can support all communications.)

The ATM switch is connected to a bank of 64-QAM modulators supplied by Scientific Atlanta. 152 unidirectional DS3 links provide a total of 5,600 Mbps of payload capacity from the ATM switch to the neighborhoods (after accounting for SONET and ATM overhead).

The QAM modulator outputs are tuned in the frequency range 50 to 735 MHz, and spaced at 12 MHz. This allows the outputs to each neighborhood to be combined into a broadband RF signal. Conventional analog television channels (spaced at 6 MHz) are also combined. The spectral frequency diagram is shown in Figure 9-2.

Figure 9-2 *Full Service Network*

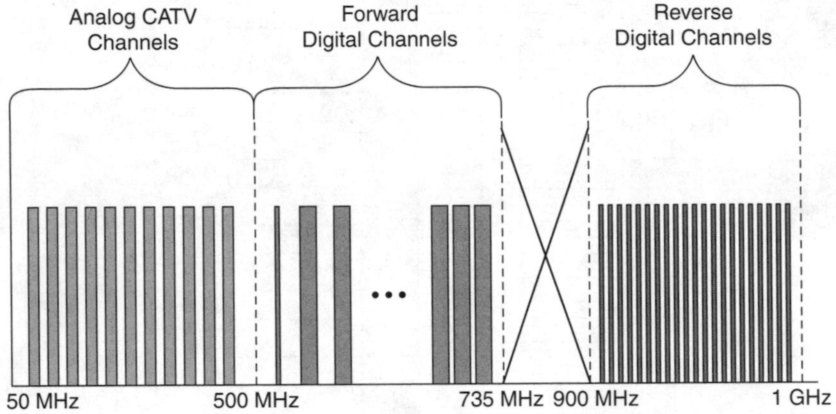

The composite RF signal from 50 to 735 MHz is used to amplitude-modulate a laser. The laser is coupled to a single-mode fiber, which takes the signal out to the neighborhood about 10 miles away. At the neighborhood, the optical signal is converted back into the RF domain by the fiber node and used to feed a coaxial feeder network, which passes about 500 subscribers.

The RF signal enters the subscriber residence and feeds the home communications terminal (HCT) or digital set-top converter. The HCT is actually a powerful RISC-based multimedia computing engine with video and audio decompression and extensive graphics capabilities. The HCT also incorporates an analog set-top converter (the Scientific Atlanta 8600X) to tune analog channels.

An ATM addressing scheme is designed to allow any server to send data to any HCT.

Reverse Path

The HCT transmits a QPSK-modulated signal in the 900 to 1000 MHz band. Reverse carrier frequencies are defined at a spacing of 2.3 MHz. The QPSK channel supports a data rate of 1.152 Mbps (after accounting for ATM overhead). Each reverse channel is slotted using a time division multiple access (TDMA) scheme. This allows a single reverse channel to be shared among a number of HCTs. The time-slot assignments are made at the headend and sent to the HCT over a forward channel so that only one HCT is enabled to transmit in any given time slot. By default, each HCT has access to a constant bit rate ATM connection with a bit-rate of 46 Kbps. More importantly, the access latency of a typical packet is 25 ms, worst-case.

The reverse channels from a neighborhood are transported by the coax plant back to the fiber node. At this point, the reverse spectrum is used to modulate a laser, which is coupled to a single-mode fiber. Separate fibers (in the same cable sheath) are used for the forward and reverse directions.

At the headend, the optical signal is first converted back into the RF domain, and then it is fed to a bank of QPSK demodulators. These convert the cell stream into an ATM-format T1 link.

The outputs of the demodulators are combined by seven Hitachi AMS5000 ATM multiplexers. A standard, bidirectional ATM-format DS3 is used to connect each multiplexer to the ATM switch.

The ATM switch passes the reverse data to the media servers. An ATM addressing scheme is designed to allow any HCT to send data to any server.

ATM Addressing

The ATM switch and multiplexers are configured with a mesh of permanent virtual connections (PVC).

In the forward path, ATM virtual paths are configured from each OC3 port to each DS3 port. This allows the server to address any forward applications channel (FAC) by selecting the appropriate VPI. The HCTs tuned to a FAC ignore the VPI and reassemble connections based on VCI. This creates a two-level switching hierarchy—VP switching in the ATM switch and VC switching in the neighborhood—and allows any media server to send data to any HCT.

In the reverse path, the ATM multiplexers perform a traffic aggregation function from DS1 to DS3 rates. A mesh of virtual paths is provisioned from the multiplexer DS1 ports to the server OC3 ports. This allows any HCT to send cells to any server by using the appropriate VPI.

Connection Management

The connection manager is composed of a distributed set of processes that run on the media servers. In response to an application request for a connection with a given quality of service, the connection manager determines a route, allocates connection identifiers, and reserves link bandwidth. The connection identifiers are passed to the server and client applications at the media server and HCT, respectively.

On-demand services use the connection manager to establish a constant bit rate ATM connection for each media stream from a server to the HCT. This approach is used to guarantee the quality of service of the connection so that the cell loss rate is less than 10^{-10}, sufficient for high-quality delivery of MPEG compressed video streams.

Connectionless Signaling

The allocation of a connection for each *application* request would create far too much overhead in the distributed application environment of the FSN. In practice, only on-demand services generate requests to the connection manager, and all other communications sessions are created using a connectionless network.

Figure 9-3 illustrates how the forward application bandwidth is shared between on-demand connections for audio and video (labeled AV) and static connections for IP networking (labeled IP).

Figure 9-3 *Forward Applications Channel Partitioning*

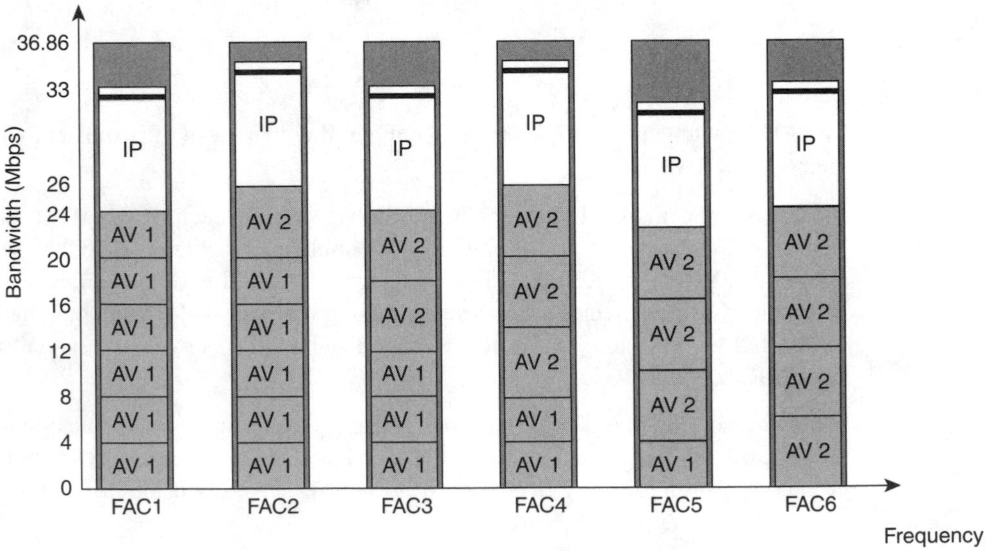

Each HCT is allocated *three* IP addresses when it is booted—one for each of the three IP networks:

- Fast IP—This network is created using a fixed, 8 Mbps connection in each forward applications channel.
- Slow IP—This network is created using a fixed, .714 Mbps connection in each forward applications channel.
- Control IP—This network is created using the forward QPSK channel and has an approximately 1 Mbps capacity.

Three IP networks are used for different applications and to work around some of the deficiencies of the HCT:

- A fast IP network is mapped into an 8 Mbps ATM connection over each Forward Applications Channel. Fast IP is used for application download, which is initiated by a file transfer request from the HCT. The HCT is capable of receiving data at bursts of up to 8 Mbps when it is dedicated to downloading a file. Applications are compressed to reduce download time even further, and the largest application can be reliably loaded in less than one second.
- The slow IP network is mapped into a 0.714 Mbps ATM connection over each Forward Applications Channel. Slow IP is used for general communications between the client and server parts of a distributed application. The HCT is capable of receiving and transmitting data at this lower rate while the client application is executing.
- The control IP network is mapped into a 1 Mbps ATM connection over each Forward Control Channel. Control IP is used for general control signaling to all HCTs in a neighborhood.

Although the requirement for connection management of on-demand sessions was obvious at the start of the development of the FSN, the need for connectionless signaling was less apparent. Distributed applications typically have less stringent quality of service requirements than on-demand applications, but distributed applications might use multiple sessions for short bursts of communication. For this reason, distributed applications require a connectionless signaling mechanism, such as that provided by IP networking.

Figure 9-4 summarizes the communications protocol stack for the FSN. The connectionless signaling protocols that support the distributed applications environment are on the left of the diagram. The connection-oriented protocols that support the streaming services are on the right of the diagram.

Figure 9-4 *FSN Protocol Stack*

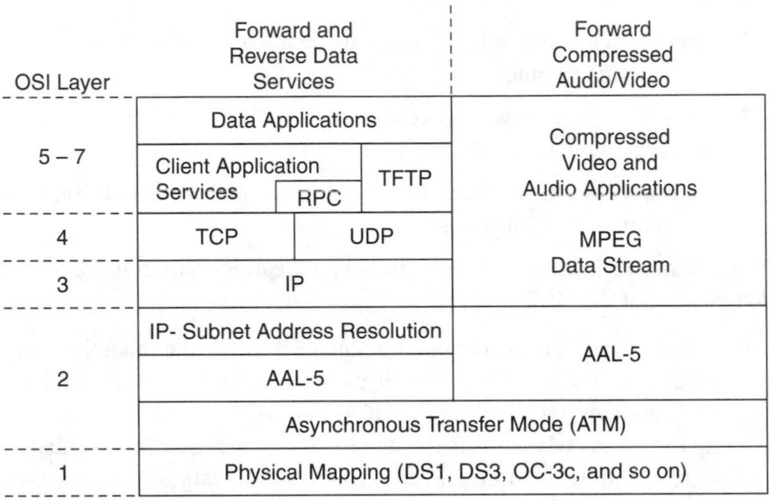

Services

Interactive services provided by the FSN include navigation, games, and home shopping. (VOD services are described in Chapter 11, "On-Demand Cable System Case Studies.")

Navigation

Navigation services provided by the FSN include

- Analog tuning
- Interactive program guide—The Preview guide look-and-feel is implemented on the HCT by an application that allows the customer to scroll through a grid of program descriptions over time and channel. (The Preview guide is now known as *TV Guide*.)
- Parental control—Parental control allows the customer to block programs based on rating or channel.
- Subscriber preferences and configuration—This part of the navigation service allows the customer to customize the configuration of the HCT.

In addition, the navigator maps each major category of interactive service (or *venue*) to a channel number between 90 and 99, as shown in Table 9-1.

Table 9-1 *Interactive Services and Channel Assignments*

Channel	Service
90	Music
91	Sports
92	Education
93	News
94	Services
95	Controls
96	Games
97	Shopping
98	Movies
99	TV

Mapping interactive services to channel numbers provides an alternative to the three-dimensional *Carousel* navigator. When the HCT is turned on, the FSN Carousel provides an effective showcase for the range of services. As customers become more familiar with the services, however, they want a shortcut to select the desired service without going through a series of menus.

Video Games

The FSN provides two ways for the customer to play video games: *native* video games, which are integrated into the HCT, and *console* games, which are played on an external game console.

Native games include card games, Klondike and Gin, and two 3D action games (PODS and TVBots). The native games are networked so that the player enters into a contest with another FSN customer. The FSN provides no mechanism to select a specific opponent, using the first-come, first-served model. PODS is a 3D flying game in which the successful player wins by dragging and dropping worms onto squares to capture the most territory on a board. TVBots puts the player into a 3D game in competition with up to 15 other players. The game is everyone for him- or herself, and players are vanquished from the maze when they take a given number of hits from other players. (An interesting phenomenon occurred when a group of younger customers started playing as a team, effectively wiping out individual players by playing cooperatively.)

Console games were provided on the Atari Jaguar console. Each game was downloaded on request over the Fast IP channel into the memory of the Jaguar console. The Jaguar console was connected to the HCT by means of a high-speed parallel interface.

Home Shopping

The home shopping venue allows the customer to select from a number of different stores: Crate and Barrel, Chrysler, LL Bean, The Nature Company, Sharper Image, Spiegel, The U.S. Post Office, Viewers Edge, Warner Brothers Studio Store, Williams Sonoma, and others. Each store provides its own unique user interface, personalized by the applications developer. Most of the stores support catalog-style ordering of goods that are delivered to the customer. Payment is by credit card.

Online shopping is now a multibillion-dollar-a-year business over the World Wide Web. There is no reason why interactive television should not take a share of this market if these same services can be delivered via a set-top box.

Enhanced Television

The Full Service Network was originally conceived as a highly enhanced television service; all the interactive services used supporting video. This approach creates an entirely new kind of television service with its own requirements for production. (The FSN even had its own Digital Production Center, which was responsible for authoring the interactive *content*, or programming.)

To support a mass rollout of interactive services, interactive programming must be adopted by existing programmers. But this will not happen until there is a significant population of set-top boxes that can support this type of service. Therefore, there has been considerable interest in interactivity that uses existing programming so that the cost of production is not incurred twice.

The FSN demonstrated this approach of enhancing existing broadcast television by adding an interactive application that displayed sports scores as an overlay. This application enables the customer to watch NFL Sunday football and browse through the other sports scores without missing any part of the game.

Applications Model

The FSN applications model was based heavily on a distributed computing model. Each application is distributed between the HCT and the server complex and includes a client and set-top part that communicates via the slow IP network. A *Remote Procedure Call* (RPC) mechanism provides a convenient abstraction of the communications layer to the applications layer. The RPC mechanism allows a procedure in the client application to invoke a remote procedure in the server application in the same way as a local procedure, greatly simplifying the development of distributed applications.

FSN client applications rely on the considerable resources in the HCT to perform the lion's share of processing, and are considered to be *thick* clients. A thick client is responsible for all the presentation layer functions and performs these functions with no assistance from the server. Several advantages are gained from the thick client model:

- The abstraction of the data is high. As an example, if a simple string of text is retrieved from the server and presented as an animated overlay by the client, the communications requirements are tiny compared to the server sending an animated overlay for display by the client. In other words, less communications resources are required, resulting in less demand on the network compared to a thin client model.
- Less processing resources are required by the server because it is primarily retrieving data objects. Moreover, a server can be designed to support many client instances without having to maintain a separate context for each client.

The combination of an RPC mechanism and a thick client allows scaling of the FSN applications. Nevertheless, the FSN applications model has its limitations because it is dependent on the availability of the network and the server components. For example, the FSN navigation application is implemented as a distributed application and is dependent on the availability of the slow IP network and the server resources. Thus, navigation of broadcast channels is tied to interactive resources, and a server failure affects some customers.

Application Requirements

The FSN applications described (navigation, games, and shopping) require significant network resources in each area identified in Chapter 8, "Interactive Services":

- Software download—All FSN application client software is downloaded in response to a user action—for example, selecting a channel or responding to an on-screen dialog. Thus, all FSN applications can be classified as solicited applications.
- Activation—All FSN applications are activated in response to a user action and can be classified as menu applications.
- Communications—All FSN applications require two-way communications with varying quality of service requirements. The navigation and home shopping services used best-effort quality of service in most cases, but when streaming media was used to support the application, guaranteed quality of service was required to deliver it. The game services required a bounded delay, especially for the action games, and this quality of service was achieved through careful management of the connectionless delivery network.
- Streaming media—All FSN services are independent of broadcast programming and are correctly classified as media-independent interactive services. However, this is misleading because many of the interactive services use on-demand streaming media to provide multimedia support (see Chapter 11).

Applications Resources

The FSN offers considerable resources to its distributed applications, both at the HCT and at the server. The network resources are engineered to support on-demand services to 25% of customers at any given time, and this dictates most of the 5 Gbps of forward network capacity. In comparison to this figure, the network resources allocated to interactive services are relatively small (about 250 Mbps or 5% of the total network capacity). This demonstrates the potential cost savings of an interactive service over an on-demand service.

Digital Set-Top

The central processing unit (CPU) performance of the first prototype FSN HCT was approximately 100 mips. This seemed like an unbelievable and inexhaustible resource in 1993 but soon proved not to be the case. Real-time compositing of live video and graphics in software puts a tremendous load on the CPU. At 60 fields per second, the CPU has just 16 milliseconds to render graphics before the field is displayed, and the field cannot be late. Even though video and audio decompression was done in hardware, a faster, 140 mips, version of the R4000 CPU was required to support FSN applications.

Software Download

Software download in the FSN allows remote upgrades to the operating system and applications. This is essential in an interactive system so that new applications can be downloaded to provide new services. However, the FSN downloads each application as a solicited application—that is, as a result of a user action. This model has some serious drawbacks when the size of the network is increased:

- There is a possibility that many users could request a new service at the same time; statistically, this is unlikely in an uncorrelated system. However, when a popular broadcast ends (or goes to commercial break), a significant fraction of customers might decide to switch to interactive services. Engineering the system for a maximum download time can be very expensive if peaks of activity are taken into account.
- Each time an application is loaded, it generates a transactional load on a server. Once again, server capacity must be engineered for peak activity.
- Any failure in any part of the network or server complex might cause an application download to fail. The navigator application is also used to select broadcast channels, and their availability can be compromised if the supporting interactive services are not completely reliable.

Although the FSN developed a broadcast carousel technique to reduce transactional load due to HCT boot, availability of all services was dependent on the two-way operation of the network and correct operation of the servers.

Communications

FSN applications required some communications resources that were not anticipated at the start of development:

- Lightweight remote procedure call (RPC)—See the section Applications Model, earlier in this chapter.
- Distributed naming service—After the client application is loaded, it needs to bind to a specific server resource in the headend. Use of a physical address does not allow server resources to be distributed across servers, so a logical address, or name, is used. At the server, a naming service is used to resolve the name, and the naming service must be distributed to provide high availability.

Lessons Learned

The Full Service Network provided some surprising and valuable lessons that can be applied to interactive service development.

Interactive services require a different communications model from on-demand services. Interactive services tend to use multiple sessions for short bursts of communication, so they require a connectionless signaling mechanism, such as that provided by IP networking. In contrast, on-demand services require a continuous stream of data that is best provided by a connection-oriented network, such as that provided by ATM. In particular, the TDMA reverse scheme was found to be very wasteful of return spectrum because it used a fixed bit rate allocation to each HCT, and the allocation is wasted most of the time. As a result, the DAVIC out-of-band protocol was developed to include a reservation protocol that allows many more set-tops to share a given return channel.

Application development cost is significant and must be carefully managed by the choice of development tools and execution environment. Application development tools must allow rapid prototyping and testing of the application in an environment that accurately simulates the cable network. The execution environment must provide some level of hardware independence so that applications can be ported from one set-top to another without the need for a complete rewrite. A robust execution environment is also very important so that applications cannot crash or permanently disable the set-top.

In addition, certification of interactive applications becomes critical to ensure that a new application does not disrupt other applications on the set-top or other functions on the network. In the FSN, a separate certification network was required to perform quality assurance of new applications before they were placed on the production network. Quality assurance of applications is key to ensuring reliable services in the cable environment.

Interactive television must have similar production values to the television programming that it accompanies. This means that applications must provide a rich graphical interface that is designed for a television display (not a computer display).

Pegasus

The Pegasus program is a direct descendant of the FSN. The program started in early 1995, even as the FSN was being rolled out to customers and the Orlando staff was grappling with stability and maintenance of the FSN. Originally, Pegasus was known internally as the Deployable FSN but this name was soon changed to Pegasus. The Pegasus name is derived from the Trojan horse strategy that it uses.

In 1995, the major stumbling block was the cost of an interactive set-top. Cost was not really an issue for the 4000 Orlando set-tops, but for general deployment of interactive services the cost of the set-top is critical. The Trojan horse strategy defines an advanced digital set-top that includes interactive features at a small cost premium over a basic digital set-top (see Chapter 6, "The Digital Set-Top Converter"). This set-top is universally deployed—initially to provide broadcast services but with future interactive services following soon after. This not only makes the set-top future-proof but also allows applications software and interactive services to be provided on the same platform. To make the interactive features cost-effective, they are included in every digital set-top; but, like the Greeks in the Trojan horse story, they appear only when interactive services are developed and delivered by the cable operator.

In much the same way, the Pegasus network architecture is designed to support interactive services as they are deployed. To minimize costs, the network communications paths are engineered to support interactive services at a relatively low service penetration, but are designed to be easily scaled up to handle additional signaling traffic as service penetration increases.

Pegasus Phase 1.1 Goals

The Pegasus Phase 1.1 goals were articulated in a Request for Quotation (RFQ) issued in 1997, one year after the initial Pegasus RFQ. Phase 1.1 adds to the interactive services provided by the resident navigation application. To enable new interactive services the RFQ identified two major goals:

"A true applications platform that will allow developers of new programs and services to use ubiquitous tools and, to the extent possible, ignore the details of the underlying broadband network architecture. This leaves the deployment of these programs and services as purely a business decision (much as deploying a new analog broadcast TV channel is today).

"Deploying a network and hardware platform architecture that will incent more vendors to enter the market in addition to the initial three mentioned above. In particular, it is hoped that the basic Pegasus hardware and network standards (with the exception of Conditional Access) will allow vendors of those products to build modulators, set-top terminals, etc., with ever better cost/performance benefits.

"The addition of a ubiquitously-supported, software runtime (execution) environment on top of, or as part of, the set-top native operating system is seen as the way to achieve both of the goals above. The execution environment and associated tools give software developers the ability to create new services and applications independent of the underlying hardware and, to some degree, the network architecture. At the same time, this abstraction allows set-top hardware vendors the flexibility to pick the best CPU's, memory architectures, graphics capabilities, operating systems, etc., to improve the cost/performance equation while supporting all applications developed for the runtime environment."

The complete RFQ is available on the Web (see the section Internet Resources at the end of this chapter).

Network Overview

The Pegasus network is described in Chapter 7, "Digital Broadcast Case Studies." The important aspects of the network for the support of interactive services are the real-time, two-way network that links the Pegasus set-top to the headend equipment.

The two-way network is based on standard networking protocols and equipment and is engineered to support interactive services (albeit at relatively low service penetration). These standards are described in Chapter 5, "Adding Digital Television Services to Cable Systems."

Lessons learned from the FSN allow the Pegasus network to support all the same interactive services as the FSN at considerably reduced network cost. This is possible because

- DSM-CC data carousels are used wherever possible to reduce the transactional and network traffic required for downloading interactive applications.
- The DAVIC OOB protocol definition is designed to support many bursty traffic sources in the shared-media cable return environment. This reduces the number of QPSK demodulators per distribution hub by a factor of 15 compared to the FSN.
- The operating system software and navigation software are always resident in the Pegasus set-top. This greatly reduces the network resources required for software download.

In addition, network resources can be further reduced by careful application design. The design of these so-called *green* applications is discussed in the next sections.

Services

Pegasus is designed to support all the interactive services described in Chapter 8. These can be summarized as

- Navigation—Navigation services include analog and digital tuning, interactive program guide, IPPV interface, VCR remote control, parental control, subscriber preferences and configuration, digital music service, messaging, and EAS support.
- Information—Informational services provide news, weather, sports, stocks, and calendar-of-events information.
- Communications—Communications services include e-mail and chat.

- Electronic commerce services—E-commerce services include home shopping and home banking (including the ability to withdraw electronic cash).
- Video games—Video games include single-player games, where the user plays against the computer, and networked games, where the user plays against other users over the network.
- Enhanced television—Enhanced television services include interactive commercials, play-along game shows, opinion polls, and surveys.

Applications Model

The Pegasus applications model supports both client and distributed applications. Client applications provide local interactivity, in which the customer interacts with the client application. This model is used for all navigation functions to reduce transactional load on the headend servers.

In addition, Pegasus separates the interactive applications functions from other system functions, allowing multivendor applications to be supported. This is illustrated by the example in Figure 9-5.

Figure 9-5 *Pegasus Applications Model*

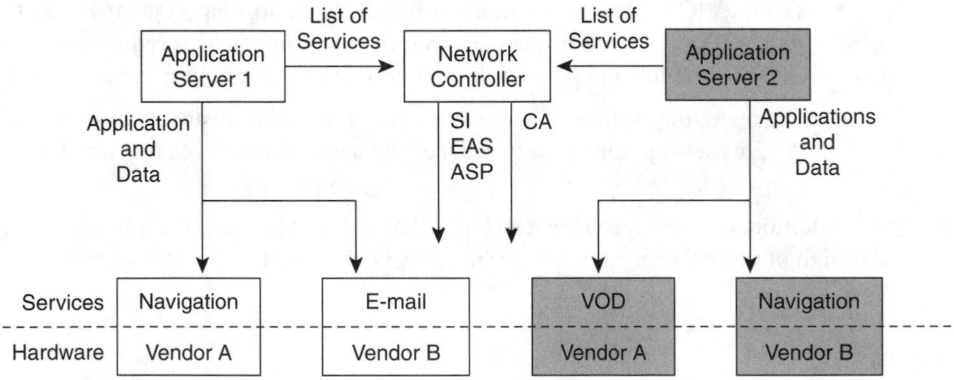

In Figure 9-5, a single network controller is responsible for broadcast functions common to all customers. These services include the delivery of service information (SI), emergency alert system (EAS) messages, application service protocol (ASP), and conditional access (CA) system messages, in which

- Service information defines the MPEG source identifier mapping for broadcast services on the cable system according to SCTE (proposed) standard DVS-234.
- Emergency alert system messages are used to signal emergencies according to SCTE standard DVS-208 (EIA 814).

- All services are accessed by the Pegasus navigator using the application service protocol (SCTE proposed standard DVS-181). There is a conscious effort to abstract all services into a single channel space at the user interface level. The application service protocol (ASP) *advertises* services available on the cable system, effectively providing a naming service to allow the set-top to locate broadcast and interactive services. Interactive services are provided by the application servers, and each application server supplies a list of services to the network controller for insertion into the ASP carousel.
- Conditional access (CA) system messages deliver entitlement and de-scrambling keys according to the selected conditional access system (in this case, PowerKEY).

Application Portability

Application portability is designed to allow applications to run on multiple hardware platforms—in this case, digital set-tops. All digital set-tops are built to conform to the common network protocol specifications described in the section Applications Model, earlier in this chapter. Figure 9-5 shows two digital set-top implementations, from Vendor A and Vendor B, and two application servers, Application Server 1 and Application Server 2.

Each application server provides interactive services to either type of set-top by providing applications code and data. Applications code is continuously broadcast over a DSM-CC data carousel. Applications data is distributed over a DSM-CC data carousel or is accessed using the two-way IP network that connects the set-tops to the servers.

In the example shown in Figure 9-5, Vendor A set-tops have loaded a navigation application from Application Server 1 and a VOD application from Application Server 2. The VOD application is a special case of interactive application because it requires a media server and a connection management service to operate. (VOD is discussed in more detail in Chapter 10, "On-Demand Services.") Vendor B set-tops have loaded an email application from Application Server 2 and a navigation application from Application Server 2.

For this scenario to work, there must some mechanism to ensure that applications can execute on the two different vendor set-tops. There are three ways to achieve this goal, which defines the level of *application portability*:

- Each application is individually authored to each type of set-top—in other words, there is no application portability. This approach quickly becomes unmanageable as the number of set-top types and applications increases.
- Each application is authored to a common operating system. In this case, the operating system provides the portability layer, but the operating system has to be ported onto every set-top. In the PC world, the dominant operating system is Windows, and it provides a portability layer between different hardware vendors.

- Each application is authored to a portable *middleware* layer of software. To support different operating systems, only the middleware has to be ported to each operating system, which is much less effort than porting all applications. In the computer industry, the Web browser provides the middleware for application portability and enables Web applications to be independent of both the hardware platform and the operating system.

The Pegasus system uses the second and third options to promote portability. *Native* applications are authored to the PowerTV operating system. *Portable* applications are authored to a middleware software, which includes Hypertext Markup Language (HTML), JavaScript, and, optionally, Java components.

In Pegasus Phase 1.0, the only applications required are those that support navigation. These are implemented as native applications and can be ported to a new operating system if required. A wide range of interactive services requires a portable applications environment, and the Pegasus 1.1 RFQ was issued to select a middleware software to support such an environment.

Applications Resources

Pegasus applications require the same set of resources as the FSN applications; these resources are the set-top, network, and server resources.

Set-Top

The FSN experience taught us that many of the video, graphics, and communications functions should be implemented in hardware in the Pegasus set-top; because hardware state machines operate in parallel, they provide considerable performance improvement over a software implementation, which operates serially.

The Pegasus set-top relies on a sophisticated multimedia operating system to manage the basic set-top resources: CPU, graphics, memory, and communications. The operating system is responsible for delivering these resources to applications so that they can operate properly. It provides support for both broadcast and interactive applications, and through the PowerTV operating system application programming interface (API), provides access to the set-top terminal functions for other applications. The operating system components are shown in Figure 9-6.

Figure 9-6 *PowerTV Operating System Components*

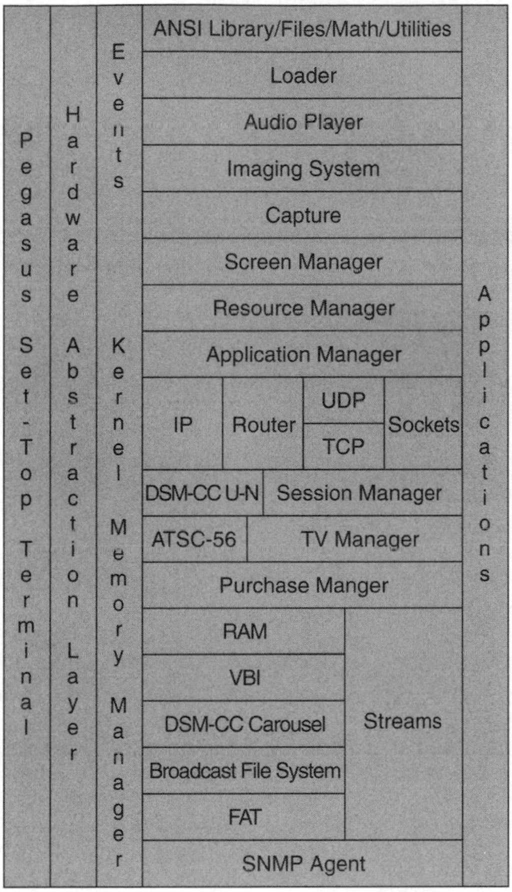

The PowerTV operating system components are described in the following sections.

Operating System Kernel

At the heart of the operating system is a high-performance, multitasking kernel, which serves as the system administrator, and the set-top terminal Memory Resource Manager. For optimal real-time performance, the operating system kernel provides

- Priority-based, preemptive task scheduling, supporting multithreaded applications
- Unified events system
- Dynamic linking and dispatching of functions and modules

- Interprocess communication facilities
- Interrupt and exception handling services
- Efficient dynamic memory management

Because all system and application modules are position-independent, complete modules or single functions can be dynamically loaded in place. The operating system is fully reentrant, allowing multiple tasks to execute the same module, while each task uses separate stack and data spaces.

The kernel manages all memory resources on a dynamic basis with a flat memory model, using the hardware memory protection and management unit available in the Pegasus platform.

The operating system includes a subset of the ANSI C libraries that provide string manipulation, character testing, memory allocation and deallocation, and date and time functions. These functions are optimized for the Pegasus environment.

A loader module supports dynamic linking of resident modules, operating system extensions, applications, shared libraries, and resources into the system at runtime. The loader is stream-based, supporting dynamic relocation of system and user modules as well as forward referencing.

Audio Functions

Abstract devices called audio players provide multichannel pulse code modulation (PCM) audio playback for one or more applications, masking the differences of underlying hardware implementations and assuring the best possible audio playback.

Audio players support the following types of audio, stored in AIFF data format:

- Uncompressed 8-bit mono/stereo PCM audio
- Uncompressed 16-bit mono/stereo PCM audio
- International Multimedia Association (IMA) ADPCM compressed audio
- 8-bit μlaw compressed audio

Audio players enable applications to

- Add and remove audio players.
- Play sounds, allowing the audio mixer to perform any necessary sample rate or bit depth conversions.
- Play any portion of a sound.
- Loop any portion of a sound any number of times.
- Pause and resume playback.
- Adjust the audio playback volume and stereo balance.
- Adjust playback pitch.

Five basic system sounds (ActionAccept, ActionReject, Attention, KeyAcknowledge, and KeyClick) are provided with the system.

Imaging Functions

The imaging system provides graphics rendering support by including a set of graphics primitives: lines, circles, ellipses, rectangles, round rectangles, arcs, and polygons. A set of graphics functions and effects enables rendering of complex images with extensive pixel map manipulations, including scaling, transparency, and translucency support. In addition to its support for pixel maps and graphics primitives, the imaging system supports

- Filling shapes with solid colors and patterns
- Drawing with brushes of application-defined widths and patterns
- Creating drawing patterns using brush masks

The imaging system supports drawing in the following color formats:

- 8-bit red green blue (RGB)
- 16-bit RGB
- 8-bit color lookup table (CLUT)
- 8-bit CLUT with an 8-bit alpha plane value

The imaging system supports opaque, transparent, and translucent graphics overlays on the video plane. In addition, the digital video can be captured in real-time with arbitrary vertical and horizontal scale factors and then manipulated as a standard pixel map.

Antiflutter and horizontal smoothing filters are controlled by the imaging system to provide high-quality graphics on interlaced television displays.

Supported fonts include monospaced fonts, proportional bitmap fonts, and their anti-aliased equivalents in a variety of styles. The system utilizes the NFNT font format definition, enabling applications to take advantage of a wide range of pre-existing font families as well as existing font creation tools on desktop platforms.

Screen Manager

The Screen Manager oversees the screen requirements of applications and controls which screen of the active application is currently visible. The Screen Manager provides support for applications using shared, private, and private-purgeable screens (that is, private screens created from purgeable memory). The use of private-purgeable screens allows the operating system to reclaim these memory resources when there is a critical memory requirement and the application that owns the purgeable screen is in the background.

Application Manager

Multiple applications must be able to execute concurrently on networked consumer devices. Although some subscribers are familiar with multiple windows-based applications within a PC environment, consumer devices using televisions as their display require a different viewer metaphor. The operating system is designed to allow the viewer to interact directly with one application at a time while all other applications continue to execute in the background.

In the operating system, applications use a messaging protocol that supports multiple applications sharing the same system. The Application Manager, which provides this protocol, is responsible for launching, releasing, switching, and monitoring applications within the system, as well as identifying and removing errant applications. The Application Manager makes resource switching optional at the application level. If an application enables resource switching, it can request that the Application Manager inform it when it regains focus and it can control which features —for example, channel or screen—of the application context are subject to resource switching.

Memory Resource Manager

The Memory Resource Manager keeps track of resources in memory and allows applications to acquire (that is, read) resources. A resource is data of any kind stored in the Apple-defined resource format in a module's resource partition. For example, the operating system has a built-in resource partition that includes system fonts and sounds.

Applications and system software interpret the data for a resource based on its resource type. Developers typically use resources to store descriptions of user interface elements, such as menus, fonts, sounds, and text. Because resources are separate from application code (which is usually stored in a module's data partition), developers can create and manage resources without recompiling their applications.

A developer can create resources using a resource compiler, resource editor, or other resource tools, such as ResEdit. Those resources are then put into a resource partition and the partition added to a module using a supplied packaging program. After the module is loaded into the set-top terminal, an application can ask the loader for the location of the resource partition and pass the handle returned to the Memory Resource Manager, thereby gaining access to the resource data.

The operating system provides an RFC-compliant Transmission Control Protocol/User Datagram Protocol-Internet Protocol (TCP/UDP-IP) network stack with a Berkeley Sockets application programming interface. The TCP/UDP-IP network stack provides transparent access to the RF broadband and Ethernet interfaces provided on the Pegasus set-top terminal.

Session Manager

The Session Manager is responsible for establishing, maintaining, monitoring, and tearing down network sessions between set-top terminal client applications and content-provider servers. It supports multiple, simultaneous sessions, administering the set-top terminal resources associated with each session.

The Session Manager supports the DAVIC 1.2 standard lower- and mid-layer protocol and physical interfaces, and implements the DSM-CC user-network signaling protocol.

In addition, the Session Manager supports client/server application download services, enabling applications and associated data to be downloaded on demand into the set-top terminal.

TV Manager

The TV Manager provides a logical channel-tuning interface to guarantee that an application is able to tune to a particular service, regardless of whether the channel is analog or digital. It provides a consistent programming interface to analog and digital services.

The TV Manager also interfaces with the PowerKEY conditional access system to guarantee that subscribers have access to only those channels for which they are authorized.

The TV Manager provides a logical interface for applications to the system information (SI) delivered across the network. The TV Manager controls the set-top terminal's master volume, stereo sound, and muting.

Purchase Manager

The Purchase Manager provides an interface for performing secure transactions for services such as pay-per-view and impulse pay-per-view. It simultaneously supports multiple purchase devices, internal as well as plug-in devices. Applications may retrieve a list of available events and request access to such events.

Streams Management

The operating system provides a streams component that provides an abstracted interface to data delivery sources in the set-top terminal. The streams interface provides access to streams whose origin is

- RAM, stored in the set-top terminal (can also be ROM or FLASH)
- VBI, delivered in the vertical blanking interval
- Data carousel, delivered in the digital domain using the DSM-CC data carousel standard both in-band on the carousel FAT channel and out-of-band on the forward data channel

For development purposes, the streams component also supports a SCSI interface, stored on a locally attached device such as a hard drive. PowerTV supports the FAT filing system standard for PCs.

In addition, a broadcast file system is supported, enabling applications to traverse a hierarchical broadcast delivery system with indications of file updates relayed automatically to applications.

By modifying one line of source code, applications can retrieve data from different sources. Thus, local storage media, such as hard drives, can be used for development; the application can then be moved to the real RF network with a change to only one line of code on the client.

The operating system also incorporates an SNMP agent that provides an interface to system diagnostic information thatcan be interrogated over the RF network.

The development environment for applications is Windows 95–based with C and C++ compiler support in addition to source-level debugging capabilities. Development set-top terminals are available that include Ethernet and SCSI interfaces with additional operating system support for FTP and FAT file systems to aid development.

Software Download

Pegasus supports all the download mechanisms described in Chapter 8:

- Data carousel—The data carousel is the preferred means of software download. The broadcast file system (BFS) layers a file system abstraction onto the DSM-CC data carousel to provide a hierarchical naming space for software files. (SCTE proposed standard DVS-111 describes the BFS.)
- MPEG-2 private data—A separate MPEG-2 packetized elementary stream (PES) is used to download synchronous applications.
- Out-of-band channel—Software download over the out-of-band channel is discouraged to preserve the out-of-band channel capacity for two-way communications.

The size of each of these download files becomes very critical, and general traffic analysis, which is not really currently done, becomes a new requirement in launching interactive applications, especially as more applications are launched on a single system.

Synchronization

The PowerTV operating system provides facilities for application synchronization to the MPEG-2 display timestamp by dispatching events to the application at the appropriate display time.

Communications

Pegasus provides one-way communications and two-way communications facilities (see Chapter 8, "Interactive Services"). One-way communications channels can support a limited subset of local interactive services in a one-way cable plant. (One-way operation might be dictated for business reasons in some areas or might be the result of a temporary operational problem; in either case, it is important to support as many services as is technically possible over a one-way system.) The DAVIC out-of-band channels provide two-way communications channels.

Lessons Learned

The Pegasus design, implementation and deployment experience has provided a number of valuable lessons:

- Broadcast services generate the primary source of revenue for cable systems and will continue to do so for the foreseeable future. This fact dictates that interactive services are layered onto a cable system with great care so as not to detract from the total value of services provided to the customer.
- Application development cost is significant and must be carefully managed by paying attention to application development tools and application portability. Application development tools must be able to simulate a cable system environment for ease of development and testing. Application portability enables multivendor set-top hardware and is best achieved through a middleware strategy.
- To be successful, interactive television services must incorporate the same production values as television programming. This represents a tremendous challenge to the application developer but can be mitigated by a rich suite of multimedia operating system facilities.
- Communications facilities must be carefully engineered to consider the most efficient way of delivering resources to the application. Total network traffic, transactional server capacity, availability, and reliability must all be considered when selecting the communications channel and data transfer mode.

Summary

This chapter summarized two interactive cable systems: the Time Warner Full Service Network and the Pegasus system. In each case, the interactive services, applications model, and applications resources are described.

The FSN provides a model for a fully interactive system and describes the ATM-based connection-oriented approach to network design. In addition, the connectionless signaling support required to support a distributed applications environment is described. FSN services and the applications model are summarized; this leads to a discussion of applications resources and how these are delivered in the FSN. The lessons learned during the FSN development include the communications infrastructure required by interactive services and the application development issues surrounding a television-centric environment.

Pegasus builds on the lessons learned from the FSN development experience and focuses on cost-effective solutions for the delivery of interactive services; the connectionless network infrastructure is optimized for interactive applications, and applications are designed to make efficient used of network resources. The Pegasus applications model is layered onto broadcast services and supports client and distributed applications to support a wide range of services. The issue of application portability is addressed through the selection of a middleware strategy that supports maximum application portability.

References

Standards

SCTE DVS-111. "Revision 1, Digital Headend and Distribution CFI Response System Description (Digital Broadcast Delivery System)." November 24, 1997. Society of Cable Telecommunications Engineers.

SCTE DVS-181. "Revision 1, Service Protocol." February 4, 1999. Society of Cable Telecommunications Engineers.

SCTE DVS-208. "Revision 3, Proposed Draft Standard: Emergency Alert Message for Cable." April 19, 1999. Society of Cable Telecommunications Engineers.

SCTE DVS-234. "Service Information for Out-of-Band Digital Cable Television." June 23, 1999. Society of Cable Telecommunications Engineers.

Internet Resources

Pegasus requirements

http://timewarner.com/rfp

PowerTV

http://www.powertv.com

CHAPTER 10

On-Demand Services

What are on-demand services? Generally, an on-demand service provides a dedicated multimedia stream to the customer and provides controls to manipulate the multimedia stream. The most common example provides a video and audio stream to the customer—video-on-demand (VOD). However, on-demand services are not limited to video-on-demand; they include any service that manipulates a dedicated multimedia stream.

Some examples of on-demand services are

- Movies-on-demand
- Music-on-demand
- Post-broadcast on-demand
- Special interest (or niche) programming
- Distance learning
- Library access
- Video mail

From a network developer's point of view, these services have the following in common:

- They require a session that provides some quality of service (QoS) guarantees to an individual client. This implies either a connection-oriented session establishment or a connectionless network that can guarantee QoS.
- They require some form of stream control. The client application controls the stream by signaling to the server application. For example, in a video-on-demand application, the client application sends play, pause, and fast-forward commands to the media server.

On-demand services represent the Holy Grail for the developer and the *killer* application for the marketer. On-demand services can be added to the real-time, two-way network infrastructure by adding new server applications and hardware.

On-demand services can support the dominant set-top application, which is watching television, and transform it by putting control into the customers' hands. Although interactive services based on computer technology might fail in the living room due to static or uninteresting appearance, on-demand services are a sure thing because the user-interface can use full-screen video and high-quality audio.

Video-on-demand has been in development for many years and has experienced various trials and tribulations (see Chapter 11, "On-Demand Cable System Case Studies"). Why has it taken video-on-demand so long to reach the market place?

There are a number of reasons:

- A video-on-demand service requires a tremendous increase in bandwidth from the cable system. For example, in a system serving 100,000 digital set-tops at 10% peak utilization, 10,000 discrete video streams must be simultaneously delivered over the cable system.
- Allowing the control of each video-on-demand session to be placed in the hands of the customer requires an efficient and reliable signaling mechanism for all 10,000 simultaneous video-on-demand sessions.
- The cost of the video servers, storage, modulation, and transport has to be reduced to the point where a business case can be made for video-on-demand services.

In a remarkably short period of time, all the technical and economic problems have been solved and video-on-demand is ready for prime time. In fact, multiple solutions exist for most problems, and this chapter describes and compares the alternatives for on-demand services.

Interactive Versus On-Demand Services

The distinction between interactive services (see Chapter 8, "Interactive Services") and on-demand services is the need for a session with some well-known QoS. Interactive services can be designed to reduce the network bandwidth requirements to a minimum (green applications) but there is no equivalent in on-demand services. In general, on-demand services have very different QoS requirements than interactive services. See Table 10-1.

Table 10-1 *Comparison of QoS Requirements for On-Demand and Interactive Services*

QoS	On-Demand	Interactive
Bit rate	2–6 Mbps (standard definition)	20–200 Kbps
Delay	Constant	Variable
Loss	10^{-10}	10^{-6}
Error	10^{-10}	10^{-6}
Retransmission	Not allowed	Allowed

Internet Comparisons

On-demand services are appearing on the World Wide Web and are called *streaming media* applications. Streaming media applications allow the user to listen to radio stations, preview CDs, and view movie clips. In contrast to the strict QoS requirements for on-demand services based on MPEG-2, streaming media applications are designed to work in an Internet environment where QoS guarantees are often nonexistent. This leads to some very different approaches for the delivery of video and audio (see Tables 10-2 and 10-3).

Table 10-2 *Comparison of Streaming Video and On-Demand Video Services*

Parameter	MPEG-2 Compression	Streaming Video
Bit rate	2–6 Mbps (standard definition)	20–200 Kbps
Resolution	480 x 544; 480 x 720	120 x 160
Frame rate	30 fps	5–15 fps

Table 10-2 compares streaming video and on-demand video services. MPEG-2 video requires a minimum bit rate of about 2 Mbps and is designed to guarantee a certain constant resolution and frame rate; for these reasons, its bandwidth is relatively constant. In contrast, streaming video services use compression schemes that adapt to network bandwidth by adjusting their frame rate and resolution dynamically. At higher bit rates (about 500 Kbps), streaming video compression can support 240 x 360 resolution. Moreover, they are designed to tolerate much higher loss and error rates than MPEG-2 compression.

Table 10-3 *Comparison of Streaming and On-Demand Audio Services*

Parameter	AC-3 Compression	Streaming Audio
Bit rate	192–384 Kbps	8–100 Kbps
Frequency response	20 Hz–20KHz	20 Hz–4, 8, or 20 KHz
Channels	2–6	1–2

Table 10-3 compares streaming audio and on-demand audio services. AC-3 video requires a bit rate from about 192 Kbps (for stereo) up to 384 Kbps (for 5.1 channel audio) and is designed to guarantee a certain level of audio fidelity at a fixed bit rate. Streaming audio services use compression schemes that adapt to network bandwidth by adjusting audio fidelity while tolerating much higher loss and error rates than AC-3 compression.

Goals of On-Demand Services

On-demand services share many of the same goals as interactive services (see Chapter 8).

Successful on-demand services add value in some way for the programmer, cable operator, and customer. Added value can come from a number of sources:

- Customer-generated revenue—If an on-demand service is useful or compelling, the customer will be prepared to pay for it. Specifically, video-on-demand has demonstrated significantly higher buy rates than impulse pay-per-view in a number of trials.
- Advertiser-generated revenue—If an on-demand service can increase the effectiveness of existing commercials or allow the customer to access a company's product and service information, the advertiser will be prepared to pay the cable operator for that service.
- Enhanced customer perception and retention—Increased competition from DBS, MMDS, and others make it even more important to cable operators that their customers are happy with their cable service. Availability of on-demand services enhances the customer's perception of the overall cable service.

To be successful, on-demand services must provide a satisfying experience for the customer in the following areas:

- They must be friendly and intuitive to use. The service needs to be easily accessible from the remote control with little or no customer training.
- They must present an attractive, graphically rich interface. The customer is accustomed to the high production values of most television programming and will not tolerate an uninteresting or static user interface.
- They must be reliable and highly available. If an interactive service becomes popular with customers, they will be frustrated if it is unreliable or unavailable.

The business case for on-demand services is simple: An on-demand service is economical if the revenue generated by it can pay for the capital cost of the additional hardware in a reasonable period of time (for example, four years). Until recently, there were two fundamental barriers to on-demand services:

- The cable system could not provide sufficient bandwidth to support revenue generating movies-on-demand service; that is, too few customers would be able to access the service simultaneously to make it successful.
- The cost of the digital set-top was prohibitive and made the movies-on-demand business case uneconomic.

The first problem has been solved by hybrid fiber coax upgrades, which provide a massive increase in the bandwidth available to each customer. The second problem has been solved because the digital set-top has been cost-reduced and is now justified economically for broadcast digital services. This chapter describes how the video-on-demand architecture is tailored to provide the best economic solution to these problems.

On-Demand Services

There are many services that are enabled by on-demand technology. The following list of services provides some examples:

- Movies-on-demand
- Music-on-demand
- Post-broadcast on-demand
- Special interest programming
- Distance learning
- Library access
- Video mail

Movies-on-Demand

Usually called video-on-demand, the idea of providing access to a movie library is very appealing. The movies-on-demand (MOD) service has been extensively tested in trials, and customer response has been enthusiastic.

This service emulates the current video rental business, so it is easiest to justify from an economic point of view. The cable industry today has later *windows* (that is, the period of time at which particular movies are available) than the video rental market. However, if a movies-on-demand service can be successfully deployed, the cable industry will be well-positioned to negotiate better windows for MOD titles.

Music-on-Demand

The music-on-demand service provides access to a music library. Broadcast music services (for example, Music Choice and DMX) are effectively niche services, and it is unclear whether on-demand access to a music library will change the status of music services.

This service emulates the CD player, but allows the customer to access any musical selection. For the same reasons that there are no CD rental stores, it is unlikely that there is much business potential in a music-on-demand service. However, music-on-demand can be used to promote CD sales in the same way as the Internet.

Post-Broadcast On-Demand

Post-broadcast on-demand uses video-on-demand technology to allow access to a library of titles that have been broadcast. It allows the customer to view shows they have missed and caters to the segment of the market that is prepared to pay for this convenience.

This service emulates using a VCR to record broadcast programming for viewing at a later time. It provides convenience, because the customer does not have to remember to record the program, and flexibility, because many titles can be offered. Some early tests also showed that the success of this service is very programming type–dependent; for example, post-broadcast on-demand might work well for soap operas or hit sitcoms, but it might not be as successful for children's programming. The real question is whether this kind of service is commercially viable—will customers pay for this type of service?

Special Interest Programming

Video-on-demand can allow random access to special interest programs and provides an alternative to creating new special interest channels. New special interest channels are being created at an amazing rate; digital compression allows many more channels on a cable system, but at some point there is a limit to the number of channels. In addition, many special interest channels are hard-pressed to provide sufficient programming to fill their schedule. With the addition of each new channel, the potential audience is further subdivided, making advertiser sponsorship more difficult. Therefore on-demand delivery of special interest programming provides a solution to dedicated channel assignments and limited viewership.

Distance Learning

The capability of providing multimedia delivery of video, graphics, and text makes on-demand technology ideal for distance learning applications. Distance learning is an ideal candidate for on-demand services. In many ways, it is similar to special interest programming—appealing only to a niche audience and not justifying a dedicated channel. (Currently, distance learning channels aggregate a number of courses to justify a channel allocation, but this model can be very inconvenient for customers if the broadcast time of the course does not fit into their schedule.)

Library Access

The idea of a large online, multimedia library is not new, but the technology to retrieve titles in real-time makes this concept compelling. On-demand library access emulates the service currently provided (albeit poorly) by the WWW. This service allows retrieval of short clips of multimedia information and would primarily support research activity.

Video Mail

The store-and-forward approach to communications is often more convenient. This approach can be extended to a video mail service that allows one customer to send a video and audio message to another. Video mail is a communications service and is not really part of video-on-demand, but VOD technology could be used to provide the record and playback capabilities required for a multimedia e-mail service.

On-Demand Reference Architecture

Figure 10-1 is a reference diagram for an on-demand system.

Figure 10-1 *On-Demand Reference Architecture*

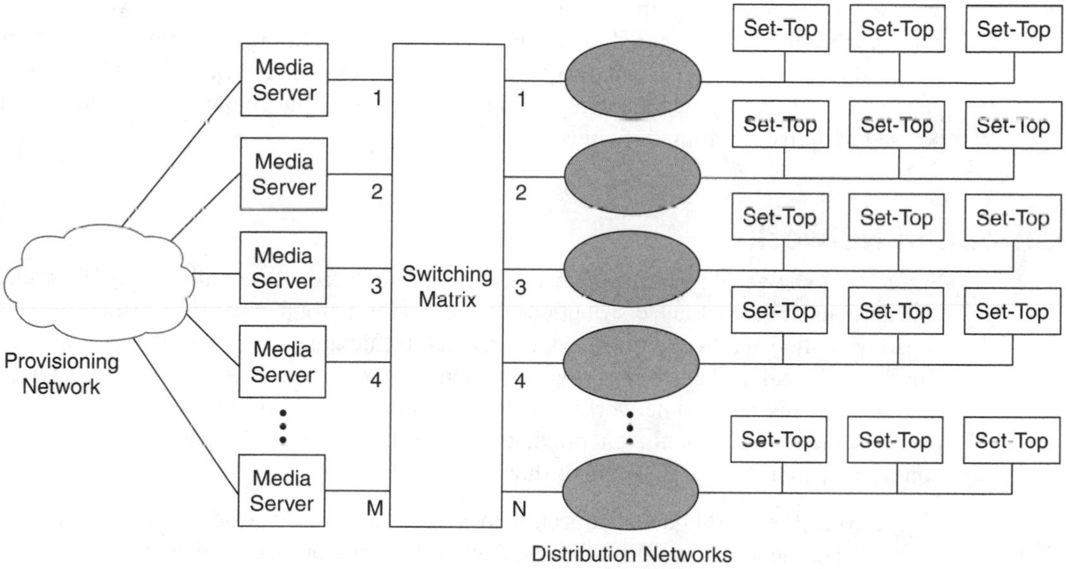

At this level of detail, the system is composed of the following major components:

- Provisioning network—This allows new content or multimedia *assets* to be loaded onto the media servers.
- Distribution networks—In a cable system, the distribution networks are formed by the hybrid fiber coax (HFC) plant. Each distribution network supplies a group of set-tops.
- Media servers—The media servers provide the streaming content for distribution to the set-tops.
- Switching matrix—The switching matrix provides a path from each media server to each distribution network.
- Set-tops—The set-top provides termination of the streaming content and adapts it to the television set.

Each of these components is described in more detail in the following sections.

Provisioning Network

The provisioning network provides secure delivery of content from the content provider to the video server location. Satellite or terrestrial links could provide this network. The important point to note is that the content provisioning can be modeled as a series of file transfers and, accordingly, the requirements for the content provisioning network are considerably relaxed compared to the distribution network. In fact, multimedia assets do not need real-time delivery, and the QoS of the provisioning network does not have to be guaranteed. Therefore, available bit rate services (on a satellite channel, for example) can be used to deliver multimedia assets.

Distribution Network

Figure 10-1 shows that in an on-demand cable system, there are actually *multiple, parallel* distribution networks. Each distribution network serves a group of set-tops so that sufficient capacity is allocated to meet the peak on-demand traffic generated by those set-tops (see Chapter 2, "Analog Cable Technologies"). Media servers are connected via a switching matrix to the distribution networks. Finally, each media server is connected to a provisioning network for content provisioning. Note that in Figure 10-1, for simplicity, the control and signaling network is not shown.

Figure 10-2 shows the channel allocation to each set-top. The analog and digital broadcast channels are the same for all set-tops (and all customers), but the on-demand channels are narrowcast to a *set-top group*.

Figure 10-2 *Set-Top Channel Allocation*

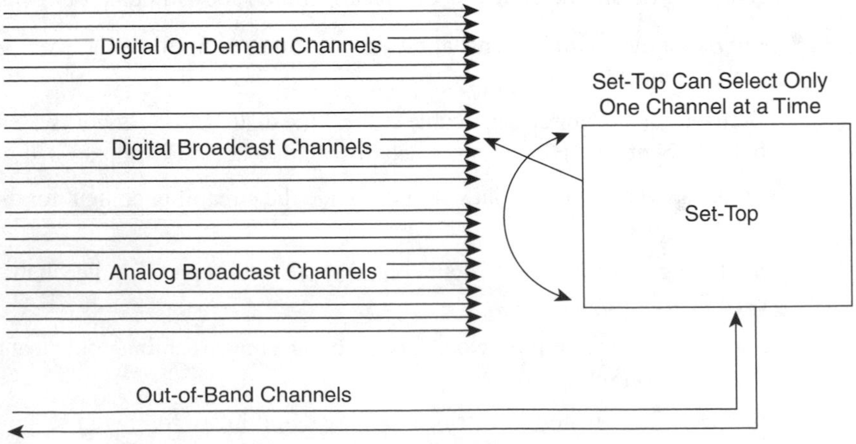

The size of the set-top group can be calculated as follows:

- The aggregate capacity of the on-demand channels is equal to the number of channels multiplied by the capacity of each channel. The more channels the better, because this provides better statistical multiplexing. For example, if 10 channels are allocated (requiring 60 MHz of cable spectrum) and 256-QAM modulation is used, the aggregate bandwidth is 10 × 38.8 Mbps, or 388 Mbps.
- The traffic generated by each set-top is determined by the on-demand session rate. For standard definition compressed digital television, 3.8 Mbps is a realistic number (and makes the math easier).
- The next factor is the peak utilization of on-demand services. This is the percentage of all customers who simultaneously request on-demand services at the busiest time. On-demand services are usually engineered for a peak-utilization rate of 10% because this number seems to be validated by on-demand trials (see Chapter 11).
- The number of set-tops per distribution network is given by the following formula:

  aggregate capacity × peak utilization ÷ on-demand session rate

  Using the numbers in the example, each distribution network can serve 1,000 set-tops. In a cable system serving 100,000 set-tops, 100 distribution networks would be required.

The distribution network provides many areas for innovation in the cost-effective delivery of on-demand services. There are a number of technology choices to be made by the network architect:

- Physical protocol—In a fiber-based network, the physical layer protocol can use a digital (for example, SONET) or analog physical layer, or a combination of both. In an HFC network, the digital payload must be modulated to traverse the analog part of the network.
- Transport protocol—There are a number of alternative transport protocols to choose from for on-demand services. The leading alternatives are MPEG-2 transport, ATM, and IP.

Physical Protocols

In an HFC cable system, the distribution network is composed of a series of cascaded fiber links and coaxial links (see Chapter 2). The physical layer protocol over the fiber link can be digital (for example SONET) or analog, but the physical layer over the coaxial links is always analog. A modulator performs the conversion from digital to analog and may be placed anywhere in the signal path between the switching matrix and the first analog link.

In practical terms, modulators are sensitive pieces of equipment that require a temperature-controlled environment; the possible locations are the headend or the distribution hub.

Modulation at Headend

Placing the modulators at the headend centralizes all the digital components of the system and uses analog fiber to transport the modulated carriers all the way to the set-tops. Centralizing the modulators might require considerable space—for example, a 100,000 set-top system would require 1,000 modulators at 10% peak utilization. However, located at the headend, the modulators can easily be reconfigured to best match the traffic pattern changes of the system as it grows.

The use of analog fiber transport is familiar to most cable operators because it is already used for analog and digital broadcast channels; the only change is that instead of one channel line-up, a separate bank of on-demand channels is required for each set-top group. However, multiple fibers or wavelength division multiplexing can be used to carry each bank of on-demand channels to the set-top group.

Modulation at Distribution Hub

Modulation at the hub allows on-demand traffic to be integrated over a single transport with other digital signals, such as cable modem, telephony, out-of-band signaling, and network management traffic. In the distribution hub, the modulators are closer to the set-top (in terms of fiber miles), and there is less analog degradation of the modulated signal. Although digital transport provides more flexibility and can be extended over greater distances than analog transport, there is a cost premium to be paid for digital transport.

Transport Protocols

There are a number of alternative transport protocols for on-demand services. The leading alternatives are MPEG-2 transport, ATM, and IP:

- MPEG-2 transport—MPEG-2 transport is optimized for compressed, streaming media.
- Asynchronous transfer mode (ATM)—ATM transport is a compromise protocol designed to handle video, data, and telephony traffic.
- Internet Protocol (IP)—IP was designed for data traffic but is being extended to add features for streaming media.

These transport protocols are discussed in more detail in Chapter 4, "Digital Technologies." There is no *correct* choice for all circumstances, but the following guidelines will help you select the best choice for your application:

- If a single traffic type dominates, select the best transport for that traffic type. For example, the best choice for a video-on-demand application is MPEG-2 transport.
- The choice of transport type is closely related to the need for distributed switching and routing. MPEG-2 transport switches are just now becomning available commercially, and ATM or IP might be a better choice for flexibility if the additional cost can be justified.

- What transport protocol is used by set-tops that are already deployed? Nearly all first-generation digital set-tops accept only MPEG-2 transport streams, and protocol conversion back to MPEG-2 in the distribution network will be required to support these set-tops if ATM or IP are selected. (Figure 10-5 provides an example of this case.)

Media Servers

The server has a number of functions and can be broken down into a number of functional elements to aid description (however, note that a specific implementation might not follow these lines):

- Asset management—Each file stored on the media server is called an *asset*. Assets must be managed to allow them to be provisioned and retrieved by the streaming service.
- Streaming service—The streaming service delivers an asset or group of assets according to the requirements of the on-demand service.
- Directory service—The directory service provides a list of assets to the server application.
- Server application—The server application provides the intelligence and control of the media server. Different applications are used to provide different on-demand services.

Asset Management

Asset management is the function responsible for making sure that assets are available to the streaming service when they are required. Asset management supports a number of functions:

- Provisioning—Each asset must be downloaded onto the media server via the provisioning network. The asset is the movie file and related elements, such as the trailer video file, the poster image, the text description, the price, and so on.
- Storage management—Each asset must be placed into the media server storage. Multiple copies of assets might be required based on server design and viewing demand.
- Deletion—Assets must be deleted when they are no longer required.

Streaming Service

The streaming service delivers an asset or group of assets according to the requirements of the on-demand service. For example, to stream a movie requires that the video and audio streams are synchronized and delivered at the precise rate for the set-top decoder. The streaming service is often implemented with special hardware to satisfy the stringent real-time requirements for streaming MPEG-2 encoded assets.

Directory Service

The directory service provides a list of assets to the server application via an API. The directory service is responsible for keeping track of assets and liberates the application program from this task. A directory service is useful for providing asset search functions, for example, to locate a movie based on genre or actor.

Server Application

The server application allows the media server to be used for many different on-demand services—typically, there is a different server application for each on-demand service. For example, a movies-on-demand application might support functions such as providing a list of available movies, movie previews, movie purchase, fast-forward, pause, and so on.

Conditional Access

Conditional access (CA) is required for the distribution of any streaming media that have value and must therefore be protected from signal theft. There are two approaches to providing conditional access to streaming media from the server:

- Encrypt the signal at the output of the server. This approach follows the broadcast model and can conveniently use the same conditional access system that is already in place for digital broadcast signals. The conditional access system must support additional interfaces to support secure session establishment and key distribution to the on-demand client application.
- Encrypt the stored assets on the server. This approach requires no stream encryption at the headend because the preencrypted assets are streamed directly from the server storage. Secure key distribution to the on-demand client could use the broadcast conditional access system or a separate conditional access system. The disadvantage to preencrypted assets is that the encryption is static and might be less resistant to pirate attacks. Preencryption also does not allow statistical multiplexing because the MPEG stream is encrypted and cannot be reencoded. Finally, updating preencrypted content to fix expired keys places an additional load on the server.

Server Placement

In theory, the server can be placed at any point in the distribution network between the headend and the set-top. However, the server requires a controlled environment, and the practical server locations are the headend, the distribution hub, or the customer premises.

Server at Headend

Placing the media server at the headend allows it to serve the entire cable system. The distribution networks aggregate the traffic from all customers, and the law of large numbers allows efficient statistical multiplexing. In early deployment, when some distribution hubs support relatively few customers, centralizing the servers makes good sense.

However, a centralized server farm might grow to require considerable resources in terms of space and power. A centralized facility is also vulnerable to disasters such as fire or flood. In addition, the distance-bandwidth product of the distribution networks is much larger than when the servers are placed nearer to the customer. Consider that every asset must be transferred across the distribution network for all customers individually—even if they live next door to each other.

Despite these caveats, placing the media server at the headend is viable for cable systems with several hundred thousand subscribers. Distribution networks with sufficient capacity can be engineered using the almost unlimited bandwidth of fiber optic links, and the physical footprint and power requirements of media servers are being constantly reduced by Moore's Law.

Server at Distribution Hub

Placing the media server at the distribution hub reduces distribution network capacity at the expense of asset replication. The media server is closer to the set-top and effectively provides a cache function, holding all the assets that might be required by the set-top. This works for systems with relatively few assets, but the provisioning traffic and media server storage increases in direct proportion to the number of assets.

The media server must be designed for unattended operation and must be managed remotely if it is located at the distribution hub. Any regular maintenance of the media server necessitates travel to and from the distribution hub.

Server in Set-Top

With the advent of multigigabyte storage at affordable prices, why not put the VOD server in the set-top? The set-top server is dedicated to a single customer, and therefore its cost cannot be amortized across a number of customers like a centralized server. However, the server complexity is considerably reduced because it plays only a single stream at a time. Moreover, server failure affects only a single customer and redundant hardware is not required.

The main problem with placing the server in the set-top is the amount of storage and the provisioning bandwidth required. In a time-shifting application, where broadcast programming is cached by the server for subsequent playback, no incremental provisioning bandwidth is needed; but in an on-demand service, every asset that might be required by the customer must be provided, using one of two approaches:

- Popular assets—for example, new movie releases—are broadcast to all set-tops to reduce provisioning bandwidth.
- Random assets—for example, library video-clips—are delivered on-demand in real-time (or faster than real-time). Media servers are still required in the headend, and set-tops generate much the same traffic load as other on-demand approaches.

In the first approach, considerable set-top storage is required to provide customer choice. In addition, because every set-top contains a copy of each new movie release, piracy is a concern; the set-top server assets must be protected by a bulletproof conditional access system. In the second approach, there is little or no advantage to the cable operator except when assets are downloaded and then played several times.

In summary, placing the set-top in the server can provide only very limited on-demand selection unless servers in the network provide a second level of support.

Switching Matrix

With reference to Figure 10-1, the media server output is routed to the set-top via one of a number of distribution networks. (To understand why there are multiple distribution networks, please refer to the section Distribution Network, earlier in this chapter.) Therefore, a switching function is required to connect a media server to a set-top in a particular distribution network. In general, an *M* by *N*, nonblocking switching matrix is required, and Figure 10-1 illustrates the use of a such a switching matrix to allow any of the *M* media servers to be connected to any of the *N* delivery networks.

There are a number of approaches to the requirement for a switching matrix (these are described in the next sections):

- Content replication—In the content replication approach, each media server holds a copy of all the potential assets required by the set-top. This allows the media server to be directly connected to the distribution network.
- Massively parallel server—Proponents of massively parallel media servers (notably, N-Cube) argue that the switching matrix can be best incorporated into a scalable media server. Such a server can output any asset on any output port and can be connected directly to the distribution network (at the headend or the distribution hub).
- ATM switching—ATM is an effective switching technology for the switching matrix. A connection manager is required to set up ATM connections from the media server to the distribution network.

- IP routing—Until recently, IP routing did not scale to meet the throughput demands required for the switching matrix. However, recent advances in multiple protocol label switching (MPLS) and IP QoS have made IP routing a potential technology for this application. The great advantage of IP is that it is self-routing—that is, no explicit connection management function is required.
- QAM matrix—It is possible to build a matrix of QAM modulators in such a way as to form a space/frequency/time switch. The switching matrix is connection-oriented, so it requires a connection management function similar to an ATM network.

Asset Replication

Asset replication places a copy of all assets on every media server and allows the media server to be directly connected to the distribution network, as shown in Figure 10-3.

Figure 10-3 *Asset Replication*

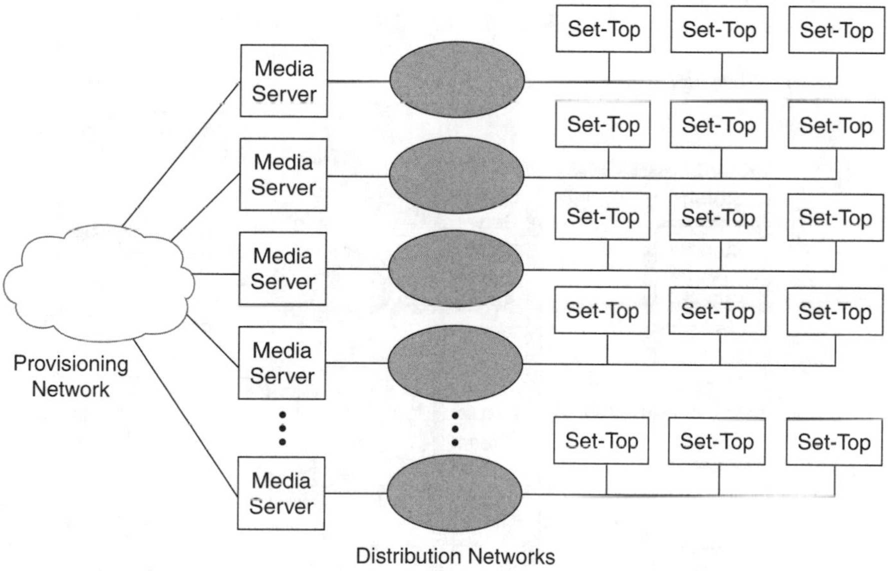

This approach is simple and eliminates the switching matrix but has a number of disadvantages that make it unsuitable for wide-scale deployment:

- Asset replication increases the amount of storage required and directly increases storage cost. In a limited movies-on-demand application, where only 10 titles are offered at any given time, asset replication is acceptable, but it does not scale to larger systems. For example, in a time-shifting or library application, asset replication in each media server requires massive amounts of storage. Worse still, the provisioning bandwidth increases linearly with the number of media servers and with the number of new assets. Eventually, as system size increases, asset provisioning generates most of the activity in the system for assets that might never be retrieved.

- The availability of such a system is the same as the availability of the media server; if it fails, no other path exists to the distribution network. This problem can be mitigated by using two media servers per distribution network, but this doubles the media server cost.
- For efficiency, the demand of each distribution network must be accurately matched to the capacity of the media server. This is difficult to achieve as the customer base grows.

Massively Parallel Server

In a massively parallel server, the switching matrix is incorporated into a large, scalable media server, as shown in Figure 10-4.

Figure 10-4 *Massively Parallel Server*

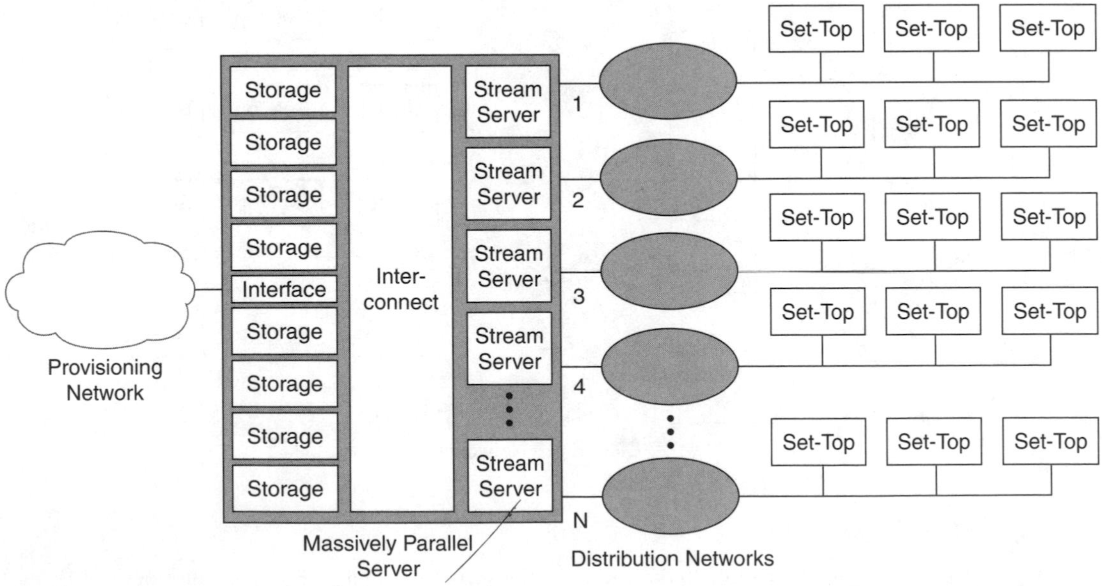

Such a server can output any asset on any output port and can be connected directly to the distribution network. Massively parallel servers provide an excellent solution to the switching problem but must satisfy rigorous availability metrics because of their design:

- Massively parallel servers must be highly available, because if they fail, no service is available to all customers.
- It must be possible to increase server capacity by increments while the server is online.
- The failure of individual disk drives, processors, memory banks, or power supplies cannot cause the server to fail (but might reduce total capacity).
- Massively parallel servers must be cost-competitive with smaller servers over the life cycle of their operation. In other words, they cannot be prohibitively expensive for early, lower-demand operation and cost-effective only in a fully subscribed system.

If massively parallel servers are built to satisfy these requirements, this technology will be very successful for the provision of on-demand services.

ATM Switching

Figure 10-5 illustrates the use of an ATM switch as a switching matrix. The ATM switching function can be distributed by building a network of switches located at the headend and distribution hubs.

Figure 10-5 *ATM Switching*

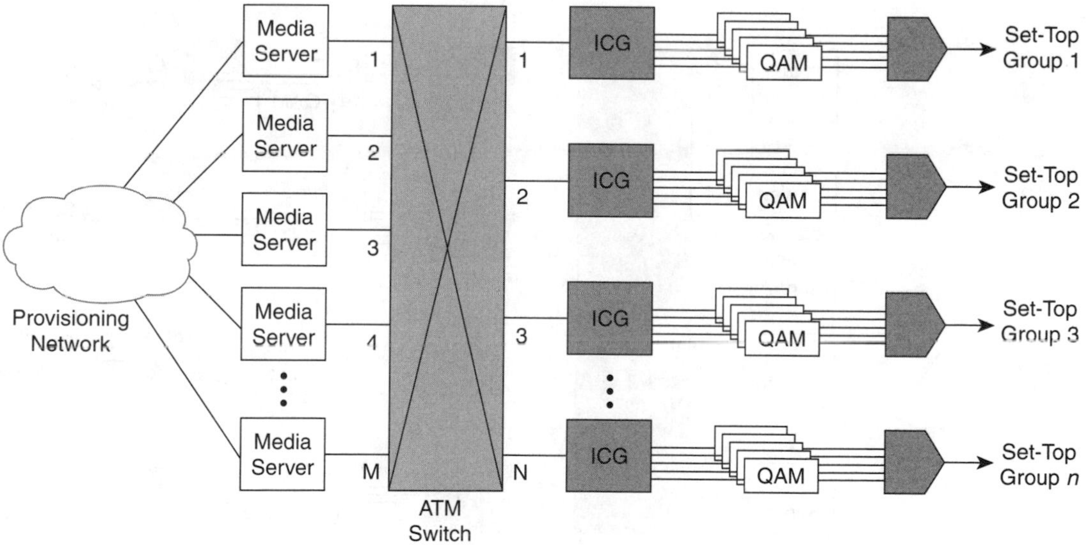

ATM is a connection-oriented protocol, and a connection manager is required to set up ATM connections from the media server to the distribution network.

Incremental cost of ATM switching includes the adaptation of MPEG-2 packets to ATM cells and reassembly back into MPEG-2 packets before they are fed into the MPEG-2 decoder. In Figure 10-5, ATM adaptation is done by the output interface of the media server. MPEG-2 streams are reassembled by the Integrated Cable Gateway (ICG) before QAM modulation to support an MPEG-2 digital set-top. (See Chapter 11 for an ATM-to-the-home case study.)

ATM switching provides flexibility and efficiency for multimedia transport but requires sophisticated connection management services that are directly accessible from the on-demand application. Some approaches, notably X-Bind, show considerable promise toward meeting these requirements. (See "A Programmable Transport Architecture with QoS Guarantees," by Jean-Francois Huard and Aurel A. Lazar, in *IEEE Communications.*)

IP Routing

Figure 10-6 illustrates a routed network approach to media server to distribution network interconnection.

Figure 10-6 *IP Routing*

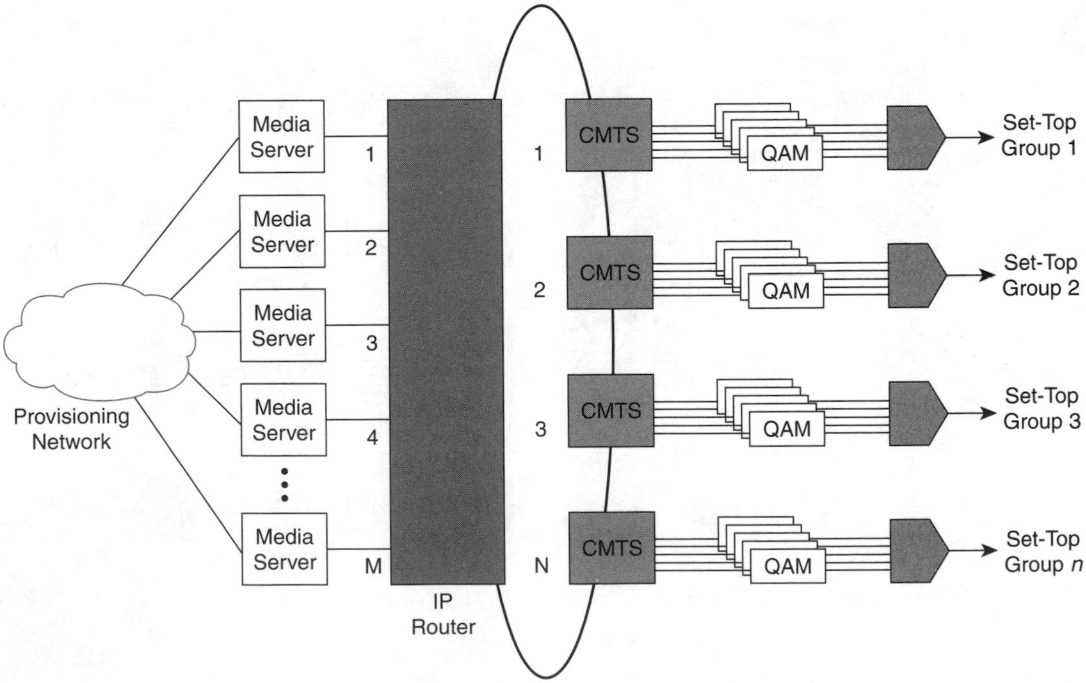

Until recently, IP routing did not scale to meet the throughput demands required for the switching matrix. However, recent advances in multiple protocol label switching (MPLS) and IP QoS have made IP routing a potential technology for this application. The great advantage of IP is that it is self-routing—that is, no explicit connection management function is required.

A routed design allows the switching matrix to be distributed by placing routers in the headend and hub locations. Figure 10-6 shows the headend router interconnected to the Cable Modem Termination System (CMTS) routers by means of an optical ring technology. Distributed routing provides a number of advantages:

- The same network can be used to provide the out-of-band channel support (see Chapter 5, "Adding Digital Television Services to Cable Systems").
- The same network can provide support for cable modem and IP telephony services.

This level of integration multiplexes cable modem, telephony, and on-demand traffic into each QAM channel. Although this is possible, there are several reasons why this level of integration might not be advisable:

- Some cable operators run their cable modem, telephony, and television services as separate businesses.
- The only practical way to integrate these traffic types is to use IP transport for all of them, which incurs increased overhead for MPEG-2 traffic.

Additionally, routed networks are still significantly more expensive than other approaches, although let's hope this is not a long-term trend. In addition, IP encapsulation of MPEG-2 transport packets is not very efficient. Finally, minimum bit rate guarantees must be provided by the routed network to ensure video and audio quality. (See "QoS Support for Integrated Services over CATV," by Richard Rabbat and Kai-Yeung Siu, in *IEEE Communications*.)

QAM Matrix

With the QAM matrix, it is possible to build a matrix of QAM modulators in such a way as to form a space/frequency/time switch, as shown in Figure 10-7.

Figure 10-7 *QAM Matrix*

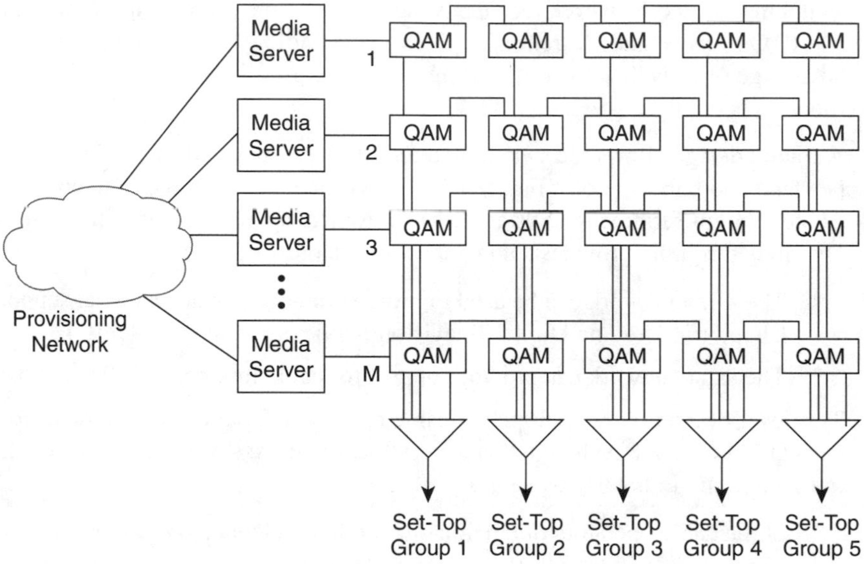

The QAM matrix deliberately connects different server output ports to each set-top group to provide alternative server choices into each group, with load balancing and redundancy. In Figure 10-7, *M* different servers (one per QAM frequency) feed each set-top group.

The switching matrix is connection-oriented and requires a connection management function similar to an ATM network. When a request is received for a particular asset, the connection manager determines which servers hold the asset and have a path to the set-top. The path is allocated according to which media server is least loaded to balance the traffic across all servers. If a server fails, the maximum capacity to the set-top group is reduced by only one QAM channel (38.8 Mbps). Any set-tops that were streaming assets from the failed server lose their stream but recover by requesting the same asset and being reassigned to another server.

The QAM matrix provides a low-cost alternative to ATM or IP switching because it uses the broadband network and the set-top tuner as a distributed switching matrix. This approach is discussed in more detail in Chapter 11 in the Pegasus Phase 2 case study.

Set-Top

The incremental requirements for a broadcast digital set-top (see Chapter 4) are quite simple to support on-demand services:

- The set-top must support an on-demand client application. An on-demand client is an example of an interactive client application that supports the manipulation of streaming media; on-demand clients can be quite simple if the existing broadcast digital hardware is used to decode and display the streaming media. For this reason, there is much interest in media servers that can provide MPEG-2–compliant transport streams that are identical to broadcast MPEG-2 transport streams.
- The set-top must support two-way, real-time signaling for session and stream control. The signaling required for on-demand services can be supported by DAVIC or DOCSIS out-of-band channels. A client-server application model is used to implement on-demand services.

Summary

This chapter described on-demand services and their application in cable systems. The following major topics were covered:

- Comparison with interactive and Internet services—The connection bit rate and quality of service requirements are higher for on-demand services than for interactive and Internet services in a television-centric environment, which provides a challenge for the on-demand service provider.
- The goals of on-demand service are summarized, and some examples of on-demand services are described, including movies-on-demand, music-on-demand, post-broadcast on-demand, special interest programming, distance learning, library access, and video mail.
- A reference architecture is proposed for an on-demand cable system that includes a provisioning network, a distribution network, media servers, a switching matrix, and a digital set-top. The alternative technologies and location of media servers is described in detail. In addition, a number of different switching matrix implementations are compared.

References

Huard, Jean-Francois, and Aurel A. Lazar. "A Programmable Transport Architecture with QoS Guarantees." *IEEE Communications.* October 1998.

Rabbat, Richard, and Kai-Yeung Siu. "QoS Support for Integrated Services over CATV." *IEEE Communications.* January 1999.

CHAPTER 11

On-Demand Cable System Case Studies

This chapter discusses two on-demand cable systems—the Time Warner Full Service Network (FSN) and the Time Warner Pegasus program. These systems have already been discussed from an interactive services standpoint in Chapter 9, "Interactive Cable System Case Studies"; this chapter focuses on those aspects specific to on-demand services. The FSN and Pegasus are closely related; the same core team of engineers is responsible for both programs, and the Pegasus program has many of the same goals as the Full Service Network.

Time Warner Full Service Network

The Full Service Network (FSN), was conceived primarily as a vehicle for video-on-demand (VOD) services, and this chapter focuses on them. VOD was the major goal of the FSN for a number of reasons. First, VOD has been the Holy Grail of engineers for many years. The idea that video can be captured, stored, and manipulated using digital techniques is fascinating, if only because it is such a wonderful engineering challenge. Second, the limitations of pay-per-view programming can be frustrating, and there is some evidence to suggest that the customer really wants a VOD service and is prepared to pay for it. This evidence is backed up by the success of the video rental business. In a short time, the (once-laughable) idea of renting videotapes of movies to customers for a fee has become a multibillion-dollar-per-year business. (For more information, see the section FSN Network Architecture Goals in Chapter 9.)

Full Service Network Overview

The FSN is designed to provide full video-on-demand with instant access over a broadband HFC network to 4,000 customers. At any given time, up to 1,000 concurrent video streams from eight video servers must be delivered over 16 parallel distribution networks. Figure 11-1 illustrates that at the core of the FSN architecture is a single, large ATM switch that provides nonblocking interconnection of the servers to the distribution network.

Figure 11-1 *Full Service Network Overview*

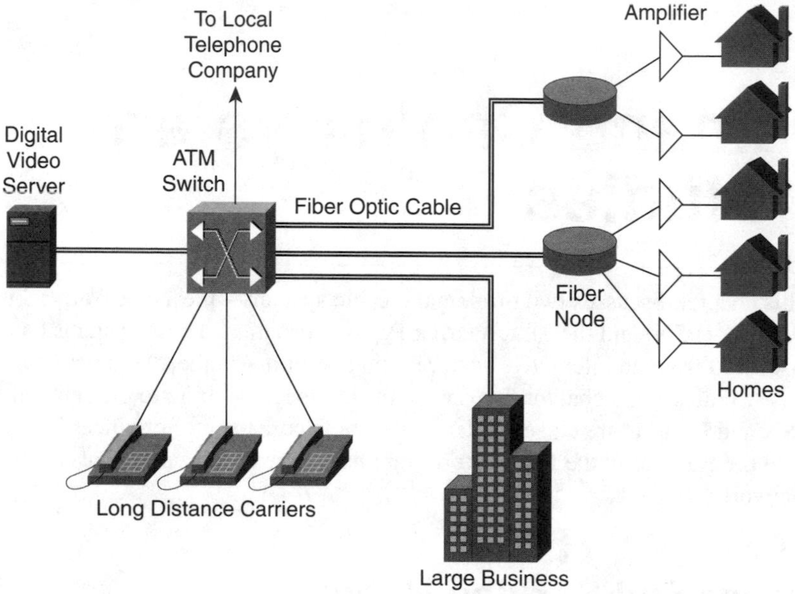

Figure 11-1 also explains why ATM was chosen as the core switching and transport technology for the FSN; the ATM switch provides an integrated solution for interconnection of telephony, data, and video services.

Basic Star Architecture

The FSN architecture places most of the equipment (media servers, ATM switch, and modulation equipment) in a network operations center (NOC). The NOC is located at a distribution hub site with the intention that it be replicated for every 20,000 homes passed. Figure 11-2 shows the basic star architecture that radiates from the distribution hub to the fiber nodes. From the fiber nodes, the signal is distributed over the coaxial portion of the network to the customer.

Figure 11-2 *Basic Star Architecture*

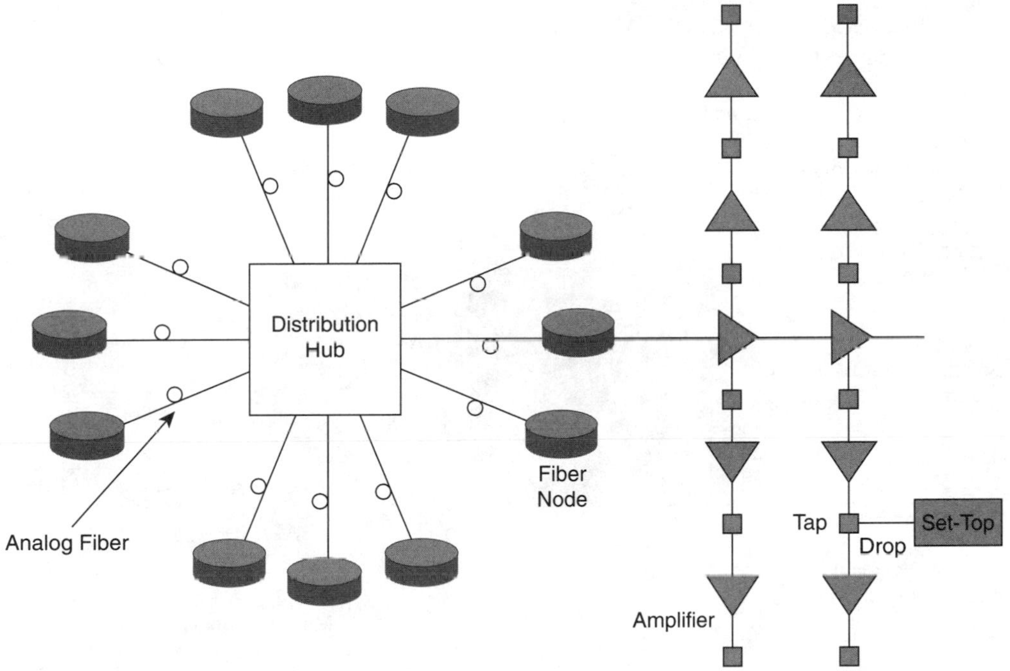

The NOC was located at the distribution hub because of the physical volume of the equipment that is required to deliver video-on-demand services. The media servers, storage vaults, ATM switching equipment, and modulation equipment was initially located in a computer room that measured approximately 60 by 22 feet, or 1320 square feet. This space was subsequently doubled with the addition of telephone switching and trunking equipment. Since 1993, most of this equipment has increased in density by a factor of between 5 and 10 (as in Moore's Law). Assuming this trend continues, this equipment may be centrally located at the headend to reduce operational costs (see the section Server Location in Chapter 10, "On-Demand Services").

A second advantage of locating the NOC at the distribution hub is that it allows direct access to the distribution networks. In Figure 11-2, each fiber node is fed by a dedicated 1310-nanometer DFB laser over a dedicated fiber, effectively forming a separate distribution network for each 500 homes passed. Each fiber node receives a unique bank of on-demand channels from the equipment in the distribution hub allowing *spacial reuse* of that portion of the cable spectrum.

(For more information, see the section FSN Network Overview in Chapter 9.)

Logical ATM Connectivity

In the FSN network, the ATM switch is used to establish ATM connections from the servers to the set-top. Figure 11-3 shows the logical view of the ATM connection service.

Figure 11-3 *Logical ATM Connectivity*

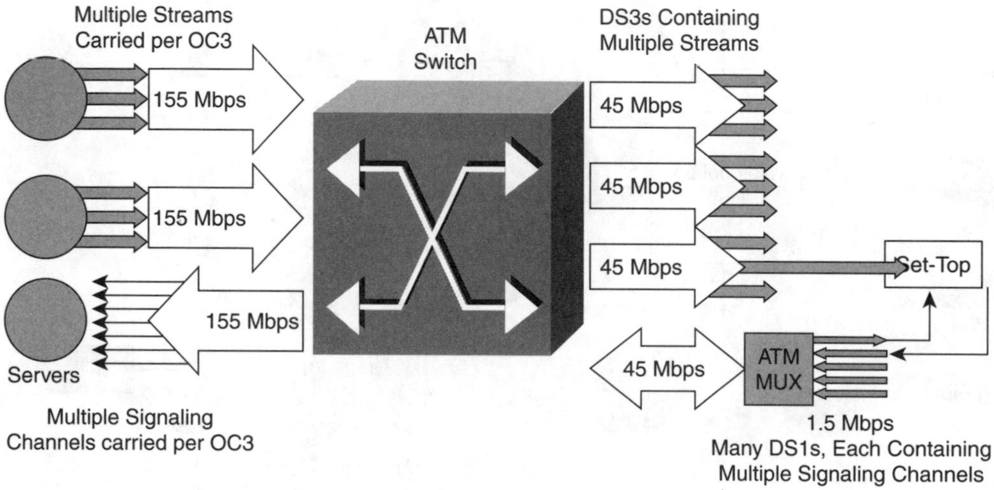

For a video-on-demand stream, an end-to-end connection is established from the server to the set-top with the following characteristics:

- The connection provides a Constant Bit Rate (CBR) service at the rate required by the compressed MPEG-1 stream; in the FSN, full-motion video events were coded at 6 Mbps and movies were coded at 4 Mbps.
- The connection flows over a 155 Mbps OC3 link from the server to the ATM switch, followed by a 45 Mbps DS3 link from the switch to the set-top.
- The connection is unidirectional; almost all the traffic flow in the network flows from the server to the set-top, so the network is constructed with one-way OC3 and DS3 links. This is unusual because OC3 and DS3 links are designed for bidirectional operation in standard telecommunication applications.

Telecommunications equipment, which is designed for symmetrical traffic flows, is inefficient for video-on-demand applications. Each OC3 link is actually bidirectional at the physical layer to provide for SONET performance measurement and alarming functions, but, because traffic flow is unidirectional, only 50% of the link capacity is used. The ATM switch is constructed for symmetrical traffic and only 50% of its total capacity is used. Each DS3 link is unidirectional (alarm monitoring functions are disabled).

The ATM switch used by the FSN is an AT&T Globeview 2000 switch with a maximum capacity of 20 Gbps, but the total traffic capacity to the distribution networks is only 6.8 Gbps. A relatively small amount of capacity (about 600 Mbps) is used for control and signaling traffic, which *is* bidirectional. Overall, the maximum switch utilization is about 37%.

Figure 11-3 shows how control and signaling traffic uses the traffic aggregation and switching functions of the ATM network. The set-top requires relatively little signaling bandwidth and a 1.5 Mbps DS1 link is used. The DS1 link is formatted to carry ATM cells and is shared by about 24 set-tops. From each set-top to the server, an ATM connection is established for return signaling traffic with the following characteristics:

- The connection provides a constant bit rate (CBR) service at the signaling rate of 48 Kbps. A variable bit rate (VBR) service would be better for bursty signaling traffic, but the shared media access layer can support only fixed-rate TDMA access to the link (see Chapter 5, "Adding Digital Television Services to Cable Systems").
- The connection flows over a 1.5 Mbps DS1 link from the set-top to an ATM multiplexer, followed by a 45 Mbps DS3 link from the multiplexer to the switch, followed by a 155 Mbps OC3 link from the switch to the server.
- The connection is unidirectional because the DS1 links are unidirectional. The ATM multiplexer provides access to a DS1 link to the set-top to close the loop for timing and signal level adjustment.

MPEG Mapping into ATM

Figure 11-4 shows the various protocol layers that are required to deliver MPEG streams over an ATM infrastructure. It also shows how ATM is adapted for transmission over a broadband, analog cable system.

At the base of the protocol stack is the frequency-division multiplexing layer; in this layer, multiple carrier frequencies separate the broadband spectrum into a number of channels. In the FSN, there are three channel types:

- NTSC—Existing analog television channels are carried according to the analog frequency plan.
- QAM—Digital services are mapped into Quadrature Amplitude Modulator (QAM) channels. QAM channels provide a high-capacity bit pipe that can be used for data, video, or audio traffic.
- QPSK—Signaling and control traffic are mapped into a quaternary phase shift keying (QPSK) channel. QPSK channels provide a medium-capacity bit pipe that is more robust than QAM modulation.

Figure 11-4 *Communications Stack*

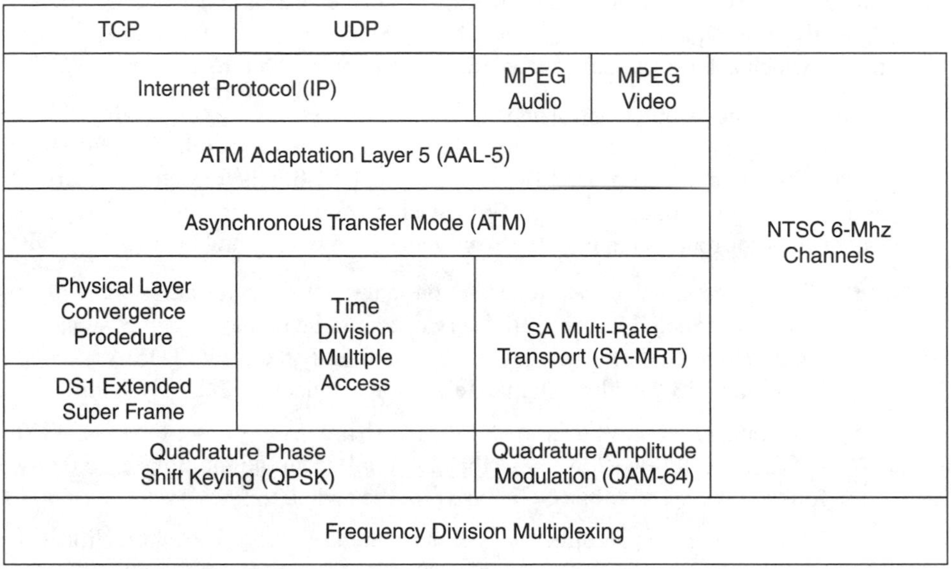

For the QAM channel to carry MPEG audio and video, an adaptation layer is required to provide error-correction and framing functions; in the FSN, this adaptation function is provided by SA-MRT (Scientific Atlanta multi-rate transport). SA-MRT packs ATM cells into a framing structure so that the set-top can recognize the individual cells in the QAM bit pipe (see the section Error Correction and Protection in Chapter 4, "Digital Technologies"). SA-MRT allows ATM cells to be reliably delivered from the server to the set-top, but another adaptation layer is required to map the MPEG streams into ATM cells.

In Figure 11-4, the ATM Adaptation Layer (AAL) is provided by AAL-5 (see Chapter 4 for more details). AAL-5 allows large blocks of MPEG data to be segmented into cells for delivery through the ATM network. When the cells arrive at the set-top, AAL-5 is used to reassemble the original block of data, which is decoded to provide audio or video.

IP data blocks are segmented, transmitted, and reassembled using AAL-5 to provide data delivery from the server to the set-top. The set-top can distinguish between audio, video, and data by the Virtual Channel Identifier (VCI) carried in the header of every ATM cell; thus, a set-top can simultaneously receive audio, video, and data streams over a single QAM channel without confusion.

MPEG Delivery from Server to Set-Top

The delivery of MPEG video and audio streams in the FSN implementation had to be carefully controlled to ensure that the customer saw a smooth, high-quality video with correctly synchronized audio (Figure 11-5 shows how this is achieved):

Figure 11-5 *MPEG Delivery from Server to Set-Top*

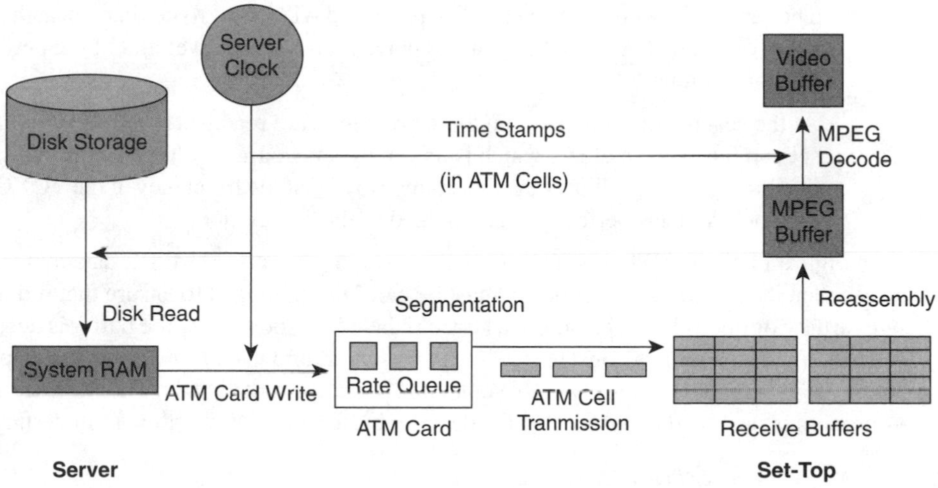

- The MPEG data is stored on a disk storage subsystem (called a *vault*). The MPEG data is fetched from the disk in large blocks to optimize access to the disks and is double-buffered so that the next disk read completes before the current block is exhausted.
- The MPEG data is written to the ATM output card. The ATM output card segments the MPEG data into cells for transmission over the network using the AAL-5 adaptation protocol. The card includes a rate queue designed to transmit the stream of ATM cells at a constant rate. If the cells are sent too fast, the set-top drops cells and video quality suffers.
- The set-top filters the ATM cells based on their VCI and selects only those cells for the chosen video flow. It receives those ATM cells and reassembles them into the original MPEG data blocks using the AAL-5 adaptation protocol.
- The MPEG data blocks are sent to the MPEG decoder, which reconstructs the original video signal.

Video signals are extremely time-sensitive, and the delivery of the MPEG data must happen at exactly the same rate as MPEG decoding. In analog video delivery, the horizontal and vertical synchronization pulses synchronize the television display to the transmitter; but there is no such mechanism in ATM networks because they use multiple, asynchronous physical links. This problem is solved in ATM by the transmission of timestamps from a master clock at the server:

- The server clock ensures that the disk reads and ATM card writes happen at the correct time to ensure that the MPEG data is played out of the server and of the network at the correct rate.
- At the set-top, timestamps from the server clock are received at regular intervals. The set-top has its own clock, which is driven by an accurate voltage controlled crystal oscillator (VCXO). It uses the timestamps to adjust the frequency of the VCXO so that its clock remains perfectly synchronized to the server clock.

In Figure 11-6, the MPEG buffer is designed to hold compressed MPEG data for the MPEG decoder. The fullness of this buffer must be carefully managed to ensure that it does not overflow or underflow. The unbroken trace (labeled A) shows how the buffer is designed to work: Data arrives at a constant rate from the server, and each time a frame is displayed, the MPEG decoder reads a variable amount of data from the buffer. The MPEG encoding process is designed to ensure that the decoder buffer will not overflow or underflow.

Figure 11-6 *MPEG Decoder Buffer Management*

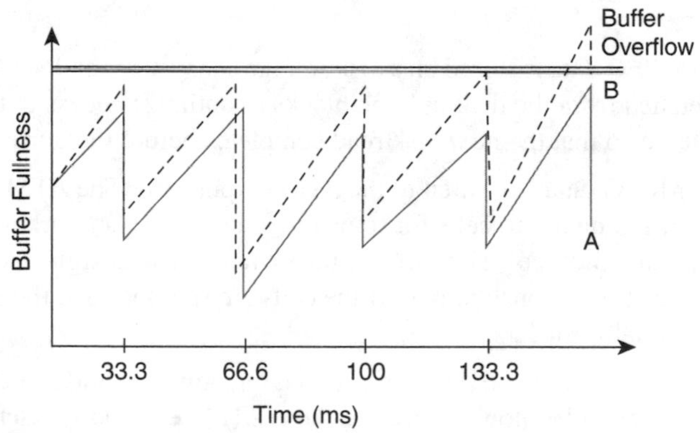

The dashed trace (labeled B) illustrates the effect of the incoming data rate being slightly high. The buffer slowly fills up and overflows—the effect is exaggerated in the diagram, but over several hours the rate has to be extremely accurate to prevent this effect. Over shorter time intervals, more rate variance can be tolerated, but only if it averages zero over the longer term. If the display rate at the set-top is not exactly the same as the effective rate delivered by the server, the same effect (buffer overflow or underflow) occurs.

Lessons Learned

The Full Service Network provided some valuable lessons that are useful in on-demand service development:

- Simultaneous peak usage—The FSN was built to operate at a maximum peak usage of 25%. After accounting for navigation demands (which required *two* open streaming media sessions per set-top in the FSN), a more reasonable design goal is 10% peak usage.
- Required automation—In a deployable, large-scale VOD system, many tasks (for example, provisioning of new assets) must be automated to reduce operational costs.
- Fault tolerance—A VOD system must continue to operate during single component failures. Customers will become frustrated if an on-demand service is unreliable or unavailable.

FSN Summary

The FSN demonstrated the successful use of ATM to deliver interactive multimedia all the way to the home over hybrid fiber coax networks. ATM provides a single transport and switching protocol for video, audio, and data, but the flexibility of ATM is expensive:

- The basic overhead of ATM (mainly associated with the 5-byte ATM header) is about 12%. For unidirectional services (for example, video-on-demand), only half the capacity of current ATM equipment can be used, because it is designed for bidirectional operation.
- There is additional cost for ATM adaptation at the headend and in every set-top.
- Digital broadcast services are all based on the MPEG-2 transport protocol; this means that either the set-top must support both ATM and MPEG-2 transport protocols or, alternatively, every digital broadcast service must be adapted to ATM at the headend.

For these reasons, MPEG-2 transport is a better alternative than ATM for *integrated* delivery of digital broadcast and on-demand services.

Pegasus Phase 2.0

Pegasus Phase 2 adds on-demand services to the broadcast services of Pegasus Phase 1 (see Chapter 7, "Digital Broadcast Case Studies") and the interactive services of Phase 1.1 (see Chapter 9). The challenge in Pegasus Phase 2 is to add on-demand services to make best use of the infrastructure that is already in place. The existing infrastructure includes the following facilities:

- A broadband network with available channel capacity for on-demand services
- A real-time, two-way control and signaling network provided by the DAVIC OOB protocol

- A set-top with built-in MPEG-2 transport, MPEG-2 video decoding, and AC-3 audio decoding functions
- A multimedia operating system with support for interactive applications and the manipulation of video and audio streams
- An EPG that allows application sharing and application hand-off for additional services
- A digital conditional access system

Pegasus Phase 2 has a different focus from the FSN; the existing facilities dictate many of the technology choices for on-demand services. For example, the FSN set-top was capable of terminating ATM virtual channels, but this function was omitted in the Pegasus set-top (after much soul-searching) to reduce cost. The Pegasus set-top expects MPEG-2 transport streams and this dictates that the network send broadcast *and* on-demand services in MPEG-2 transport stream format.

FSN Learning Experience

Pegasus Phase 2 owes much to the FSN learning experience and differs from the FSN in a number of key architectural areas. Each change solves one set of technical issues but also creates new challenges:

- Server location—In the FSN, the servers are located at the distribution hub, whereas the Pegasus architecture allows servers to be placed at the headend or distribution hub.
- Transport protocol—The FSN uses ATM as a switching and transport protocol, but ATM is replaced by MPEG-2 transport in Pegasus. MPEG-2 transport provides significant advantages, including the integration of broadcast and on-demand services into a single format and reduction in set-top cost. However, MPEG-2 transport assumes a constant delay network because it was designed for broadcast applications (see Chapter 4).
- Switching matrix—The FSN uses ATM to provide the switching function between the media server and the distribution network. ATM switching is very inefficient for unidirectional traffic and Pegasus replaces it with a distributed MPEG-2 transport switch. Nevertheless, there are limitations to this approach, including the maximum capacity of the matrix and its flexibility.

This chapter focuses on solutions to each of these challenges.

On-Demand Services

Figure 11-7 provides an overview of the Pegasus Phase 2 architecture. Pegasus Phase 2 reuses many components from the Phase 1 architecture and adds two new components for the support of on-demand services.

Figure 11-7 *Pegasus Phase 2 Architecture*

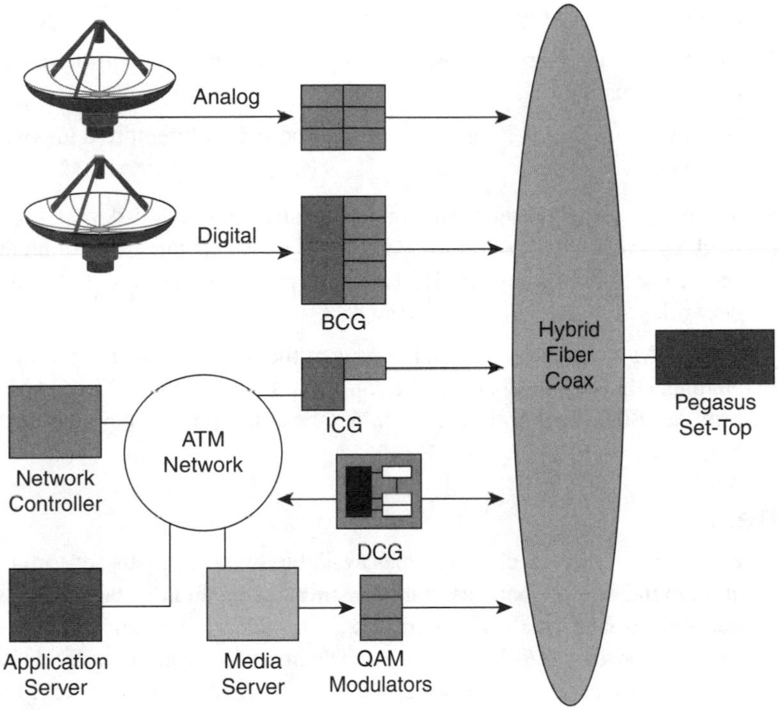

The following Phase 1 components are reused:

- The network controller provides provisioning, management, and conditional access support for on-demand services. A software module called the *interactive control suite* is added to provide additional services for on-demand services, notably creation of on-demand sessions over the network.
- The application server provides a platform for the server-side part of on-demand client/server applications. Multiple application servers may be used to provide load sharing or to support different on-demand or interactive services.

- The ATM network connects headend components, including the media server, and provides connection to a wide area network. The ATM network is used to provision on-demand assets (see Chapter 10).
- The interactive cable gateway (ICG) provides support for the broadcast carousel channels, which are used to deliver software applications code and data to the set-top.
- The data channel gateway (DCG) provides two-way, real-time control and signaling support to the set-top.
- The hybrid fiber coax distribution network is reused to add on-demand channels to the existing broadcast channels.

In addition to these Phase 1 components, the Phase 2 architecture adds two new components:

- The media server provides support for the streaming of on-demand services. Multiple media servers are used to provide scaling, load sharing, and redundancy. The media server uses the existing ATM network for provisioning of assets over a wide-area network.
- The QAM modulators are used to convert the output of the media servers into 6 MHz channels that can be distributed through the HFC network. The QAM modulator also provides digital encryption support for the conditional access system.

New Channels

Figure 11-8 illustrates the channel types available to the Pegasus set-top. Pegasus Phase 2 adds on-demand digital channels to the existing analog and digital broadcast channels and broadcast carousel channels. In contrast to the broadcast channels, which are shared by all customers, the on-demand channels provide dedicated services to individual customers. For example, a customer that purchases a video-on-demand event is allocated a dedicated stream from the media server that is carried in one of the on-demand channels. Sufficient on-demand channel capacity must be allocated to each group of customers so that the video-on-demand service is always available. How much on-demand capacity is required? And how many customers can share a bank of on-demand channels?

Figure 11-8 *Pegasus Channel Types*

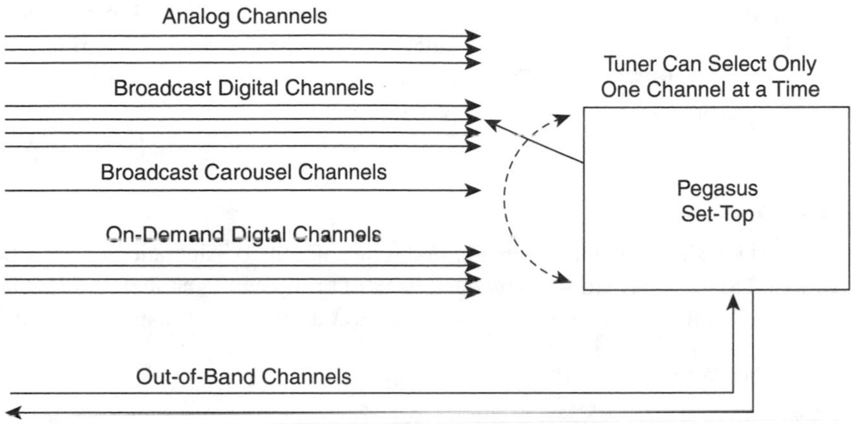

The answer to these questions is based on the existing broadcast architecture of the HFC network (see Chapter 2, "Analog Cable Technologies"). In Time Warner Cable's upgraded systems, a single DFB laser at the distribution hub feeds approximately 2,000 homes passed. On average, about 60% of homes passed receive cable service, a total of 1,200 customers. Assuming that 50% of customers would like to sign up for on-demand services, up to 600 on-demand customers are fed from a single laser. Therefore, 600 is the *least* number of customers that can share a bank of on-demand channels. (More customers can easily be arranged by aggregating two or more lasers into a single customer group.)

How much on-demand capacity is required to support 600 customers? The answer depends on how much capacity is required by each customer and how many customers simultaneously request the on-demand service. Assuming that the peak-utilization is 10%, up to 60 on-demand streams are required. For standard definition material, a single on-demand channel can carry about 10 streams; therefore, a minimum of 6 on-demand channels are required per 600 customers. (Note: this math is linear and is easily calculated at various bit rates, modulation schemes, and channel allocations.)

Server Location

There are a number of advantages to locating the server at the headend; server operations and maintenance can be centralized and the statistics of load sharing are improved. This is particularly important if the customer demand is unevenly distributed across the system. In early deployment of on-demand services, it might be difficult to justify the cost of a server at a distribution hub with few customers, whereas serving all the customers from a single headend location can be viable even at low service penetrations.

Nevertheless, there are significant advantages to locating the server at the hub as service penetration grows. If a cable system has 100,000 *on-demand* customers, a headend server would require 1,000 on-demand channels from the headend to the distribution hubs (a payload of almost 40 Gbps!). Therefore, it becomes more cost-effective to locate the servers at the hubs at some level of service penetration.

Fiber Transport

Figure 11-9 shows how Pegasus Phase 2 transports the on-demand channels from the headend to the distribution hubs. Each bank of on-demand channels is modulated and combined at the headend before being sent over a fiber to the distribution hub.

Figure 11-9 *Pegasus Phase 2 Implementation*

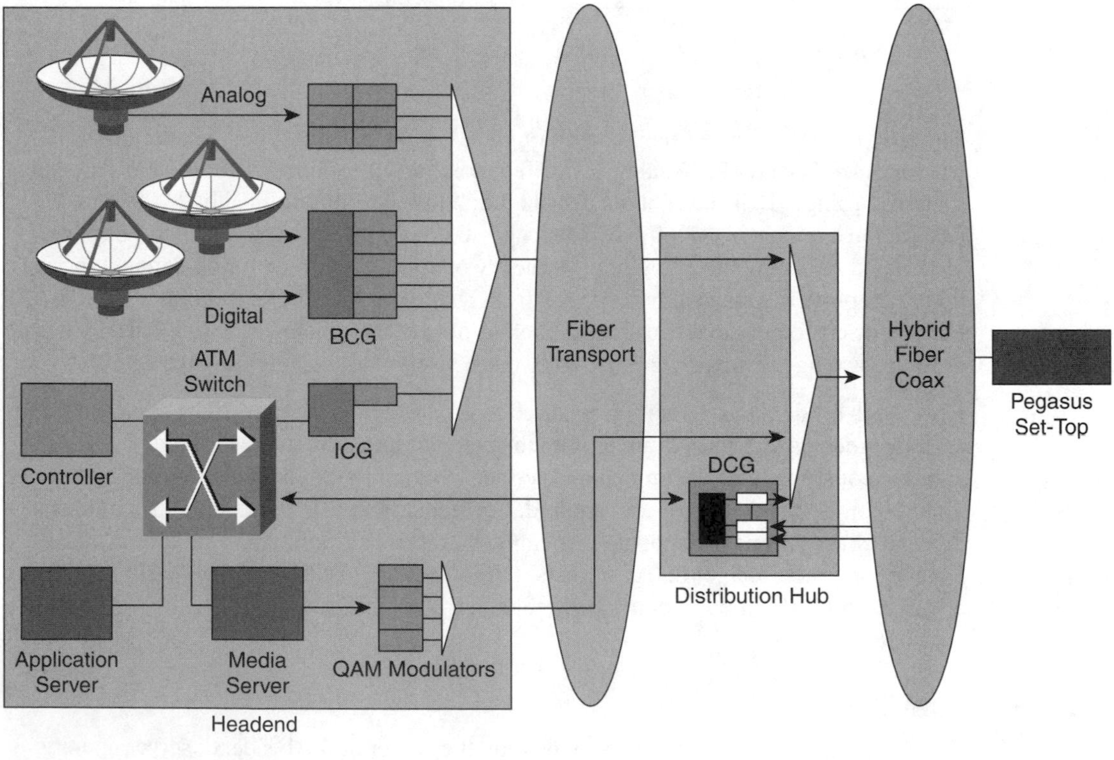

In a system with 100,000 subscribers, 167 banks (each containing six on-demand channels) are required. This solution also requires 167 fibers—far too many in practice. However, there are a number of strategies to reduce the fiber count and reduce cost:

- If the number of on-demand channels in each bank is increased, the number of fibers and lasers at the headend can be reduced proportionately. However, there is only a certain amount of available spectrum for on-demand services; in a 750 MHz system they might be placed between 700 and 750 MHz above all the broadcast frequencies.
- If the full spectrum of the fiber link to the distribution hub could be used—from 50 to 750 MHz—many more on-demand channels could be over a single laser. However, the on-demand channels would require block conversion at the distribution hub to place them in the correct frequency band before being combined with the broadcast channels.
- DFB lasers are now available with different optical wavelengths (or colors). By combining eight or more wavelengths onto a single fiber, the fiber count can be dramatically reduced in most cases to one fiber per distribution hub. This approach is called wavelength division multiplexing (WDM).

The most promising solution appears to be WDM of the on-demand channels onto a single fiber.

Transport Protocol

The Pegasus set-top is designed to work with MPEG-2 transport streams and this dictates the transport protocol selection for the on-demand channels. In fact, this is the ideal choice for video-on-demand for the following reasons:

- The efficiency of MPEG-2 transport is superior to other transport protocols, such as ATM and IP.
- MPEG-2 transport includes support for synchronization, statistical multiplexing, and conditional access functions.

Nevertheless, on-demand services might include high-speed data transport as well as video and audio services. Fortunately, the designers of MPEG-2 transport included support for mapping arbitrary data into MPEG-2 private sections. In addition, the DSM-CC specification includes an efficient segmentation function for mapping large data packets into a series of MPEG-2 transport packets (see Chapter 6, "The Digital Set-Top Converter").

In summary, the choice of MPEG-2 transport streams is both efficient and flexible.

Switching Matrix

MPEG-2 transport was not designed as a wide-area network protocol. It does not include any connection management protocols or any connectionless routing mechanisms. Although MPEG-2 transport is ideal for broadcast applications, it has limited applications in switched networks.

Nevertheless, an MPEG-2 transport switch can be constructed as shown in Figure 11-10. Each media server is connected to a row of QAM modulators using the DVB asynchronous serial interface (ASI) described in Chapter 6. This interface operates at a maximum payload rate of 216 Mbps and can saturate more than 5 256-QAM channels. Moreover, it is a native MPEG-2 transport interface and no protocol translation is required to meet the set-top requirements.

Figure 11-10 *QAM Switching Matrix*

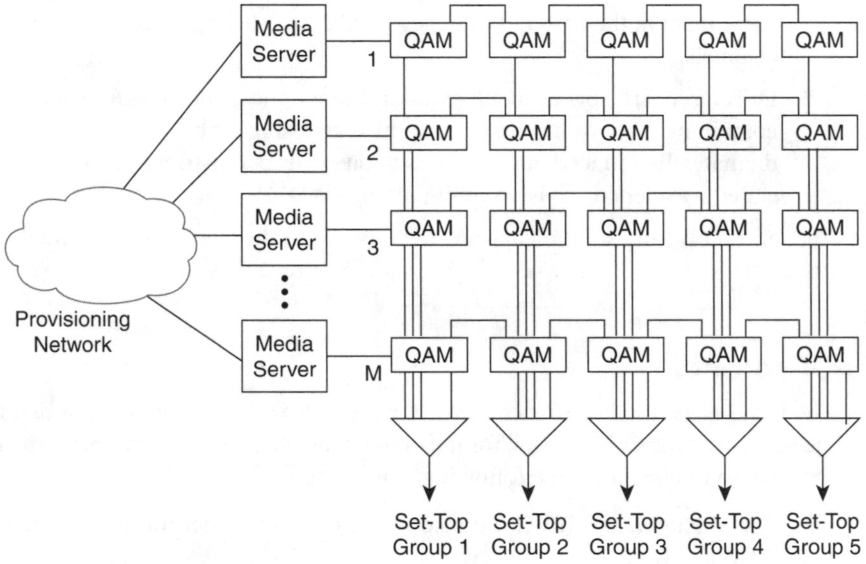

Each set-top group shares a bank of on-demand channels, which contains M (between 6 and 8) QAM channels. A different media server feeds each on-demand channel in the bank to provide load balancing and redundancy. This arrangement provides the following advantages:

- If a media server fails, the on-demand capacity of any bank of on-demand channels is reduced by only one channel. Customers connected to a media server that fails will lose service but can recover by reordering the event and will be allocated to a different media server.
- Load sharing across media servers can be easily accomplished by choosing the least busy on-demand channel in the bank.
- On-demand channel selection can be used to connect a set-top to a server based on the requested asset, avoiding the need to replicate assets across all media servers.

The QAM matrix provides only limited switching because the dimensions of the switch matrix is determined by M, the number of on-demand channels in a bank, multiplied by N, the number of QAM modulators per media server, multiplied by the number of streams in an on-demand channel. In the Pegasus Phase 2 implementation, each QAM matrix supports approximately 320 streams, or 3,200 customers.

In addition, a connection manager must be implemented to support the QAM matrix. The connection manager algorithm is relatively simple; when an on-demand request is received by the network, the connection manager determines the best route according to media server and QAM loading.

Pegasus Phase 2 Summary

Pegasus Phase 2 is one of the first applications of MPEG-2 transport to deliver interactive multimedia over a switched network. MPEG-2 transport provides an integrated transport solution for broadcast and on-demand services, and provides the following advantages:

- The overhead of MPEG-2 transport is extremely low (approximately 2%), and it is designed for unidirectional services (for example, video-on-demand).
- The MPEG-2 set-top is capable of broadcast and on-demand services.
- MPEG-2 supports data as well as video and audio encapsulation using the private data section mapping.

For these reasons, MPEG-2 Transport provides an ideal solution for *integrated* delivery of digital broadcast and on-demand services.

Summary

This chapter has provided a brief overview of two on-demand systems:

- FSN—The Full Service Network used an ATM to the home network to provide a wide range of interactive and on-demand services, including video-on-demand. It provided a valuable research tool into customer behavior and the operational challenges of on-demand services. The network architecture was not very efficient, mainly because of the asymmetric traffic pattern generated by on-demand services.
- Pegasus—The Pegasus program adds incremental on-demand services to an existing broadcast digital network that supports real-time, two-way signaling. Significant transport cost reductions are made by using native MPEG-2 transport from media server to set-top and by using the network as a distributed switching matrix.

References

Standards

ISO-IEC 13818-6 DSM-CC.

Internet Resources

Pegasus requirements

http://timewarner.com/rfp

PART III

OpenCable

CHAPTER 12

Why OpenCable?

The old model of cable television, in which each cable system is an island of proprietary technology, is changing rapidly due to competition from Direct Broadcast from Satellite (DBS), recent government regulation, digital television, silicon integration, and the Internet. The Federal Communications Commission (FCC) regulations now provide for retail availability of the set-top (or *navigation device*) with the goal of reducing the cost to the customer by facilitating free-market competition. In a digital world, effective standards are required to provide compatibility between the cable system and consumer electronic devices. Silicon integration continues to produce cost-performance breakthroughs, particularly in set-top components, such as microprocessors and memory. Finally, the Internet is an interactive model that has shown explosive growth, and much of the same networking technology can be applied to enhance television services.

OpenCable is an initiative led by Cable Television Laboratories (CableLabs) on behalf of the cable operators. OpenCable seeks to set a common set of requirements for set-top equipment so that new suppliers from the consumer electronics and computer industries can start to build equipment for connection to cable systems.

The genesis of OpenCable is due to a number of factors:

- A sense that the advanced technology being developed by the consumer electronics and computer industries is not being made available by traditional cable suppliers
- The rapid growth of DBS competitors that have used digital technology to leapfrog the cable industry
- The observation that while other industries have thrived through interoperable standards, the cable industry has stayed relatively closed and proprietary in its approach to new technologies

These factors led to the standards-based approach of OpenCable. OpenCable specifies an architecture based on standards where they are already in place. Where no applicable standards exist, OpenCable will develop such standards that are necessary and pass them into the appropriate industry-approved standards organizations for adoption. (An example is the specification for a point-of-deployment module interface, initially proposed by OpenCable as document OCI-C2 and subsequently developed and adopted as the DVS 131 standard by the SCTE Digital Video Subcommittee. DVS 131 is discussed in detail in Chapter 18, "OCI-C2: The Security Interface.")

In addition, OpenCable defines functional requirements for equipment that connects to the cable system (see Chapter 14, "OpenCable Device Functional Requirements").

Goals of OpenCable

OpenCable was first conceived as a way to encourage new suppliers from the consumer electronics and computer industries to build products for the cable industry. However, the goals were soon expanded as a result of the FCC's Report and Order (R&O) in the proceeding implementing Section 304 of the Telecommunications Act of 1996. Section 304 called upon the FCC to adopt rules to ensure the commercial availability of navigation devices, while not jeopardizing the signal security of the cable operator.

The following summarizes the expanded goals of OpenCable:

- Encourage entry of new suppliers into the cable industry, particularly for set-tops.
- Support the introduction of new services, particularly those based on the convergence of the computing and entertainment industries.
- Support retail availability of set-tops.

New Suppliers

The entry of new suppliers, particularly for digital set-tops is intended to promote competition and to provide enhanced features at lower cost. Previous efforts by individual cable operators to broaden the supplier base failed, mainly because the cable marketplace is small and highly segmented. To address this, OpenCable started to work on a set of purchase requirements for an OpenCable set-top that were consistent across the cable industry (made possible by digital standards and the natural discontinuity due to introduction of new technology). The consistent purchase requirements are intended to make the entire North American cable industry a single, unified market with sufficient volume to generate interest from large consumer electronics and computer equipment vendors.

New Services

The cable industry experiences considerable difficulty in bringing new services to market, particularly those services that rely on Internet and computer technology. This has caused considerable frustration with those traditional cable suppliers that have been slow to adopt any technologies they did not invent themselves.

Retail Availability

The OpenCable initiative was already addressing many of the issues of separable security to enable the entry of new suppliers and services, and it was natural to use the OpenCable approach to propose a solution that could be used to satisfy the FCC's Report and Order in the proceeding addressing the retail availability of navigation devices.

Market Forces

The OpenCable initiative is a response to a number of competitive market forces and technical factors. The market forces include competition from direct broadcast satellite services, digital terrestrial broadcasting, and the Internet. DBS services provide an example of successful partnering between satellite operators and consumer electronics companies where the customer base has grown rapidly using retail distribution channels (in some cases, the satellite receiver is integrated into the television receiver). Digital terrestrial broadcast looks to the same model. The Internet has grown exponentially and follows the retail model because it relies on the customers' purchase of a personal computer. All these services plan rapid deployment of new services based on retail sales where new equipment features are used to generate increased sales and to enable new services.

Competition

Competition is a positive force for any industry as long as there is no fundamental or overwhelming advantage of one player over another. In a rapidly evolving digital world, the cable industry seems to have missed out on many technological breakthroughs that have been used very effectively by competing industries. In particular, the digital satellite broadcasting (DBS) companies have made significant inroads into cable's core video distribution business by the use of standard definition MPEG-2 compression. The broadcasters are swiftly following DBS and have persuaded congress to allocate a second channel so they can transition to high definition and multiple standard definition digital services. The Internet has generated explosive growth and is starting to look hungrily at the video distribution business as its next killer application, which it calls *streaming media* (see the Internet section in Chapter 10, "On-Demand Services").

Although the cable industry is holding up well in face of this competition it has been slow to upgrade its technology for these new battlefronts. (Chapter 1, "Why Digital Television?" details the advantages of digital television technology over analog technology.) To compete effectively, the cable industry needs to recruit new suppliers that are skilled in the art of these new technologies—not just digital television but also the latest computing and networking techniques.

DBS

DBS is, without doubt, the biggest competitive problem for the cable industry. DBS has been very effective in marketing digital television to differentiate its service from cable. The cable industry has responded by promising digital cable services but has been relatively slow to deliver on this promise. Currently, cable companies have a significant advantage over DBS in providing local channels, and this has been one of the biggest weaknesses of satellite-delivered television. The DBS industry continues to lobby for permission to retransmit local channels, and it is probably only a matter of time before they are successful. At the time of writing, bills have passed in both the Senate and the House and await a conference between the two.

The DBS companies have successfully allied themselves with the consumer electronics manufacturers and retailers—most satellite receivers are built by consumer electronics giants such as RCA and Sony, and are distributed by all major consumer electronics retailers. This strategy has generated several generations of satellite receivers while the cable industry has struggled to built its first-generation digital set-top.

Cable still has a fundamental advantage over DBS—its ability to deliver interactive and on-demand services by using real-time, two-way communications over the cable plant. However, the supplier of these services must be competent in advanced networking and computing disciplines, areas where existing cable suppliers are weak.

Digital Terrestrial Broadcasting

Digital terrestrial broadcasting is still in its infancy but promises to emerge as another competitive threat to cable. Digital compression allows the terrestrial broadcaster to transmit a single high-definition signal or four to five standard definition signals. The error correction techniques used by VSB-8 modulation can deliver a perfect picture when the customer is within the footprint of the transmitter, so snowy pictures will no longer force the customer to subscribe to cable (although there are still some significant problems due to multipath interference in cities). By transmitting four to five standard definition signals during certain times of the day, a typical market with six affiliates and independent television stations will provide 30 channels.

The broadcasters are aligned with the consumer electronics manufacturers and retailers to provide additional services to customers in exchange for generating new television sales. New services include built-in interactive program guides that use digital program guide information, which is transmitted as part of the MPEG-2 transport stream, and *datacasting* services, which use spare transport stream capacity to broadcast data. Datacasting services may include enhanced television and informational services.

Internet

The Internet has emerged as a powerhouse of rapidly developing services and has grown explosively since the introduction of the World Wide Web. Many of the services that were demonstrated by the Time Warner Full Service Network (see Chapter 9, "Interactive Cable System Case Studies") have arrived in lower-bandwidth, browser-based incarnations over the Internet. In particular, the Internet is supporting many thriving electronic commerce applications, such as electronic trading (led by E-Schwab) and electronic retailing (for example, Amazon.com).

The Internet is also starting to be viewed as an entertainment service by many subscribers. The development of streaming media protocols that can distribute audio and video over the Internet provides a threat to cable's core business (see the Internet section in Chapter 10).

Many of the services offered by the Internet can be provided as part of an interactive or on-demand television service provided by the cable operator. However, development has been slow compared with that of the Internet and the cable industry now has to play catch-up.

Technology

There are two main areas of technology where the cable industry is in danger of falling behind the competition: silicon integration and software. Silicon integration allows very complex functions to be placed on a chip and allows dramatic cost reduction, but the cost of developing integrated circuits is high and cannot be justified unless millions of units can be sold. Software technology is developing rapidly and requires more processor performance and memory space as it becomes more sophisticated.

Government Regulation

During the 1990s, the cable television industry has been subject to regulation from two acts of Congress, the 1992 Cable Act and the 1996 Telecommunications Act. The FCC is often the agency charged with interpreting and implementing the the applicable portion of these Acts into regulations. The FCC, created by the 1934 Communications Act, describes itself as "An independent government agency with a mission to encourage competition in all communications markets and to protect the public interest" (see the section Internet Resources at the end of the chapter).

When developing regulation, the FCC often will open a proceeding on the various aspects. This usually begins with a Notice of Proposed Rulemaking (NPRM) to solicit comments and reply comments from all affected parties. At the conclusion of this process, a Report and Order is issued that specifies the rules that must be adhered to. These rules are then incorporated into the Code of Federal Regulations (CFR). In some cases, affected parties petition for changes in the rules.

1992 Cable Act

Section 17 of the 1992 Cable Act, based on a bill first introduced the previous year by Senator Leahy (D-Vermont), was intended to promote compatibility between cable systems and consumer electronics devices. In particular, the so-called "Leahy amendments" were addressed:

- To allow unattended recording of multiple cable channels using the timer features provided by VCRs

- To allow simultaneous viewing and recording of different channels (known as *watch-and-record*)
- To allow the use of Picture In Picture (PIP) features provided by television receivers

The 1992 Cable Act directed the FCC to consider the cost and benefits to the consumer in their proceeding, but also to allow the cable operators to protect against signal theft. The FCC was given considerable authority over cable operators to permit or restrict scrambling of cable channels. The FCC was also directed to promote the commercial availability of set-top converters and remote controls, and to give the customer a bypass option to allow direct connection of televisions and VCRs to the cable system. In comparison, the FCC has considerably less authority over the consumer electronics industry; the FCC is allowed to specify only the technical requirements for a cable ready or cable-compatible receiver.

1994 FCC Report and Order

After going through the usual process of issuing a notice of proposed rule making, the FCC issued a Report and Order on May 4, 1994. The Report and Order does not allow scrambling basic channels and mandates a bypass option, but the cable industry was able to persuade the FCC that retail availability of de-scrambling equipment would cause increased signal theft, so that idea was abandoned. However, the option of a decoder interface, to allow retail equipment to use an external de-scrambler, was recommended as a longer-term measure. To address the Leahy requirements, the cable operators were told to make set-tops with multiple tuners and de-scramblers available. (In most cases, this is achieved in practice by connecting two set-tops with an umbilical link and modifying the set-top software to make them behave as a single, watch-and-record, set-top—see the section Data Port in Chapter 3, "The Analog Set-Top Converter.")

The FCC postponed the issue of digital compatibility of set-tops to a later order (see the July 1998 Report and Order). However, it did state the opinion that digital standards and methods should be used to avoid future compatibility problems.

1996 Telecommunications Act

The 1996 Telecommunications Act includes two sections that relate to compatibility between cable systems and consumer electronic devices: Section 301, known as the Eschoo Amendment, and Section 304 which addresses "Competitive Availability of Navigation Devices."

Section 301 reduces the scope of the cable compatibility requirements in the 1992 Cable Act, limiting action to "a minimum degree of common design and operation, leaving all features, functions, protocols and other product and service options for selection through open competition in the market." In other words, the FCC is not allowed to specify or choose particular standards for cable compatibility but must leave development of these to those industries involved. In practice, a joint approach between cable operators and consumer electronics manufacturers is required to develop these standards, and any such standards that are developed are voluntary (see the section Standards in Chapter 13, "OpenCable Architectural Model").

Section 304 introduces new FCC language for a cable set-top, describing it as a *navigation device*, presumably because it performs the task of navigating from one service to another. Another new term is *multichannel video programming distributor* (MVPD), which is used to describe all providers of video services, including cable and satellite operators. The main purpose of Section 304 is to make navigation devices available at retail. However, to promote competition, the act states that they must be available from manufacturers and retailers that are not affiliated with the MVPD (that is, the cable operator). In addition, the security of service should not be compromised by any FCC regulations.

1998 Report and Order on Competitive Availability of Navigation Devices

On June 24, 1998, the Commission released its Report and Order in this proceeding implementing Section 304 of the Telecommunications Act of 1996. Section 304 calls upon the Commission to adopt rules to ensure the commercial availability of navigation devices, while not jeopardizing the signal security of an affected MVPD. As part of that R&O, the Commission determined that one means of implementing these twin goals was to separate security (that is, conditional access) functions from nonsecurity functions and to require that only the nonsecurity functions be made commercially available in equipment provided by entities unaffiliated with the MVPD. The security functions would reside in a separate security module to be obtained from the MVPD.

In its decision, the Commission repeatedly referenced the ongoing effort of CableLabs to develop specifications for both a digital security module and a digital security module interface. That OpenCable effort is focused on digital set-top converters and cable ready digital televisions. After such specifications are developed and the interface is adopted as an industry standard, manufacturers can produce digital navigation devices with the standardized digital security module interface and make such equipment available at retail. Cable operators would then supply a compatible digital security module to the customer.

In the course of the navigation devices proceeding, the Commission requested from the cable industry a schedule of milestones by which the FCC could monitor CableLabs' progress in meeting the OpenCable forecast of September 2000 for having digital security modules available for cable operators. The schedule submitted to the Commission included milestones for the development of specifications for the digital security module and the digital security module interface. It also included a post-specification time-line for development and production of the digital security module.

The Commission adopted a more aggressive schedule than CableLabs and ordered that digital security modules be available to cable operators by July (not September) 2000.

Nevertheless, in the R&O, it also included (without change) the industry-provided schedule of interim milestones.

To "assure itself that the schedule was being met," the Commission ordered that eight multiple system operators (MSOs) involved in the OpenCable project, whose statements concerning their commitments to that project were included in the record of the proceeding, file semi-annual progress reports with the Commission. The Commission established filing dates of January 7, 1999, July 7, 1999, January 7, 2000, and July 7, 2000, for the MSOs to detail "the progress of their efforts and the efforts of CableLabs to assure the commercial availability to consumers [of navigation devices]."

Providers of DBS and open video services (OVS) are exempt from these provisions; in other words, they are directed specifically at cable operators. Moreover, only security functions used to provide conditional access to video services are included and the rules do not apply to Internet security functions such as privacy, encryption, and authentication.

Digital Carriage

Digital carriage regulation, so called *digital must-carry*, is as yet undecided. The FCC issued a wide-ranging notice of proposed rule-making on the carriage of digital broadcast television signals by cable television systems on July 9, 1998. The FCC tentatively concluded that it has "broad authority" under the Cable Act and the Balanced Budget Act of 1997 to define the scope of a cable operator's signal carriage of digital television signals during the transition period from analog to digital broadcasting.

The FCC has identified seven distinct options for dealing with the carriage of digital television signals during transition:

- No digital must-carry—In this case, it will be left to the broadcasters to work out retransmission agreements with the cable companies without government regulation.
- Deferral—Digital must-carry would be deferred until a specific date.
- Equipment penetration—Digital must-carry requirements would be triggered by a specific penetration of digital receivers (or digital-to-analog converters), for example, 10%.
- Either/or—A broadcaster could choose must-carry for either its analog or digital channel, but not for both.
- Phase in—A cable system's required addition of digital television channels would be limited to a specified number per year.
- System upgrade—Only higher-channel capacity (for example, 750 MHz) systems would be forced to carry digital television signals.
- Immediate carriage—Must-carry regulations would be enforced immediately.

In the meantime, digital retransmission agreements are being hammered out between the broadcasters and cable operators.

Emergency Alert Systems

The primary purpose of the emergency alert system (EAS) is to provide emergency communications from the President during times of national emergency; thankfully, the EAS system has never been used for this purpose. In practice, the EAS is used to notify customers of state and local emergencies (which is a voluntary service provided by the cable operator).

The FCC adopted new EAS rules on September 29, 1997. These rules incorporated an agreement between cable operators and the National Association of the Deaf. The rules vary according to the size of the cable system:

- Cable systems with 10,000 customers or more must implement full audio and video override on all channels by December 31, 1998.
- Cable systems with between 5,000 and 10,000 customers must implement full audio and video override on all channels by October 1, 2002.
- Cable systems with fewer than 5,000 customers must implement full audio override on all channels with video override on a minimum of one channel by October 1, 2002.

Retail Issues

The cable industry has been reluctant to support a retail model. As a result, premium cable services are generally available only through a proprietary set-top converter (see Chapter 3 and Chapter 6, "The Digital Set-Top Converter"), which is leased to the customer. Nevertheless, the cable industry relies heavily on analog cable ready televisions to deliver basic cable to more than half of all cable customers. As the television industry moves toward a more digital world, the cable industry has to decide whether to provide every customer with a digital set-top at enormous capital expense or to embrace the development of a digital standard for the attachment of retail devices to the cable system. This choice is very difficult to make because

- The cable industry is concerned about its ability to manage cable services going forward. Management of the customer relationship—in particular, the user interface—is critical to the cable operators.
- In the past, cable operators have made the investment in new technology and taken on the cost of deployment to drive new services with associated revenues. CE manufacturers might be less likely to incorporate new features without a proven service. How will cable operators influence feature definition in retail devices?

- The current suppliers to the cable industry have a vested interest in perpetuating proprietary systems to protect their market share. Does the cable operator have sufficient leverage with its current suppliers to force them to build to open standards? Can current suppliers anticipate the move to open standards and shift their business model to take advantage of the new environment?
- The potential for increased signal theft makes the cable operator understandably concerned about standardizing the interface to the cable system.

The following sections examine these concerns in more detail.

Cable Service Management

Cable operators have considerable influence over the features of a set-top converter that they purchase and subsequently lease to the customer. In particular, the user interface is precisely specified by the cable operator to ensure that it is as user friendly as possible and does not have a negative impact on the operation of the cable system. For example, one vendor initially designed a digital set-top to display an error screen containing a telephone number if a problem occurred when ordering an IPPV event. The cable operator asked the vendor to remove the telephone number, dryly remarking: "We have spent years trying to reduce our call volume and this error screen would double it overnight!"

Typically, a cable operator deploys only a single model of set-top (in a given market) to ensure the user interface is consistent across all customers; this also simplifies the job of the customer service representative in answering customer queries. Even minor differences in the user interface can result in operational costs from increased call volume to lost revenue.

The introduction of retail devices might lead to a proliferation of different user interfaces because vendors see the user interface as a way of differentiating their products. A cable customer will naturally call the cable customer service representative (and not the retailer or manufacturer) with any questions about operation of the device on the cable system.

The issues of look and feel are not limited to operational impacts; the navigation and presentation of services are an integral part of the cable service. For example, a retail device could change the display order of channels, make certain channels more accessible and others difficult to find. These concerns are usually answered by the old chestnut: "The market will decide." However, cable operators naturally fear a bumpy ride while the market is making up its mind!

New Services

Although the introduction of new cable channels into the cable industry has been rapid and innovative, introduction of advanced services has been slow. In the case of a new cable channel, there are few technical challenges—adding a new channel requires satellite distribution to the headend and spectrum on the cable system. An advanced service is a much more difficult proposition; new types of equipment might be added to the cable system, new channel types might be defined, and the functions of the set-top might be extended. Of these, functional changes to the set-top are the most difficult for the cable operator. Most set-tops are analog (see Chapter 3) and are hard-wired for a fixed set of functions. Although many efforts have been made to extend the functions of advanced analog set-tops by software download, the memory size and processor performance limitations make this very difficult. Even in those cable systems that have deployed digital set-tops, most set-tops are almost as limited in their functions when they end up in the customer's home.

Chapter 8, "Interactive Services," and Chapter 10 describe the architectural models for advanced services on cable systems. It should be clear from these chapters that, although they often require additional set-top features, these types of services also require additional hardware and software components in the cable system itself. The following is current engineering practice:

- The cable operator specifies the new service, including any new system and set-top features that are required.
- The cable operator subcontracts design, implementation, integration, and testing of an end-to-end system from a single vendor.

In the retail model, the set-top is no longer built as part of an integrated system. The interface to the set-top must be specified precisely and frozen, so that it can be designed, built, and tested independently. How can new services be offered in a retail environment with these limitations?

Existing Suppliers

There is considerable resistance from existing cable suppliers to the migration to retail set-tops, which is hardly surprising because they face considerable erosion of their market share. An analogy is the development of the NTSC color standard; within a fairly short time, nearly all American television suppliers were wiped out by imports. The dominant suppliers of set-tops to the cable industry are General Instrument, with about 60% market share, and Scientific Atlanta, with about 30%. Both GI and SA are much smaller than the consumer electronics giants such as Sony, Toshiba, and Panasonic and fear that they will not be able to compete with them. (Sony owns 5% of GI.)

The existing suppliers to the cable industry have developed highly integrated cable systems that feature a headend controller that is tightly coupled to the set-top converter. The controller development cost is often subsidized by set-top sales, and the cable operator typically pays only a small fraction of its true cost. The interfaces between the controller and the set-top are highly proprietary, and it is questionable whether they are even fully documented in some cases. In particular, the conditional access system is kept a closely guarded secret in an attempt to combat signal theft.

The business relationships between the suppliers and the operators are often symbiotic, and many senior executives have moved from supplier companies to operator companies. Cable suppliers have an intimate understanding of the operator's requirements gleaned through many years of working closely together. The suppliers provide a full-service, turnkey solution to the operator, including new feature development, on-site maintenance and support, and even funding. In some cases, the operator has considerable equity ownership in the supplier, and stock warrants have been used as an inducement to sell set-tops. In short, the customer-supplier relationship in the cable industry is a complicated web of intricate business deals that might be hard to unravel. (See *The Billionaire Shell Game* by L. J. Davis.)

Signal Theft

Theft of service was estimated to have cost the cable industry $6 billion in 1997, and cable piracy has become big-business with multimillion-dollar companies pitting their wits against the cable and satellite operators (see Web resources on piracy). Nationally, 11.5% of homes passed do not pay for basic services and 9.23% do not pay for premium services. As a result, an Anti-Theft Cable Task Force has been created and has conducted focus groups to better understand the customers' attitude to signal theft. (See the article, "Task Force Outlines Stats, Initiative," by Thomas Umstead in *MultiChannel News*.) The focus group results indicated that

- Most cable consumers are not concerned about the problem and don't believe that cable operators are either.
- There is little visible enforcement of legal penalties against perpetrators.
- Cable employees are the most accessible source of *free* cable.
- Signal theft is a *victimless crime*.

In this environment, the cable operator is in a continuous struggle to control signal theft and is usually only one step ahead of the pirates. To protect revenues from premium services, cable operators rely on the conditional access system, which grants selective access to those services in exchange for payment from the customer (see Chapters 3 and 6). If the conditional access system is compromised, the cable supplier changes the conditional access to defeat the pirate set-tops while maintaining service to paying customers. (A standard conditional access system would be hacked and rendered useless in weeks, if not days.) There is justified concern that the deployment of retail set-tops might compromise the ability of the cable operator to introduce remedies in the case of a breach to the conditional access system.

OpenCable Solutions

Solutions to all the issues described in the previous section do not yet exist. Nevertheless, the OpenCable initiative has made considerable progress in a number of areas, notably the separation of security functions and the cable network interface. Other areas, such as the development of a portable software environment, are still under study.

Chapter 13 describes the OpenCable architecture in detail, and the remaining chapters of this book describe and discuss each of the OpenCable interfaces. It is helpful to look at some of the OpenCable initiatives in more general terms to show how they are intended to address the issues raised in this chapter.

The OpenCable initiative addresses these issues in a number of ways:

- OpenCable provides the cable industry with a process that makes it possible to address these issues in a concerted and industrywide manner.
- OpenCable specifies an architectural framework to enable new technologies to be structured into the existing cable systems and allow evolution to future cable systems.
- OpenCable also specifies set-top and system specifications that communicate the cable industry requirements to new and existing suppliers.
- OpenCable provides a blueprint for retail availability of navigation devices.

The following sections discuss each of these facets of OpenCable in more detail and serves as a preamble to Part III, "OpenCable."

The OpenCable Process

The OpenCable process is based on the following guiding principles:

- Embrace open standards—Accurate and complete standards are very important in a digital world, because a digital system cannot tolerate slight imperfections in the same way as an analog system. A digital system generally has only two major operational states: *working perfectly* and *not working at all*. Chapter 13 discusses the standards organizations that are most relevant to cable systems.
- Include installed systems—The currently deployed cable systems represent the *existing practice* of the cable industry. (An equally used, but less popular, term is *legacy systems.*) The OpenCable process is designed to support existing practice and allow gradual migration toward fully OpenCable-compliant systems.
- Seek input from all quarters—There are many interested parties in the OpenCable process, including the FCC, cable operators, equipment suppliers, retailers and broadcasters, and the customer. The OpenCable process is designed to allow each of these interested parties to have their say by issuing a series of document drafts and providing for review periods according to a published schedule.

- Develop and maintain a specification—The OpenCable specification is broken into a number of parts and actually forms a hierarchy of documents. The major specifications include the OpenCable device functional requirements and specifications for the major interfaces defined by the OpenCable architecture.
- Submit to standards bodies—When the OpenCable interface specification is complete, the specifications are submitted to the public standards process. (See Chapter 13 for more details.)
- Test interoperability—An important part of the OpenCable process is to test and verify interoperability of different implementations to the common set of specifications. The complexity and ambiguity inherent in specification documents often leads to slightly different implementations that are not interoperable. Interoperability testing allows any bugs to be discovered and resolved in a controlled laboratory environment and prevents them from reaching the real world.
- Certify compliance—Finally, after successful interoperability testing has been completed, products are certified as being OpenCable-compliant.

The OpenCable Architecture

The OpenCable architecture is based on the existing practice of modern cable systems:

- Hybrid fiber coax is recommended for systems that adopt the OpenCable architecture, because this can be used to support additional services such as video-on-demand. Nevertheless, the OpenCable architecture is applicable to any cable system that can support digital carriage.
- The OpenCable architecture is designed to take advantage of real-time, two-way capabilities of cable systems if they exist.
- In September 1997, the two largest suppliers of digital set-tops (General Instrument and Scientific Atlanta) agreed to cooperate on the use of a set of common digital transmission formats. The Harmony agreement specifies the modulation, encryption, system information, and transport protocols used across the network interface. OpenCable specifies these formats as OCI-N, the network interface (see Chapter 16, "OCI-N: The Network Interface").
- The OpenCable architecture does not specify any microprocessor and operating system (OS) choice.
- The OpenCable architecture is intended to provide a flexible software platform to support new services (based on new software applications). This part of the architecture is still under study and is described in Chapter 14.
- The OpenCable architecture is designed to be extensible to allow evolution. New techniques and initiatives will be layered onto the baseline OpenCable specifications over time.

The OpenCable Specifications

The OpenCable process generates a set of specifications that are published and submitted into the standards process if appropriate. The current suite of specifications envisioned by OpenCable includes

- Specifications for a family of set-tops, or *OpenCable devices*—The baseline specification is described in Chapter 14.
- OpenCable Interface Specifications for the headend, network, and consumer interface—These interface specifications are fundamental to OpenCable and are known as the OCI series specifications. The three headend interfaces defined (OCI-H1, OCI-H2, and OCI-H3) are described in Chapter 15, "OpenCable Headend Interfaces." The network interface (OCI-N) is described in Chapter 16. The interface to consumer electronics equipment (OCI-C1) is described in Chapter 17, "OCI C-1: The Consumer Interface," and the security interface (OCI-C2) is described in Chapter 18.
- Future OpenCable interfaces might be defined to allow further evolution.

Retail Availability

OpenCable represents the cable industry's chosen strategy to address FCC regulations as a result of the 1996 Telecommunications Act and the subsequent Report and Order in 1998. These include the following issues:

- Retail strategy—OpenCable is the strategy to enable the development of competitive devices for sale at retail for connection to the cable system.
- OpenCable provides solutions for digital and high definition connection of the set-top to the display device. This is the purpose of the OCI-C1 specification (see Chapter 17).
- Portability across cable systems—To support retail availability of devices, the issue of portability must be solved. In other words, it must be possible for customers to move from one cable system to another and still be able to use the retail devices that they have purchased for connection to the cable system. Portability is addressed by the OCI-N and OCI-C2 specifications.
- Point-of-deployment (POD) module specification—The POD module provides replaceable security functions in a small format PCMCIA module. The POD module is specified and purchased by the cable operator and is leased to the customer to provide access to encrypted services. The POD module is described in Chapter 18.

Summary

This chapter discussed the cable industry's reasons for initiating the OpenCable process, which are summarized in Table 12-1.

Table 12-1 *Issues and OpenCable's Response*

Issue	Description	OpenCable Response
Competition	Competition is growing from DBS, Terrestrial Digital Broadcast, and the Internet.	Publish baseline specifications to promote new services on cable.
Consumer compatibility	Digital television requires new interfaces.	OCI-C1 specification.
Retail availability	The 1998 Report and Order mandates "Competitive Availability of Navigation Devices."	OCI-N specifies network interface. OCI-C2 specifies separable security.
Digital cable ready	FCC has mandated the development of a cable ready digital television.	OCI-N specifies network interface. OCI-C2 specifies security module interface.
New suppliers	New suppliers find entry difficult because of the proprietary nature of cable systems.	Publish baseline specifications for an OpenCable device.
New services	Introduction of new services has been slow.	Define new services and adopt industry protocol specifications.
New technology	Introduction of new technology has been slow.	Encourage new suppliers skilled in these technologies to enter the cable industry through the RFP process.
Service management	Cable operators might lose their ability to manage the user interface and the look-and-feel of retail devices.	Educate new suppliers through OpenCable process whether they supply to the cable operator or directly to the customer. Foster business relationships between cable operators and CE manufacturers.
Digital carriage	Regulations are unclear, but digital carriage is expected for the cable industry.	Not specifically addressed by OpenCable.
Signal theft	Cable industry loses $6 billion per year to signal theft.	Specification of POD replaceable digital security that remains the property of the cable operator.

References

Books

Abe, George. *Residential Broadband.* Indianapolis, IN: Cisco Press, 1997.

Ciciora, Walter, James Farmer, and David Large. *Modern Cable Television Technology; Video, Voice, and Data Communications.* San Francisco, CA: Morgan Kaufmann Publishers, Inc., 1999.

Davis, L. J. *The Billionaire Shell Game.* Doubleday, 1998.

Periodicals

Umstead, Thomas. "Task Force Outlines Stats, Initiative." *MultiChannel News*, October 1998.

Internet Resources

Federal Communications Commission Web site

http://www.fcc.gov

OpenCable Web site

http://www.opencable.com

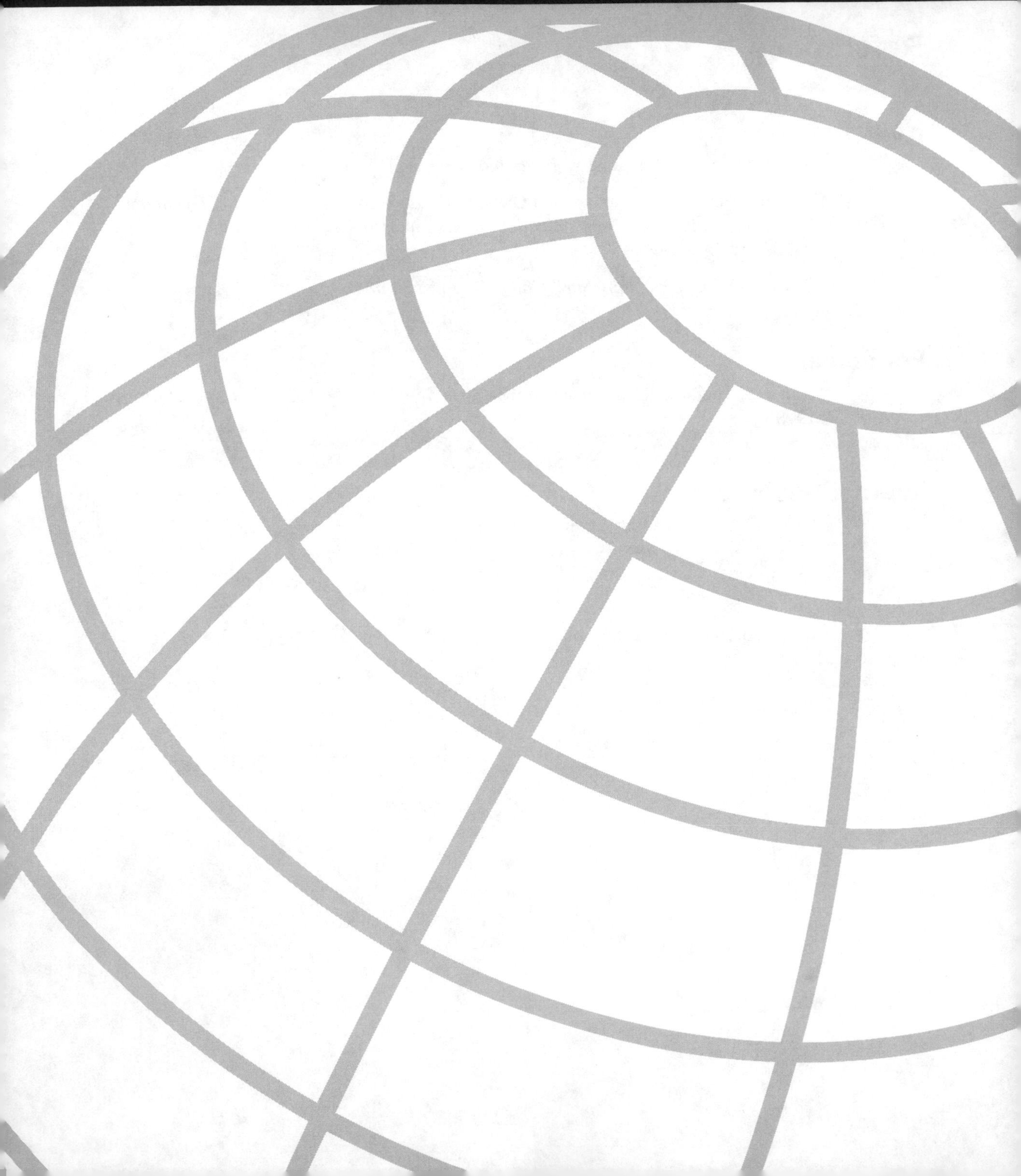

CHAPTER 13

OpenCable Architectural Model

The OpenCable initiative is designed to provide solutions to many of the following issues, which were described in Chapter 12, "Why OpenCable?":

- Competition in the marketplace is growing due to the emergence of new players, including DBS, terrestrial broadcasters, and the Internet. Competition is healthy for the cable industry, but cable can compete effectively over the long term only if it can harness digital technology.
- The cable industry represents a fragmented marketplace to new suppliers looking at the potential of supplying digital technology because of the proliferation of proprietary interfaces and the lack of generally accepted standards. This tends to block entry of new suppliers.
- New services are becoming more and more software-intensive, and it is critical that the cable industry develop a software application strategy to support introduction of new services.
- The recent acts of Congress have mandated the competitive availability of navigation devices, but the consumer electronics manufacturers need specifications to enable them to build navigation devices that will work when connected to cable systems.

To address these issues, OpenCable defines an architectural model, an approach that is often used in the standards development process. A reference diagram serves to define the major interfaces in a cable system and to identify a set of defined interfaces between system components (the network interface, the point at which the cable system arrives at the customer's home, is the most important). In addition, OpenCable defines a set of baseline functional requirements for any device that attaches to the cable at the network interface. A device that meets the baseline functional requirements is considered to be OpenCable-compliant.

The OpenCable specification addresses the issues listed at the beginning of this section:

- Competition—By specifying the reference diagram and interfaces, OpenCable provides a clear strategy for incorporating digital technology into cable systems.

- Marketplace fragmentation—Although there are many cable operators, there is considerable consensus within the cable industry about how digital technology should be applied within cable systems. OpenCable captures and formalizes this consensus so that new suppliers can build to it. This has the effect of unifying the marketplace and making it more attractive to new suppliers.
- Software application strategy—The OpenCable baseline functional requirements provide a platform specification that is capable of supporting downloaded software applications.
- Retail—OpenCable defines the network interface to the cable system and also defines the separation of security functions into a separate Point Of Deployment (POD) module. The OpenCable specifications have been presented to the FCC, and a process is in place to deliver the first POD modules by the FCC target date of July 2000.

In many ways, the OpenCable process has formalized initiatives, which were already in progress (and still continue), between some cable operators and the computer and consumer electronics industries. It is important to recognize that OpenCable is intended to promote innovation and, therefore, OpenCable does not completely specify how to build digital cable systems. Instead, OpenCable provides an architectural model that can be extended by implementers to provide considerable flexibility and promotes competition between suppliers on the basis of features and performance.

OpenCable History

The OpenCable history started with a series of high-level meetings between the cable and computer industries in April 1997. The computer industry executives expressed an interest in entering the cable marketplace, specifically in providing advanced set-top devices that would look more like network computers than consumer electronics products. The computer industry's pitch was very attractive: a hardware platform that could be supplied for close to the cost of its components, a software architecture that enabled rapid innovation, and development time-scales measured in *Internet years*—of which there are seven in a normal calendar year.

To investigate the potential of the computer industry's proposals, an Advanced Set-top Taskforce was formed under the auspices of CableLabs. The taskforce drew its members from the larger cable operators (Time Warner Cable, TCI, Cox, Comcast, and Rogers) and started work on a Request For Information (RFI) for an advanced set-top. The RFI, which was modeled on Time Warner Cable's Pegasus RFP for convenience as much as anything, was issued in September 1997. The RFI was deliberately very brief (11 pages) to not limit the imaginations of the respondents. The introduction outlined the goals as follows:

> The goal of the OpenCable specifications process is to explore the range of costs of the variety of products, ranging from *Digital Cable Ready TVs* and *VCRs* to *Digital Set-tops* to *Cable Ready Digital PC cards*, that may be connected to the cable system. Information is presented in this document in order to help define the

range of capabilities and applications that can be supported by digital set-top boxes. Further, the requirements contained in this document are intended to help us qualify the vendor authors for developing the OpenCable specifications.

(The functional requirements for the OpenCable device are described in Chapter 14, "OpenCable Device Functional Requirements.")

The last sentence of the introduction introduces the concept of *vendor authors*, which are a means to solicit help from the vendor community in the development of OpenCable specifications. Cable operators are notoriously understaffed in senior technical positions and often lack the necessary personnel to author specifications. As a result, cable operators have come to rely on their traditional suppliers for technical advice and it is natural to extend this model to the OpenCable process.

Twenty-three companies responded to the initial OpenCable RFI. Most of the responses were in the form of PowerPoint presentations and none were judged complete enough to provide a solution. The OpenCable process was established to provide more guidance to responding companies by developing a set of specifications. The 23 respondents to the initial OpenCable RFI were

- ACTV/Sarnoff
- Criterion Software
- General Instrument
- IBM (IP issues only)
- Intel Group—Cisco, Netscape, Network Computer Inc. (NCI) Oracle, Thomson CE
- Intel/NCI
- Lucent Technologies
- Microsoft
- Oracle/NCI/Netscape
- Panasonic
- Pioneer Digital
- Samsung
- Scientific-Atlanta
- Scientific-Atlanta Group—IBM, Pioneer Electronics, PowerTV, Sun, Toshiba
- SCM Microsystems
- Sony
- Texas Instruments
- Thomson CE/NCI

- Thomson Sun (OpenTV)
- Wink Communications
- Worldgate Communications
- Zenith Electronics

OpenCable Process

The OpenCable process is highly collaborative, allowing input from the cable operator and vendor communities throughout the development of OpenCable specifications and implementations. The OpenCable process is managed by the Advanced Platforms and Services organization, which is part of CableLabs. The OpenCable process is divided into two main parts:

- Specification development
- Interoperability

Specification Development

The specification development process is illustrated in Figure 13-1. Initial drafts of OpenCable documents are written by *member authors*, that is, by the technical staff of cable operators, which are members of CableLabs. Input from vendors is solicited at this stage either by an OpenCable RFI or by direct consultation with companies that have previously responded to an OpenCable RFI.

Figure 13-1 *Specification Development Process*

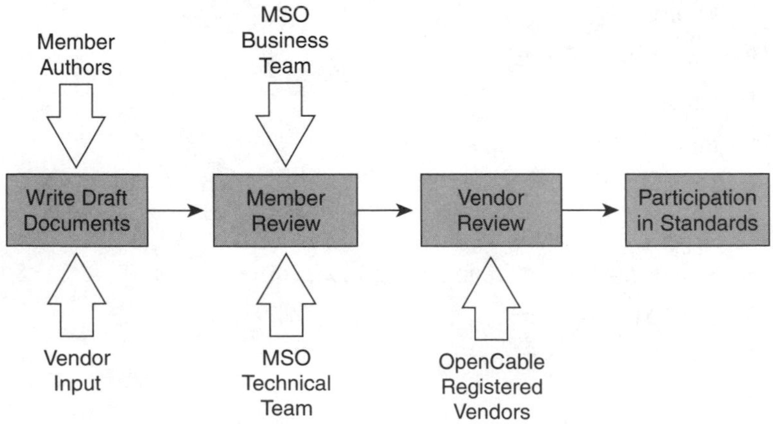

The next step is member review by the OpenCable Technical and Business teams. Technical and business staff of cable operators, which are members of CableLabs, make up these teams. This step is particularly important because it tends to drive consensus across the cable operators and allows compromises to be made that impact existing practices. A cable operator naturally fears the economic consequences of a migration to a standard that might cause operational changes and ultimately affect the bottom line. Discussions often center on the long-term benefits for the cable industry versus short-time pain for individual operators. Fortunately, most cable operators are just starting the process of introducing digital services into their cable systems and have some flexibility in their digital strategy.

The next step in the process is vendor review, which allows OpenCable registered vendors to submit comments of any specification. Any vendor is welcome to register with CableLabs; to date, several hundred vendors have completed the registration process.

The final step is to generate a standard for the specification. This is not a rubber-stamp process by any means, and a good example is the OCI-C2 specification (see Chapter 18, "OCI-C2: The Security Interface"), which was introduced to SCTE DVS as DVS-131. The DVS-131 document went through seven revision cycles before being approved as a U.S. cable standard. The standards forum requires considerable attention to the nuances of language and must consider input from all the participants regardless of which industry or faction they represent.

Interoperability

The interoperability testing process is illustrated in Figure 13-2. Reference implementations, as well as test beds, are used to demonstrate interoperability. These are developed by cooperation between the OpenCable technical team and the OpenCable vendors. To provide focus and visibility, interop events are scheduled; in the case of the OCI-C2 interface, the cable operators have committed to a schedule of interop events that were adopted as part of the FCC's Report and Order on the commercial availability of navigation devices (see Chapter 18 for more details).

Figure 13-2 *Interoperability Testing Process*

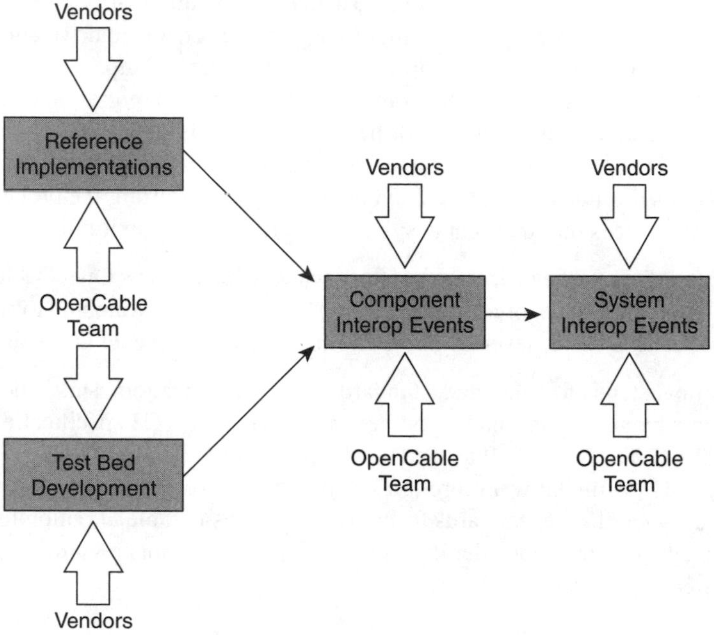

Interop events are divided into two stages that demonstrate component and system-level interoperability. The interop process is modeled on the DOCSIS cable modem incubator laboratory.

OpenCable Reference Diagram

Figure 13-3 shows the OpenCable reference diagram. The reference diagram describes the system at a very high level and deliberately hides much of the detail of a *real* cable system; for example, the cable delivery network is abstracted away completely. A cable system is reduced in the diagram to a small number of *black-box* components, and most of the complexity is hidden inside these components. An exception to this rule is the *OpenCable device*, which is modeled as a *gray box* to describe some of its internal mechanisms.

Figure 13-3 *OpenCable Reference Diagram*

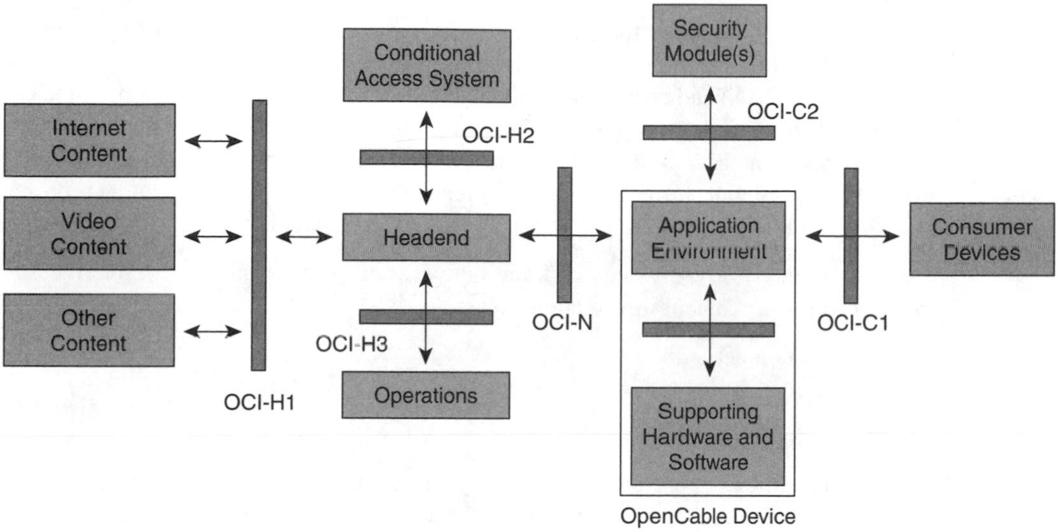

The importance of the OpenCable reference diagram is that it specifies a number of standard interfaces between the components of a cable system. By specifying these interfaces, it is possible to replace certain components with others without redesigning the entire system. The most important interfaces are the OCI-N, OCI-C1, and OCI-C2 interfaces because they allow substitution of a wide range of different products that satisfy the functional requirements of the OpenCable device.

Specified Interfaces

OpenCable defines three headend interfaces (OCI-H1, OCI-H2, and OCI-H3), a network interface (OCI-N), and two consumer interfaces (OCI-C1 and OCI-C2). Each of these interfaces is very broad in scope and each includes several different interface specifications that meet the information transfer requirements. For example, the OCI-C1 interface function can be performed by an analog or digital link between the OpenCable device and the consumer device. Therefore, each OpenCable interface is a family of interface specifications, which can be extended to include new members over time.

Each OC-series interface will be discussed in more detail in the following chapters:

- Chapter 15—OCI-H1, OCI-H2, and OCI-H2
- Chapter 16—OCI-N
- Chapter 17—OCI-C1
- Chapter 18—OCI-C2

OCI-H1 Interface

The information flow across the OCI-H1 interface in Figure 13-1 consists of *programming content*, which has three main sources. Internet content is generally received from a wide-area network (WAN) and represents a two-way flow of information, although, in the case of Web browsing, the flow is predominantly from the content provider to the customer. Video content is a one-way flow of information and arrives from a number of content providers over satellite, terrestrial, or wide-area networks. Finally, other content represents any other kind of information that arrives at the headend, which has yet to be defined.

The OCI-H1 interface is divided into three subtypes according to the content interfaces that are defined for the content information flows:

- Internet content
- Video content
- Other content

In many cases, the content flows transparently through the headend to the network; in other words, its appearance is not changed by the headend even though its physical format may be changed. For example, a QPSK signal received from satellite encrypted with DigiCipher II conditional access might be transcoded into a QAM signal encrypted with PowerKEY conditional access, but the customer is generally unaware of this fact when viewing the content. In the case of Internet content, the appearance of the content often depends on the software application at the OpenCable device; for example, a Web browser resizes and reformats content to fit the screen. Nevertheless, the headend acts as merely a relay point in the network established between the content provider and the customer.

In the case of on-demand services, the headend provides temporary storage of the content without changing its appearance. In the case of video-on-demand services, the entire movie title is provisioned on a server at the headend (see Chapter 10, "On-Demand Services") so it can be streamed out to the customer when requested. In the case of Internet services, it is becoming more common to cache Web pages on a server at the headend or hub.

In some cases, the content might be created by the cable operator, but this is really a case of vertical integration of the business, and the reference diagram in Figure 13-1 still represents the flow of content from the content provider to the customer over the network.

OCI-H2 Interface

The OCI-H2 interface provides for the separation of the conditional access function from the rest of the headend functions. This interface is the headend equivalent of the OCI-C2 interface. In both cases, the security function must remain as secure as possible and relies on shared secrets in the headend conditional access system (CAS) and the point-of-deployment (POD) security module. The definition of the OCI-H2 and OCI-C2 interfaces must provide for a number of contingencies:

- CAS upgrade—The conditional access system might require periodic upgrade, either to combat signal theft or to add new features.
- CAS replacement—The complete replacement of the conditional access system might be required under certain circumstances.

OCI-H3 Interface

The OCI-H3 interface provides operational and control flows between the headend components and the other systems that are required to operate the cable system, including billing systems, subscriber management systems, operational support systems, network management systems, and so on. These systems might be located in the headend or at a nearby business office, or they might be remote from the cable system. In any case, the interface requirements are similar, and include

- Subscriber management
- Event provisioning
- Purchase collection
- Network management

OCI-N Interface

NOTE The OCI-N interface is discussed in detail in Chapter 16, "OCI-N: The Network Interface."

In network design, the User-Network Interface (UNI) is often standardized to allow different kinds of equipment to attach to the network. The OpenCable UNI is designated as OCI-N. A standard OpenCable UNI is essential to support a family of OpenCable devices, where each family member can be built by multiple vendors to a set of open standards.

Unfortunately, in today's cable networks, the UNI is not uniform across all cable system providers; to use a telephone analogy, a telephone connected to one network would not work when connected to another network. The *existing practice* (or *legacy*) of deployed cable systems makes selection of an OCI-N standard difficult. Why are there so many variations in existing practice?

The telephone analogy is an oversimplification because a cable UNI is far more complicated than a telephone UNI. This complexity allows considerable implementation choice:

- The cable UNI is a broadband interface (whereas the telephone UNI is a narrowband interface). The frequency spectrum extends from about 5 MHz up to 870 MHz.

- The cable UNI is channelized into a large number of frequency bands (whereas a telephone UNI uses a single frequency band). This provides tremendous capacity and flexibility, but it also allows each cable operator to build differences into the UNI.
- Each channel defined across the cable UNI can be of a number of different types, and some services use multiple channel types (see Chapter 5, "Adding Digital Television Services to Cable Systems").
- The information content provided in the channel has an intrinsic value, and the cable operator generates revenue by charging for service rather than bandwidth. In contrast, most UNI definitions in the telecommunications and data communications provide a connection, where the tariff is dependent merely on the information capacity and endpoints of the communications link.

These factors have caused the cable UNI to evolve differently across different cable systems. Fortunately, there are also a number of forces that have provided some standardization across the UNI:

- The Joint Engineering Committee of the EIA and NCTA developed a standard frequency plan for cable, which is now an ANSI-approved standard EIA-542. (See *Modern Cable Television Technology; Video, Voice, and Data Communications* by Walter Ciciora and others, page 354.)
- The Joint Engineering Committee of the EIA and NCTA developed a standard RF interface for cable, EIA-23 to meet the FCC Part 76 regulations for cable (47 C.F.R. Part 76) and the FCC Part 15 regulations for television receiving devices (47 C.F.R. Part 76).
- CableLabs announced the Harmony agreement in October 1997. The Harmony agreement, reached between Scientific Atlanta and General Instrument at the prompting of the cable industry, formalized the acceptance of five open standards, including MPEG-2 video, Dolby Digital audio, MPEG-2 transport, ASTC system information, and ITU-J83 Annex B modulation.

OpenCable builds on these standards and agreements to provide a single UNI specification that is compatible across all cable systems. Although there are some differences to support variations in existing practice, these are accommodated by options to a baseline specification. For example, one of three different out-of-band signaling choices can be selected at the option of the cable operator.

OCI-C1 Interface

NOTE The OCI-C1 interface is discussed in detail in Chapter 17, "OCI-C1: The Consumer Interface."

The OCI-C1 interface connects the OpenCable device to any consumer electronics devices in the home, including a television, a VCR, and any external audio systems. As with the other interfaces, OCI-C1 is a family of analog and digital interfaces (as described in the section Set-Top Outputs in Chapter 6, "The Digital Set-Top Converter"), which are

- RF channel 3/4 output
- Baseband video
- Baseband audio
- Component video
- IEEE-1394
- S/PDIF digital audio

The OCI-C1 interface must support consumer electronics compatibility as defined by the 1992 Cable Act. In addition to standard definition television signals, cable requires a solution to high definition interconnect. For both standard and high definition interfaces, the OCI-C1 must support copy protection mechanisms designed to prevent illegal copying of the signal.

OCI-C2 Interface

NOTE The OCI-C2 interface is discussed in detail in Chapter 18.

The OCI-C2 interface provides the interface to a Point Of Deployment (POD) module for digital signals provided over the cable system. The POD module is a PCMCIA-format device supplied by the cable operator, which provides two important functions:

- Separation of security—The FCC Report and Order on the Retail Availability of Navigation Devices mandates the separation of security and navigation functions in a navigation device by July 2000. Moreover, cable operators will not be allowed to deploy set-tops with integrated security after January 1, 2005. The POD module is designed to satisfy the FCC requirements for separable security.
- Signaling support—The greatest variation in existing practice is in the choice of out-of-band signaling protocol. The POD module terminates the lower layers of the signaling protocol and adapts a navigation device to the signaling scheme for that cable system. The POD module supports signaling according to DVS 167 and DVS 178 (see Chapter 5).

A third aspect of the OCI-C2 interface is that it transfers programming content across a digital interface. In recognition of the concerns of the Motion Picture Association of America (MPAA), the OCI-C2 interface supports a copy protection technology designed to ensure that copyrighted material sent over this digital link is protected from illegal copying.

Specified Components

The OpenCable architecture specifies the functional requirements for two components, the OpenCable device and the POD module.

OpenCable Device

NOTE The functional requirements for the OpenCable device are discussed in detail in Chapter 18.

The OpenCable device performs all the functions of a hybrid analog/digital set-top converter (see Chapter 6). It terminates the OCI-N interface; it hosts the OCI-C2 interface; it provides tuning, demodulation, navigation, and decoding functions; and it supports outputs, as specified by the OCI-C1 interface. A set-top converter might perform the functions of an OpenCable device, or the functions might be incorporated into a television receiver or VCR, or even by a card designed to be inserted into a personal computer.

There is a wide range of possible OpenCable device designs that support different advanced features and services. For this reason, the OpenCable device functional requirements specify a set of *core requirements* that must be satisfied by all OpenCable devices. The core requirements specify an OpenCable device that approximates the functions of digital set-tops currently being deployed (that is, the General Instrument DCT-series set-tops and the Pegasus set-top—see Chapter 6).

OpenCable also specifies *extension requirements* for the OpenCable device, which are supplemental to the core requirements. These requirements specify a wide range of additional features and services that might be required by individual cable operators.

There are a number of important receiver performance requirements that *all* OpenCable devices must satisfy:

- Connection of an OpenCable device must not adversely affect the operation of the cable network.
- The OpenCable device must meet certain RF performance requirements according to EIA-23.
- In addition, the cable operator has a long list of performance parameters specified in the OpenCable device functional requirements.

POD Module

NOTE The Point Of Deployment (POD) module is discussed in detail in Chapter 18.

The Point Of Deployment (POD) module adapts a single device to any cable system. This is possible largely because of standardization of the OCI-N interface. However, there are a number of options built into the OCI-N interface to account for variations in the existing practice of different cable operators. The most significant of these are the out-of-band signaling protocol and the conditional access system.

Standards

OpenCable is committed to the use of open standards—that is, international standards (for example, ISO standards), North American standards (for example, standards approved by ANSI), or *de facto* industry standards. All standard interfaces must be in the public domain or must be freely available on payment of nominal licensing fees. OpenCable will avoid use of closed, proprietary systems.

OpenCable draws on many existing standards. Many standards are optional, so it is important for OpenCable to make the use of them mandatory. This provides vendors with explicit guidance on the appropriate set of standards used by the cable industry. By making these standards universal and mandatory across all cable systems, OpenCable promotes portability from one system to another.

Where no standards exist, OpenCable will develop appropriate standards by submitting the applicable specifications to standards bodies. In the case of the OCI-C1 and OCI-C2 interfaces, submissions have already been made to SCTE DVS and have resulted in approved SCTE standards.

Relevant Standards Bodies

There has been an explosion of activity in standards over the past decade, and the section Internet References, located at the end of this chapter, provides a partial list of Web sites of relevant standards bodies for digital television. The OpenCable process focuses on cable systems, so it is appropriate that the Society of Cable Telecommunications Engineers (SCTE) Digital Video Standards (DVS) subcommittee is the primary vehicle for standardization of OpenCable documents. In addition, the work of the Joint Engineering Committee (JEC), which is a group sponsored by the National Cable Television Association (NCTA) and the Consumer Manufacturers Association (CEMA), is also relevant to OpenCable. Finally, the Advanced Television Systems Committee (ATSC) is very active in the development of standards for television.

SCTE DVS

The SCTE mission statement includes the development of training, certification, and standards for the broadband industry. The SCTE was formed in 1969 to promote the sharing of operational and technical knowledge in cable television and broadband communications. Since that time, it has worked to promote technical awareness in the industry and to establish standards and practices. (See the NCTA paper "SCTE's Digital Video Subcommittee: Introduction and Update," by Paul J. Hearty.)

In August 1995, the SCTE was granted accreditation as a standards-setting body by ANSI (American National Standards Institute). On April 19, 1996, the SCTE established the Digital Video Subcommittee (DVS). The original mandate assigned to the DVS was

> to explore the need for SCTE involvement in the development of standards for digital video signal delivery…

In its inaugural meeting on June 9, 1996, the DVS affirmed the need for timely standards in a number of areas. To meet this need, the subcommittee established five *working groups*, each chaired by a cable operator, a programmer, or an employee of CableLabs. The working groups (WGs) are as follows:

- WG-1 Video and Audio
- WG-2 Data (Transport Applications)
- WG-3 Networks Architecture and Management
- WG-4 Transmission and Distribution
- WG-5 Security

The subcommittee meets approximately six times per year. The membership includes system operators, equipment manufacturers, programmers, and service providers. At last count, more than 50 companies and organizations are taking part in the work.

Each submission to SCTE DVS is assigned to one or more working groups according to the following work plan. To date, there have been approximately 200 submissions to SCTE DVS.

Working Group 1

- Video profiles and levels
- Video formats
- Audio specification
- MPEG-1 support
- Statistical multiplexing support
- Video user data (for example, VBI) applications

Working Group 2

- Base system information (SI)
- SI extensions for cable and satellite
- Program guide
- Subtitling methods
- Transport data services
- Program navigation requirements

Working Group 3

- Network/headend architectures and interfaces
- Functional requirements
- Emergency alerting requirements and methods
- Bit stream editing and commercial insertion—an *ad hoc* working group has been formed to consider Digital Program Insertion (DPI)

Working Group 4

- Cable modulation and forward error correction
- Out-of-band modulation (forward and reverse path)
- Satellite modulation and forward error correction
- Other media modulation

Working Group 5

- Core encryption
- Security interfaces

JEC

The Joint Engineering Committee is jointly sponsored by the National Cable Television Association (NCTA) and the Consumer Manufacturers Association (CEMA) and was formed in 1980. The JEC developed the EIA-542 Cable Television Identification Plan (frequency plan) and the EIA 105 Analog Decoder Interface Standard. The JEC has two subcommittees actively working on cable standards, which are

- National Renewable Security Standard (NRSS) subcommittee—NRSS developed two alternatives for a replaceable security module known as NRSS EIA 679 Part A and Part B. The EIA 679 Part B standard forms the basis for the OpenCable POD module.
- Digital Standards Sub-Committee (DSSC)—Until recently, this group was a working group (DSWG) but it became a subcommittee in early 1999. The DSSC has the mandate to consider requirements for a cable ready digital television.

ATSC

The Advanced Television Systems Committee (ATSC) was formed to establish voluntary technical standards for advanced television systems, including high definition television (HDTV). The ATSC is not ANSI-accredited but operates under ANSI procedures.

Summary

This chapter described the broad structure of the OpenCable architecture and the relevant standards bodies for OpenCable. Later chapters in this book describe specific details of OpenCable in more detail. This chapter described the following four major sections:

- History—The OpenCable initiative was started in 1997 with the creation of an Advanced Set-Top Taskforce. The initial 23 respondents have since grown to more than 300 vendors that are now involved in the OpenCable specification process.
- Process—The OpenCable process is a collaborative effort between CableLabs, cable operators, and vendors. The process generates a set of interface and device specifications, and includes a series of interoperability tests.
- Reference diagram—the OpenCable reference diagram defines a set of headend interfaces (OCI-H1, OCI-H2, and OCI-H3), the network interface (OCI-N), the consumer interface (OCI-C1), and the security module interface (OCI-C2). In addition, the OpenCable device (for example, a digital set-top, a cable ready digital television, or a cable ready personal computer) is defined. Specifications for OCI-N, OCI-C1, OCI-C2, and the OpenCable device have been released by OpenCable.
- Standards—The most relevant standards bodies to OpenCable are the SCTE Digital Video Standards subcommittee (DVS), the NCTA Joint Engineering Committee (JEC), and the Advanced Television Systems Committee (ATSC).

References

Books

Ciciora, Walter, James Farmer, and David Large. *Modern Cable Television Technology; Video, Voice, and Data Communications.* San Francisco, CA: Morgan Kaufmann Publishers, Inc., 1999.

Hearty, Paul J. "SCTE's Digital Video Subcommittee: Introduction and Update." *1997 NCTA Convention Technical papers.* NCTA, Washington, D.C.

Internet Resources

OpenCable Web site

http://www.opencable.com

CableLabs Web site

http://www.cablelabs.com

The International Organization for Standardization (ISO) is a worldwide federation of national standards bodies from 130 countries, one from each country. ISO is a nongovernmental organization that was established in 1947. The mission of ISO is to promote the development of standardization and related activities in the world with a view to facilitating the international exchange of goods and services and to developing cooperation in the spheres of intellectual, scientific, technological, and economic activity. ISO's work results in international agreements that are published as International Standards.

http://www.iso.ch/welcome.html

Founded in 1906, the International Electrotechnical Commission (IEC) is the world organization that prepares and publishes international standards for all electrical, electronic, and related technologies. The IEC was founded as a result of a resolution passed at the International Electrical Congress held in St. Louis (USA) in 1904. The membership consists of more than 50 participating countries, including all the world's major trading nations and a growing number of industrializing countries.

http://www.iec.ch/

The ITU, headquartered in Geneva, Switzerland, is an international organization, within which governments and the private sector coordinate global telecom networks and services.

http://www.itu.int/

The American National Standards Institute (ANSI) has served in its capacity as administrator and coordinator of the United States private sector voluntary standardization system for 80 years. Founded in 1918 by five engineering societies and three government agencies, the Institute remains a private, nonprofit membership organization supported by a diverse constituency of private and public sector organizations.

http://web.ansi.org/default.htm

SMPTE is the preeminent professional society for motion picture and television engineers, with approximately 10,000 members worldwide.

http://www.smpte.org/

European Digital Video Broadcasting Web site

http://www.dvb.org/

Dolby Web site of technical information on audio compression and related matters

http://www.dolby.com/tech/

The Advanced Television Systems Committee (ATSC) was formed to establish voluntary technical standards for advanced television systems, including digital high definition television (HDTV). The ATSC is supported by its members who are subject to certain qualification requirements.

http://www.atsc.org

The Advanced Television Technology Center is a private, nonprofit corporation organized by members of the television broadcasting and consumer electronics products industry to test and recommend hardware solutions for delivery and reception of the new U.S. terrestrial transmission system for digital television (DTV) service, including high definition television (HDTV).

http://www.attc.org/

CHAPTER 14

OpenCable Device Functional Requirements

The OpenCable device performs all the functions of a hybrid analog/digital set-top converter (see Chapter 6, "The Digital Set-Top Converter"). It terminates the network interface (OCI-N); hosts the POD module interface (OCI-C2); provides tuning, demodulation, navigation, and decoding functions; and supports the interface to the display device (OCI-C1). The functions of an OpenCable device might be built into a set-top converter, integrated into a television, or incorporated into a PC expansion card. When an OpenCable device is integrated into a television, it is called a cable ready digital television (CR-DTV). When the OpenCable functions are integrated into a PC, the result is a *cable ready personal computer (CRPC)*—a new term that is not yet clearly defined.

There is a wide range of possible OpenCable device designs that might support different advanced features and services. For this reason, the OpenCable technical team has concentrated on specifying the *core requirements* for an OpenCable set-top terminal that approximates the lowest common denominator functions of digital set-tops currently being deployed (that is, the General Instrument DCT-series set-tops, Scientific Atlanta Explorer-series set-tops, and Pioneer Voyager-series set-tops—see Chapter 6).

In addition, extended functional requirements for the OpenCable device have been discussed and specified, but it is more difficult to reach agreement on them. Naturally, vendors are free to innovate as to which extended features they include into more advanced OpenCable devices, and customers will make their decision to purchase based on their personal preferences. This is an excellent model to promote competitive availability at retail, but there are also some reasons for caution:

- The features and functions of an OpenCable device depend on the cable system, and cable networks will not universally support extended features in the foreseeable future. For example, a customer who buys an OpenCable device that provides video-on-demand functions will be able to use those functions only on cable systems that support video-on-demand.
- Portability from one cable system to another is not guaranteed for the same reason, and there is potential for customers to be stuck with a stranded investment if they move.

Nevertheless, these restrictions are also true today for DOCSIS cable modems purchased at retail. The important thing is to manage customers' expectations so that these limitations do not come as a surprise. Moreover, the OpenCable process is designed to support the existing leased model as well as a retail model.

Goals

The overall goals of the OpenCable specification process are clearly stated in the OpenCable Set-top Functional Requirements specifications [CableLabs]. It is worth discussing how these goals relate to the OpenCable device requirements in some detail because they are often more difficult to achieve in practice than in theory:

- Integrated service environment—The OpenCable device must provide consistent services to those provided by existing set-tops and all other types and models of OpenCable device when deployed, side by side, in the same cable system.
- Open and interoperable—The OpenCable device shall use *open* computing and network architectures, wherever possible, to reduce costs and incorporate new technologies as they are developed.
- Portability—The OpenCable device must be portable across OpenCable-compliant cable systems.
- Renewable security—The OpenCable device must support renewable security by means of the OCI-C2 interface.
- User interface—The OpenCable device must provide some means for displaying information relating to the navigation and access of services (video, Internet, and so on) that are offered by the cable operator.
- Scalable—The OpenCable device must continue to function (to its *original* specification) in cable systems during the migration to real-time, two-way systems providing interactive and on-demand services.
- Efficient application and network design—The OpenCable device must follow certain network behavior rules that are designed to ensure the efficient use of network resources.
- Operational compatibility—The OpenCable device must be compatible with existing operational, customer support, and billing systems.
- Backward compatibility—The OpenCable device must be backward-compatible and interoperable with the embedded base of existing set-top terminals.

Provide for Integrated Service Environments

This goal is designed to allow the cable operator to provide a broad range of services tailored to the cable system using a range of different OpenCable device models and existing set-tops. (This is a logical extension of the existing cable industry business model, where new services have been introduced using new set-tops; for example, advanced analog set-tops were introduced to provide EPG and IPPV functions.)

The tiered service model allows programming services to be packaged into groups of services according to marketing requirements. An integrated service environment preserves the cable operator's ability to tier services independently from the technology that is used to deliver them. For example, HBO is often delivered as an analog channel, but digital technology allows the cable operator to provide the multichannel HBO multiplex. The transition must be seamless from the customers' standpoint even though both packages are offered at the same time over the same cable system.

As interactive and on-demand services are offered, it is an important marketing requirement that they can be packaged alongside, or with, existing services. An integrated service environment allows the service to be separated from the technology used to deliver it and enables a smooth migration to enhanced television services over time.

Open and Interoperable

OpenCable is committed to the use of open standards—that is, international standards (for example, ISO standards), North American standards (for example, standards approved by ANSI), industry standards (for example, standards approved by SCTE), or *de facto* industry standards. All standard interfaces must be in the public domain or must be freely available on payment of nominal licensing fees. OpenCable avoids the use of closed, proprietary systems except where required to protect copyrighted material or preserve the presentation format.

The specification of the OCI-series interfaces draws on existing standards where possible (see Chapter 15, "OpenCable Headend Interfaces," through Chapter 18, "OCI-C2: The Security Interface"). In addition, the technologies used to build OpenCable devices must be available competitively to minimize costs. For example, the OpenCable specifications do not specify the use of a particular operating system, so each vendor can choose to purchase or build this technology.

Network interoperability of the OpenCable device is achieved through standard interface specifications of the OCI-N, OCI-C1, and OCI-C2 interfaces. To provide service interoperability is more challenging because it involves interoperability at the software applications layer. The Internet defines standards for text, graphics, and portable applications. Groups such as ATVEF, W3C, and DASE are using Internet standards to extend the existing content standards for broadcast digital television.

Portability

Although the 1996 Telecom Act and the subsequent FCC Report and Order on Navigation Devices did not require portability, portability is a requirement reflecting OpenCable's (and subsequently the cable industry's) commitment toward making retail successful. The OpenCable device requirements for interoperable standards at the OCI-N interface provides the basis for portability, but is not sufficient to achieve full portability. The reason is that there are fundamental differences between the specific set of interfaces used by different cable operators. The Harmony agreement (see Chapter 13, "OpenCable

Architectural Model") was designed to provide as much convergence as possible between digital systems provided by Scientific Atlanta and General Instrument, but there remain fundamental differences in security, out-of-band signaling mechanisms, and user interfaces.

OpenCable addresses this issue by allowing a *point-of-deployment* (POD) decision to accommodate these differences. The first two differences (security and out-of-band signaling) are hardware functions and are solved by a replaceable POD module, which is supplied by the cable operator (see Chapter 18). The third difference (user interface) can be solved by downloadable applications software but requires agreement on a common application environment for OpenCable devices.

Renewable Security

This goal supports the 1998 FCC Report and Order on Navigation Devices mandating the separation of security from non-security functions (see Chapter 12, "Why OpenCable?"). Renewable security accommodates multiple requirements in the OpenCable device:

- Making the security system renewable allows it to be replaced in case of a breach of security.
- Making the security system renewable allows it to be provisioned according to the particular security system selected by the cable operator, thus allowing a point-of-deployment decision.
- Making the security system renewable separates all the security functions from the other functions of the navigation device and satisfies the FCC requirements for separation of security.

User Interface

The cable operator needs to be able to provide navigation and access information to services offered by the cable system. (The issues associated with the management of the user interface are discussed in the section Retail Issues in Chapter 12.) Often, access to services is as important as the services themselves. The electronic program guide (EPG) in advanced analog set-tops increased customer acceptance of the set-top and customer satisfaction with the service.

Naturally, the cable operator would like to provide the same navigation functions on an OpenCable retail device (for example, a cable ready digital television) as are provided on a leased digital set-top. There is a significant technical challenge and business challenge in doing this. The technical challenge includes porting and provisioning of the software applications that provide the user interface. The business challenge is to reach agreements with the suppliers of the OpenCable devices to allow the cable operators' applications to run.

Scaleable

The cable network capabilities are expected to migrate toward a more general availability of real-time, two-way signaling and the introduction of interactive and on-demand services. It is important that the OpenCable device continues to function in these environments. Newer models with extended requirements will be required to take advantage of extended network capabilities in most cases. Software upgrade of the OpenCable device is a goal in the longer term.

Efficient Application and Network Design

The set-top is an integral part of the larger, interdependent network created by the cable system. It is important that the OpenCable device requirements support an efficient network design. For example, it is possible to build an OpenCable device that uses dedicated resources while providing only a broadcast service, and this approach must be discouraged to prevent network resources from being wasted. In other words, not all the services have to be interactive and not all the services have to be broadcast. A balance is required. And as technology progresses, decision points will most certainly change.

Operational Compatibility

The OpenCable device must be compatible with existing operational, customer support and billing systems. In existing cable systems, a headend controller provides the bridge between the set-top and these systems (see Chapter 7, "Digital Broadcast Case Studies"). The OpenCable device is physically split into two separately managed components:

- The POD module—This module is responsible for all conditional access functions, including the authorization of service and collection of purchase records. The POD module is supplied by the cable operator and is managed by the existing headend controller.
- The OpenCable host—The OpenCable host is responsible for all other functions. Service provisioning and user interface parameters must be separately managed. (In the Pegasus system, this is achieved by a separate applications server for each application provider.)

Backward Compatibility

The OpenCable device must be backward-compatible and interoperable with existing set-top terminals. There are a number of aspects to this requirement:

- The OpenCable device must be able to support existing services using existing technologies. For example, a digital-only OpenCable device would be useless to a consumer, because many services are available only in analog form.

- The OpenCable device must not interfere in any way with the operation of existing set-tops. This is ensured at the physical level by the performance parameter specification.

Goals for the OpenCable Set-Top Terminal

The specific goals for the OpenCable set-top terminal are

- To enable new digital broadcast services and support on-demand services in the future
- To be application developer–friendly
- To support nonscrambled analog services as well as encrypted or nonencrypted digital services.
- To be sold through retail channels directly to the consumer
- To be upgradable for support of additional features by the cable operator or the customer when required via the extensions defined in the OpenCable specification process.

OpenCable Device Models

OpenCable devices can be categorized according to a number of different characteristics: whether they are leased or sold at retail, whether they support two-way communications, or whether they are integrated into a digital television or VCR. There are three main types of OpenCable devices:

- OpenCable set-top—This represents the traditional approach of using a separate set-top to provide OpenCable functions. Such a set-top could be leased to the customer by the cable operator or made available at retail.
- OpenCable ready digital television—This incorporates the OpenCable functions into a cable ready digital television or VCR. Such devices would be available only at retail.
- OpenCable ready personal computer—This incorporates the OpenCable functions into a personal computer by means of an expansion card. Such devices would be available only at retail.

In all these types, the security functions are separated into a separate security module called the point-of-deployment (POD) module. The POD module is leased by the cable operator to control conditional access functions. Please refer to Chapter 18 for specific details of the POD module and its interface to the OpenCable device.

The first OpenCable device that has been specified is the OpenCable set-top, and the next sections concentrate on the function requirements for it. The other OpenCable devices have yet to be specified, and the following sections discuss the open issues and choices to be made.

All OpenCable devices fit into two main categories: leased and retail. There are some fundamental differences in requirements between these two categories of devices that follow from the leased or retail model.

Leased

If the OpenCable device is leased, it is a pretty safe assumption that it is a digital set-top. It is unlikely that set-tops will become obsolete, because they provide some distinct advantages to the cable operator and the cable customer.

The advantages for the cable operator of a set-top are

- The digital set-top can be rigorously specified in terms of performance and operation. This includes every aspect of the digital set-top behavior, from the out-of-band signaling protocol to the user interface.
- As new services are developed, new digital set-top hardware and software is often required. The cable operator can provide the digital set-top and the service (although the set-top lease charge must be shown separately on the cable bill by law, it can be blended into the *equipment basket* to reduce the impact to early adopters).
- Less advanced set-tops, which do not support a new service offering, can be redeployed to customers who do not subscribe to the new services. This is a well-established tenet of cable operations where nothing is wasted.

For the customer, this model also has advantages:

- The cable customer does not have to be concerned about owning obsolete equipment—if he subscribes to a new service, either his existing set-top will work or it will be replaced by the cable operator.
- The customer service support can help the customer with any equipment and service issues related to the set-top hardware or the new service, because each customer has the same hardware and software configuration.

This model is being challenged because the consumer electronics manufacturers are continuously adding new features to televisions and VCRs. Sometimes these features do not work with a set-top and the customer is disappointed. In addition to analog compatibility problems that led to language in the 1992 Cable Act (see Chapter 12), there are some new compatibility issues associated with digital television that have to be addressed:

- As yet, most digital televisions have no provision for a digital connection to a set-top. The cable industry and NAB have agreed that a baseband digital interface between the set-top and the digital television is required for cable ready operation (see the FCC Roundtable on Compatibility between Digital TV and Cable). However, not all consumer equipment manufacturers are in favor of putting a baseband interface on every television set, saying it is too expensive. The OpenCable specification for a base-band digital interface is called the host digital network interface (HDNI) and is part of the OCI-C1 specification (see Chapter 17, "OCI-C1: The Consumer Interface").

- There is a requirement from the Motion Picture Association of America (MPAA) for some means of copy protection for premium content. The HDNI specification uses the digital transmission content protection (DTCP) scheme but here again, not all consumer electronics manufacturers are in full suppport of this technology.

Nevertheless, new services will likely appear first on leased digital set-tops before they migrate to a retail digital set-top or cable ready digital television.

Retail

If the OpenCable device is sold at retail, it will probably be incorporated into a digital television or a personal computer, because relatively few additional components are required to make such devices OpenCable-compliant. This can readily be seen in Figure 14-1; the additional components required for a digital television are

- A 64/256 QAM demodulator
- An out-of-band QPSK tuner and demodulator
- An interface to support the POD module
- An HDNI interface

It is expected that these components would be integrated into future television designs and that silicon integration of the functions would reduce the cost premium to the manufacturer. The additional components required to make a PC OpenCable-compliant are

- A 6 MHz cable tuner
- An NTSC demodulator
- A 64/256 QAM demodulator
- An out-of-band QPSK tuner and demodulator
- An interface to support the POD module
- An HDNI interface

Although this is slightly more than the digital television, these components could easily be placed on an expansion module and sold separately at retail.

The issues associated with providing an OpenCable-compliant DTV or PC are that only basic services are currently defined by OpenCable specifications. Services currently not standardized include

- Extended navigation—Although basic tuning functions are supported by in-band PSIP carriage and DVS-234 out-of-band service information (see Chapter 16, "OCI-N: The Network Interface"), rich guide functions offered by the cable operator on digital set-tops require more work. Two potential solutions exist: First, the cable operator could support DVS-234 profile 4 or higher for all services; second, the

OpenCable device could download and execute a guide application provided by the cable operator. In either case, because the guide information is not the property of the cable operator, some kind of business relationship needs to be established.

- Impulse pay-per-view (IPPV)—The POD module specification (see Chapter 18) defines a method for purchase of IPPV events and a mechanism for collection of purchase information using the RF return path. However, the same issues exist for navigation with regard to the user interface. In addition, the OpenCable device must include a return transmitter.
- Video-on-demand (VOD)—The OpenCable team is developing a set of signaling protocols for video-on-demand services. The POD module supports a two-way signaling channel (if the OpenCable device supports a return transmitter), but a VOD software application is required in addition to the signaling framework. Therefore, the OpenCable device must support a download and execution environment.
- Interactive services—A wide range of interactive services could be supported by an OpenCable device, but like VOD, a download, application sharing, and execution environment must be supported by the OpenCable device.

Why is it so difficult to define a standard mechanism to download and execute applications on an OpenCable device? The main issue is software portability; the retail OpenCable device must be able to download and execute applications from any cable operator, and to do this a common software environment must be defined and agreed to by all OpenCable members. Although groups such as ATVEF, W3C, and DASE are making considerable progress on portable application environments, these environments are only now becoming practical. There are considerable technical challenges to overcome:

- Applications must run on all OpenCable devices so that advanced features and functions are used if they exist, but the application still functions on less capable devices.
- There must be no possibility that a faulty application or virus could affect the basic operation of an OpenCable device.
- Portable applications typically require considerably higher levels of processor performance and more memory than embedded applications.

Nevertheless, the advantages to the customer of an integrated OpenCable device make this effort potentially invaluable:

- The customer can expect an unprecedented level of integration of functions provided by the DTV (or PC) and the services provided by the cable operator—for example, a single remote control that provides access to all features and the potential that new features, such as video-on-demand, will just show up as the cable operator invests in the necessary infrastructure.

There are also advantages for the cable operator and the consumer electronics manufacturers. However, it will take time to work out the necessary business relationships to enable this level of integration.

Set-Top Core Requirements

The core requirements for the set-top are similar to first generation set-tops being deployed by the cable industry (see Chapter 7). In addition, any features that are mandated by law or FCC regulation (for example, emergency alert system support) are part of the core requirements.

Core Services

The core services provided by the basic OpenCable set-top are

- Analog NTSC video—Because there is no support for analog de-scrambling in the basic set-top, only in-the-clear analog channels are supported.
- Digital television—In-the-clear digital television services (for example, terrestrial digital broadcast retransmission) are supported. In addition, encrypted digital television is supported by means of a POD module supplied by the cable operator. The encrypted services are limited to subscription and reservation pay-per-view services because the basic set-top does not include a reverse transmitter.

The core services provided by a basic OpenCable set-top are very limited but do provide considerably more functionality than a cable ready analog television.

Core Functions and Features

The core functional requirements for the OpenCable set-top are illustrated by Figure 14-1. The block diagram is derived from the Pegasus set-top (see Figure 6-1 in Chapter 6) and has a single, 6 MHz tuner that is shared for analog and digital channels. The most importance difference from Pegasus is the separation of security functions into the POD module.

Figure 14-1 can be subdivided into the same major sections as Figure 6-1:

- The cable network interface (functions labeled as RF/Baseband and Preprocessing in Figure 14-1)—The interface circuitry between the cable system and the set-top includes the cable tuner, NTSC demodulator, and QAM demodulator and an OOB receiver. The interface to the cable system is a 75 ohm F-connector.
- Transport processing (labeled as Main Processing in Figure 14-1)—This function is required to break the transport multiplex into the specific streams that are required for the selected service. Transport processing is linked into the conditional access system because different services in a multiplex are typically encrypted using different session and working keys.

Figure 14-1 *The Core OpenCable Set-Top*

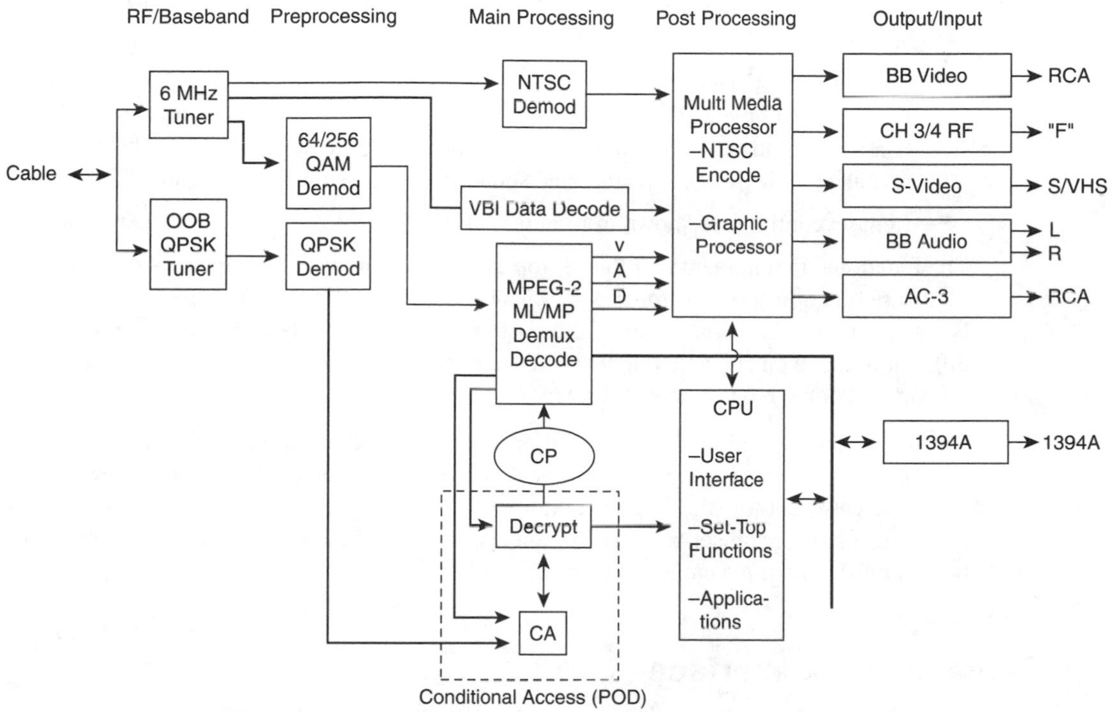

- Conditional access (POD)—The means by which access to specific services is granted to the user based on payment for those services. A digital decryption circuit (Decrypt), in conjunction with a secure microprocessor (CA), performs the conditional access functions for digital services. There is no provision for analog conditional access in OpenCable.
- Video and graphics processing (these functions are labeled as Main Processing and Post Processing in the Figure 14-1)—This subsystem is responsible for MPEG-2 transport de-multiplexing and decoding and on-screen display generation. In the OpenCable set-top, an additional function, copy protection (labeled CP), is required to protect the digital programming content that flows across the POD module interface.
- Audio processing (not shown in Figure 14-1)—This subystem includes a Dolby AC-3 decoder.

- Microprocessor subsystem (labeled CPU in Figure 14-1)—The microprocessor subsystem is the brains of the set-top. This subsystem typically includes a microprocessor together with ROM, Flash, NVRAM, RAM memory, LED display, and keypad.
- Outputs—All OpenCable set-tops have an F-connector output for an NTSC channel modulated at broadcast channel 3 or channel 4. In addition, the set-top has baseband (BB) video and audio, S-Video, AC-3, and IEEE 1394A outputs to allow the customer to realize higher-quality picture and sound than is possible via the channel 3/4 output.
- Remote control (not shown in Figure 14-1)—This is not specified by OpenCable.

The functional requirements for the set-top can be accurately and completely specified for hardware functions, such as tuner performance, MPEG-2 transport functions, and so on. But as the higher-layer functions of the set-top are specified, it becomes more and more difficult to agree on and accurately specify requirements. For this reason, the OpenCable set-top functional requirements are silent on higher-level functions.

The higher-level functions include the user interface and the software behavior of the set-top and are the most visible aspects of the set-top from the customer's point of view. In the case of a leased set-top, the cable operator will completely specify these aspects of the set-top, whereas in a retail set-top it is still unclear whether these will be under the control of the manufacturer or the cable operator.

The Cable Network Interface

The cable network interface (CNI) is designed to meet the OCI-N specification (see Chapter 16). In addition to the basic parameters defined by the OCI-N specification, the OpenCable functional requirements specify the performance parameters of the cable network interface.

There is a clear distinction between the OCI-N specification and the performance parameters of the set-top. This is best explained by example; the OCI-N specification specifies the channel bandwidth (6 MHz) and the frequency plan (EIA-542), but this information is not sufficient to build a set-top. The performance parameters specify the sensitivity of the tuner (its input level range), the local oscillator leakage (into the cable plant), the adjacent channel rejection ratio, and so on. Thus, for successful operation both an interface specification and the performance parameters are required.

The OpenCable set-top performance parameters specify 35 parameters for RF and Modulation Performance, which include the parameters of the cable network interface and the channel 3/4 outputs. Some of these parameters are covered by FCC Part 15 and FCC

Part 76 requirements and are legally required; for more information on FCC requirements, see Chapter 13 of *Modern Cable Television Technology; Video, Voice, and Data Communications* by Walter Ciciora and others.

Tuner

The OpenCable set-top requirements specify a single, 54 to 860 MHz tuner to support the widest frequency range to which cable systems are currently being built. Tuner performance is specified to support NTSC, 64-QAM, and 256-QAM channels over a range of input levels normally found in cable plants.

Input levels are specified for analog carriers by FCC Part 76 requirements as

- >= 3dBmV at the end of a reference 100-foot drop cable connected to any subscriber tap port
- >= 0dBmV at the input to each subscriber's television

In practice, the tuner performance must exceed these requirements for digital carriers because they are typically transmitted at 6 to 10 dBmV lower signal levels than analog carriers to reduce overall RMS power loading of the HFC plant.

QAM Demodulator

The block labeled QAM demodulator in Figure 14-1 is actually responsible for a number of related transmission functions, as specified by DVS-031:

- Adaptive equalization of the received signal to compensate for reflections introduced by the cable plant
- 64-QAM or 256-QAM demodulation according to the type of channel tuned
- Trellis code interpolation (see Chapter 4, "Digital Technologies")
- Deinterleaving (see Chapter 4)
- Forward error correction (see Chapter 4)

The output of the demodulator is a baseband digital stream at 27 or 38.8 Mbps per 6 MHz channel.

NTSC Demodulator

The NTSC Demodulator is carefully specified to provide acceptable video performance.

Out-of-Band Channel Termination

There are two alternative out-of-band channel specifications currently being used in North America:

- DVS 178, as specified by General Instrument
- DVS 167, as specified by DAVIC

(Please refer to Chapter 5, "Adding Digital Television Services to Cable Systems," for a detailed description of the out-of-band channel.)

The out-of-band channel type is one of two major differences between the two digital systems that have been deployed in North America (the other is conditional access). The General Instrument DigiCable system uses a proprietary out-of-band channel definition (which is now specified in DVS 178), and the Scientific Atlanta Digital Broadband Delivery System (DBDS) uses the DAVIC out-of-band channel definition (which is specified in DVS 167). The two out-of-band channel types are fundamentally different and cannot interoperate although they are used for very similar purposes in the two systems.

In a leased set-top, the manufacturer can simply build the set-top to one out-of-band specification or another based on the order received from the cable operator, and this is the case for currently deployed digital set-tops. However, this model clearly does not work in a retail environment:

- When a customer purchases a set-top, he must make an informed decision based on his cable system operator. Moreover, the retailer must stock double the inventory to accommodate two types of every set-top.
- If a customer moves from one type of system to another, the set-top will no longer work. In other words, the set-top is not portable.

The OpenCable solution to this problem is to make the out-of-band termination decision a point-of-deployment choice. There are a number of ways to make a point-of-deployment choice in OpenCable:

- When a cable operator leases a set-top, he has made the point-of-deployment choice for the customer.
- When the customer buys a set-top, the point-of-deployment choice is deferred until the set-top is connected to the cable system (that is, it is deployed).

In the second case, the set-top either must contain both types of out-of-band termination and dynamically adapt to the cable system, or the out-of-band circuitry can be separated into a replaceable module. The OpenCable specification allows a set-top manufacturer to make this decision based on economic considerations.The mechanisms to support replaceable out-of-band circuitry are described in Chapter 18.

Out-of-Band Receiver

The out-of-band channel can be one-way or two-way. An out-of-band receiver is required in either case, and all digital set-tops include an out-of-band tuner and QPSK demodulator.

Figure 14-1 shows that the output of the QPSK demodulator is fed to the POD module. The out-of-band front end is specified to receive at two rates—1.544 Mbps (DVS 167) and 2.048 Mbps (DVS 178)—and the appropriate type of POD module adapts the set-top to the signaling system used in the cable system.

An alternative approach is to build a dual-standard, out-of-band termination circuit into the set-top (at least one silicon vendor believes this to be feasible). In this case, the out-of-band termination interfaces directly with the CPU, and the CPU forwards conditional access messages to (and from) the POD module (please refer to Chapter 18 for more details).

Out-of-Band Transmitter

Figure 14-1 does not include an out-of-band transmitter because this is not part of the core functional requirements for the OpenCable set-top. There are a number of reasons for this omission:

- One-way plant—Many cable operators have not yet upgraded their cable systems to support two-way operation.
- DOCSIS—Some cable operators believe that the OpenCable device can share a DOCSIS channel (deployed for cable modem service). The POD module supports the use of a DOCSIS modem for two-way operation (see Chapter 18).

An out-of-band transmitter is required for two-way operation of the out-of-band channel. Two-way signaling supports impulse-pay-per-view (IPPV), video-on-demand (VOD), and interactive applications.

An out-of-band transmitter is optional for set-tops deployed in a one-way cable plant, although if an upgrade to two-way is planned it makes good economic sense to deploy a set-top with an out-of-band transmitter.

Media Access Control

The media access control (MAC) function supports the out-of-band transmitter and allows a number of set-tops to share a common return path. In the OpenCable set-top, the MAC circuit might be embedded into the POD module or implemented by the set-top.

Telephone Modem

A telephone modem provides an alternative to the out-of-band transmitter in a one-way plant. The POD module interface supports the use of a telephone modem if it exists. The telephone modem is then used off-hours for non–real-time data transfers, such as IPPV buy collections.

Conditional Access System

The conditional access system provides the means by which access to specific services is granted to the user based on payment for those services. The OpenCable digital conditional access system is contained in a POD module that connects to the OpenCable device by means of the OCI-C2 interface (see Chapter 18).

OpenCable does not provide any means for analog de-scrambling. Although a standard for replaceable analog security exists in the EIA-105 specification, it has never been implemented. Recently, the FCC has reconsidered its requirements for separable conditional access for analog-only set-top boxes in recognition of the fact that there is no retail market for this type of device.

The digital conditional access system is described in Chapter 6. This discussion will focus on the differences relating to the separation of security.

POD Module

The POD module contains all the conditional access system components within a single PCMCIA module. The input to the POD module is an encrypted MPEG-2 transport stream. The POD module performs the following operations on the transport stream:

- The POD decrypts services in the transport stream for which it is authorized.
- The POD applies copy protection to those services that have copy control information indicating there are copy restrictions.

In addition, the POD module supports a generic impulse pay-per-view API that allows the OpenCable device to purchase, cancel, and view history for pay-per-view events. For the support of IPPV, the POD requires a return channel resource.

Video and Graphics Processing

The OpenCable device provides MPEG-2 main profile at main level (MP@ML) de-multiplexing and decoding in accordance with DVS-241 and DVS-033. Support for high-level decoding (that is, high definition television) is an optional extension. However, the OpenCable device must support high definition pass-through to the IEEE 1394A output port.

Graphics processing requirements for on-screen display are not directly specified by the functional requirements, but certain minimum capabilities are required to support the DVS-194/EIA 775 output standard required at the IEEE 1394A output port (see Chapter 17 for more details).

Audio Processing

The OpenCable device provides Dolby AC-3 digital audio decoding according to ATSC A/53 Annex B.

Microprocessor Subsystem

The core OpenCable functional requirements do not specify any performance requirements for the microprocessor subsystem. Future extensions to the OpenCable specifications might set minimum performance and memory footprint parameters for a portable software execution environment.

Remote Control

The OpenCable device specification does not include any requirements for a remote control, although it is expected that a remote control would be supplied with the OpenCable device.

Extension Requirements

The extended requirements for the set-top are effectively unbounded and will be defined by OpenCable as part of the continuous improvement process. Although the extensions have not been finalized, there are a number that have been discussed:

- Two-way support by means of a QPSK transmitter or DOCSIS modem
- Impulse pay-per-view
- Multiple tuners for picture-in-picture operation
- High definition television support
- Software download, application sharing, and execution environment
- Video-on-demand
- Internal hard drive for local video record and playback functions

Performance

The OpenCable functional requirements include a table of about 120 performance parameters. These parameters are designed to ensure that the set-top meets FCC part 15 requirements and that all OpenCable set-tops provide a consistent standard of video and audio quality.

Summary

The OpenCable device can take a number of different forms: a set-top, a cable ready digital television, or a cable ready personal computer. The core requirements for an OpenCable set-top have been published in draft form by CableLabs, and it is expected that requirements for an OpenCable-compliant cable ready digital television will follow.

The functional requirements for the OpenCable device are very broad and include support for the following:

- FCC-mandated requirements for separable security, competitive availability of navigation devices, and cable compatibility
- Performance parameters to ensure acceptable network operation and audio and video quality
- Digital conditional access support by means of a replaceable POD module
- Out-of-band signaling
- High definition pass-through to a IEEE 1394A connection
- Copy protection that meets MPAA requirements for premium programming

As yet, the OpenCable device functional requirements do not specify mechanisms for download and execution of software applications. This capability is required for many advanced services in a retail environment, and until they are specified, a leased set-top will continue to bridge the gap for new services.

References

Book

Ciciora, Walter, James Farmer, and David Large. *Modern Cable Television Technology; Video, Voice, and Data Communications*. San Francisco, CA: Morgan Kaufmann Publishers, Inc., 1999.

Standards

CableLabs. CFR-OCS-UDC-WD04-990805. "OpenCable Set-top Terminal Functional Requirements for Unidirectional Cable." Draft Specification. Cable Television Laboratories, Inc.

CableLabs. CFR-OCS-BDC-WD04-990805. "OpenCable Set-top Terminal Functional Requirements for Bidirectional Cable." Draft Specification. Cable Television Laboratories, Inc.

Internet Resources

Pegasus RFP at the Pegasus Web site

http://timewarner.com/rfp

FCC Roundtable on Compatibility between Digital TV and Cable, May 20, 1999; Realaudio

www.fcc.gov.

CHAPTER 15

OpenCable Headend Interfaces

The OpenCable headend interfaces allow interconnection between the headend and other components of the cable system using standard interfaces. Three headend interfaces are defined in the OpenCable reference architecture:

- OCI-H1, programming content—The headend provides a central point in a cable system where programming is received, from satellite or a wide-area network (WAN), and is then converted into a standard format for transmission over the network interface (OCI-N) to the customer. The OCI-H1 interface is a family of interfaces for content provisioning. Broadcast content can arrive in analog or compressed digital formats to be streamed in real-time over OCI-N. Interactive and on-demand services make use of stored content that is usually copied from the content provider to a server in the headend. Finally, Internet services provide a real-time, two-way stream of HTML pages, Java applets, and streaming media (and many other data types) over a session between the customer and the Internet content provider.

  In all cases, content interchange standards are essential to ensure that the content can be efficiently managed and converted into the desired OCI-N format.

- OCI-H2, conditional access system—In nearly all headends deployed in North America, the conditional access system (CAS) is integrated into the headend equipment, forcing the cable operator to choose the same supplier for the headend and the CAS. In contrast, the European Digital Video Broadcast (DVB) model defines a separation of CAS from other headend functions, allowing one or more independent CAS vendors to connect to the headend equipment via a standard interface. The OCI-H2 interface follows a similar approach to support multiple CAS vendors.
- OCI-H3, billing and operational support—All services require an interface into the billing and operational support system. This interface must be able to support the existing billing systems and the existing operations of deployed digital cable systems. It must also be extensible so that new services can be introduced without requiring new development by the billing vendor. Standardizing the OCI-H3 interface also allows migration from one billing system to another.

OpenCable has defined only OCI-H1 at the current time. However, there is growing interest in OCI-H2 and OCI-H3.

OCI-H1

The information flow across the OCI-H1 interface in Figure 15-1 consists of *programming content*, which has three main sources. Internet content is generally received from a wide area network and, although there is a two-way exchange of information, the flow is predominantly from the content provider to the customer. Video content is a one-way flow of information and arrives from a number of content providers over satellite, terrestrial, or wide-area networks. Finally, other content represents any other kind of information that arrives at the headend, which is yet to be defined.

Figure 15-1 *OpenCable Reference Diagram*

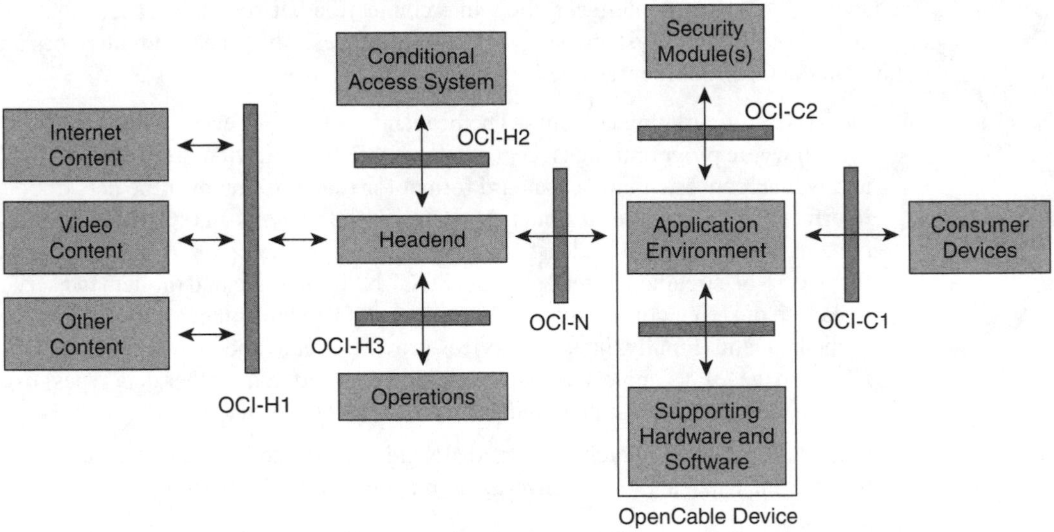

The OCI-H1 interface is divided into three sections for the following content types:

- Internet content
- Television (video and audio) content
- Other content

In many cases, the content flows transparently through the headend to the network; in other words, its appearance is not changed by the headend even though its physical format might be changed. For example, a QPSK signal (containing MPEG-2 compressed video) received from a satellite encrypted with DigiCipher II conditional access might be transcoded (and transmodulated) into a QAM signal encrypted with PowerKEY conditional access. The customer is generally unaware of this fact when viewing the content. In the case of Internet content, the appearance of the content often depends on the software application at the OpenCable device; for example, a Web browser resizes and reformats content to fit the screen. Nevertheless, the headend acts as merely a relay point in the network established between the content provider and the customer.

In the case of on-demand services, the headend provides temporary storage of the content without changing its appearance. In the case of video-on-demand services, the entire movie title is provisioned on a server at the headend (see Chapter 10, "On-Demand Services") so that it can be streamed out to the customer when requested. In the case of Internet services, it is becoming more common to cache Web pages on a server at the headend or hub. This takes advantage of the high-speed link between the home and the distribution hub to allow the most popular content to be accessed quickly.

Goals

The goal of the OCI-H1 interface is to define a standard content format for all digital services. A standard format for content eases delivery from the content provider to the headend and enables retransmission agreements between content providers and cable operators. Standard content formats help enable rapid deployment of new services by providing a standard framework for which new services can be designed. Because the range of digital content types is much broader than in analog systems, more standardization is required.

Issues

There are many issues that must be resolved to achieve the goal of defining a standard content format for all digital services. For example:

- Audio levels—The encoding of digital content does not specify a consistent audio level. This means that on channel change from analog to digital, there can be a substantial difference in the audio level.
- Progressive refresh—The encoding of video with the MPEG-2 standard allows a great deal of flexibility at the encoder. The General Instrument encoder does not encode I-frames like most other MPEG-2 encoders, but distributes intracoded macro-blocks throughout the frames. This is easy to observe on channel change because the picture progressively builds with a tiling effect. Progressive refresh makes it more difficult to splice one MPEG program to another, a technique that is used for digital program insertion.
- Meta-data—Preencoded material, such as movies, requires considerable descriptive and promotional information to be packaged with the compressed video and audio. The format of this *meta-data* (data about data) needs to be defined for electronic interchange of on-demand assets.
- Integration of digital video and Internet content—Many interactive services (see Chapter 8," Interactive Services") blend digital video and Internet techniques to enhance the viewing experience. There is currently no standard way of integrating digital video and Internet content.

Reference Architecture

Figure 15-2 illustrates some of the interfaces required to supply programming content to a modern digital headend. Starting from the top of the diagram, the types of content available to the headend are

- NTSC analog video—Sources for analog video are satellite and off-air programming.
- Compressed digital video and audio—Sources for digital video and audio are satellite and off-air programming.
- On-demand assets—An example is compressed movies or other programming intended for delivery as an on-demand service.
- Commercial insertion assets—Commercials that have been produced and edited and are ready for commercial insertion.
- Internet assets—This includes any Web-based, streaming media or other content that can be accessed with the appropriate applications software for interactive services.
- Wide-area networking—The two-way communications resource can be viewed as a type of asset because it enables services such as email and chat.

NTSC Analog Video

For analog video, a composite IF signal (intermediate frequency 41 to 47 MHz) carrying NTSC with BTSC audio provides the standard interface between equipment in the headend.

The two main sources for analog video are satellite-delivered (C-band) feeds, local broadcast (off-air) programming and the locally generated public access, education, and government (PEG) channels. Satellite channels are transmodulated, and other channels are fed through signal processors so that they are suitable for transmission over the cable plant. (See Chapter 7 of *Modern Cable Television Technology; Video, Voice, and Data Communications* by Walter Ciciora and others.)

In the case of satellite feeds, which are usually scrambled, an authorized satellite receiver is required to obtain a clear signal.

The signal might be switched (at IF) before it is sent to the plant for three main reasons:

- Shared-use channels—In some cases, a cable channel is fed by one of two input sources according to the time of day.
- Commercial insertion—Many advertiser-supported channels allow the cable operator to override a national advertising slot with a locally generated ad.
- Emergency alert system (EAS) overrides—The cable operator is obliged to provide override of all channels to support the national EAS.

Finally, the signal might be scrambled before it is sent out over the cable plant.

Figure 15-2 *External Content Reference Model*

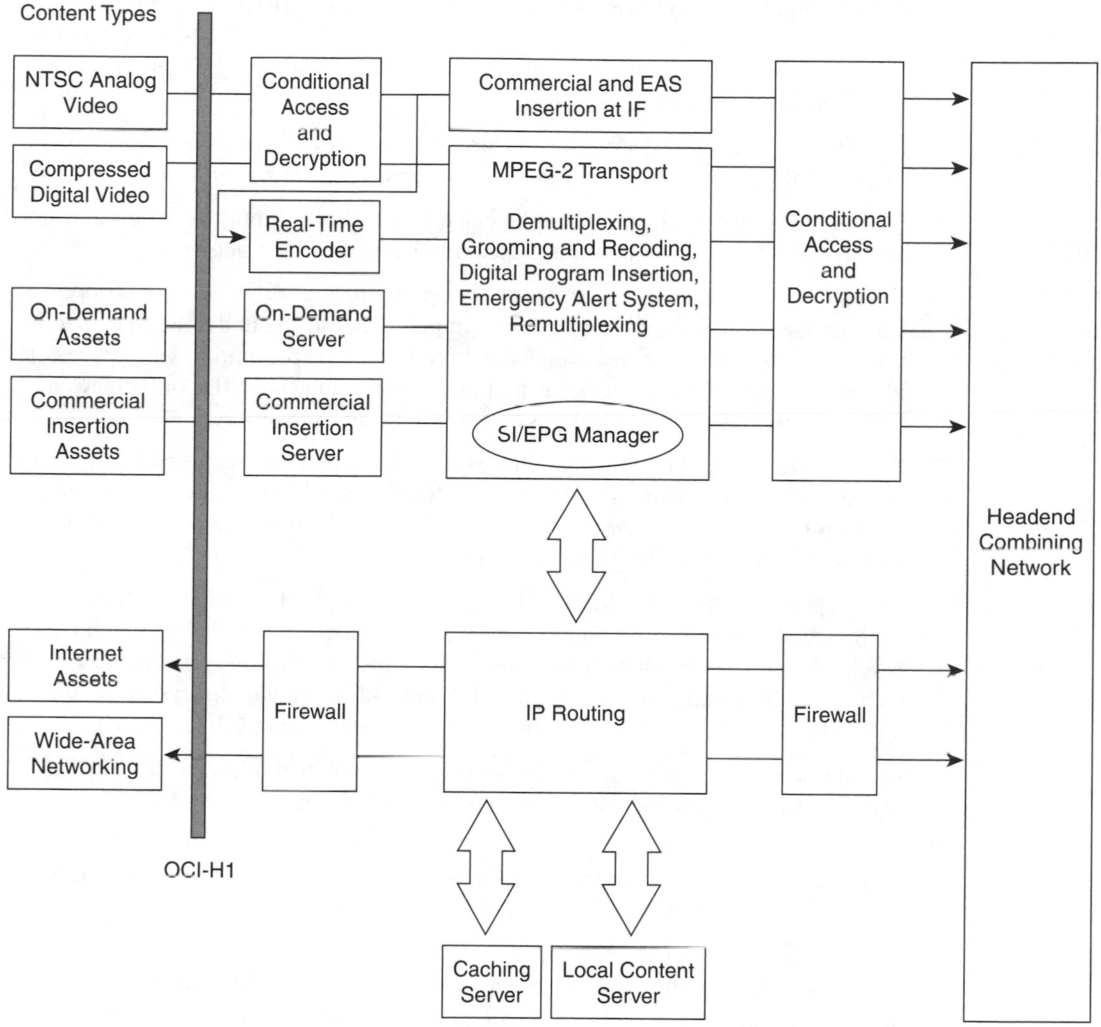

Compressed Digital Video and Audio

For digital video and audio, a number of different physical protocols can be used to support the MPEG-2 multi-program transport stream (see the section Baseband Transmission in Chapter 4, "Digital Technlogies"):

- The two main sources for compressed digital video and audio are satellite-delivered (C-band and Ku-band) feeds and local digital broadcast (off-air) programming. In both cases, the channels are demodulated to baseband digital signals for subsequent processing before they are sent to the cable plant (see Chapter 7, "Digital Broadcast Case Studies," for two case studies).
- Conditional access and decryption—This removes any encryption used to secure satellite links and provides an in-the-clear baseband digital signal.
- De-multiplexing—Each source digital channel is actually a multi-program transport stream (MPTS), which is de-multiplexed into its discrete components.
- Grooming—Individual single-program transport streams (SPTS) can be dropped by deleting the packets used to carry them. (In practice, this is often done by replacing the packets with null packets, which are discarded in the re-multiplexing process.) PID remapping is often required as part of grooming to avoid PID conflicts when SPTSs from different source MPTSs are re-multiplexed together.
- Reencoding—The bit rate of individual MPEG-2 elementary streams can be modified by reencoding the stream in real-time. This technique allows a tradeoff of quality versus bit rate (see *Rate-remultiplexing: An Optimimum Bandwidth Utilization Technology* by Richard S. Prodan and others).
- Digital program insertion (DPI)—Many advertiser-supported channels allow the cable operator to override a national advertising slot with a locally generated ad. Unlike the analog case, which is a relatively simple switch, sophisticated DPI techniques are required to replace the video and audio components so that the MPEG-2 decoder in the set-top continues to function normally (see SMPTE 312M).
- Re-multiplexing—Finally, the various inputs are combined into 27 or 38.8 Mbps channels suitable for modulation into a 6 MHz QAM channel.
- Conditional access and encryption—Conditional access (CA) provides selective access to the content and supports the premium channel subscriber business model. CA uses encryption of the digital channels to secure them over the cable system.
- In addition to the process steps required to produce the digital channels themselves, it is necessary to describe the channel lineups to support tuning and navigation. The service information/electronic program guide (SI/EPG) manager is responsible for generating and inserting information to support the navigation application.

This process can be used to combine compressed digital feeds, the output from real-time encoders, and the output from on-demand servers. However, in some architectures the on-demand server outputs are handled separately (see Chapter 11, "On-Demand Cable System Case Studies").

On-Demand Assets

On-demand assets include compressed movies or other programming intended for delivery as an on-demand service. The audio/video component of the asset is quite straightforward and could be specified as a compressed digital video source. However, there are many other related pieces of information associated with the movie or program, which is collectively known as the meta-data:

- Video meta-data includes duration, aspect ratio, MPEG-2 profile and level, data rate, closed captioning, and so on.
- Audio meta-data includes duration, language(s), data rate, number of audio channels, and so on.

The meta-data must also contain a complete description of supporting material, such as

- MPAA rating (G, PG, R, NC-17, NR) or television rating (TV-Y, Y7, 14, MA)
- Window of availability—the start and end dates when the program might be shown
- Title
- Credits (actors, director, producer, music, and so on)
- Plot summary

All the information about an on-demand asset must be organized as a self-describing data structure so that the entire asset can be provisioned at the on-demand server by means of a file copy (see Pegasus Functional Requirements for Video-On-Demand (VOD) Systems V2.0).

Commercial Insertion Assets

Commercial Insertion is an automated process that allows overriding of the national advertising in special time slots (called *ad. avails*). However, the asset distribution is currently a manual process that usually involves sending videotapes from the content provider to the headend.

However, as targeted advertising and narrow-casting becomes more common and as assets are distributed in digital (rather than analog) form, the same techniques described for on-demand assets will be applied to commercial insertion assets. The meta-data will require some new fields:

- Insertion schedule—a list of times, channels and duration when the asset is to be inserted
- Demographics—a description of the targeted audience for the commercial

In addition, a cue message is used in addition to the schedule control to trigger the insertion of a particular commercial (see the DPI Ad Hoc Working Group, Preliminary V8.5).

Internet Assets

The Internet provides both a source of programming content and a communications resource. The content is structured around the World Wide Web (WWW) framework, which is created by an open, extensible set of de facto protocols, specified by the Internet Engineering Task Force (IETF) through the Request for Comment (RFC) process:

- Internet Protocol (IP)
- Transmission Control Protocol (TCP)
- Hypertext Transmission Protocol (HTTP)
- Hypertext Markup Language (HTML)

Many WWW extensions rely on the download of applications to enable local execution at the client. These include such applications as QuickTime, Shockwave, Macromedia Director, RealMedia and Pointcast, which are application-specific. Internet applications often use software-based video and audio decoders designed for low bit rates because of the bandwidth limitations of the Internet. In addition, the Java virtual machine (JVM) allows arbitrary, portable applications (called *applets*) to be downloaded to the client and executed within the JVM.

At the headend, the Internet content must pass through a firewall before streaming to the network or being provisioned or cached onto headend servers. The firewall provides protection from hackers who might otherwise be able to access and corrupt the headend servers.

There is a second firewall between the cable access network and the headend computer resources, which provides protection from hackers and also restricts access to services according to customer profile; this is the online equivalent to conditional access of television channels.

Wide-Area Networking

The Internet is an example of a wide-area network (WAN) that provides both a source of programming content and a communications resource. The wide-area communications are provided, at the physical layer, by a variety of interfaces, from T1 and T3 carriers through to SONET facilities at OC-3, OC-12, and OC-48 rates. The facilities may support frame relay, asynchronous transfer mode (ATM) or packet over SONET (PoS).

Content Convergence

Figure 15-2 shows a double-ended arrow between the MPEG-2 Transport and IP Routing functions; this indicates that the migration to digital television allows content exchange, or convergence, between digital television and personal computer users. This convergence is enabled by

- The ability to adapt IP-based content into MPEG-2 transport streams for delivery to the OpenCable device
- The ability to stream video and audio assets to personal computers using IP-based streaming media protocols (for example, RealMedia)

Although the transport protocols exist to support content convergence, many advanced content representations require extensions to the set-top or PC. In the PC world, extensions are incorporated in the browser or downloaded and installed as plug-ins, or applications, by the user. The set-top environment is more constrained by ease-of-use and memory space considerations. To provide content convergence, a standard software environment for the download and execution of applications is required.

Development Status

The OCI-H1 interface is at first-draft level. The current document summarizes the current standards that exist for content interchange. At the time of writing, there is still considerable work needed to define the interfaces to support more sophisticated types of content, such as interactive and on-demand content.

OCI-H2

The OCI-H2 interface provides separation of the conditional access function from the rest of the headend functions. This interface is the headend equivalent of the OCI-C2 interface at the OpenCable device. In both cases, the security function must remain as secure as possible and relies on shared secrets in the headend conditional access system (CAS) and the point-of-deployment (POD) security module. The definition of the OCI-H2 and OCI-C2 interfaces must provide for a number of contingencies:

- CAS upgrade—The conditional access system might require periodic upgrade either to combat signal theft or to add new features.
- CAS replacement—The complete replacement of the conditional access system might be required under certain circumstances.

Goals

The goal of the OCI-H2 interface is to define a standard interface that supports the separation of conditional access functions from service delivery functions. By separating conditional access, the OCI-H2 interface provides the option of supporting multiple conditional access systems with a single cable system. This mode is called *simulcrypt* operation.

Issues

There are a number of issues that must be resolved to achieve the goal of separation of conditional access functions:

- Separation in currently deployed systems—In existing practice, the conditional access is tightly coupled into the other headend functions.
- Definition and agreement of interfaces—Work has not yet started on the OCI-H2 interface definition.
- Separation of conditional access from programming and features—This task has not yet started.

Reference Architecture

Figure 15-3 illustrates an approach to separation of the conditional access functions based on the European DVB simulcrypt model (see ETSI TS 101 197—DVB Simulcrypt Specification Part 1). The main difference is the delivery of entitlement management messages (EMMs), which are sent to the OpenCable device via an out-of-band channel (rather than in-band as described by DVB).

Figure 15-3 *DVB Simulcrypt Model*

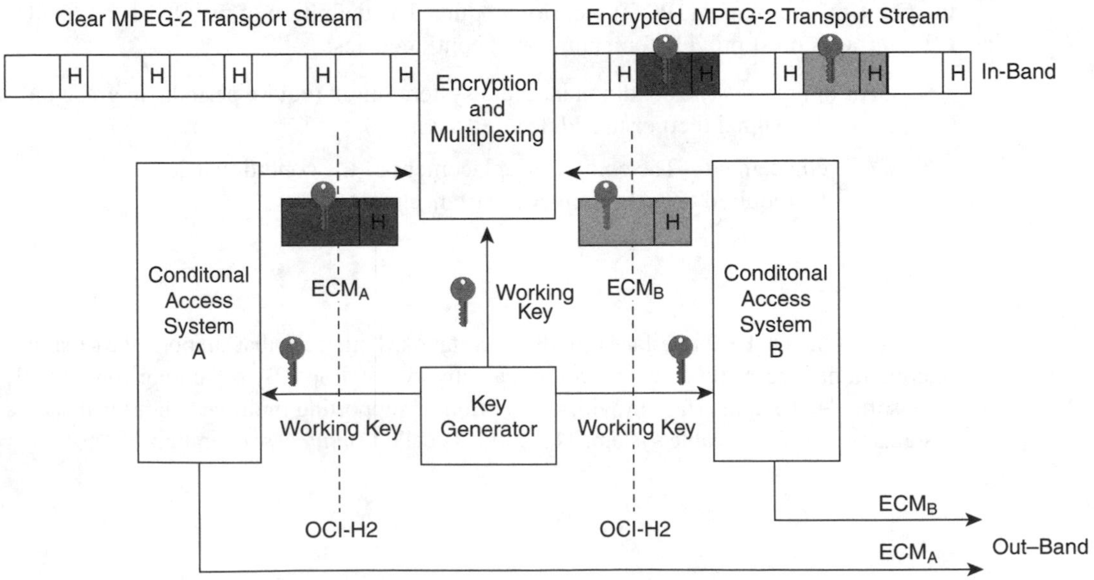

Figure 15-3 shows an example of simulcrypt operation, in which two conditional access systems can be used simultaneously. In this arrangement, the MPEG-2 multi-program transport stream is encrypted and sent once to all OpenCable devices using an agreed common encryption algorithm. In Europe, the DVB consortium licenses the common scrambling algorithm (CSA) for this purpose. In North America, General Instrument and Scientific Atlanta have cross-licensed the Harmony encryption algorithm to allow *key sharing* (simulcrypt) operation.

The system works by sharing a single key generator—a source of random *working keys* that are used to encrypt the MPEG-2 transport stream (in practice, different working keys are used to encrypt each service). The working key is also sent to the conditional access system(s). The job of the conditional access system is to authorize each customer for those services for which he has paid. This is done by sending an encrypted working key in an in-band entitlement control message (ECM). The ECMs are sent in-band so that they can be changed frequently to increase security and so that they can quickly be acquired on channel change.

In Figure 15-3, each conditional access system sends its own ECM stream to an MPEG-2 multiplexer for insertion periodically (usually about 10 times per second) in the multi-program transport stream. The conditional access system also sends entitlement management messages (EMM) to the OpenCable device via the out-of-band channel. The EMM contains the key that the OpenCable device uses to decrypt the ECMs and provide access to a service. The EMMs are addressed to individual OpenCable devices, and CAS_A sends EMMs to OpenCable devices with only CAS_A security in them. Likewise, CAS_B sends EMMs to OpenCable devices with only CAS_B security in them.

Development Status

At the time of writing, the OCI-H2 interface is undefined by OpenCable. There is considerable work to define all the interfaces to make separation of conditional access functions a reality.

The Open Conditional Access group (OpenCAS) is a collection of companies working together to define open interfaces to conditional access components for U.S. cable headends and U.S. broadcast installations.

The OpenCAS charter is

"Define interfaces between Head-End (HE) equipment and Conditional Access (CA) equipment. Interface should allow for systems to be interoperable, separable and replaceable. Provisions should be made for CA data to be delivered via in-band and out-of-band channels. The defined system and interfaces must be considered for compatibility with over-the-air (satellite and terrestrial) systems and achieve consumer friendliness. The group will deliver finished document(s) to ANSI-sanctioned standards bodies (SMPTE & SCTE) for due-process standardization. In keeping with the ANSI standardization model, participation in the group is open to all parties interested in fulfilling this charter. The group does not intend to specify interfaces to billing systems or specify a scrambling algorithm."

For more information on OpenCAS, see the OpenCAS Web site (http:/www.opencas.com).

OCI-H3

The OCI-H3 interface provides operational and control flows between the headend components and the other systems that are required to operate the cable system, including billing systems, subscriber management systems, operational support systems, network management systems, and so on. These systems might be located in the headend, at a nearby business office, or might be remote from the cable system. In any case, the interface requirements are similar, and include

- Subscriber management—This interface allows the selective enabling of service to each subscriber. It provides the interface between the subscriber management system and the conditional access system.
- Event provisioning—This interface allows the definition of pay-per-view events (which have a specific start and end time) and on-demand events (which have flexible start and end times). This interface is between the event scheduling system and the conditional access system.
- Purchase collection—This interface allows purchase reports to be sent to the billing system. Purchase reports are collected by the conditional access system.
- Network management—This interface provides the network management view into the headend, hub, and customer premises components of the cable system. This interface is designed to support an external network management system.

Goals

The goal of the OCI-H3 interface is to define a standard interface that supports all the operational functions for the cable system. This interface should be able to support the existing billing systems and the existing operations of deployed digital cable systems. Standardizing the OCI-H3 interface provides ease of migration from one billing system to another. The OCI-H3 interface must also be extensible to allow new service definitions to be added over time.

Issues

There are a number of issues that must be resolved to achieve the goal of standard operational interfaces:

- Support of legacy deployments—In existing practice, most operational interfaces are pair-wise proprietary agreements between headend system suppliers and billing system suppliers. This causes a proliferation of interfaces and limits flexibility.
- Definition and agreement of interfaces—There is much work to do to define a standard interface definition for OCI-H3.

- Support of new billing models (for example, VOD and e-commerce)—the current operational interface for billing recognizes only subscription and pay-per-view events. The operational interface must be flexible enough to support new types of service that have different billing models.

Development Status

At the time of writing, the OCI-H3 interface is undefined by OpenCable. There is considerable work to make a standard operations interface a reality. However, an initiative by Time Warner Cable and Scientific Atlanta has defined a standard Billing and Operational Support System (BOSS) interface, which is supported by all of Time Warner Cable's billing system vendors.

Summary

This chapter summarized the current issues and development of the OpenCable headend interfaces. Three headend interfaces were defined:

- OCI-H1, programming content—The goal of the OCI-H1 interface is to define a standard content format for all digital services. A standard format for content eases delivery from the content provider to the headend and enables retransmission agreements between content providers and cable operators.
- OCI-H2, conditional access—The OCI-H2 interface provides separation of the conditional access function from the rest of the headend functions. This interface is the headend equivalent of the OCI-C2 interface. The OpenCAS group is actively working on these interfaces at the time of writing.
- OCI-H3, billing and operational support—The goal of the OCI-H3 interface is to define a standard interface that supports all the operational functions for the cable system. This interface must support the existing billing systems and the existing operations of deployed digital cable systems. Scientific Atlanta's BOSS interface is becoming the *de facto* standard for billing system interfacing.

References

Book

Ciciora, Walter, James Farmer, and David Large. *Modern Cable Television Technology; Video, Voice, and Data Communications*. San Francisco, CA: Morgan Kaufmann Publishers, Inc., 1999.

Papers

Kar, Mukta, Majid Chelehmal, Richard S. Prodan, and Chezhian Renganathan. "Cable headend architecture for Delivery of Multimedia Services." *NTCA Convention Papers,* 1999.

Prodan, Richard S., Mukta Kar, and Majid Chelehmal. "Rate-remultiplexing: An Optimimum Bandwidth Utilization Technology." *NTCA Convention Papers,* 1999.

Standards

SMPTE 312M. SMPTE Standard for Television. "Splice Points for MPEG-2 Transport Streams.Digital Program Insertion Cueing Message for Cable." DPI Ad Hoc Working Group, Preliminary V8.5, September 1, 1999.

ETSI TS 101 197. "DVB Simulcrypt Specification Part 1." (Available at the ETSI Web site—see the following section.)

Internet Resources

Pegasus Functional Requirements for Video-On-Demand (VOD) Systems V2.0. Time Warner Cable, 1997.

http://timewarner.com/rfp

Open Conditional Access (OpenCAS) Web site

http://www.opencas.com

European Telecommunications Standards Institute (ETSI) Web site

http://www.etsi.org

CHAPTER 16

OCI-N: The Network Interface

The OpenCable Network Interface (OCI-N) is the most important of all the OpenCable interfaces because it supports plug-and-play of set-tops, cable ready digital televisions, or other devices to the OpenCable network (see Figure 16-1). Standardizing the OCI-N interface allows different kinds of equipment to attach to the network, supporting a family of *OpenCable devices*, where each family member can be built by a different vendor to a set of open standards.

This chapter describes the OCI-N interface as follows:

- Scope—The scope of OCI-N includes all analog and digital channels used for television services.
- Issues—The OCI-N specification raises many issues related to performance and protocols. Performance specifications must be agreed to by all devices connecting to the cable network. Protocol specifications must be agreed to for all network interface functions.
- Frequency-domain view—The OCI-N interface is a broadband interface that allows many channels to coexist within the passband of the HFC network.
- Channel types—The OCI-N interface defines several channel types: in-band channels that carry an analog NTSC channel or a 64-QAM or 256-QAM channel and forward and reverse out-of-band channels that are used to provide a two-way data communications link between the headend and the OpenCable device.
- Protocol layering—Each of the different channel types is described using a layered protocol model. The protocol layers for in-band channels follow a single standard. In contrast, three alternatives exist for out-of-band channels: DVS-167 (DAVIC OOB V1.2), DVS-178, and DOCSIS V1.0.

Figure 16-1 *OpenCable Reference Diagram*

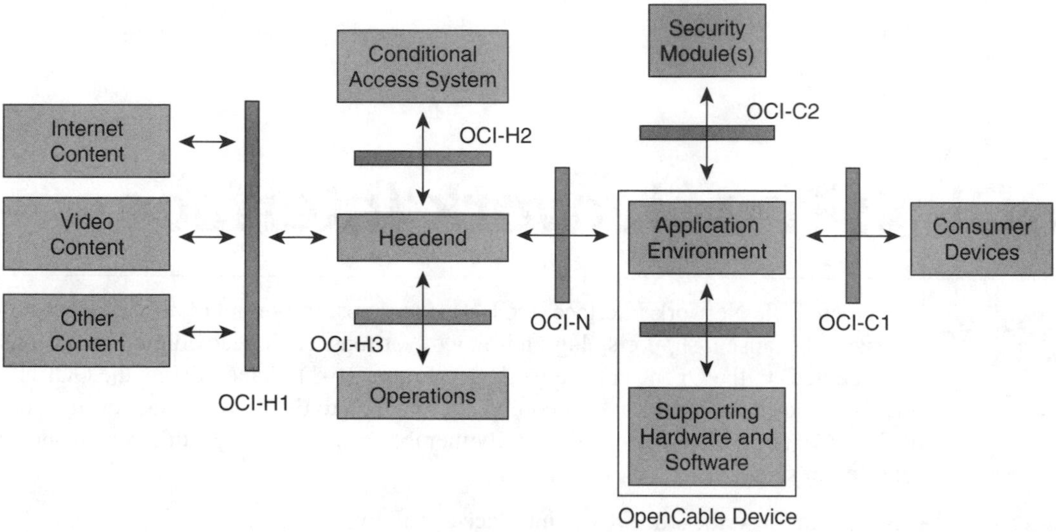

Scope of OCI-N

The OCI-N defines all the digital channels (in-band and out-of-band) and in-the-clear analog NTSC channels. OCI-N defines all aspects of the network interface that are common to cable systems and that are based on open standards. The conditional access system protocols are not fully defined by the OCI-N interface, but this is acceptable because they are terminated by the point-of-deployment (POD) module.

Issues

The network interface to a cable system is evolving from a variety of proprietary protocols toward a more standards-based approach. There are still many issues associated with the definition of the OCI-N interface that are at various stages of resolution:

- Performance parameters—In an HFC broadband network, the performance of each terminal device that attaches to the network affects the performance of the shared-media network. Thus, one terminal device can adversely effect the service to many customers. Consumer electronics (CE) manufacturers and cable operators will probably continue to disagree about the stringency of performance parameters; the CE manufacturers are focused on cost and the cable operators are more concerned about performance. An example of this can be found in the EIA-23 standard (see EIA-23 RF Interface Specification for Television Receiving Devices and Cable Television Systems), which contains two different values for the signals between 30 and 54 MHz because no agreement could be reached after years of negotiations. The CE and cable proposals from Annex A of EIA 23 are shown in Table 16-1. As you can see, the cable-proposed levels are higher, which makes the tuner design more difficult and costly. The reason is to reject spurious signals generated by return transmitters in set-tops and cable modems.

Table 16-1 *Maximum RMS Value for 30–54 MHz Individual Signals*

Frequency Range	CE Proposal	Cable Proposal
30–41 MHz	+24 dBmV	+35 dBmV
41–48 MHz	0 dBmV	0 dBmV
48–54 MHz	–10 dBmV	–10 dB relative to channel 2 visual carrier or + 10 dBmV

- Service information (SI)—There has been considerable discussion regarding the SI standard for OCI-N. The existing practice is based on ATSC standard A/56 and is part of the Harmony agreement. The standard for terrestrial broadcast was changed and extended as A/65 after the cable industry had adopted A/56. As a result, there are now two competing standards for service information.
- Program guide information—As each cable vendor developed electronic program guides (EPG), they created or licensed one of several different proprietary guide formats. The guide information itself is purchased by the cable operator and sold as part of a package that includes the set-top, which decodes and displays the EPG. Thus, an OpenCable device would have to support multiple guide formats to be truly portable across multiple cable systems.
- Emergency alert system (EAS)—All cable operators with more than 10,000 subscribers are required to support EAS override for all channels (analog and digital) as of January 1, 1999. Video override of compressed digital channels is technically more complex because of the transport multiplexing layer. Moreover, a digital set-top might be *tuned* to a Web page or an e-mail session, so the concept of video override does not always make sense.
- Network management—Digital set-tops provide network management features, such as reporting signal levels and error rates. However, set-tops might use proprietary protocols and have varying network management capabilities.
- On-demand services—On-demand services have special signaling requirements, as described in Chapter 10, "On-Demand Services," to create on-demand sessions and to provide stream control. Although the Digital Storage Management—Command and Control (DSM-CC) standard (ISO-IEC 13818-6) provides a framework that is widely adopted for on-demand service, there are many variations from one implementation to another.

- Interactive Services—No standards have yet been agreed on for the description of interactive services that do not conform to traditional broadcast content–oriented services. A proposal for an application service protocol (DVS-181) to advertise all services, such as broadcast, e-mail, Web browsing, e-commerce, and games, has been submitted to the SCTE Digital Video Standards subcommittee but there has been little progress toward adoption of this as a standard.

The Frequency-Domain View

Figure 16-2 shows the frequency-domain view of a typical upgraded cable system, which is capable of supporting up to 135 6-MHz channels in the forward path (providing a maximum information rate of more than 5 Gbps!). The forward spectrum is divided between analog channels and digital channels, the latter usually occupying the higher frequencies above 550 MHz. The boundary between analog and digital channels is flexible and, over time, analog channels will be retired and replaced with digital channels. The digital channels can be transmitted at a lower signal level (about 6 to 10 dB lower) to reduce overall loading on the HFC system.

Figure 16-2 *OCI-N at the F-Connector*

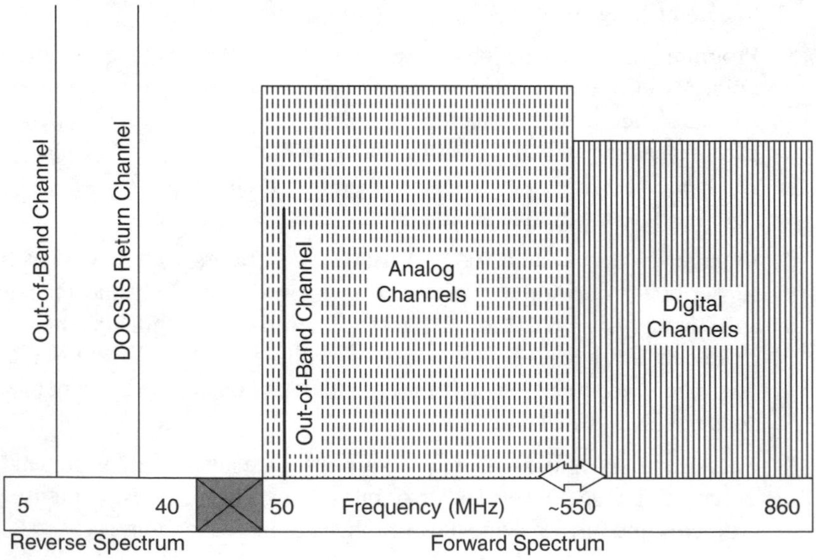

The frequencies of the forward channels are defined by the Cable Television Channel Identification Plan (EIA-542). (See Chapter 8 of *Modern Cable Television Technology; Video, Voice, and Data Communications,* by Ciciora and others.)

Some cable systems support two-way operation by providing a return path from the home to the cable network. A passband of 5 to 42 MHz is typical although there are variations between different systems. The return spectrum is used predominantly for digitally modulated carriers generated by set-tops, cable modems, and cable telephony equipment. As illustrated in Figure 16-1, considerable amplitude is required to send these signals back through thc cablc systcm, duc to attenuation at the tap by as much as 29 dB.

There are, as yet, no standards for frequency allocation in the return spectrum, and cable operators are specifying agile transmitters in new equipment so that the return spectrum can be used efficiently.

Channel Types

The broadband cable system allows the luxury of defining a number of different channel types that are used for different purposes (see Figure 16-3).

Figure 16-3 *OCI-N Channel Types*

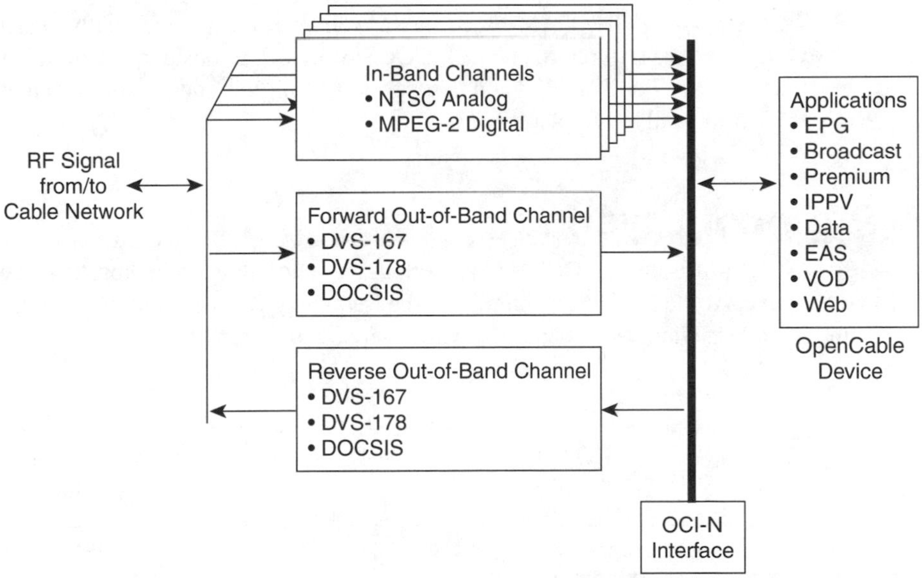

As shown in Figure 16-3, there are three main types of channels:

- In-band channels—These are further subdivided into analog and digital subtypes. These channels are 6 MHz in bandwidth in North America and Japan (or 8 MHz in Europe), and are called in-band channels because usually only one channel is tuned at any given time.

- Forward out-of-band (OOB) channel—The forward and reverse OOB channels work together to provide a two-way data communications link across the OCI-N interface. These channels are called out-of-band channels because they are always tuned by the OpenCable device, providing *always-connected* properties similar to a local area network.
- Reverse out-of-band (OOB) channel—The reverse OOB channel works in conjunction with the forward OOB channel. The reverse OOB channel is optional according to the requirements of the cable operator, but it provides the resource for many advanced services, including impulse PPV, on-demand, and interactive services (see Part II, "Interactive and On-Demand Services").

As shown in Figure 16-3, there are three choices for the out-of-band channel pair:

- DVS-167—A narrow-band QPSK-based format developed by DAVIC and used by the Pegasus system. (See Chapter 5, "Adding Digital Television Services to Cable Systems.")
- DVS-178—A narrow-band QPSK-based format developed by GI and used in the DigiCable system. (See Chapter 5.)
- DOCSIS—A 6 MHz QAM-based forward channel is combined with a narrow-band QPSK or QAM-16 return channel. DOCSIS provides considerably more bandwidth than DVS-167 or DVS-178 and is supported by higher-end set-tops, such as the GI DCT-5000 and SA Explorer 6000.

OCI-N Protocol Layering

Figure 16-4 illustrates the OCI-N from both a frequency-domain and protocol-layered perspective. At the base of the diagram is the frequency-division multiplexing layer that supports a large number of channels, which may be of different types.

Figure 16-4 *OCI-N Protocol Layers*

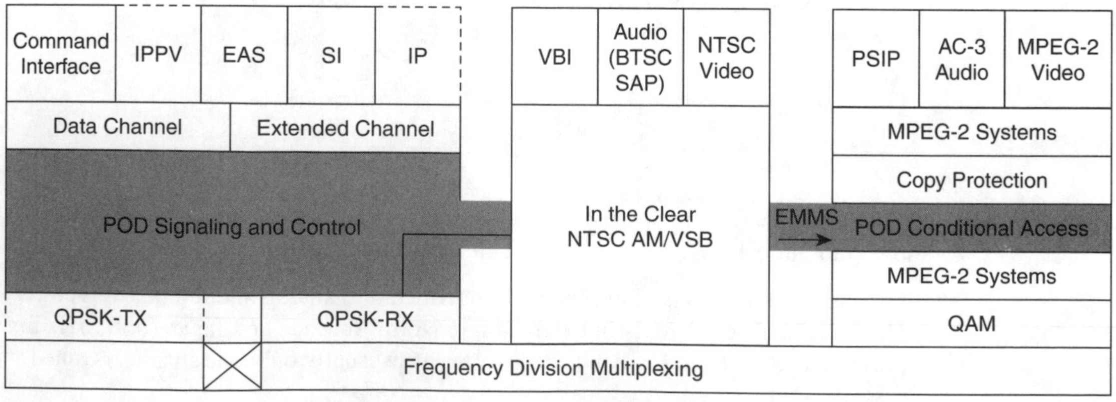

The left side of Figure 16-4 illustrates the protocol stack for the DVS-167/DVS-178 out-of-band channels. The modulation layer (QPSK) is used to adapt the baseband signal to the analog network (see Chapter 4, "Digital Technologies," for QPSK operation). Above the QPSK layer, the data-link and network layer protocols for the DVS-167/DVS-178 out-of-band channel are implemented in the point-of-deployment (POD) module because multiple standards exist (see Chapter 18, "OCI-C2: The Security Interface"). The POD effectively hides this complexity from the OpenCable device (or host) to allow a manufacturer to build a single type of OpenCable device for all of North America. The POD module and its interface (OCI-C2) is described in detail in Chapter 18. At the upper boundary of the POD, two control and signaling channels are presented to the OpenCable device; the data channel and the extended channel.

The data channel provides communications to the POD module for initialization and configuration via a set of defined commands that are carried across the command interface. The data channel also supports a generic impulse pay-per-view (IPPV) interface to allow the OpenCable device to communicate with the conditional access function in the POD module.

The extended channel provides for communications to the headend via the out-of-band channel. The signaling flows include emergency alert system (EAS) messages, service information (SI), and, optionally, Internet Protocol–based communications for applications support.

The center of Figure 16-4 illustrates the protocol stack for NTSC analog channels. The OCI-N interface does not include any definition of scrambled analog channels because the POD module does not support analog de-scrambling. NTSC video channels employ amplitude modulation vestigial sideband (AM-VSB). The video vertical blanking interval (VBI) is used to carry a limited amount of data. Audio is carried by means of a separate subcarrier. (See Chapter 2 of *Modern Cable Television Techology; Video, Voice, and Data Communications,* by Ciciora and others.)

The right side of Figure 16-4 illustrates the protocol stack for digital channels. All in-band digital channels use QAM modulation to impose a digital bit stream onto a 6 MHz RF carrier. Above the QAM layer is the MPEG-2 systems layer, which is used to transfer encrypted digital data to the POD module. The POD module is responsible for providing the conditional access function for digital signals, which varies from one cable system to another. The entitlement management messages (EMMs) are delivered via the out-of-band channel to provide the POD module with the necessary authorization for premium services (see Chapter 18). Above the conditional access layer is a copy protection layer, which is required to protect the digital data as it flows across the OCI-C2 interface. The MPEG-2 systems layer multiplexes compressed audio and video content into a single multi-program transport stream (see Chapter 4). In addition, in-band program and system information protocol (PSIP) might be carried to describe the contents of the multi-program transport stream.

The optional DOCSIS channel is not shown in Figure 16-4 and will be described separately in the DOCSIS section.

This overview provides a summary of the various protocol layers for each channel type. The following sections describe the standards associated with each layer and channel type.

In-Band Channels

In-band channels can be divided according to modulation into analog and digital channels, which are described in the following sections.

Analog

Figure 16-5 illustrates the protocol layers for the analog channels. At the base is the frequency-division multiplexing layer, which is channelized according to the EIA-542 tuning plan into 6 MHz channels.

Figure 16-5 *Analog Protocol Stack*

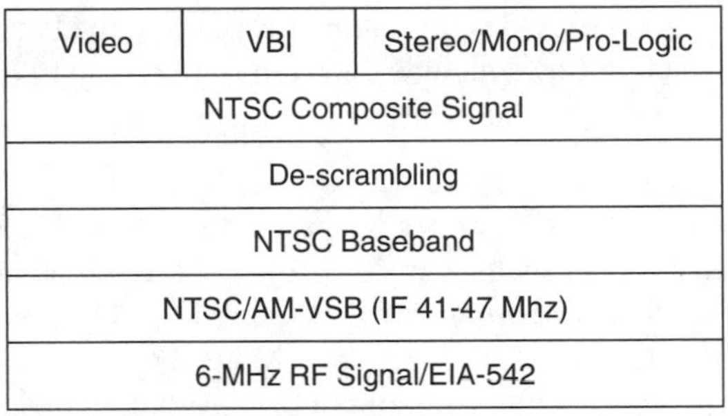

After tuning, an intermediate frequency (IF) signal with a center frequency of 44 MHz is standard. The NTSC baseband signal might be scrambled according to a number of different techniques to prevent signal theft. After demodulation and de-scrambling, an NTSC composite signal is recovered, which includes luminance information at baseband combined with modulated chrominance and audio carriers as defined by SMPTE-170M. The composite signal can be further processed to output other video/audio formats, such as S-Video stereo, mono, and pro-logic audio. VBI data is sent in the NTSC vertical blanking interval (VBI) lines and is then processed by the OpenCable device or television receiver in compliance with FCC 47 CFR part 15.119.

The analog channels deliver broadcast, subscription, and impulse pay-per-view services. The analog channels might be in the clear or scrambled, but the de-scrambling algorithms are closely guarded and proprietary to each cable vendor. The decoder-interface standard EIA 105 was designed to provide a replaceable analog security device but was not implemented by consumer electronics or cable operators. The OCI-N interface defines only in-the-clear analog services.

Digital

The in-band digital channels provide video, audio, and data services. Figure 16-6 shows the protocol stack for digital channels. At the base is the frequency-division multiplexing layer, which is channelized according to the EIA-542 tuning plan into 6 MHz channels. After tuning, the QAM intermediate frequency is recovered and demodulated to a baseband signal that is an MPEG-2 multi-program transport stream as defined by DVS-241.

Figure 16-6 *Digital Protocol Stack*

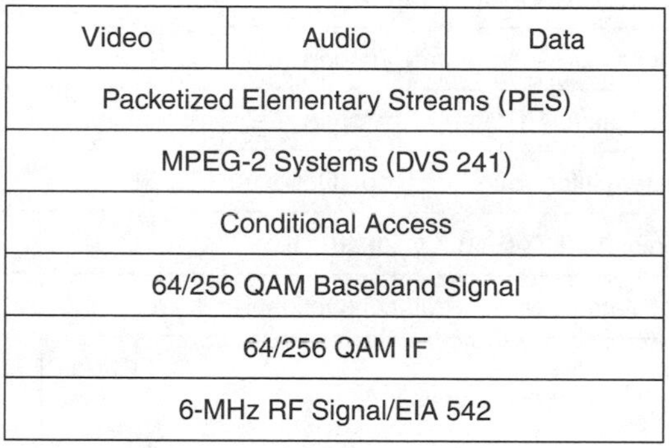

As with analog channels, the digital video channels are secured by conditional access technology that remains the closely guarded and proprietary property of each cable vendor. Unlike analog, a separable security module (the POD module, see Chapter 18) has been adopted by the cable industry. The OCI-C2 interface specifies the interface to the POD module.

Digital channels make extensive use of the MPEG-2 systems layer for multiplexing, as shown in Figure 16-7.

Figure 16-7 *In-Band Digital Channels*

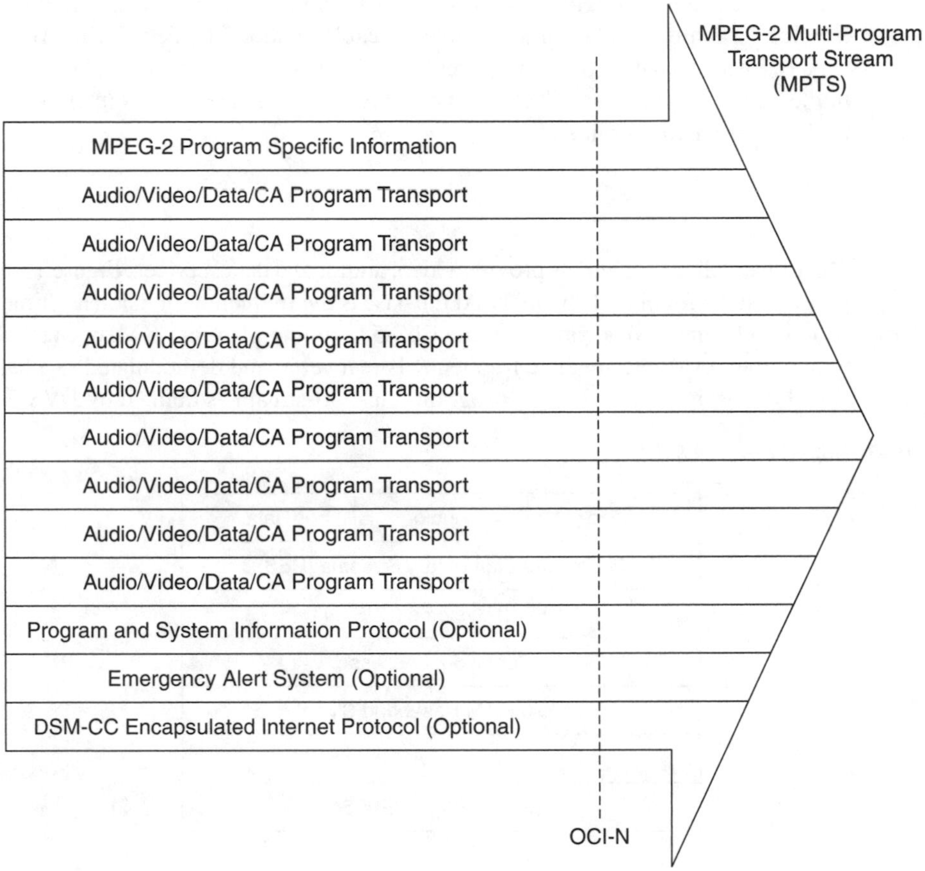

The MPEG-2 systems layer multiplexes a number of different types of information. Figure 16-7 illustrates the different stream types that might be incorporated into a digital video channel:

- MPEG-2 program specific information (PSI)—The role of the PSI tables is to describe the rest of the transport stream (see Chapter 4).
- Audio, video, data, and CA packetized elementary streams (PES)—Each MPEG-2 program consists of several packet identifiers (PIDs) for audio, video, data, and conditional access ECMs. As illustrated, these program transports account for the majority of the bandwidth of the multiplex.

- Program and system information protocol (PSIP)—The PSIP standard (ATSC A/65) might be used to describe the audio and video services within the transport stream. This standard is used for terrestrial broadcast, so a retransmission over cable will include a PSIP description (unless the cable operator explicitly removes it). However, cable-originated channels do not typically include any PSIP description because the out-of-band channel carries equivalent information for all in-band channels.
- Emergency alert system (EAS)—The CEMA/NCTA Joint Engineering Committee has developed a standard for the transmission of EAS messages in the form of MPEG private table sections (DVS-208, EIA 814). This standard allows emergency alert messages to be sent to the OpenCable device to communicate EAS events in a standard format. In-band EAS messages are optional on encrypted in-band channels because the cable operator has the option of sending them on the out-of-band channel (the logic is that to decrypt the channel, the receiver must have an out-of-band receiver). However, in-band EAS messages are mandatory on in the clear in band channels because of the possibility that a cable ready receiver without an out-of-band receiver can tune these channels.
- Internet Protocol(IP)—IP messages can be encapsulated into MPEG-2 private data sections according to the DSM-CC standard (see DSM-CC, Digital Storage Media—Command and Control). IP messages can be used to carry data to support interactive applications, such as Web browsing, which might require more bandwidth than can be supported by the narrow out-of-band channel.

The DSM-CC data carousel provides a standard mechanism for continuously transmitting any type of information over a channel. In practice, a data carousel is typically used to transmit PSIP and EAS messages on in-band digital channels.

Out-of-Band Channels

The forward and reverse out-of-band channels are designed to provide a two-way connectionless signaling path between the OpenCable device and the headend. Figure 16-8 shows the logical message flows supported by the out-of-band channel.

Figure 16-8 *Out-of-Band Channels*

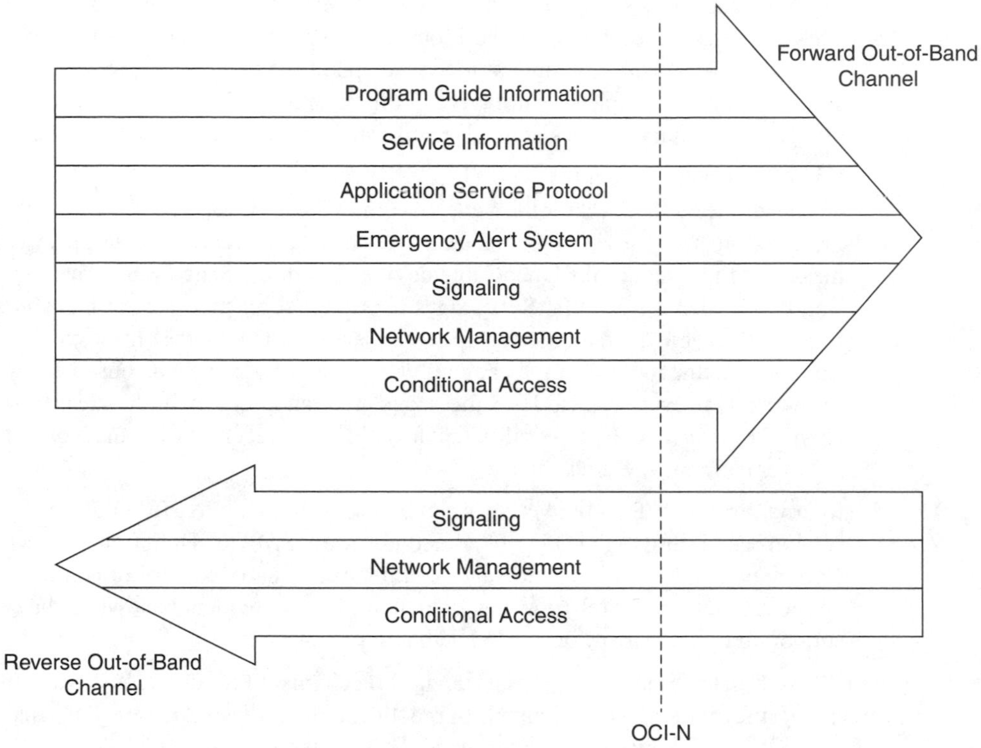

There is considerable controversy about the need for a reverse out-of-band channel, which is required for interactive and on-demand services but not for broadcast services. As a result, the return transmitter is currently defined only in the OpenCable device functional requirements for bidirectional cable systems (see Chapter 14, "OpenCable Device Functional Requirements"). The following sections separate one-way and two-way flows for clarity.

One-Way Flows

It is important to understand one-way operation of the out-of-band channel because this mode of operation can occur for a number of reasons:

- The OpenCable device does not include a reverse transmitter.
- The cable system has not been upgraded to support two-way operation.

- There is a failure in the reverse path due to excessive ingress, attenuation, or a return amplifier failure.

In any of these cases, it is a requirement that the cable system gracefully degrades into one-way operation and continues to support broadcast services. The one-way flows are

- Program guide information—This is continuously broadcast for all channels supported by the cable system. The format is proprietary and often tied to the EPG application in the set-top.
- Service information—This is continuously broadcast for all channels supported by the cable system. The format is specified by DVS-234, which is based on A/56. However, in response to requests from the CE industry, DVS-234 has added several features from PSIP as optional profiles to include support for parental control and a standard program guide data representation.
- Application service protocol—This is continuously broadcast to advertise interactive services available to the OpenCable device. The proposed format is contained in DVS-181, but little progress has been made to adopt it as a standard to date.
- Emergency alert system—During an alert, messages are sent that contain information about the alert condition. The OpenCable device is required to display the alert condition as a graphics overlay. In certain cases, a message might be sent to force-tune the OpenCable device to the appropriate alert channel.
- Conditional access—This consists of addressed messages (EMMs) to individual OpenCable devices and set-tops. The same EMM must be sent repeatedly when a system is in one-way operation because there is no way for the OpenCable device to acknowledge message receipt.

The DSM-CC data carousel provides a standard mechanism for continuously transmitting any type of information over a channel. In practice, a data carousel is used to transmit these information flows on the forward out-of-band channel.

Two-Way Flows

The two-way flows are

- Signaling—There are many possible signaling flows to support interactive and on-demand applications. The TCP/IP protocol suite provides addressing and multiplexing facilities that may be used to support a number of different concurrent signaling flows to different entities in the headend from an OpenCable device.
- Network management—The simple network management protocol (SNMP) may be used to monitor and control the OpenCable device or POD.
- Conditional access—The reporting of purchase information is required for the support of impulse pay-per-view services. A secure protocol is used by the conditional access system, which is not specified by the OCI-N interface.

Forward OOB Channel

Figure 16-9 compares the protocol stacks for the three alternative forward out-of-band channels.

Figure 16-9 *Protocol Stack for Forward Out-of-Band Channel*

SCTE DVS 167	SCTE DVS 178	DOCSIS
Payload	Payload	Payload (DPU)
		IP, ICMP
		LLC/DIX
		Link Security
ATM Cell Format	Data Link Layer	MAC
Reed-Solomon	MAC Sublayer	Transmission Convergence
Interleaving	MPEG-2 Transport	MPEG-2 Transport
SL-ESF Frame Payload Structure	Randomizer	Randomizer
SL-ESF Format	Reed-Solomon	Reed-Solomon
Randomizer	Interleaving	Interleaving
QPSK/Differential Coding	QPSK/Differential Coding	64/256 QAM

Reverse OOB Channel

Figure 16-10 compares the protocol stacks for the three alternative reverse out-of-band channels.

Figure 16-10 *Protocol Stack for Out-of-Band Return Channel*

<table>
<tr><td>SCTE DVS 167</td><td>SCTE DVS 178</td><td>DOCSIS</td></tr>
<tr><td rowspan="2">Payload</td><td rowspan="2">Payload</td><td>Payload (DPU)</td></tr>
<tr><td>IP, ICMP</td></tr>
<tr><td>Data Link Layer/AAL-5</td><td>Data Link Layer/AAL-5</td><td>LLC/DIX</td></tr>
<tr><td>MAC Sublayer</td><td>ATM Cell Format</td><td>Link Security</td></tr>
<tr><td>ATM Cell Format</td><td rowspan="2">MAC Packet Sublayer</td><td>MAC Packet Sublayer</td></tr>
<tr><td>Time Slot Structure</td><td>Time Slot Structure</td></tr>
<tr><td>Reed-Solomon</td><td>Randomizer</td><td>FEC</td></tr>
<tr><td>Randomizer</td><td>Reed-Solomon</td><td>Scrambler</td></tr>
<tr><td>QPSK/Differential Coding</td><td>QPSK/Differential Coding</td><td>QPSK/16-QAM</td></tr>
</table>

Summary

OCI-N is still under development, but progress is being made and OCI-N includes the following standards (which are part of existing cable practice):

- ATSC Digital Television Standard (A/53)—This standard describes the overall system characteristics of the U.S. Advanced Television System.
- RF Interface Specification for Television Receiving Devices and Cable Television Systems (EIA-23)—This standard provides RF performance recommendations for the digital set-top.
- Cable Television Channel Identification Plan (EIA-542)—This standard specifies the frequencies of all cable channels. (See Chapter 8 of *Modern Cable Television Technology; Video, Voice, and Data Communications,* by Ciciora and others.)
- Digital Transmission Standard for Cable Televisions (DVS-031)—This standard specifies the modulation (64-QAM or 256-QAM), forward error correction, and framing of the digital payload (see Chapter 4).
- Digital Video Service Multiplex (DVS-093)—This standard references the MPEG-2 systems layer (see Chapter 4).
- Service Information for Digital Television (DVS-234)—This standard specifies the out-of-band format and is based on A/56.

Retransmission of terrestrial digital broadcast channels adds a new protocol for tuning and guide information:

- Program and System Information Protocol for Terrestrial Broadcast and Cable (DVS-097)—This standard specifies that the in-band format is based on A/65. A/65 is the terrestrial broadcast standard for system information.

References

Book

Ciciora, Walter, James Farmer, and David Large. *Modern Cable Television Technology; Video, Voice, and Data Communications*. San Francisco, CA: Morgan Kaufmann Publishers, Inc., 1999.

Standards

CableLabs. "OpenCable Network Interface Specification." Cable Television Laboratories, Inc.

EIA-23. "RF Interface Specification for Television Receiving Devices and Cable Television Systems." October 1998.

ISO-IEC 13818-6. EIA Engineering Department. "Digital Storage Media—Command and Control (DSM-CC)."

SCTE DVS-241 "Draft: Digital Video Service Multiplex and Transport System Standard for Cable Television." August 6, 1999.

Internet Resources

The SCTE DVS FTP site for DVS documents is maintained by CableLabs

http://www.cablelabs.com.

CHAPTER 17

OCI-C1: The Consumer Interface

The OCI-C1 interface connects the OpenCable device to the consumer devices in the home. The OCI-C1 interface is of paramount importance for cable operators because it allows them to deploy a digital set-top, which provides the service delivery gateway between the cable network and the consumer device. Conversely, the OCI-C1 interface is less important when a cable ready digital television is envisioned because the set-top functions are integrated into the television. In this case, the consumer interface becomes the territory of the consumer electronics manufacturers.

Figure 17-1 illustrates that the intelligence is to the left of the OCI-C1 interface, within the applications environment. To the right of the OCI-C1 interface, the functions are predominately associated with the display of the service rather than the presentation of it. In other words, the user interface and service management functions are done prior to the OCI-C1 interface in the OpenCable device.

This chapter is organized as follows:

- Goals—The OCI-C1 interface is intended to provide a digital content delivery mechanism from the digital set-top to a digital television with support for content protection. It must also support high definition services and user interface functions.
- Issues—OCI-C1 issues include providing for high-quality transfer of video and audio from the set-top to the consumer display device, the challenges of effective copy protection, and carriage of the high bit rates of digital television signals.
- OCI-C1 Family—The OCI-C1 interface describes a family of analog and digital interfaces between the digital set-top and the consumer display device. The analog interfaces (RF channel 3/4, composite, S-video, and component video) are summarized. The digital interface defined by OCI-C1 (the home digital network interface) is described in detail with descriptions of video, audio, and graphics transfers and the digital transmission content protection mechanism.

Figure 17-1 *OpenCable Reference Diagram*

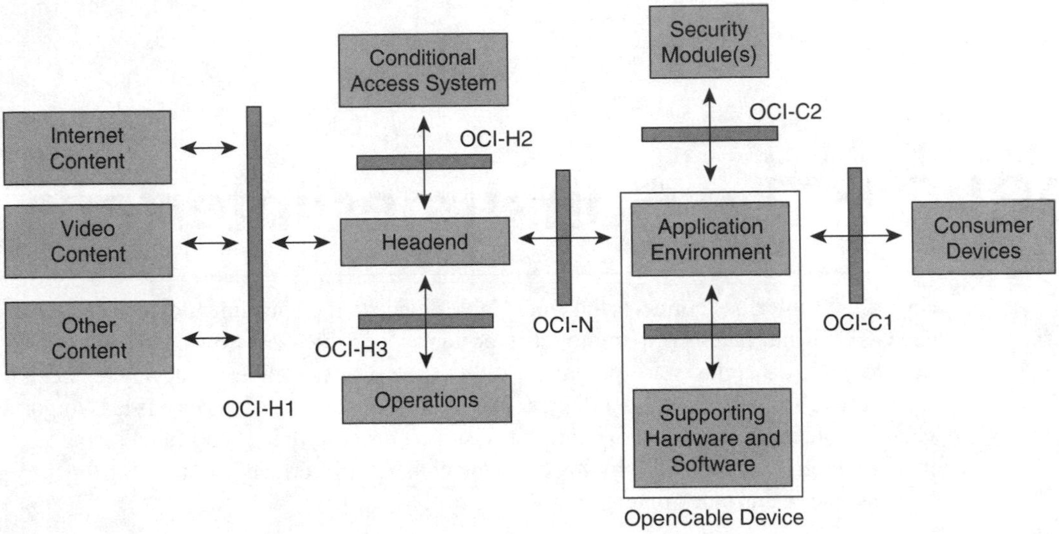

Goals

The goals of the OCI-C1 interface are

- To support a digital interface from a digital set-top to the television receiver—Until recently, the analog NTSC interface from the set-top to the television receiver provided the only way to display television services. With the advent of digital cable services, the analog link reduces the quality of the signal from the set-top and becomes a bottleneck for new services.
- To provide content protection—Traditionally, the limited quality of the analog NTSC signal and limited analog duplication capabilities makes theft of the signal from an analog set-top uninteresting to the serious pirate. In addition, the Macrovision copy protection techniques for NTSC signals and VHS videocassette recorders achieve the desired result of "keep the honest people honest" despite the fact that they can be easily circumvented.

Today, the combination of digital services, multimedia PCs and the Internet are changing the ground rules of content protection. Signal quality is improved almost to the quality of the master copy, multimedia PCs provide multiple generation digital copying without quality loss, and the Internet provides an inexpensive and rapid distribution mechanism for digital content. For these reasons, digital content protection is based on the same principles of digital cryptography as digital conditional access systems (see Chapter 6, "The Digital Set-Top Converter" and the section Content Protection later in this chapter).

- To support high definition services—An interface is required to carry high definition signals (at 720-line progressive or 1080-line interlace vertical resolutions) from the set-top to the display device. Analog standards exist (see the section OCI-C1 Family later in this chapter), but there is no effective copy protection mechanism. For this reason, the content owners are insisting on the use of digital interfaces that can support encryption.
- To support the cable user interface with a single remote control in the cable environment—As the display device (the television in most cases) becomes more sophisticated, there is more potential for features to clash in the set-top and the television. Examples from the analog world, such as watch-and-record and picture-in-picture (see Chapter 3, "The Analog Set-Top Converter"), transfer to the digital world. In addition, new interactive features (see Chapter 8, "Interactive Services"), implemented in both the set-top and the television receiver, might cause more confusion. In the OCI-C1 model, the set-top provides the user interface and remote control, and the television receiver provides only display functions.

Issues

There are many issues regarding the consumer interface that is associated with the transition to digital television and with advanced services, such as interactive and on-demand services. In general, the more advanced the service, the more local (or client) involvement in the composition and presentation of the user experience. For example, digital broadcast requires only the well-understood MPEG-2 decoding function, whereas an interactive service requires additional graphics, user input, and computational functions.

The following issues are important in the consumer interface:

- To maintain quality of a digital signal, it should be transferred from the set-top to the display device in digital form if possible.
- Associated with the digital transfer of video from the set-top to the display is the issue of content protection. The Motion Picture Association of America (MPAA) has decided that this is a beach to die on. The prospect of unlimited digital copies with no degradation combined with mass electronic communication over the Internet is frightening to any copyright owner. Moreover, the recent Digital Millenium

Copyright Act has made it necessary to physically encrypt digital bit streams to provide the legal basis for content protection. Unfortunately, there are at least five content protection schemes that are currently being promoted by various companies or groups of companies—which one do we pick?

- The required bit rate of *uncompressed* digital video is enormous (especially at higher resolutions) see Table 17-1. Until recently, most digital interconnections were designed for *compressed* digital transfer (for example, IEEE 1394). Unfortunately, the compressed digital video cannot be modified, preventing the addition of graphics overlays for a user interface. Uncompressed digital links are under development (for example, VESA's Plug & Display).

Table 17-1 *Resolution and Frame Rate Versus Bit Rate*

Video Resolution	Compressed Bit Rate	Uncompressed Bit Rate
Standard (30 fps) 480 x 720	3–8 Mbps	124 Mbps
High (60 fps) 720 x 1280	15 Mbps	664 Mbps
High (24 fps) (1080 x 1920)	12 Mbps	597 Mbps
High (30 fps) (1080 x 1920)	18.8 Mbps	746 Mbps
High (60 fps) (1080 x 1920)	Not yet established	1493 Mbps

The home digital network interface (HDNI) uses IEEE 1394 with extensions designed to overcome the limitations of compressed video transfer by separately sending graphics information and establishing that the digital receiver is responsible for compositing the video and graphics. This approach, which comes with its own set of advantages and disadvantages, is explained in some detail in this chapter.

OCI-C1 Family

Although OCI-C1 defines new interfaces required for digital services (both standard and high definition), OCI-C1 is an umbrella definition that includes the current practice for connecting set-tops to consumer electronics equipment. There are many potential interface standards to choose from, as illustrated by Figure 17-2:

Figure 17-2 *Consumer Interface Family Tree*

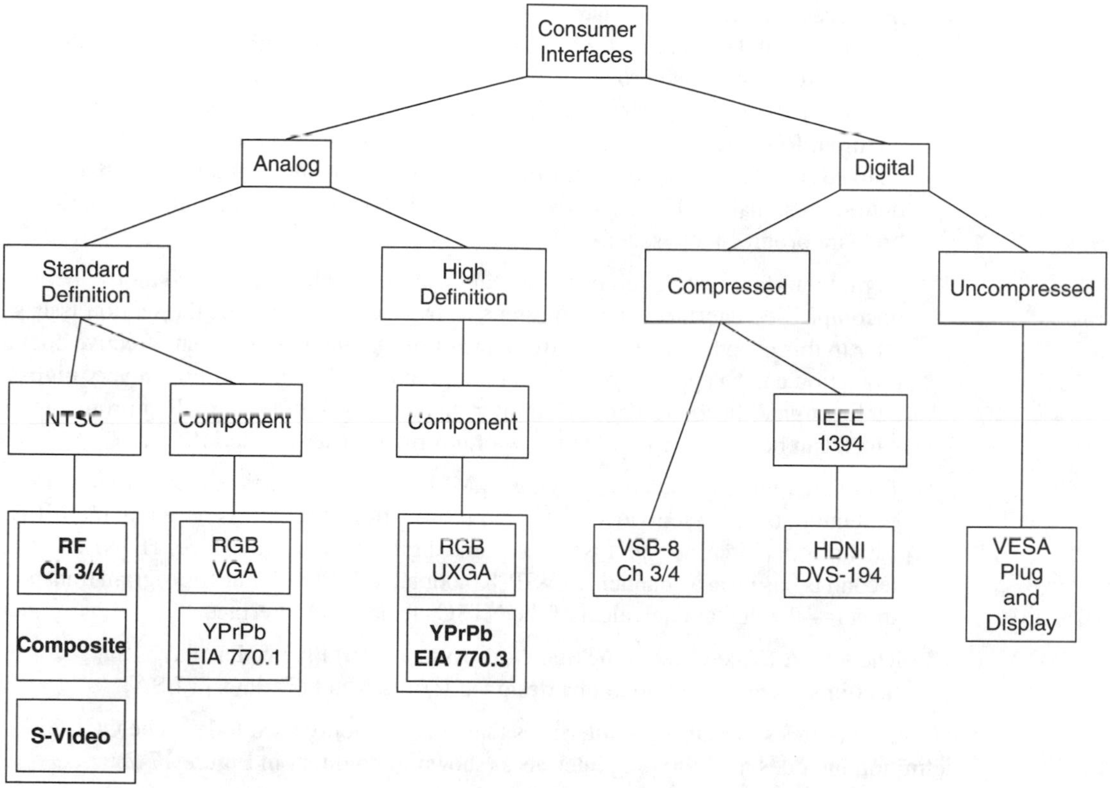

- NTSC interfaces—Although limited to standard definition signals, NTSC still provides the basis for 99% of today's OCI-C1 connections. The RF channel 3/4 variant is most common and provides a single 75 ohm coaxial connection for video and audio. The channel 3/4 connection is particularly useful because it allows bypass operation of the set-top (see Chapter 6). Composite (or baseband) NTSC video requires separate audio (usually left and right) and solves the problem of delivering a stereo audio signal from a set-top to a separate amplifier. Finally, S-video separates the luminance and chrominance components of the NTSC signal to increase horizontal resolution and to avoid certain NTSC artifacts associated with luma-chroma separation. (See *Video Demystified: A handbook for the digital engineer,* Second Edition, by Keith Jack, Chapter 4.)

- Analog interfaces—Limited because of their lack of copy protection, analog interfaces extend from standard definition to high definition signals. The most important standards are EIA 770.1 and EIA 770.2 (for standard definition 480-line interlaced and 480-line progressively scanned signals) and EIA 770.3 (for high definition 1080-line interlaced and 720-line progressively scanned signals). In addition, RGB (red-green-blue) interfaces for computer monitors are sometimes adapted for use as a video interface: VGA (640 × 480) approximating standard definition signals and UXGA (1600 × 1200 pixels) approximating high definition—both are progressively scanned.
- Digital interfaces—Digital interfaces can be divided into compressed and uncompressed interfaces. Each presents its own set of issues (see the section Issues later in this chapter). The main advantage of digital interfaces is that effective copy protection can be applied (based on cryptography), while maintaining a very high-quality signal. In addition, a digital interface can also support signaling protocols, which can be used to control the flow of information across the interface.
- There are two proposals for carrying an MPEG-2 multi-program transport stream containing compressed video and audio information. The first is based on the IEEE 1394 physical interface and is called home digital network interface (HDNI). The second is based on a channel 3/4 VSB-8 modulated MPEG-2 multi-program transport stream—the digital equivalent of the NTSC channel 3/4 interface.
- The VESA (Video Electronic Standards Association) Plug & Display is an uncompressed digital video link designed for flat panel displays [VESA].

OCI-C1 embraces the subset of interfaces that are commonly used today. The OCI-C1 definition includes the following interfaces (shown in bold text in Figure 17-2):

- NTSC RF channel 3/4—The NTSC signal is modulated onto RF channel 3 or 4 with the audio signal, which might be BTSC-encoded.
- Composite—Composite (or baseband) video uses a single RCA connector to carry the NTSC video signal.
- S-video—S-video provides the highest-quality alternative for NTSC-encoded signals and uses a 4-pin mini-DIN connector.
- Component video—High definition component video provides an interim method for transferring video from a set-top to an HDTV or monitor.
- Home digital network interface (HDNI)—Specified by DVS-194, HDNI is designed to provide the digital equivalent of the analog channel 3/4 interface.

Analog NTSC

Analog video connections that use the NTSC standard have provided the only way of interconnecting set-tops with the television receiver until now. The NTSC standard is the basis for several interfaces:

- NTSC RF channel 3/4—This interface provides a single 75 ohm coaxial connection for video and audio and is the most common variant. The channel 3/4 connection is particularly useful because it allows bypass operation of the set-top (see Chapter 6).
- Composite (or baseband) video—This interface allows separate audio (usually left and right) and solves the problem of delivering a stereo signal from a set-top to a separate amplifier.
- S-video—This interface separates the luminance and chrominance components of the NTSC signal to increase horizontal resolution and avoid certain NTSC artifacts associated with luma-chroma separation. (See Chapter 4 of *Video Demystified: A handbook for the digital engineer,* Second Edition, by Keith Jack.)

Component Video

High definition analog component video provides an interim method for transferring video from a set-top to an HDTV or monitor. Unfortunately, the EIA 770.3 standard (for high definition 1080-line interlaced and 720-line progressively scanned signals) provides, as yet, no content protection mechanism approved by the MPAA. Nevertheless, EIA 770.3 is the only available high definition output for the small numbers of currently deployed high definition capable set-tops, such as the Explorer 2000-HD from Scientific Atlanta.

EIA 770.3 is also commonly used to provide the connection from a digital receiver to the monitor in an HDTV receiver. Many consumer electronics manufacturers have elected to build their HDTV receivers in two components—a digital receiver that includes tuning and MPEG decoder functions, and a high definition monitor. This allows the digital receiver to be upgraded separately and preserves the lifetime of the high definition monitor, which currently represents the most costly items: cathode ray tubes, mirrors, lenses, and power supply.

Home Digital Network Interface

Home digital network interface (HDNI) uses a digital interface to replace the analog link. The digital interface is a high-speed serial bus called IEEE 1394.

1394 Media

Initially developed by Apple Computer as FireWire for plug-and-play networking for multimedia, IEEE 1394 has become the preferred solution for digital interconnect of consumer electronics devices. The IEEE 1394 connectors are hot-pluggable, and IEEE 1394 equipment (or *nodes*) are designed to autoconfigure into a network when they are daisy-chained together with IEEE 1394 links.

IEEE 1394 defines a family of bit rates of approximately 100, 200, 400, and 800 Mbps over serial or fiber-optic (1394b) connections. The IEEE 1394 network supports guaranteed bandwidth connections for transport of isochronous data (such as audio and video). Nevertheless, IEEE 1394 has insufficient bandwidth for uncompressed, high definition video (refer to Table 17-1) and is designed to carry compressed video and audio streams.

Figure 17-3 shows a digital set-top connected to a digital television (DTV) via an IEEE 1394 interface. This arrangement allows transfer of the compressed MPEG-2 transport stream without modification. This has the advantage of maintaining the signal quality and allows the DTV to provide the tightly coupled decode and display functions. The problem with this arrangement is that graphics cannot be added to the compressed signal before it leaves the set-top, providing no mechanism for user interface display functions.

Figure 17-3 *The IEEE 1394 Interface*

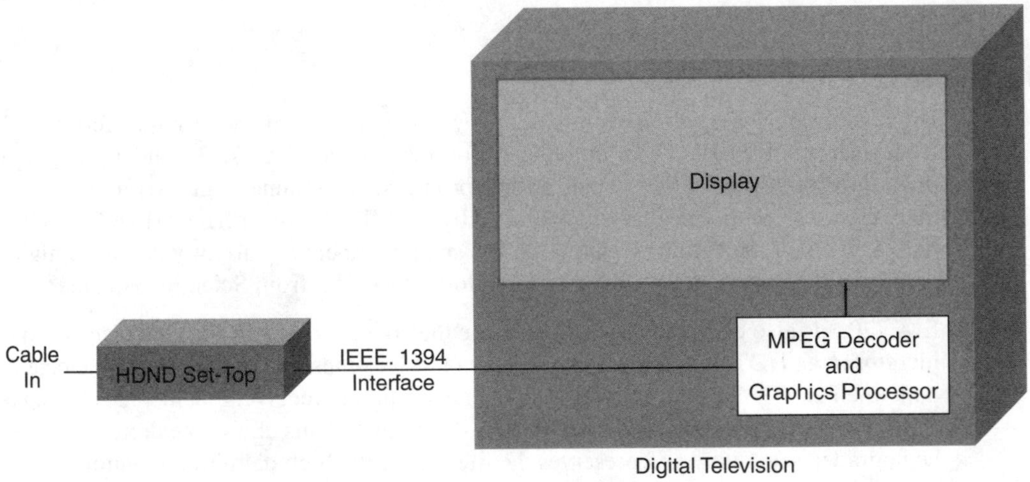

HDNI extends the IEEE 1394 syntax to allow separate transfer of graphics to the DTV. The DTV is responsible for compositing the graphics with the decoded video and presenting them on the television display.

In addition, HDNI specifies a content protection mechanism for the compressed digital signal to prevent unauthorized copying of copyrighted material.

Figure 17-4 illustrates the HDNI concept. A home digital network device (HDND), which is a modified digital set-top, provides the cable network interface and conditional access functions. The HDND is connected to a digital television (DTV) via an IEEE 1394 network and, optionally, by an analog audio and video link. The DTV provides audio, video, and user interface display functions.

Figure 17-4 *HDNI Reference Diagram*

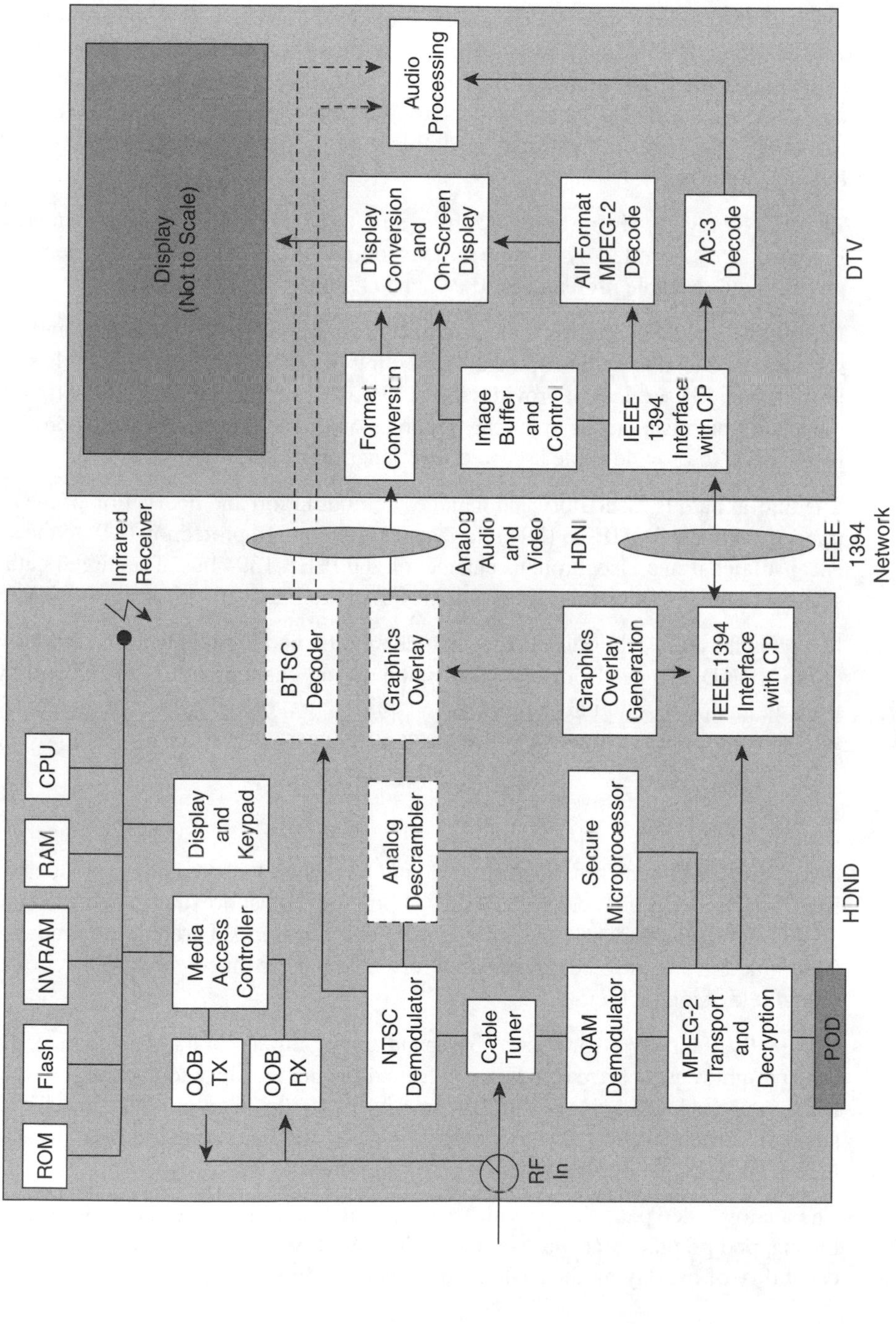

Home Digital Network Device

The home digital network device (HDND) can be compared to the digital set-top described in Chapter 6 (see Figure 6-1). The HDND performs all digital set-top functions except MPEG-2 and AC-3 decoding. As shown in Figure 17-4, the HDND includes two-way, out-of-band communications and a CPU and memory subsystem, which provides an application platform that the cable operator manages. The HDND could be leased or sold at retail; a POD interface provides separable security (see Chapter 18, "OCI-C2: The Security Interface").

The HDND receives infrared signals from a remote control. All cable user interface functions are controlled by a single remote control; these include tuning, electronic program guide, cable preferences, IPPV, or VOD ordering.

In Figure 17-4, there are two separate paths through the HDND for analog and digital services. The analog path is optional (according to DVS 194), but if the cable network provides analog services, it provides the only way to get them to the DTV. Also optional in the analog path is a means to overlay graphics on the analog signal, which provides a mechanism to provide cable user interface functions.

The digital path is mandatory and includes demodulation and decryption of the MPEG-2 transport stream. The IEEE 1394 interface applies content protection (CP) to the signal and encapsulates it in an isochronous channel on the IEEE 1394 bus. The digital path also supports asynchronous transfer of graphics over the IEEE 1394 bus to the DTV.

In a typical hybrid cable system that includes analog and digital channels, the active output of the HDND changes from analog to digital during channel surfing as the user switches from an analog to a digital channel. When this occurs, the HDND instructs the DTV to select the appropriate input by sending a control message.

Digital Television

Figure 17-4 shows the functions of the digital television when connected to the HDNI. The IEEE 1394 interface receives the MPEG-2 program transport stream, which is fed to an MPEG-2 decoder and AC-3 decoder. In addition, bit-mapped graphics arrive via the IEEE 1394 link and are buffered before being forwarded to the on-screen display circuitry of the digital television (DTV).

Optionally, the DTV also supports baseband analog inputs for audio and video. The NTSC video might require format conversion from 480-line interlace to the native display of the DTV, which is likely to be 720-line progressive or 1080-line interlace format. The DVS 194 standard does not specify the exact type of analog input, but either composite or S-video NTSC with a separate analog stereo pair is assumed.

The analog video path also provides another optional alternative for the user interface to bit-mapped graphics transfer over the IEEE 1394 link. In this case, the DTV provides the capability of overlaying the analog video over the digital video.

Video/Audio Payload

The video and audio payload is transferred over the IEEE 1394 link as an isochronous payload with a guaranteed bit rate allocated on the bus. The payload is in MPEG-2 transport stream format, but several variations exist depending on the implementation of the HDND:

- Single program transport stream—This approach is recommended by the cable operators because it fits the tuning and control model envisioned for OCI-C1. When a program is tuned by the HDND, the audio and video is decrypted and assembled into a single program transport stream and forwarded to the DTV. There is additional implementation cost because the new transport stream needs to be re-timestamped to adjust for re-multiplexing from a multi-program transport stream received over the cable.
- Multi-program transport stream—This approach is favored by the broadcasters and consumer electronics manufacturers and recommends that the entire multiple program transport stream is forwarded over the IEEE 1394 interface (a maximum payload of 38.8 Mbps in a 256-QAM environment). The problem with this approach is the split navigation paradigm; the DTV has to select which program to display from the multiplex and requires PSIP information to provide the user with guide information for the multiplex. This leads to a *dueling remote control* scenario where the user must juggle the set-top and DTV remote controls continuously to obtain the desired service.

Graphics

The DVS-194 specification includes a variety of bit-mapped graphics formats from 4- or 8-bit color lookup tables to 16-bit uncompressed graphics. The HDND and DTV use a discovery process to negotiate the highest common graphics format that they both support.

Graphics capabilities are divided into two EIA DTV profiles. Profile A supports only a 4-bit color lookup table for on-screen display and a single, 16-bit pixel format. Profile B supports all the graphics formats in DVS-194. There is some concern from cable operators that the user interface provided by profile A DTVs will be limited compared to existing analog capabilities.

Hypertext Markup Language

A future profile (profile 2) is discussed in DVS-194. The main purpose of profile 2 is to reduce the data traffic on the IEEE 1394 bus. Because Hypertext Markup Language (HTML) is at a much higher level of abstraction than a graphics bitmap (profile 1), it typically requires much less data to describe the same graphics overlay.

Content Protection

The combination of digital services, multimedia PCs, and the Internet pose a serious threat to any owner of copyright material. Picture quality is improved almost to the quality of the master copy, multimedia PCs provide multiple generation digital copying without quality loss, and the Internet provides an inexpensive and rapid distribution mechanism for digital copies. For these reasons, the movie studios adopted a consistent position that they will not release digital content until adequate content protection mechanisms exist. As such, the launch of the digital versatile disk (DVD) was delayed by more than a year while content protection was developed.

The Copy Protection Technical Working Group (CPTWG) is responsible for developing content protection technology. The CPTWG meets about six times a year, usually in Burbank, California, and is sponsored by the member companies of the Motion Picture Association of America (MPAA). The CPTWG is a completely open forum but does not work as a due-process standardization body.

Content protection is obviously important for stored media (for example, DVD) but is equally important for the transmission of digital media. Digital transmission content protection (DTCP) addresses the need to prevent unauthorized copying of entertainment content. DTCP is developed by the Digital Transmission Working Group (DTWG), which is part of CPTWG.

5C Content Protection Overview

The content protection specified by HDNI is 5C digital transmission content protection Volume 1, which defines

> a cryptographic protocol for protecting audio/video entertainment content from unauthorized copying, intercepting, and tampering as it traverses digital transmission mechanisms such as a high-performance serial bus that conforms to the IEEE 1394-1995 standard.

The name 5C refers to the five companies that jointly authored and agreed to use the specification: Hitachi, Intel, Matsushita Electric Industrial (MEI—better known in America as Panasonic), Sony, and Toshiba. The 5C content protection specification represents a hard-won compromise developed by DTWG. The 5C group was formed in February 1998 to break an impasse that had developed between two alternative proposals in DTWG. After much work, the version 1.0 specification was issued in February 1999.

To implement 5C content protection (5C CP), a manufacturer is required to obtain a license from the Digital Transmission Licensing Administrator (see Web page at http://www.dtla.com). A license is required primarily to enforce the conditions under which the intellectual property contained in the 5C CP might be used. These conditions are the set of rules under which copies are allowed and include the types of output that are allowed. The intellectual property hook is used because it is often easier to enforce patent infringement than it is to enforce copyright infringement. Therefore, the goal of any content protection mechanism is to ensure that copies cannot be made without using a chosen, patented technology. If a manufacturer builds a device that makes illegal copies (known as a *circumvention device*), that manufacturer can be sued for patent infringement.

The Content Protection Chain

5C content protection is link-based and forms only one link in the copy protection chain. In a cable television environment this chain has several links:

- The satellite link from the content provider to the headend is protected using a proprietary conditional access system (for example, GI's Digicipher II or SA's PowerVU, see Chapter 7, "Digital Broadcast Case Studies").
- The cable system from the headend to the set-top (HDND) is protected using a proprietary conditional access system (for example, GI's Digicipher II or SA's PowerKEY, see Chapter 6).
- The IEEE 1394 link from the set-top to the digital television is protected by 5C content protection.

5C Content Protection Mechanisms

5C content protection uses a number of techniques to prevent unauthorized copying, which are described using a layered model:

- Copy control information (CCI)—The content owner tags the content with the copying restrictions placed on it using the CCI. The CCI is carried by the encryption mode indicator (EMI) in the sy field of the 1394 isochronous packet header and is also embedded in the MPEG content (to prevent tampering). There are four possible states for CCI: *copy-free*, *no-more-copies*, *copy-one-generation*, and *copy-never*. Table 17-2 shows how these CCI states are expected to be used in a cable environment.

Table 17-2 *Copy Control Information*

CCI State	EMI Value	Content Type
Copy-free	00	Broadcast services
No-more-copies	01	Not applicable
Copy-one-generation	10	Pay services, PPV or VOD
Copy-never	11	PPV or VOD

- Device authentication and key exchange—This step allows the source device (the HDND) to authenticate the sink device (the DTV). There are two levels of authentication: restricted and full. Full authentication is required if copy-never material is to be transferred, so both the HDND and DTV must support full authentication to carry all types of material. Full authentication uses the public key–based elliptic curve digital signature algorithm (EC-DSA) for signing and verification and the elliptic curve Diffie-Hellman (EC-DH) key exchange algorithm to generate a shared authentication key. The elliptic curve intellectual property was contributed by

Toshiba and is a critical part of the 5C system. Some manufacturers have expressed concern that others might contest the ownership of the elliptic curve intellectual property.

Device authentication allows both devices (in this case, the HDND and the DTV) to verify that the other has a device certificate that is a valid public/private key pair issued by the DTLA.

A shared authentication key is then generated using an EC-DH exchange. The source device uses the authentication key to encrypt the content encryption key.

- Content encryption—This part of the 5C scheme protects the content itself using digital encryption. The selected algorithm is a 56-bit block cipher called M6, which was contributed by Hitachi. Export approval for M6 has been granted by MITI (the Japanese Government department for security).

  The source device selects a random key (which is periodically changed) and uses it to encrypt the MPEG-2 transport stream with the M6 algorithm. It also sends a message to the sink (or destination) device containing the random key encrypted using the shared authentication key.

  The sink device decrypts the message using the shared authentication key to recover the random key. It then decrypts the MPEG-2 transport stream with the random key.

- Device renewability—The final part of 5C content protection is a mechanism that allows the DTLA to revoke a device certificate. The DTLA might periodically issue system renewability messages (SRM), which are digitally signed with the DTLA EC-DSA private key (this allows all 5C-compliant devices to verify the authenticity of the SRM message using the EC-DSA public key). The SRM contains a list of device certificates that are no longer valid (for example, they might have been cloned by a pirate manufacturer to build circumvention devices).

  SRMs may be placed on recorded media or encapsulated in streaming content. They are designed to propagate through the population of 5C-compliant devices rather like a virus. Each 5C-compliant device is responsible for building a list of invalid device certificates and checking it during the authentication process. A 5C-compliant device will refuse to send (or receive) content to (or from) a revoked device.

This brief description illustrates the implementation complexity of the 5C content protection system, which has been demanded by the movie studios. It is not surprising that not all consumer electronics companies support the 5C initiative. Some commonly cited issues are

- Secrets in the box—This refers to the fact that each 5C-compliant device holds a secure secret (a private key). This arguably increases the manufacturing cost of the device.

- Intel administers DTLA—Some CE companies have expressed concern that Intel, one of the world's largest chip suppliers, holds the keys to the 5C licensing process.
- End-to-end security is superior—Thomson Consumer Electronics and Zenith have proposed an alternative content protection mechanism called XCA. In this proposal, content providers encrypt their content at the source, and it remains encrypted until it reaches the display device. A smart card in each display device would be used to enable access to protected content.
- Revocation of devices—When a 5C-compliant device is revoked, it is no longer able to exchange protected content. For example, a revoked DTV would not be able to display premium content from the set-top, doubtless causing a very negative reaction from the customer.

Summary

This chapter describes the OCI-C1 interface between the OpenCable device (typically a digital set-top) and the consumer display device (typically a television). OCI-C1 is actually a family of interfaces that embraces current analog NTSC interfaces and a proposed digital interface called the host digital network interface (HDNI).

The goals of OCI-C1 include support of standard and high definition services, transfer of the digital signal quality to the consumer device, and support for improved content protection.

The HDNI specification is based on the IEEE 1394 standard and supports compressed digital transfer of the MPEG-2 transport stream from the digital set-top to a digital television. The digital television performs MPEG-2 and Dolby AC-3 decoding functions. Graphics overlays for user interface are sent separately over the IEEE 1394 link, and the digital television is responsible for compositing the graphics overlay with video.

The HDNI specification includes provision for digital transmission content protection (DTCP). DTCP uses digital cryptography to prevent unauthorized copying of the digital video and audio content.

References

Book

Jack, Keith. *Video Demystified: A handbook for the digital engineer,* Second Edition. HighText Publications, 1996.

Standards

OCI-C1 Consumer Device Interface Specification. IS-C1-WD01-980501. CableLabs. May 1, 1998.

IEEE 1394-1995, "Standard for a High Performance Serial Bus."

P1394a, "Draft Standard for a High Performance Serial Bus (Supplement), Draft 2.0," March 15, 1998.

DVS-194 Revision 1 "SCTE DVS," December 1998.

"AV/C Digital Interface Command Set General Specification, Version 3.0," April 15, 1998.

IEC 61883, "Digital Interface for consumer audio/video equipment."

VESA Plug and Display (P&D) Standard Version 1. June 11, 1997. (Available at the VESA Web site.)

Internet Resources

1394 Trade Associate Web site

http://www.1394ta.org.

VESA "Plug & Display"

http://www.vesa.org

CHAPTER 18

OCI-C2: The Security Interface

The OCI-C2 interface provides the interface to a *point-of-deployment* (POD) module for digital signals provided over the cable system. The POD module is a Type II PC Card (commonly known as a PCMCIA module) supplied by the cable operator, which provides two important functions:

- Separation of security—The FCC Report and Order (issued on June 11, 1998) mandates the separation of a cable system's security from other functions in a navigation device available at retail by July 2000. Moreover, cable operators will not be allowed to deploy set-tops with embedded security after January 1, 2005. The POD module is designed to satisfy the FCC requirements for separable security.
- Out-of-band communications—Some variation in existing practice in digital cable systems is in the choice of out-of-band (OOB) protocol. The POD module terminates the lower layers of the OOB protocol and adapts a navigation device to the OOB scheme for that cable system. The POD module supports OOB communications according to DVS 167 or DVS 178 (see Chapter 5, "Adding Digital Television Services to Cable Systems").

A third aspect of the OCI-C2 interface is that it transfers programming content across a digital interface. The Motion Picture Association of America (MPAA) requires that the OCI-C2 interface support a content protection system to prevent illegal copying.

This chapter is organized as follows:

- Reference diagram—The OCI-C2 interface is placed in context of the OpenCable reference architecture, and the terms *host* and *POD module* are defined.
- Drivers—The drivers for the OCI-C2 interface are discussed, which include government regulation, retail set-top availability, cable ready digital television, and high definition television.
- Retail issues—The OCI-C2 interface solves some of the portability issues, the choice of conditional access system, and out-of-band communications channel, but does not address user interface and new service introduction issues.

- Opportunities—The separation of conditional access system functions provides opportunities for integration of set-top functions into a cable ready digital television (CR-DTV) and might speed introduction of new technology into the consumer's home. For the cable operator, opportunities are reduced capital expenditure and new ways of acquiring customers.
- Summary of approaches—The different approaches for conditional access system renewal and replacement are summarized to explain the choice of NRSS-B as the basis for the POD module.
- System architecture—The POD system architecture provides a single replaceable module that provides flexibility to adapt the host to all variants of the conditional access system and out-of-band communications channel types.
- POD module—OCI-C2 (SCTE DVS-131) specifies only the POD module interface. This section describes the internal structure and operation of a typical POD module design.
- Copy protection—The OCI-C2 specification includes a content protection mechanism that uses digital cryptography to prevent unauthorized copying of copy-protected material. This section describes the operation of POD copy protection in some detail.
- Applications—Three applications of the OCI-C2 interface are discussed: a digital set-top, a digital set-top with a DOCSIS cable modem, and a cable ready digital television (CR-DTV).

Reference Diagram

Figure 18-1 is the OpenCable reference diagram. The OCI-C2 interface is defined between the OpenCable device and the security (POD) module.

SCTE DVS 131 Revision 7 defines the OCI-C2 interface. DVS-131 uses the following terms for convenience:

- Host—The *host* is responsible for all functions except conditional access. There are many different kinds of host devices with a wide range of functions and capabilities; examples are a digital set-top, a cable ready digital television, or a cable ready VCR. The OpenCable device functional requirements provide a set of performance and functional specifications for an OpenCable-compliant host device.
- POD module—The *POD module* is a replaceable component that is provided by the cable operator. The POD module provides all the security functions required by the cable conditional access system.

Figure 18-1 *OpenCable Reference Diagram*

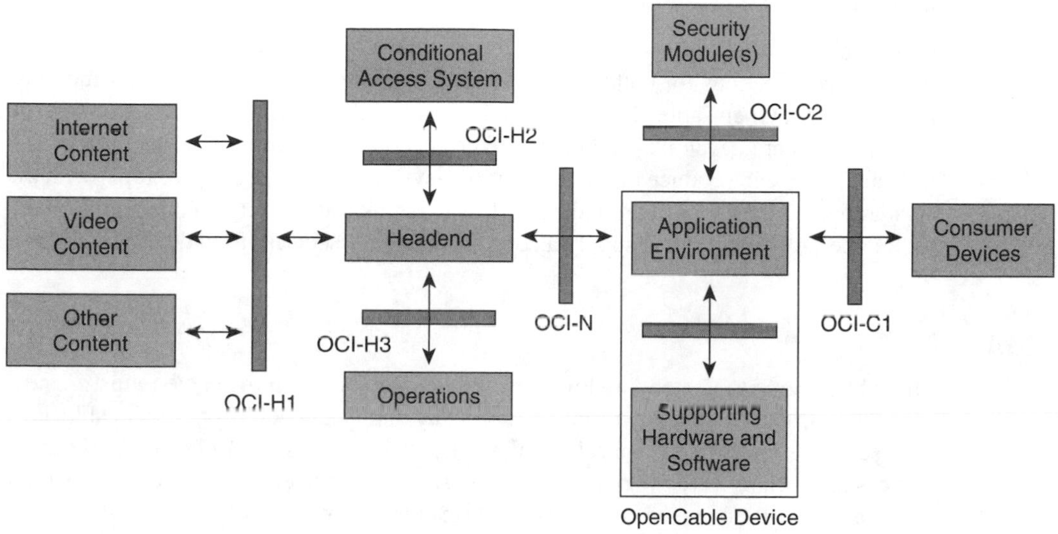

Drivers

There are a number of drivers for the OCI-C2 interface. These can be divided into

- Regulatory
- Retail
- Cable ready digital television
- High definition television

Regulatory

On June 24, 1998, the Commission released its Report and Order in this proceeding implementing Section 304 of the Telecommunications Act of 1996. Section 304 calls upon the Commission to adopt rules to ensure the commercial availability of navigation devices, while not jeopardizing the signal security of an affected multichannel video programming distributor (MVPD). As part of that R&O, the Commission determined that one means of implementing these twin goals was to separate security (that is conditional access) functions from nonsecurity functions and to require that only the nonsecurity functions be made commercially available in equipment provided by entities unaffiliated with the

MVPD. The security functions would reside in a separate security module to be obtained from the MVPD.

In its decision, the Commission repeatedly references the ongoing effort of CableLabs to develop specifications for both a digital security module and a digital security module interface. That OpenCable effort is focused on cable's *digital* set-top converters. After such specifications are developed and the interface is adopted as an industry standard, manufacturers can produce digital navigation devices (such as digital set-tops) with the standardized digital security module interface and make such equipment available at retail. Cable operators would then supply a compatible digital security module to the customer.

Retail

There has been a long-standing love-hate relationship between the cable industry and manufacturers of cable ready receivers. For many in the cable industry, retail cable devices represent a serious loss of control that threatens their business. For others, retail cable devices are seen as a way to reduce capital costs and to move more quickly to advanced services. It should come as no surprise that retail is an emotive subject as well as a complicated one.

In the analog world, cable ready televisions and video cassette recorders have gained favor with subscribers as manufacturers adopted innovations (such as the remote control) from set-top manufacturers. As cable ready television performance increased (allowing the tuning of all cable channels and providing better adjacent channel rejection), the customer's need for a set-top was reduced to de-scrambling premium channels. In addition, new features, such as picture-in-picture and VCR-plus do not work well with a set-top and cause compatibility issues (see Chapter 3, "The Analog Set-Top Converter"). More recently, advanced analog set-tops have added two major new features—the electronic program guide and impulse pay-per-view, which have increased customer acceptance of set-tops.

The fundamental problem with retail availability of analog set-tops is one of portability. For an advanced analog set-top to work in a cable system it must be exactly the correct make and model and contain the correct revision of software. The analog decoder interface attempted to address this with something called an *extended feature box.* The idea was that a separate box containing extra functions and features, such as software applications, would be plugged into the EIA 105 bus.

Cable Ready Digital Television

The POD module interface specification is designed to facilitate cable ready operation of a digital television when a POD module is inserted. Figure 18-2 shows a simplified diagram of a cable ready digital television (CR-DTV). The DTV's tuner and QAM demodulator feed a baseband digital signal to the POD module, which is responsible for conditional access functions. The output of the POD module feeds the receiver's MPEG-2 decoder and graphics processor that, in turn, drives the display.

Figure 18-2 *Cable Ready Digital Television*

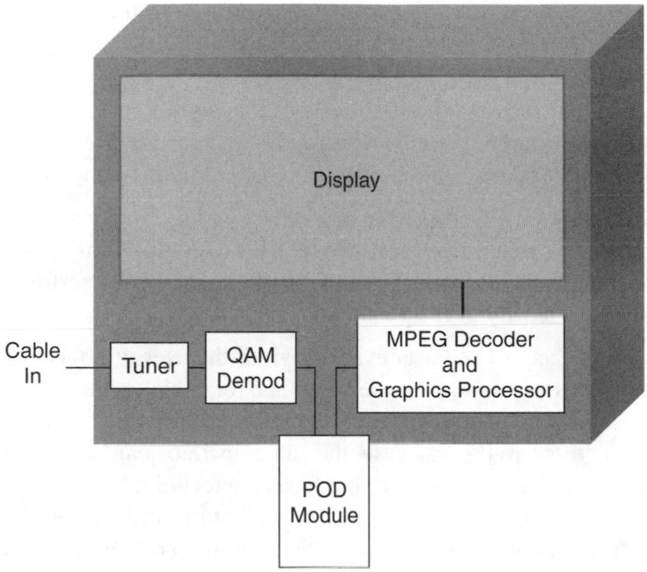

High Definition Television

The OCI-C2 interface supports standard and high definition MPEG-2 packetized elementary streams (in fact, the POD module is unaware of the difference between these stream types). Therefore, an integrated high-definition digital cable ready receiver with a POD module provides an excellent solution for premium high definition television (HDTV) services.

Retail Cable Issues

The fundamental difficulty with a cable ready retail device is the differences between cable systems. Although the 1996 telecommunication's act does not require *portability* from one system to another, it is necessary in practice to avoid leaving the customer with a cable ready device that worked in one part of the country only to become inoperative when moved to a new location.

Portability has become a critical issue because cable's biggest competitor, DBS, does not suffer from this problem. The satellite footprint is national and so, even though each operator is proprietary, there is an implicit portability to DBS services. For this reason, DBS operators were exempted from the 1998 Report and Order (although cable operators continue to contest this decision).

There is considerably more to portability than the choice of conditional access technology. As cable operators start to offer more advanced services, these differences tend to become more and more pronounced. Electronic program guides provide a good example; although simple in concept, they are provided by a small number of companies that claim intellectual property rights over the look and feel of each feature of the guide.

Portability requires technical and/or business solutions in the following areas:

- Conditional access—Conditional access is a problem that has an elegant technical solution for digital systems. The conditional access circuitry can be separated into a replaceable security module, which is leased by the cable operator.
- RF termination—Because the host device is directly connected to the cable system, it is imperative that is does not affect correct operation of the system. Cable systems are broadband, shared-media systems, so all devices must perform to specification to maintain integrity of the plant.
- User interface—The host device provides the user interface. There are two alternatives to provide the user interface for cable services: Either the user interface software is provided by the cable operator or it is independently developed by the host manufacturer. In the first case, the cable operator can provide a consistent and comprehensive user interface but faces the technical challenge of supporting all host varieties. In the second case, each manufacturer independently develops a user interface that provides only the lowest common denominator services without any consistent *look-and-feel*.
- New services—Providing new services is constrained in the same way as the user interface because new services require new application software; either the application software is provided by the cable operator or it is independently developed by the host manufacturer. Moreover, if new hardware features are required by a new service, it can be offered only by hosts that support them—a frustrating situation for customer and cable operator alike.

At the time of writing, CableLabs has issued a request for proposals for OpenCable Software. This software *middleware* addresses user interface and new services issues by providing a portability layer for software applications. The middleware is intended to "allow individual cable operators to deploy custom services and applications on all compliant host devices connected to their networks."

Retail Opportunities

Retail provides some significant opportunities if the technical issues can be resolved:

- Integration with other consumer electronic devices in the home—The best example of this is the cable ready digital television. Not only are cost savings possible by sharing a common chassis and power supply but also integration allows seamless implementation of features such as picture-in-picture.

- New technology—Retail presents a way to introduce new technologies into the host device. Examples are convergence with PC technology, such as local content storage using a hard-drive, or support for video conferencing using a digital camera.
- Less capital expense—Because the customer shares some or all of the cost of the host device, the retail model can significantly reduce the cable operator's capital investment. Moreover, customers that desire extended hardware features can pay for them, providing greater choice.
- New customer acquisition—Cable operators can use retail to acquire new cable customers in partnership with host manufacturers and retailers. For example, new services can be demonstrated on the salesroom floor and rebates on hardware can provide an incentive to service subscription.

These threats and opportunities are summarized in Table 18-1.

Table 18-1 *Retail Summary*

Issue	Threat	Opportunity
New services	How to introduce without loss of control	Sharing of risk
Economic	Loss of guaranteed rate of return	Lower capital outlay
Convergence	Threat to existing business	New business opportunities
Integration with other CE devices	Loss of control—more service calls	Happier customer, access to latest technology

Summary of Approaches

Several approaches exist for separation of security. Most advanced digital set-tops use *smart cards* (ISO-7816), which allow replacement of the secure microprocessor component of the conditional access system (see Chapter 6, "The Digital Set-Top Converter"). But the smart card does not allow complete replacement of the security system because the actual decryption of the signal still resides in the digital set-top.

The Joint Engineering Committee (JEC) of NCTA and CEMA released a specification for a National Renewable Security System (NRSS) to address the issue of conditional access and security functions. The approach is to encapsulate these functions in a replaceable module and to standardize the module interface. In this way, the security system can be upgraded or replaced over time without impacting the host.

Unfortunately, there are two versions of NRSS called Part A and Part B. Part A is a super-smart card, which uses the ISO-7816 connector to carry the entire transport stream through the card. Part B is functionally equivalent to Part A but adopts the Type II PC Card format defined by the Personal Computer Memory Card International Association (PCMCIA).

NRSS Part B is based on the DVB common interface (CI) module, which is required by many European countries (CENELEC EN 50221). The North American cable industry has adopted the Part B specification for several reasons:

- The interface of Part B is more robust and flexible than Part A. The Part B connector has 68 pins and the module is shielded.
- The Part B module is thicker than the Part A card and supports a metallic casing that provides better heat dissipation.

Although the Part B module has these technical advantages over Part A, it is likely to be more expensive. To mitigate this, the Part B module can accept a smart card, allowing security upgrades without replacement of the entire module.

System Architecture

The POD module adapts a *generic* cable ready device to any digital cable system. This is possible largely because of standardization of the OCI-N interface (see Chapter 16, "OCI-N: The Network Interface"). Although OCI-N facilitates a common interface into the device, it cannot account for the choice of OOB signaling and CA system, which vary from system to system. The POD solves this challenge by separating all these variations into a single, replaceable module.

This is possible, in practice, for the following reasons:

- Digital deployment was at an early stage during the specification of OCI-C2. Specifically, only two digital cable system architectures were deployed in North America: General Instrument's DigiCable system, developed in partnership with TCI (now AT&T BIS), and Scientific Atlanta's Digital Broadband Delivery System (DBDS), developed to Time Warner Cable's Pegasus requirements. (See Chapter 7, "Digital Broadcast Case Studies," for an overview and comparison of the two systems.)
- The Harmony agreement (see Chapter 16) established a set of standards for modulation, transport, and MPEG-2 encoding based on the DigiCable system and adopted by the DBDS during its development phase. (Note that the POD module does not rely on the Harmony core encryption because it completely replaces all security functions).
- Many standards already exist for digital television systems due to the work of the Advanced Television Systems Committee (ATSC) on high definition television. These standards include MPEG-2 video compression, MPEG-2 systems layer, and Dolby AC-3 audio (see Chapter 4, "Digital Technologies"). Moreover, the layered approach in MPEG-2 systems allows independence between the transport and application layers in digital television systems. This property is essential to the development of a cost-effective, replaceable security module.

Nevertheless, significant differences remain between the two systems and any system architecture must accommodate innovation by suppliers to promote competition. The hardware differences are accommodated by what OpenCable terms a POD decision. This decision can be made in two ways:

- In a leased set-top environment, the cable operator makes the POD decision when the set-top is ordered. Obviously this is a decision that cannot be reversed, but cable operators are comfortable with managing their set-top inventory (as they do today for analog set-tops).
- In a retail environment, the POD decision must be delayed until the customer chooses a cable television supplier. At that time, the customer might have already purchased the set-top or cable ready television, so a replaceable module is the only viable solution.

The POD module allows the choice of conditional access system and out-of-band communications to be made at the time of customer subscription to the cable service.

Conditional Access System

The POD module provides all the conditional access functions for the host device. These functions include the authorization of services as well as the decryption of the audio/video streams. This complete separation of conditional access functions allows a completely open-ended choice of conditional access system.

Within the cable system it is very expensive to replace the conditional access system, because it is embedded into many headend components and tightly coupled to operational functions (see the section OCI-H2 in Chapter 15, "OpenCable Headend Interfaces"). Therefore, the POD module provides the flexibility to adapt any host to the conditional access system chosen by the cable operator.

Out-of-Band Communications

The out-of-band communications options for cable are described in Chapter 5. There are currently three options:

- DVS-178—Developed and owned by General Instrument, this option uses a 2.048 Mbps forward channel and a 256 Kbps return channel. Modulation is QPSK.
- DVS-167—Developed and standardized by DAVIC, this option specifies a 1.544 or 3.088 Mbps forward data channel (FDC) and a 256 Kbps, 1,544 Mbps, or 3.088 Mbps reverse data channel (RDC). The DVS-131 specification supports only one variant of DAVIC 1.2 operating with a 1.544 Mbps FDC and a 1.544 Mbps RDC. Modulation is QPSK.

- DOCSIS cable modem—Developed and standardized by CableLabs, this option specifies a 27 or 38 Mbps FDC using 64-QAM or 256-QAM modulation. The RDC supports a range of bit-rates from 320 Kbps to 10.024 Mbps and uses QPSK or QAM-16 modulation [DOCSIS]. Because DOCSIS is an agreed standard, it may be built into any retail device at the option of the manufacturer. Currently, no cable operator is using DOCSIS for out-of-band communications, but some have publicly stated their plans to do so. The POD module supports DOCSIS as a host modem (see the section DOCSIS Operation, later in this chapter).

Because DVS-178 and DVS-167 use the same type of modulation, it is possible to build a unified QPSK transceiver that supports both standards. This approach has a number of advantages:

- All digital set-tops and cable ready digital televisions can include a standard RF transceiver at low cost and complexity for the support of out-of-band communications.
- The data-link and media access control protocol components are completely implemented by the POD module. This allows further development of these protocols. More importantly, the cable operator remains in control of the return channel operation, which is critical because a single *babbling* transmitter can disrupt an entire fiber node until it can be located and disabled.
- The POD terminates and processes conditional access messages with no host intervention. This reduces the threat of theft-of-service attacks.

Two-Way Operation

The POD is designed to support two-way operation, as shown in Figure 18-3.

The QPSK receiver circuit in the host tunes and demodulates the out-of-band forward data channel (FDC) under control of the POD module. The receiver circuit adapts to the 1.544 Mbps (DVS-167) or 2.048 Mbps (DVS-178) FDC bit rate, and delivers a serial bit stream and clock to the POD module. The POD module controls the tuning of the QPSK receiver circuit by means of commands delivered over the command interface. The tuning range is between 70 and 130 MHz.

Figure 18-3 *POD Two-Way Operation*

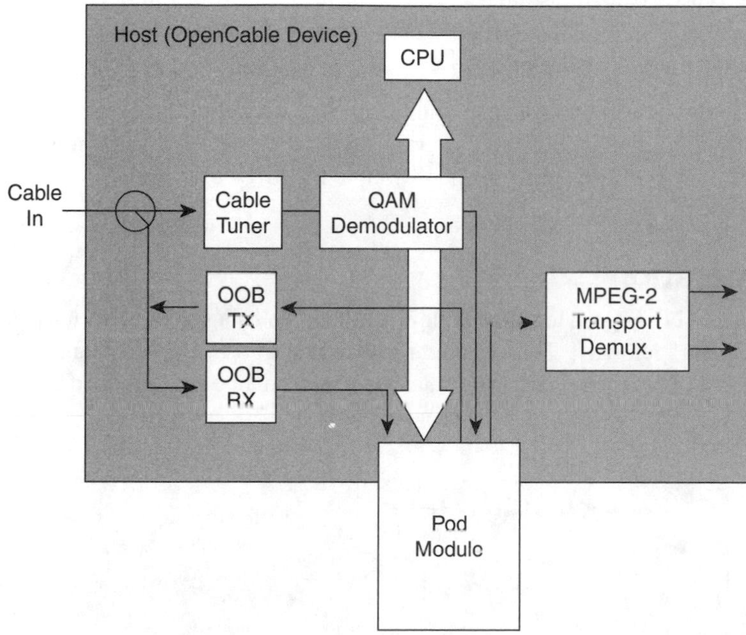

The serial data received from the out-of-band receiver carries entitlement management messages (EMMs) from the conditional access system to the POD module. These messages are not documented by the DVS-131 specification because

- There is always a one-to-one match between the conditional access system and the POD module. For example, a DigiCipher II POD module is required for hosts in cable systems that employ DigiCipher II CA.
- The exact EMM format is one of the details of the conditional access system that is not disclosed to reduce the risk of theft-of-service attacks.

In addition to EMMs, the out-of-band channel carries several other message types, which support various functions in a digital set-top, including navigation, signaling, and management. Because the host device is now responsible for these functions, these messages must be routed back into the host. DVS-131 defines an extended data channel for this purpose, and DVS-216 defines the format of these messages.

In the reverse path, the POD module generates QPSK symbols and clock and transfers them to the out-of-band transmitter circuit in the host. The transmitter circuit adapts to the 1.544 Mbps (DVS-167) or 0.256 Mbps (DVS-178) RDC bit rate and modulates the QPSK symbols onto a narrowband carrier.

The POD module controls the tuning and output level of the QPSK transmitter circuit by means of commands delivered over the command interface. The tuning range is between 8 and 26.5 MHz. The output level is variable in 1 dB steps from +26 dBmV to +55 dBmV.

One-Way Operation

The POD is designed to support one-way operation using an optional telephone modem, as shown in Figure 18-4. The QPSK transmitter in the host is not used (and is omitted from the diagram). The receiver circuit operates in the same manner as described in a two-way operation.

Figure 18-4 *POD One-Way Operation*

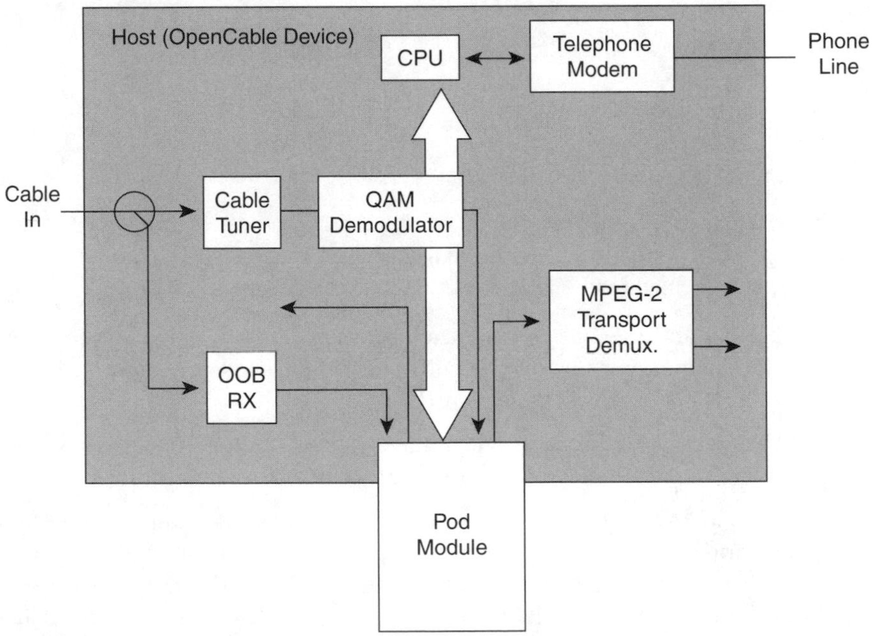

A standard telephone modem can be incorporated into the host to support impulse pay-per-view services in one-way networks. In this case, the POD module accesses the telephone modem via the extended channel interface.

The host signals an available *low-speed communication resource* to the POD module. The POD module establishes a dial-up connection with the cable headend and sends messages to the telephone modem via the data channel interface.

DOCSIS Operation

The POD module may be designed to support two-way operation using a host-resident DOCSIS cable modem, as shown in Figure 18-5.

Figure 18-5 *POD DOCSIS Operation*

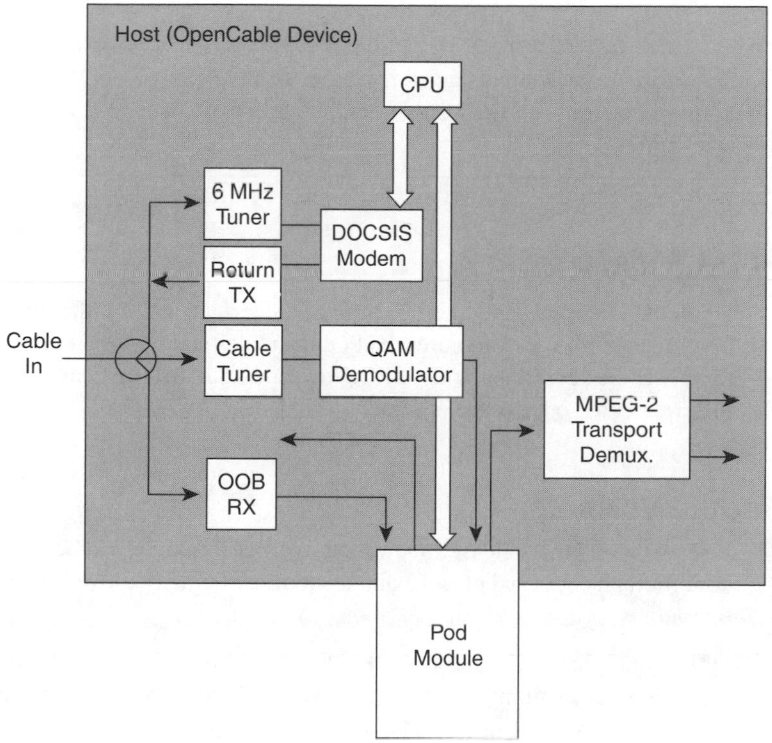

The DOCSIS cable modem is capable of completely replacing the QPSK out-of-band FDC and RDC channels but, in practice, it complements and enhances the OOB channel:

- If the cable system uses a DOCSIS-based out-of-band from day one, the host's OOB receiver and OOB transmitter are not used in that system. In this case, the host forwards conditional access messages received by the DOCSIS modem to the POD via the extended data channel (as described in DVS-216). The host terminates all other messages.
- If the cable system adds a DOCSIS channel to support additional capabilities, such as interactive or data services, the host uses the OOB receiver to receive *legacy* conditional access messages.

- Retaining the host's OOB transmitter is more problematic because it is difficult to combine its output with the DOCSIS return transmitter and achieve the required maximum transmit power levels. To ease migration to DOCSIS, the POD module may use the DOCSIS cable modem as a resource to send messages to the cable system instead of the OOB transmitter.

NOTE To ensure host portability across systems using DVS-167 or DVS-178 for out-of-band data communications, *all* OpenCable-compliant host devices require an OOB receiver and transmitter.

The POD Module

DVS-131 describes only the POD module interface and not the module itself. Each cable operator specifies and procures the POD modules and leases them to the customer. As such, there will be several variants of POD module with different capabilities according to different cable operator requirements.

POD Module Variants

It seems likely that at least three variants of POD module will be deployed according to the conditional access and out-of-band technology being deployed by North American cable operators:

- Digicipher II CA and DVS-178 OOB—This variant of POD module, developed by General Instrument (GI), supports DigiCipher-II conditional access. This POD module variant supports GI's DigiCable system, which uses GI's out-of-band specification (SCTE DVS-178).
- PowerKEY CA and DVS-167 OOB—This variant of POD module is developed by Scientific Atlanta, which owns the intellectual property for PowerKEY CA. This POD module variant supports Scientific Atlanta's Digital Broadband Delivery System (DBDS), which uses DAVIC 1.2 out-of-band (SCTE DVS-167).
- MediaGuard CA and DVS-167 OOB—At the time of writing, it seems likely that this variant of POD module will be developed by SCM Microsystems under license from SECA (Canal+). This POD module variant will support MediaOne's digital system, which uses DAVIC 1.2 out-of-band (SCTE DVS-167).

See Chapter 7 for a description of the DigiCable and DBDS systems.

As cable systems continue to evolve, it is quite likely that new POD variants will be required. If a cable operator selects DOCSIS for out-of-band communications, the POD module can be cost-reduced by removing support for DVS-178 or DVS-167. However, this places the additional cost burden of a DOCSIS cable modem on the host device. Moreover, a cable system that selects DOCSIS as the *only* OOB communications mechanism will work only with host devices that include a DOCSIS cable modem.

POD Module Architecture

The design of the point-of-deployment module varies from one implementation to another. Figure 18-6 shows an example of a typical POD design.

Figure 18-6 *POD Module Block Diagram*

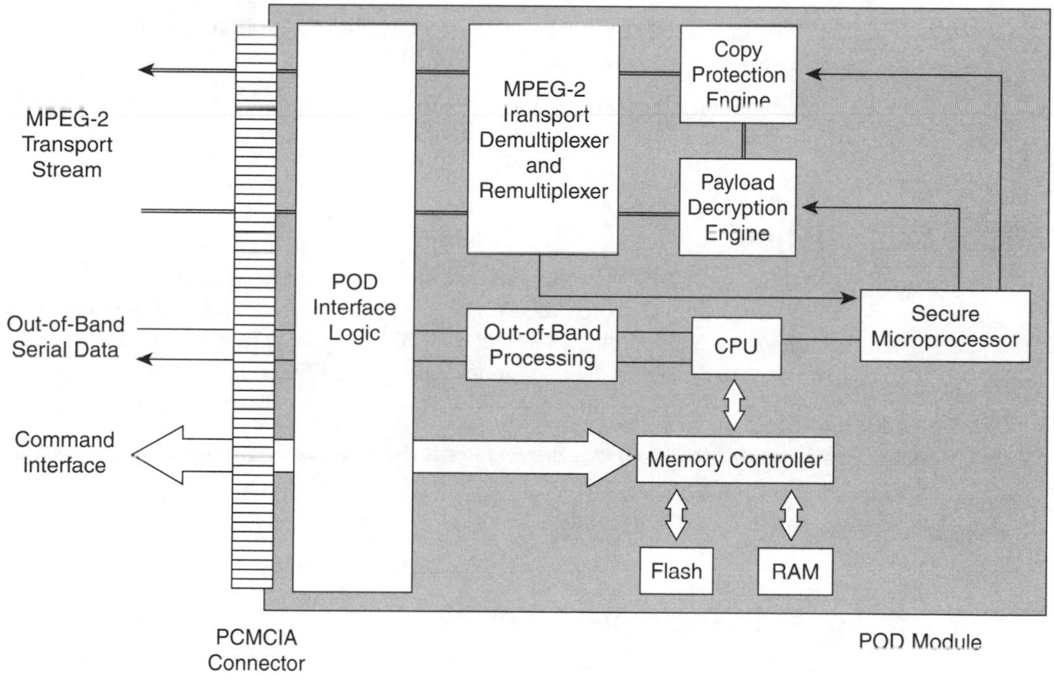

Although the POD module separates security functions into a replaceable module, system operation is identical to the integrated set-top described in Chapter 6:

- The MPEG-2 multi-program transport stream enters the POD module via the PCMCIA connector and is de-multiplexed into its component program elementary streams. The selected PIDs are filtered and sent to the payload decryption engine. In addition, the entitlement control messages are sent to the secure microprocessor where they are decrypted and fed to the payload decryption engine.

- After the payload is decrypted, it is fed into the copy protection engine, which encrypts protected content. In the example shown, the same secure microprocessor that supports CA functions generates the encryption keys for content encryption.
- The final payload is re-multiplexed into an MPEG-2 multi-program transport stream and leaves the POD module via the PCMCIA connector.
- The out-of-band data enters the POD module via the PCMCIA connector and arrives at the out-of-band processing circuit. This block contains data link and media access control functions and provides the out-of-band communications processing for the POD.
- Messages from the out-of-band processing circuit arrive at the CPU, which is the heart of the POD module. The CPU controls and coordinates all POD functions by executing applications stored in FLASH memory.
- The command interface allows messages to be exchanged between the host and the POD module by reading and writing locations in RAM.

PCMCIA Compliance

The POD module is a PCMCIA-compliant module that is registered as the OpenCable POD module custom interface. On reset, the POD behaves as a 16-bit memory-only interface. After a host device recognizes the POD, the PCMCIA signals are reassigned to carry the in-band channel and the out-of-band channels across the POD module interface.

In addition, while the first card-enable pin (CE1) is used to support the *data channel*, the second card-enable pin (CE2) is used to support the *extended channel*. This allows out-of-band messages to be exchanged over the extended channel independently from control messages, which are exchanged over the data channel.

MPEG-2 Transport Stream Interface

The MPEG-2 multi-program transport stream is transferred across the DVS-131 interface as a byte-parallel stream. There is a separate 8-bit parallel input to the POD module and a separate 8-bit parallel output, together with control signals and a byte clock. The POD module introduces a constant delay to the transport stream so that MPEG-2 timestamps do not require adjustment by the host. The maximum transport stream data rate supported is 58 Mbps.

Out-of-Band Interface

The out-of-band interface is the main distinguishing feature of the POD module interface over other replaceable security modules. It is required for the cable systems in North America because there is no single standard for out-of-band communications in digital cable systems. The out-of-band interface is designed to support both DVS-167 and DVS-178 standards using a single, unified RF front end. All cable ready devices incorporating the unified front end will be portable across all North American cable systems. The unified RF front end is designed to be simple to minimize cost, which is estimated at less than two dollars (including the diplex filter).

The out-of-band interface uses six dedicated pins to provide a serial connection from the out-of-band receiver and transmitter (in the host) to the out-of-band processing circuitry (in the POD module). Figure 18-7 shows the pin assignments:

- Two pins (DRX and CRX) pass the receive data and clock from the out-of-band receiver to the POD module.
- Two pins (ITX, QTX) are used to send transmit symbols to the host transmitter.
- The transmitter provides a symbol clock (CTX) to the POD module, which sets the transmit rate.
- The POD module controls an explicit transmit enable signal (ETX) to the host transmitter. This ensures that the transmitter cannot operate unless a POD module is inserted, and that the timing of transmit bursts in under the control of the POD module.

Figure 18-7 *Out-of-Band Interface*

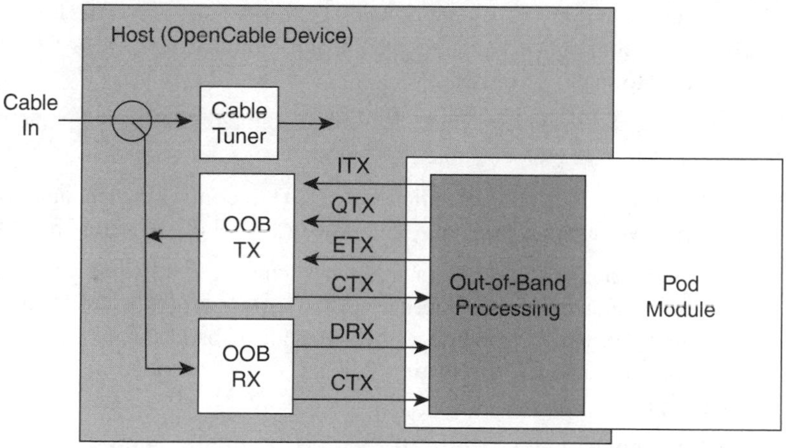

CPU Interface

The CPU interface supports command and signaling traffic between the host and the POD module via an 8-bit bidirectional data bus together with address and control signals.

The SCTE DVS-064 CPU interface defines a data channel that is designed to allow the exchange of control messages between the host and the POD module. This data channel is called the *command interface* in DVS-064. The DVS-131 CPU interface is augmented with a second channel, called the *extended channel*.

Data Channel

The DVS-131 data channel supports the DVS-064 command interface. The data channel uses four registers to control the exchange of variable length messages between the host and the POD. DVS-131 also adds two interrupt enable bits that cause the POD to interrupt the host when it has new data available or when it is free to accept data. The data channel is activated by Card Enable #1 (CE1#).

The DVS-064 command interface syntax defines a set of application level messages that define the application programming interface (API) to the POD module. DVS-131 extends the DVS-064 API in a number of areas:

- Low-speed communication—This resource is modified to describe the out-of-band communications resources provided by the host. This allows the host to describe any combination of out-of-band receiver, out-of-band transmitter, or DOCSIS modem resources to the POD module.
- Copy protection—This resource is used to define the DVS-213 content protection mechanism for the OpenCable POD module.
- Host control—This resource allows the POD to control the frequency of the out-of-band receiver and the frequency and transmit level of the out-of-band transmitter.
- Extended channel—This resource allows signaling flows to be established across the extended channel. For example, a new flow request might be used to establish the flow of on-demand signaling messages from the out-of-band channel, via the POD module, to the host on-demand application. The use of the extended channel is described in detail in DVS-216.
- Generic impulse pay-per-view (IPPV)—This resource defines a general purpose IPPV API for use between a host navigation application and the security manager (in the POD module).
- Specific application support—This resource allows a private syntax to be used between the host and the POD module. It allows the use of a specific POD driver, which would be downloaded to the host, to communicate via the POD module using a private set of objects. For example, a host might support an IPPV application that is tightly coupled to the POD module to provide a specific IPPV implementation.

Extended Channel

The DVS-131 extended channel is a second physical channel that operates identically to the data channel. The extended channel uses four registers to control the exchange of variable length messages between the host and the POD and defines two interrupt enable bits that cause the POD to interrupt the host when it has new data available or when it is free to accept data on the extended channel. The extended channel is activated by Card Enable #2 (CE2#).

The extended channel allows the POD module to act as a communications resource for the host. The out-of-band channel message flows can be directed to host applications to allow two-way, real-time communications between the host application and the cable system.

Content Protection

The content community (primarily the movie studios represented by the MPAA) requires that the POD module interface support a sophisticated content protection system that encrypts the MPEG-2 payload. The content protection system authenticates the host device and allows revocation of service to fraudulent hosts.

Why Is Content Protection Required?

The combination of digital services, multimedia PCs, and the Internet pose a serious threat to any owner of copyright material. Digital picture quality is improved almost to the quality of the master copy. Multimedia PCs provide unlimited generation digital copying without quality loss. Finally, the Internet provides an inexpensive and rapid distribution mechanism for digital copies. For these reasons, the movie studios have adopted a consistent position that they will not release digital content until adequate content protection mechanisms exist.

The Motion Picture Association of America (MPAA) consider the POD interface to be a potential source of digital media because the POD module could be inserted into the PCMCIA slot of a standard personal computer. With appropriate software, the PC could be made to emulate a host, making it possible to record a clear MPEG-2 multi-program transport stream. Some form of content protection is required to prevent unauthorized copying of the digital transport payload flowing across the POD module interface.

The Content Protection System

The POD module interface is one link in the content distribution chain from the content provider to the consumer. Figure 18-8 illustrates the path of the MPEG-2 payload from the headend via the cable network to the host. (Note that in the case of a cable ready digital television, there is one less interface to worry about because the display is integrated into the host.)

Figure 18-8 *Payload Protection*

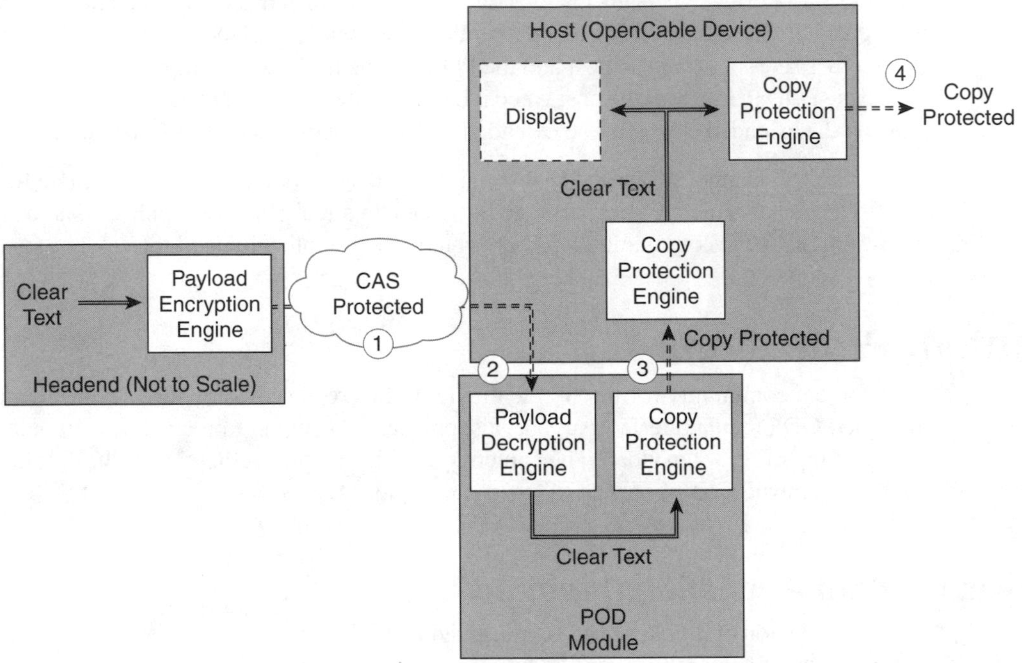

The content protection system prevents unauthorized copying of the MPEG payload when it is exposed at any interface in the content distribution chain (the numbers in the following list refer to the numbers on the figure):

- At 1 (OCI-N), the conditional access system (CAS) protects the payload from unauthorized viewing and copying.
- At 2 (OCI-C2), the conditional access system (CAS) protects the payload from unauthorized viewing and copying.
- At 3 (OCI-C2), the POD copy protection mechanism protects the payload from unauthorized copying. (At this point, the conditional access system has done its job of allowing only authorized POD modules to decrypt the payload.)
- At 4, the OCI-C2 copy protection mechanism protects the payload from unauthorized copying. Macrovision copy protection is used for analog NTSC connections. For an IEEE-1394 digital link, 5C digital transmission content protection is employed (see the section The Content Protection System in Chapter 17, "OCI-C1: The Consumer Interface").

In all exposed interfaces (OCI-N, OCI-C2, and OCI-C1), the digital payload is encrypted to prevent unauthorized copying (represented in Figure 18-8 by a dashed line).

The payload is present in *clear text* form (that is, unencrypted) *within* devices. (Clear text is represented in Figure 18-8 by a solid line.) There are three instances of clear text payload:

- Within the headend—At this location, access is securely controlled to authorized technicians.
- Within the POD module—The clear text is present only within the POD ASIC (Application Specific Integrated Circuit), making it very difficult to tap.
- Within the host—The clear text is physically protected by the case of the host. Only the serious pirate will open the case, invalidating the warranty, to make illegal copies of the payload.

Content Protection System Integrity

The content protection system is only as strong as the weakest link in the content distribution chain. Therefore, each link consists of licensed technology, and the conditions of the license dictate the copy protection methods that are employed on the *next* link in the chain. The POD module copy protection license enforces the following requirements:

- The host must monitor and respect the copy control information (CCI) associated with the content. If the host contains a recording device, it cannot be used to record *copy-never* material. (Please refer to Chapter 17 for more information on CCI.)
- The host must employ Macrovision copy protection for analog NTSC outputs.
- The host must employ 5C digital transmission content protection for IEEE-1394 outputs.

Over time, the MPAA might add additional requirements to the POD copy protection license agreement.

POD Interface Copy Protection

POD copy protection is described in detail by SCTE DVS-213. The copy protection system is very similar in operation to a conditional access system and uses some of the 5C digital transmission content protection (DTCP) technology developed for IEEE 1394. POD module interface copy protection includes several steps:

- Host authentication—The POD module authenticates the host before it releases any payload over the OCI-C2 interface. Each host contains a 5C restricted authentication device certificate that is digitally signed by the Digital Transmission License Authority (DTLA). The POD verifies that the host certificate is valid before it binds with the host. (The POD module uses the public key of the DTLA to authenticate the host certificate using public-private key cryptography.)
- Host certificate reporting—The POD module sends the host's device certificate to the headend when it binds with a host where it is stored in a database.

- Modified Diffie-Hellman key exchange—The POD module and the host exchange random numbers to generate a shared secret key. This key is refreshed periodically to reduce vulnerability to brute-force key search attacks. (A brute-force attack tries every possible key until the correct key is found.)
- Payload encryption—The POD module encrypts the MPEG-2 payload using a standard 56-bit DES algorithm. The POD module uses a session key (derived from the shared key generated by the Diffie-Hellman exchange) to encrypt the payload.
- Authentication of copy control information (CCI)—The CCI is sent to the POD, protected by the conditional access system. The POD module sends a CCI message, in the clear, to the host across the data channel. CCI authentication is achieved by using information contained in the CCI message to compute the derived session key. Any attempt at tampering with the CCI message causes the host to compute an invalid session key, preventing it from decrypting the protected content.

These steps ensure that is very difficult for the customer to make illegal copies of the payload. Nevertheless, a serious pirate could modify (or even manufacture) *fraudulent hosts*, which are hosts that are specifically designed to circumvent the copy protection system. Experience with conditional access system piracy shows that fraudulent devices are usually cloned from a single valid host. Therefore, a mechanism is implemented to *revoke* a cloned 5C restricted authentication device certificate.

Host Revocation

If a pirate modifies or manufactures hosts to produce fraudulent clones, it is usually possible to discover identity of the cloned 5C restricted authentication device certificate. This can be done in two ways:

- The POD module reports a 5C restricted authentication device certificate to the headend when it binds with a host. All valid hosts have unique certificates, so if any duplicate certificates are reported this indicates a cloned device.
- The fraudulent host can be recovered from the field.

When a cloned 5C restricted authentication device certificate has been discovered, the content providers have two ways to prevent further piracy:

- Deny service to affected channels—for example, premium movie channels.
- Deny service to affected events (or programs)—for example, pay-per-view or video-on-demand events.

This approach is called *service revocation* because it disables services using the conditional access system instead of revoking the host itself. Service revocation represents a compromise between the content providers and the consumer electronics manufacturers. In contrast, *device revocation* prevents the host from viewing any protected content. CE manufacturers are very concerned about device revocation—effectively, the screen goes dark and they have an irate customer whose digital television suddenly no longer works with any protected content. Service revocation is less draconian but still prevents piracy of premium content at the discretion of the service provider and allows the service provider to make a judgement call on which services (or events) to deny to a fraudulent host.

Applications

Now that the operation of the POD module has been described, it is possible to describe how the POD module can be used in a retail environment. There are several different classes of retail OpenCable device:

- Digital set-top
- Digital set-top with DOCSIS cable modem
- Cable ready digital television (optionally with a DOCSIS cable modem)

Digital Set-Top

Figure 18-9 shows how the POD module can be incorporated into a digital set-top (see Chapter 6, Figure 6-1) to implement a digital set-top that could be sold at retail. The POD module makes the conditional access and out-of-band communications functions *portable* by placing them in a customer-replaceable module. The customer purchases the digital set-top and leases the POD module from the local cable company (the cable company retains ownership of the POD module). Upon moving, the customer can still use the same digital set-top but must lease a different POD module from his or her new cable television supplier.

The entire MPEG-2 multi-program transport stream (from the QAM demodulator) is fed into the POD module. The POD module is responsible for all conditional access functions: authorizing services in response to messages from the headend controller and decrypting the encrypted MPEG-2 payload of services that have been authorized.

Figure 18-9 *Digital Set-Top*

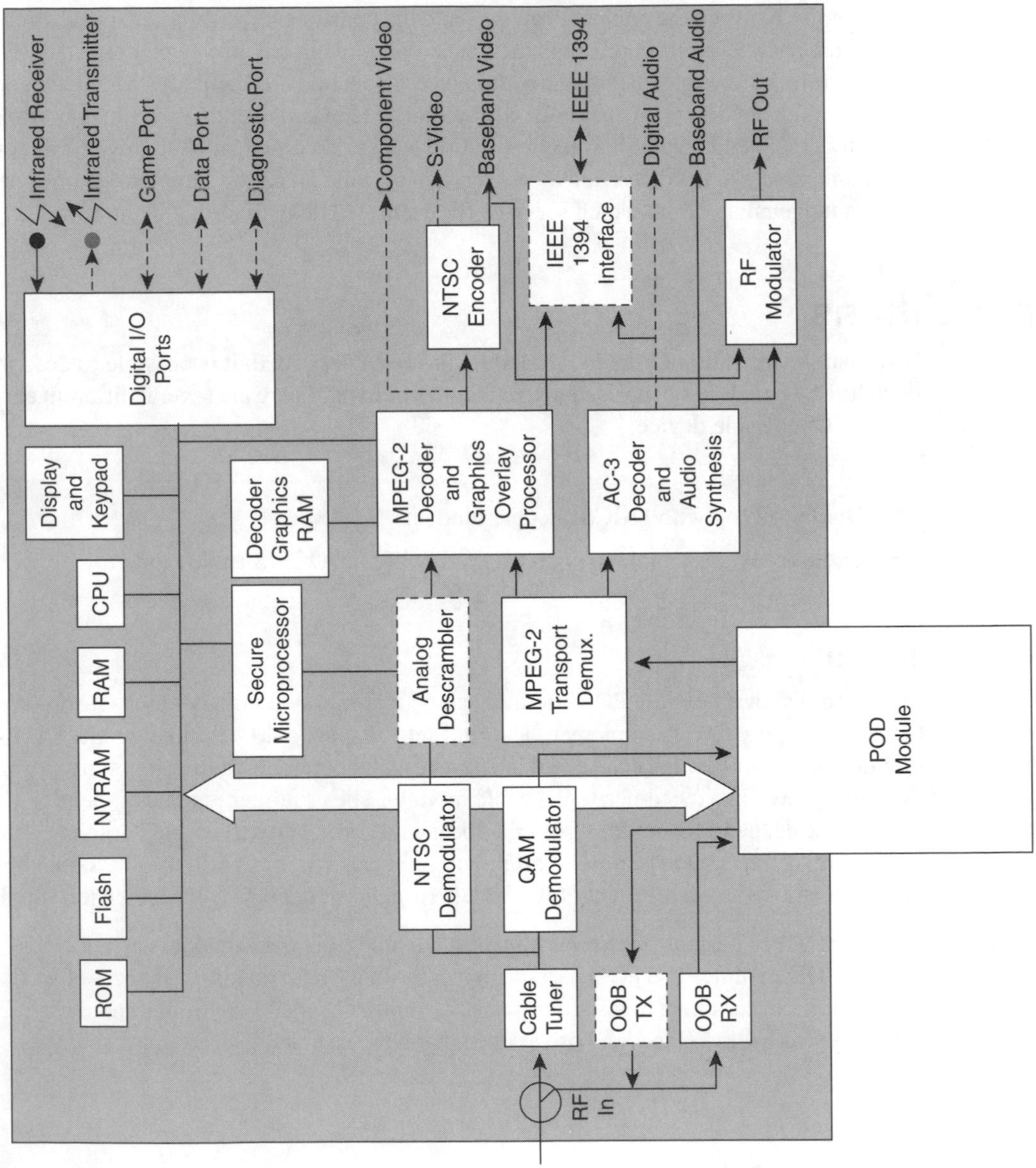

In addition, the POD module terminates the out-of-band channel. The block labeled OOB RX (out-of-band receiver) demodulates the QPSK signal and forwards it to the POD module. Two different OOB communication methods (DVS 167 and DVS 178, see Chapter 5) are currently used in digital cable systems. The appropriate type of POD module is supplied by the customer's cable operator.

The out-of-band transmitter circuit is optional (labeled OOB TX in the diagram). It is not required for subscription services, but an out-of-band transmitter is required for interactive services (see Chapter 8, "Interactive Services") and on-demand services (see Chapter 10, "On-Demand Services").

The analog de-scrambler is problematic because there is, as yet, no adopted standard for a replaceable module. It is unlikely that a retail digital set-top will contain any analog de-scrambling circuitry.

Some cable operators (notably Time Warner Cable) have decided to simulcast all analog scrambled channels in digital form so that analog de-scrambling circuitry is not required in a digital set-top. This approach requires additional investment at the headend and consumes more cable spectrum, but it reduces set-top cost and provides a migration path away from analog scrambling. There is also some early indication from the FCC that this approach satifies the Report and Order requirement for a separate analog de-scrambling module.

The retail set-top provides competition in the digital set-top marketplace by allowing the customer a choice of features and price. For example, additional features, such as a second tuner or a hard disk, could be added to the digital set-top. Another feature, which has generated a lot of interest, extends the communications capabilities of the digital set-top by adding a DOCSIS cable modem.

Digital Set-Top with DOCSIS Cable Modem

Figure 18-10 is an example of the implementation of a digital set-top with an integrated DOCSIS cable modem. Operation is identical to a standard (that is, non-DOCSIS) set-top except that the out-of-band channel is replaced by the DOCSIS channel. Nevertheless, the out-of-band receiver might still be required to receive conditional access messages for backward compatibility with existing cable systems.

Figure 18-10 *Digital Set-Top with DOCSIS Cable Modem*

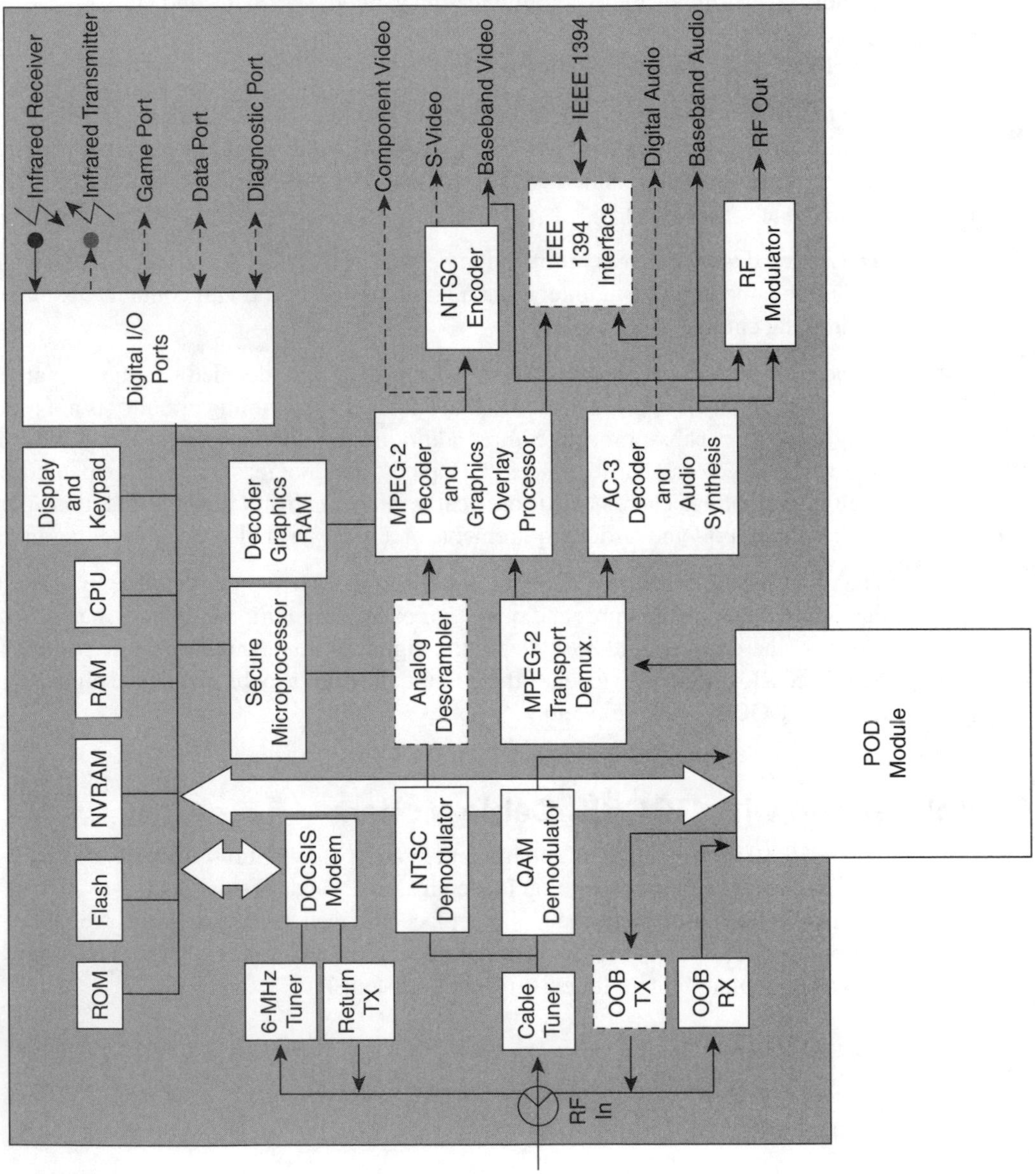

The DOCSIS cable modem provides a high-speed communications resource that can support interactive applications (particularly Internet applications). To support the DOCSIS modem, the cable operator must provide the same network infrastructure as for a standalone DOCSIS cable modem, and this infrastructure can be shared between the population of standalone cable modems and digital set-tops.

General Instrument has announced a digital set-top with equivalent functionality to Figure 18-10 called the DCT-5000. Scientific Atlanta has also announced a DOCSIS-based digital set-top called the Explorer 6000.

The digital set-top with an integrated DOCSIS modem raises some interesting issues for the cable operator and the customer:

- The cable operator would like to recover the costs associated with supporting a DOCSIS channel. These costs include provisioning of the cable modem termination s ystem (CMTS) in every hub, and building a high-speed network backbone. The cable modem business is based on a subscription service of approximately $40 per month. Will a customer who purchases a set-top with a DOCSIS modem be prepared to pay this kind of monthly premium for the additional services?
- The customer would naturally expect a wide range of new services to be associated with the addition of a DOCSIS cable modem in the set-top. However, the DOCSIS cable modem does not provide the services, only the communications link. In the personal computer model this is acceptable because every PC comes with a Web browser, and a wide range of software is available for download from the Internet. Maybe the DOCSIS-enabled digital set-top will become more like a PC to provide the new services that the customer expects.

Cable Ready Digital Television

Figure 18-11 is an example of the implementation of a cable ready digital television (CR-DTV). The integration of digital set-top and television functions allows reduction of overall cost (because components such as the power supply, tuner, MPEG-2 and AC-3 decoders, and CPU subsystem are shared). This can be seen by comparing figure 18-11 with Figure 17-4 (in Chapter 17), which provides the same functions.

Figure 18-11 *Cable Ready Digital Television*

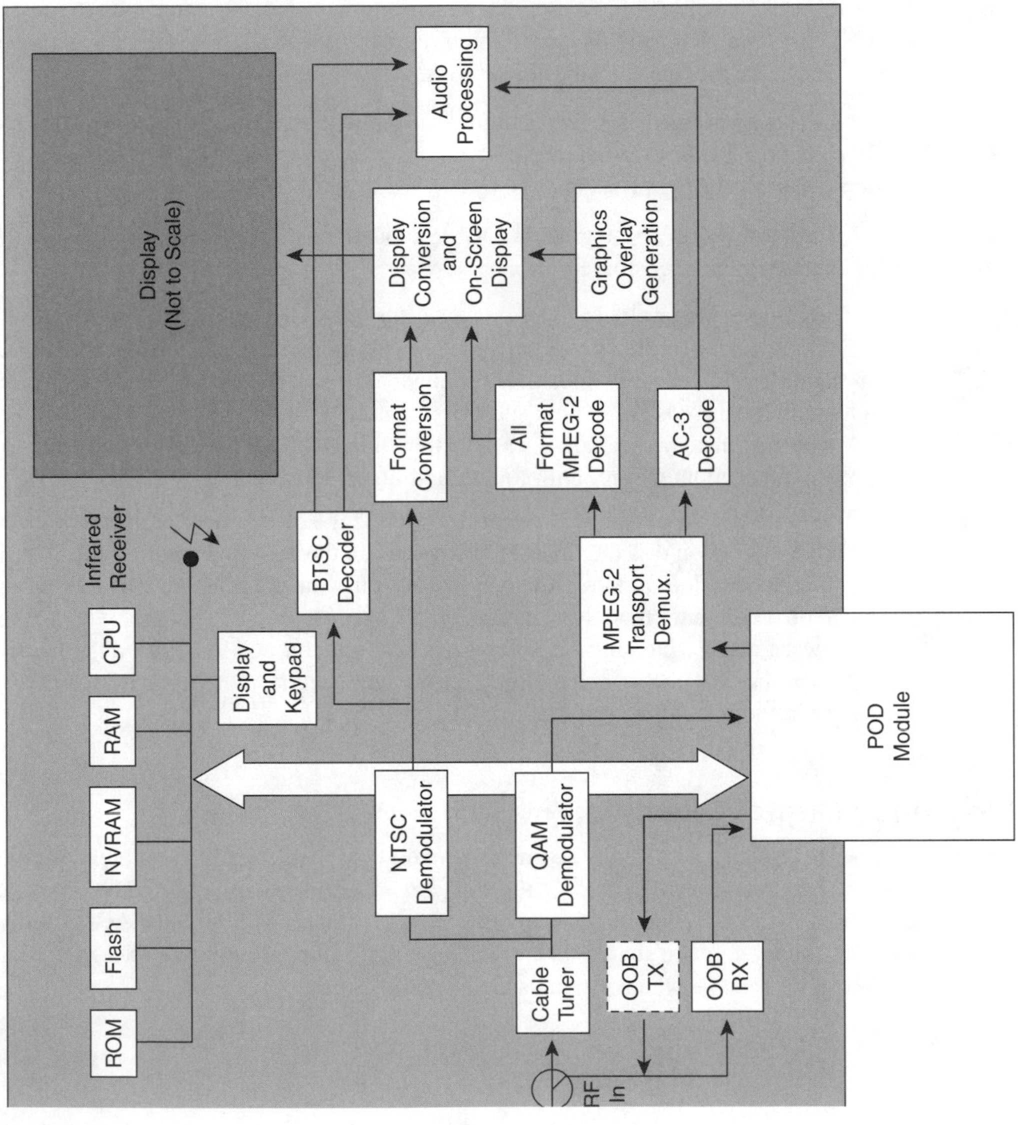

The CR-DTV has generated tremendous interest in the cable industry, in the consumer electronics industry, and at the FCC. There are some compelling advantages to cable ready devices:

- The cost of an integrated device can be considerably less than two separate devices. In fact, Moore's Law naturally pushes all consumer electronics manufacturers to higher levels of integration just to stay competitive.
- The cable operators currently provide only basic services to about 50 percent of their customers. If these customers could purchase impulse pay-per-view services without the need for a set-top, the cable operator could realize significant additional revenue.
- Many customers dislike the additional complexity introduced by set-tops. Although customers like the additional features that set-tops provide (such as electronic program guides, expanded choice of services, digital quality, and impulse pay-per-view ordering), many customers would prefer an integrated device with the same features.

Nevertheless, one of the requirements that the cable industry views as important when considering the definition of a CR-DTV is an IEEE 1394 interface so that a digital set-top can be added later to upgrade the service to a customer. Moreover, it is difficult to agree on standards for the CR-DTV. Not only does a CR-DTV have to meet a gamut of electrical specifications but it must also provide a set of services. The Joint Engineering Committee's Digital Standards Sub-Committee has been wrestling with the definition of a cable ready receiver for some time (see Chapter 13, "OpenCable Architectural Model"). This process is highly political (as well as highly technical) because there are many different interests represented.

From a cable operator's (and customer's) point of view, the CR-DTV should be able to provide all the services that are currently supported by a digital set-top. *Comprehensive cable ready* operation includes support of the following services:

- Emergency alert system (EAS)
- Navigation
- Impulse pay-per-view (IPPV)
- On-demand services
- General messaging
- Interactive services

Emergency Alert System

The FCC has mandated that cable systems support the emergency alert system (EAS), as described in Chapter 12, "Why OpenCable?" The EAS overrides *analog* channels by IF switching at the headend, but this method does not work well for digital channels:

- Overriding digital channels at the headend is difficult and expensive. For analog channels a simple IF switch is sufficient, but for digital channels this does not work because each 6 MHz QAM channel carries a multiplex of *compressed* digital programs. (To overlay text or graphics into a digital program, you have to decode it, overlay, and then reencode.)
- Some services provided in a digital system are not provided by a digital program. For example, if the customer is checking stock quotes by means of an interactive service, there is no program to override.

For these reasons, EAS is implemented using digital messaging, and the cable ready device must be able to correctly act on EAS messages. In response to an emergency alert system message, the host displays a text message, plays an audio message, or force-tunes to another channel. EAS messages are delivered to the host by means of the out-of-band and/or the in-band (QAM) channel. DVS-208 and EIA-814 (a single standard developed under the auspices of the JEC DSSC) define the format of the EAS messages. A cable ready device, with an OOB receiver, ignores in-band EAS messages in favor of out-of-band messages.

In-band carriage uses MPEG-2 private sections to insert EAS messages in the same PID used to carry in-band Service Information. Out-of-band carriage uses a data carousel (or similar) mechanism that is defined by the cable operator. The POD module forwards EAS messages across the extended channel using MPEG-2 private section syntax, as defined by SCTE DVS-216.

Navigation

Navigation includes channel numbering and electronic program guide information. Channel numbering identifies the display channel number, which is not directly related to the frequency of the channel in a digital system (channel numbering is contained in the aptly named *virtual channel table*). Cable systems use channel numbers that consist of one number, whereas the ATSC A/65 standard defines a two-part channel naming and numbering scheme for terrestrial digital broadcast.

An electronic program guide (EPG) allows the user to navigate to available services, including basic channels, premium channels, impulse pay-per-view, interactive services, and on-demand services. Program guide data can be delivered to the navigation application by means of the in-band channel and/or the out-of-band channel:

- Program and System Information Protocol (PSIP, ATSC standard A/65) describes the program numbering and the program events carried in a digital multiplex. This standard is used by digital terrestrial broadcasters and is sent in-band. In-band PSIP information typically describes only the digital multiplex in which it is sent, and this forces a single-tuner host device to periodically scan through all channels to accumulate program guide information in memory.
- The out-of-band channel is also used to deliver Service Information (SI). The format of out-of-band SI is defined by DVS-234. DVS-234 includes a number of profiles that may be used to send additional information, such as two-part channel numbering, rating information, and program guidc information.
- Cable operators use proprietary guide data formats to support specific EPG implementations. The program guide data is sent in the out-of-band channel and describes the entire range of services offered by the cable system. Sending the program guide data on the out-of-band channel conserves system bandwidth because the guide data is sent only once. The EPG is always up to date because the set-top continuously receives data via the out-of-band channel.

The POD forwards SI received on the out-of-band channel to a cable ready host over the extended channel. The POD encapsulates SI into MPEG-2 private sections for transfer across the extended channel (as defined by DVS-216). This method is designed to simplify the cable ready device design by putting the SI into the same format as in-band SI.

Impulse Pay-per-View

A cable ready digital television might support the purchase of impulse pay-per-view (IPPV) events. IPPV processing is split into two parts as follows:

- All security-related and billing functions are in the POD module.
- All user interface functions are in the host.

The IPPV API is specified by *Generic IPPV Support* in section 6.10 of DVS-131 and covers common functions related to IPPV purchase, IPPV cancel, and IPPV purchase review.

On-Demand Services

On-demand services can be modeled as an IPPV event where the program stream is dedicated to an individual subscriber. The on-demand application executes in the host and supports all the user interface functions. The generic IPPV support API can be used for VOD event purchases.

The additional streaming media control functions (that is, pause, play, fast-forward, and rewind) can be supported using DSM-CC user-to-user messages, for example. The extended channel provides the communication path for on-demand signaling (see DVS-216). After an on-demand session control is established via the session creation interface, signaling messages can be exchanged transparently between the host and the cable system.

General Messaging

General messaging supports the display of HTML 3.2–formatted text messages by the host device in response to a request from the POD module.

Interactive Services

Interactive services are supported by applications executing on the cable ready receiver—for example, an e-mail or game application. To advertise interactive services, a mechanism is required to deliver information about applications to the host, and the application service protocol (ASP) (DVS-181) is used for this purpose. Typically, interactive services are not associated with a streaming media service, so information about them is delivered via the out-of-band channel. The ASP is passed to the host via the extended channel.

The extended channel also provides the communication path for interactive service signaling. After an interactive service session is established via the session creation interface, messages can be exchanged transparently between the host and the cable system.

Issues for Cable Ready Devices

To support the services described in the preceding sections, a cable ready device must contain the appropriate software applications. There are several possible ways to provide applications:

- Each manufacturer of a cable ready device could independently develop applications. This works only for services that are fixed and standardized—for example, support of EAS messages.
- The service developers could license applications to the manufacturer of cable ready devices. This does not work very well, because each cable operator uses different licensed applications to support electronic program guides, impulse pay-per-view, on-demand services, and interactive services. To be portable, a cable ready device would have to license *all* variants of *each* application.
- The cable operator could download applications to the cable ready device to support the offered services. The drawback to this approach is that each application would have to be ported to and certified against every different model of cable ready device.

The most promising solution to the software application problem is to establish a common middleware for all OpenCable devices. Each application would have to be ported and certified against the middleware only once. In addition, each manufacturer would have to port the middleware to the OpenCable device only once.

Summary

This chapter discussed the requirements for a replaceable security module. The POD module satisfies two requirements—separation of the conditional access system and adaptation to the out-of-band communications system used to carry conditional access system messages. The POD module interface (OCI-C2) includes an MPEG-2 multi-program transport interface, an out-of-band interface, and a CPU interface. The operation of each interface is defined by DVS-131, DVS-213, and DVS-216.

The POD module can operate in one-way, two-way, and DOCSIS-based networks, and the potential advantages of using the DOCSIS cable modem standard for out-of-band communications are discussed. DVS-216 allows the POD module to provide a two-way communications resource to the host via the out-of-band channel.

The MPAA requires that the POD module interface support a sophisticated content protection system (DVS-213) that encrypts the payload to prevent unauthorized copying. The content protection system authenticates the host device and allows revocation of service to fraudulent hosts.

The POD module interface enables the development of OpenCable devices that can be made available through retail distribution channels. Nevertheless, significant issues have to be solved to make cable ready digital television a reality. These issues include the ratification of a number of standard protocols to support Emergency Alert System messaging (DVS-208, EIA-814) and navigation (DVS-234). In addition, electronic program guides, impulse pay-per-view, on-demand services, and interactive services require software applications in the OpenCable device.

References

Standards

PC Card Standard, Volume 2. "Electrical Specification." Sunnyvale, CA: Personal Computer Memory Card International Association. March 1997.

PC Card Standard, Volume 3. "Physical Specification." Sunnyvale, CA: Personal Computer Memory Card International Association. March 1997.

PC Card Standard, Volume 4. "Metaformat Specification." Sunnyvale, CA: Personal Computer Memory Card International Association. March 1997.

DOCSIS (Data Over Cable Interface Specification 1.0. "Radio Frequency Interface Specification SP-RFI-I04-980724." (Available at the DOCSIS Web site.)

DVS-064C. "National Replaceable Security Standard (IS-679 Part B)." SCTE DVS. January 27, 1997.

DVS-084. "Guidelines for Implementation and Use of the Common Interface for DVB Decoder Applications, Draft E." SCTE DVS. May 1997.

DVS-131 Revision 7. "Point-of-Deployment (POD) Module Interface Proposal." SCTE DVS. November 17, 1998.

DVS-213 Revision 2. "Copy Protection for POD Module Interface." SCTE DVS. June 1, 1999.

DVS-216 Revision 3. "Proposal for MPEG Sections in POD API." SCTE DVS. August 6, 1999.

DVS-217 Revision 1. "Point-of-Deployment (POD) Module Power Requirements." SCTE DVS. April 15, 1999.

DVS-221 Revision 1. "Point-of-Deployment (POD) Module Low Level Initialization (Informative)." SCTE DVS. April 15, 1999.

DVS-222 Revision 1. "Point-of-Deployment (POD) Module Attribute and Configuration Registers." SCTE DVS. April 15, 1999.

DVS-223 Revision 1. "Standby Power Management Control for the Point-of-Deployment (POD) Module." SCTE DVS. March 8, 1999.

Internet Resources

Personal Computer Memory Card International Association (PCMCIA)

http://www.pcmcia.org

SCTE DVS documents

http://www.cablelabs.com

DOCSIS specifications at the DOCSIS Web site

http://www.cablemodem.com

EPA ENERGY STAR Program

http://www.epa.gov/appdstar/home_electronics/

GLOSSARY

A

AAL. ATM adaptation layer, used to adapt variable length packets to fixed-length ATM cells.

analog broadcast service. One or more events transmitted via an analog transmission channel.

analog channel. An AM-VSB waveform with a bandwidth of 6 MHz used for transporting an NTSC signal from the headend to the customer's home.

ANSI. American National Standards Institute.

API. Application programming interface. The software interface to system services or software libraries.

application server. Application servers provide application services. Although some of these services will be time-critical in nature, they do not have the high-bandwidth requirement of media servers. Application servers provide services such as database services, network management services, and transactional and electronic commerce services.

artifact. Any video or audio degradation of a signal due to digital processing, particularly compression.

ASI. Asynchronous serial interface. A DVB standard for the transfer of MPEG-2 transport streams.

aspect ratio. The ratio of width to height of a picture. Standard definition television uses a 4:3 aspect ratio. High definition television uses a 16:9 aspect ratio.

ATM. Asynchronous Transfer Mode. A switching and transport protocol for efficient transmission of both constant-rate and bursty information in broadband digital networks. The ATM digital stream consists of fixed-length packets called *cells*; each one has a 5-byte header and a 48-byte information payload.

ATSC. Advanced Television System Committee.

author. A person who creates applications for digital set-top converters.

B

baseband. An unmodulated signal. Baseband video refers to a video signal before it is modulated onto an RF carrier.

BER. Bit error rate. The number of erroneous bits divided by the total number of bits over a stipulated period of time. Usually expressed as a number and a power of 10, per second.

B-frames. Bidirectional frames. MPEG-2 frames that use both future and past frames as a reference. This technique is termed *bidirectional prediction*. B-frames provide the most compression. B-frames do not propagate coding errors because they are never used as a reference.

BFS. Broadcast file system. A data carousel system by which application data can be stored on an application server and transmitted frequently to the set-top converters for application use.

block. An 8-by-8 array of pel values or DCT coefficients representing luminance or chrominance information.

broadcast. A service that is delivered to all customers. Each customer may select a particular broadcast channel out of many.

broadcast application. An application running on the set-top converter that is loaded through in-band information, inserted either at the headend or by a content provider farther upstream.

BTSC. Broadband Television Standard Committee.

C

CA. Conditional access.

CableLabs. Cable Television Laboratories. The research consortium of the cable television operating companies and originator of the DOCSIS and OpenCable specifications.

cascade. A set of series-connected components (usually amplifiers).

CATV. Community antenna television.

CBR. Constant bit rate. Transmission of data at a fixed data rate. Most frequently used in conjunction with CBR encoding of MPEG-2 video.

CEMA. Consumer Electronics Manufacturers Association.

chroma. Chrominance. The color information in a television signal.

closed captioning. A system used to transmit captioning information in the Analog VBI or MPEG-2 video user data to hard-of-hearing viewers. Since extended to support V-chip rating data.

CMOS. Complementary metal-oxide silicon.

CMTS. Cable modem termination system (for cable modems).

commercial insertion. A mechanism to insert commercials in *ad. avails* in broadcast programming. In the digital domain, digital program insertion performs this function.

conditional access and encryption. A system that provides selective access to programming to individual customers in exchange for payment.

content protection. A mechanism to protect the unathorized copying of video and audio programming.

CPTWG. Copy Protection Technical Working Group.

CPU. Central processing unit.

CRC. Cyclic redundancy check; used to detect errors in digital messages.

CSMA/CD. Carrier sense multiple access/collision detection. The shared media access control mechanism used by Ethernet.

customer. A customer who has subscribed to cable service.

D

DAVIC. Digital Audio Video Interactive Council. An international consortium working on the development of standards for interactive television.

DBDS. Digital Broadband Delivery System. Scientific Atlanta's implementation of the Pegasus architecture.

dBmV. Decibels with respect to 1 millivolt in a 75 ohm system.

DCG. Data channel gateway. The point at which a traditional IP-based network is interfaced to the HFC network.

DHCP. Dynamic Host Configuration Protocol. An Internet standard for assigning IP addresses dynamically to IP hosts.

DHEI. Digital headend extension interface. A proprietary GI MPEG-2 transport interface used by the GI Integrated Receiver Transcoder (IRT).

DigiCipher-II. GI's proprietary conditional access and encryption system for digital video.

digital broadcast service. One or more events transmitted via a digital channel.

digital channel. A QAM signal with a bandwidth of 6 MHz used for transporting an MPEG-2 transport stream from a headend to a digital set-top converter. A digital transmission channel is capable of supporting a data rate of 26.9703 Mbps (after FEC) when modulated using 64-QAM, or 38.8107 Mbps (after FEC) when modulated using 256-QAM.

digital stream. The digital equivalent of an analog television channel. A digital stream contains compressed audio and video information to provide a single program. A digital stream will typically contain a single video and multiple audio components with subtitles and other related information.

discrete cosine transform. A mathematical transform that can be perfectly undone and which is useful in image compression.

distribution hub. A signal distribution point for part of a cable system.

DOCSIS. Data-Over-Cable Service Interface Specification for retail cable modems.

Dolby AC-3. The audio encoding format adopted by the ATSC for its advanced television audio encoding. Also known as Dolby Digital.

DPI. Digital program insertion. The technique of splicing one digital stream into another to perform commercial insertion.

DSM-CC. Digital storage management-command and control. Part 6 of the MPEG-2 standard.

DTS. Decoding timestamp. A field that might be present in a PES packet header that indicates the time that an access unit is decoded in the system target decoder.

DVB. Digital Video Broadcast. A European standard for digital television.

DVS. Digital Video Subcommittee. An ANSI-sponsored standardization committee of the SCTE.

E

electrically-eraseable programmable read-only memory. EEPROM. Memory that can be electrically erased and reprogrammed.

elementary stream (ES). A generic term for one of the coded video, coded audio, or other coded bit streams. One elementary stream is carried in a sequence of PES packets with one and only one stream_id.

entitlement control message (ECM). Entitlement control messages are private conditional access information that specifies control words and possibly other stream-specific, scrambling, and/or control parameters.

entitlement management message (EMM). Entitlement management messages are private conditional access information that specifies the authorization level or the services of specific set-top converters.

entropy coding. Variable-length lossless coding of the digital representation of a signal to reduce redundancy.

EPG. Electronic program guide. An application that displays television program information, including program name, start time, and duration.

event. A unit of programming, such as a movie, an episode of a television show, a newscast, or a sports game. An event can also be a series of consecutive units of programming.

F

FAT channel. Forward applications transport channel. A data channel carried from the headend to the set-top converter in a QAM modulated channel. MPEG-2 transport is used to multiplex video, audio, and data into the FAT channel.

FCC. Federal Communications Commission.

FCS. Frame check sequence.

FDC. Forward data channel. A data channel carried from the headend to the set-top converter in a modulated channel at a typical rate of 1.5 to 8 Mbps.

FDM. Frequency-division multiplexing. A method of transmitting two or more signals by dividing the available transmission frequency into narrow bands and using each as a separate channel.

FEC. Forward error correction. A technique for regenerating lost data transmissions or error messages.

fiber node. The point at which the optical signal is converted into an electrical signal in an HFC network.

field. For an interlaced video signal, a field is the assembly of alternate lines of a frame. Therefore, an interlaced frame is composed of two fields, a top field and a bottom field.

forward path. A physical connection from a distribution hub to a digital set-top converter. A forward path can support multiple analog channels, digital channels, and forward data channels.

frame. A frame contains lines of spatial information of a video signal. For progressive video, these lines contain samples starting from one time instant and continuing through successive lines to the bottom of the frame. For interlaced video, a frame consists of two fields, a top field and a bottom field. One of these fields will commence one field later than the other.

G

green application. An application that is designed to conserve system or network resources.

GUI. Graphical user interface. A point-and-click style of interaction with the computer user, rather than a strictly character-based display.

H

Harmony DES. The DES-based encryption algorithm agreed upon through the CableLabs Harmony effort.

HDTV. High definition television. Has a resolution of approximately twice that of conventional television in both the horizontal and vertical dimensions and a picture aspect ratio of 16:9. ITU-R Recommendation 1125 further defines *HDTV quality* as the delivery of a television picture that is subjectively identical with the interlaced HDTV studio standard.

headend. The control center of a cable television system, where incoming signals are amplified, converted, processed, and combined into a common cable, along with any origination cable-casting, for transmission to customers.

HFC plant. Hybrid fiber coaxial plant. A cable network featuring optical fiber from a headend location to a fiber node, and coaxial cable from the node to individual homes.

high level. A range of allowed picture parameters defined by the MPEG-2 video coding specification that corresponds to high definition television.

HTML. A presentation language for the display of multiple media contents, typically used on the Internet.

HTTP. Hypertext Transport Protocol. The transport layer for HTML documents over IP.

Huffman coding. A type of source coding that uses codes of different lengths to represent symbols that have unequal likelihood of occurrence.

I

ICG. Interactive cable gateway. The conversion point from the core network to the HFC transport network. Core connections are terminated and MPEG-2 transport streams are reconstructed.

IEC. International Electrotechnical Commission.

I-frames. Intra-coded frames. MPEG-2 frames that are coded using information present only in the frame itself and not depending on information from other frames. I-frames provide a mechanism for random access into the compressed video data. I-frames employ transform coding of the pel blocks and provide only moderate compression.

IP. Internet Protocol. The network layer (layer 3) of the OSI Internet Protocol, providing connectionless datagram service.

IPPV. Impulse pay-per-view. A movie rental service, such as pay-per-view, but which allows the customer to purchase the right to view the movie or event through an onscreen interface.

ISO. International Standards Organization.

ITU. International Telecommunication Union.

ITV. Interactive television. All forms of interactive television applications, in which the customer can make choices in viewing. This might involve real-time transactions between the customer and the headend.

J

JEC. Joint Engineering Committee of EIA and NCTA.

K

Kbps. Kilobits per second.

KHz. Kilohertz. 10^3 of a hertz, frequency unit.

L

LAN. Local-area network.

layer. One of the levels in the data hierarchy of the MPEG-2 video and system specification.

level. A range of allowed picture parameters and combinations of picture parameters in MPEG-2.

linear optical transmission. A technique that modulates the intensity of the optical signal (from a laser), which is used in HFC systems.

local interactivity. A class of client-only applications that are downloaded to the set-top converter and interact only locally with the customer. These generate no headend impact but place considerable limitations on the application. However, this form of interactivity might become common before the wide-scale deployment of full-service networks, because it is simpler to engineer and requires only a one-way path to the set-top terminal.

luma. Luminance. The brightness of a television picture.

M

macro-block. In MPEG-2 compression, a macro-block consists of four blocks of luminance, one Cr block, and one Cb block.

main level. A range of allowed picture parameters defined by the MPEG-2 video coding specification with maximum resolution equivalent to ITU-R Recommendation 601.

main profile. A subset of the syntax of the MPEG-2 video coding specification that is expected to be supported over a large range of applications.

media asset. A movie, video clip, music clip, or any other piece of content or programming (usually when stored on a media server).

media server. Servers responsible for the delivery of time-critical media assets to client devices through the core and HFC network.

meta-data. Data that describes a media asset, such as its type, location, or duration.

modulation. The process of imposing information on an RF carrier by varying the amplitude, frequency, or phase of the carrier to allow signals to be frequency-division multiplexed in a broadband network.

motion vector. A pair of numbers that represent the vertical and horizontal displacement of a region of a reference picture for prediction.

MP@ML. Main profile at main level.

MP@HL. Main profile at high level

MPEG. Motion Picture Experts Group. An international standards-setting group, working to develop standards for compressed full-motion video, still image, audio, and other associated information.

MPEG-2. An ISO standard for the compression of video and audio assets. It supports field- and frame-based coding, which is critical for 60 field-per-second interlaced video formats. It also supports a range of resolutions and aspect ratios, and bilateral interpolation (that is, B-frames).

MPEG-2 Systems. An ISO-IEC international standard for the transport of compressed digital media (video and audio).

MSO. Multiple system operator.

N

narrowcast. A service delivered to a subset of customers. An on-demand service is narrowcast to a single customer. Other customers can receive the electrical signal but are prevented from viewing it by the conditional access system.

NATBS. Joint EIA/CVCC Recommended Practice for Teletext: North American Basic Teletext Specification (NABTS) (ANSI/EIA-516-88) (May, 1988).

navigation device. The FCC term for a set-top converter.

NCTA. National Cable Television Association.

NMS. Network management system. A system that provides fault and alarm management, configuration management, and equipment management.

NRSS-B. IS 679 Part B National Renewable Security System.

NTSC. National Television Systems Committee. The developers of a color television system that has been adopted as a national standard.

NVRAM. Nonvolatile random access memory. RAM that maintains its contents when the power is turned off.

O

OC-3. SONET Optical Carrier at 155.52 Mbps.

OOB channel. Out-of-band channel. The combination of the forward and reverse out-of-band communications channels. The OOB channel provides an IP-based communication channel between the network and the digital set-top converter.

OpenCable device. An OpenCable-compliant digital set-top converter or cable ready digital television, allowing reception of existing cable television channels and providing the user interface for future, interactive applications.

P

packet. A header followed by a number of contiguous bytes from an elementary data stream. It is a layer in the MPEG-2 system coding syntax.

payload. The bytes that follow the header byte in a packet. For example, the payload of a transport stream packet includes the PES_packet_header and its PES_packet_data_bytes or pointer_field and PSI sections, or private data. A PES_packet_payload, however, consists only of PES_packet_data_bytes. The transport stream packet header and adaptation fields are not payload.

PC. Personal computer. A computer designed for single-user operation. Examples include a Macintosh or an IBM PC-compatible.

PCMCIA. Personal Computer Memory Card International Association.

peak usage. The highest percentage of total interactive customers who are active at any given time. The network must be engineered to support a certain number of interactive sessions simultaneously.

P-frames. Predicted frames. MPEG-2 frames that are coded with respect to the nearest *previous* I- or P-frame. This technique is termed *forward prediction.* P-frames provide more compression than I-frames and serve as a reference for future P-frames or B-frames. P-frames can propagate coding errors when P-frames (or B-frames) are predicted from prior P-frames where the prediction is flawed.

PHY. Physical layers.

PID. Packet identifier. A unique integer value used to associate elementary streams of a program in a single or multi-program transport stream.

PIN. Personal identification number.

POD module. Point-of-deployment module. Used to enable retail availability of navigation devices.

PowerKEY. Scientific Atlanta's proprietary conditional access and encryption system for digital video.

ppm. Parts per million.

PPV. Pay-per-view. A movie rental service that requires the customer to call the cable company in advance of a movie or event, so the set-top converter can be programmed to receive the encrypted stream

presentation timestamp (PTS). A field that might be present in a PES packet header that indicates the time that a presentation unit is presented in the system target decoder.

profile. A defined subset of the syntax specified in the MPEG-2 video coding specification

program. A collection of program elements. Program elements can be elementary streams. Program elements need not have any defined time base; those that do have a common time base are intended for synchronized presentation.

program clock reference (PCR). A timestamp in the transport stream from which MPEG decoder timing is derived.

program specific information (PSI). PSI consists of tabular data that is necessary for the de-multiplexing of transport streams and the successful regeneration of programs.

PSTN. Public switch telephone network.

Q

QAM. Quadrature amplitude modulation. A signaling modulation scheme that greatly increases the amount of information that can be carried within a given bandwidth.

QPSK. Quaternary phase shift keying. A signaling modulation scheme in which the phase of the signal is changed. It is used for transmitting digital signals over an analog medium.

R

resident application. An application running on the set-top converter that stays resident in the set-top memory.

Reverse Data Channel (RDC). A communications channel carried from the set-top converter to the headend in a modulated channel at a typical rate of 1.5 to 3 Mbps.

reverse path. A physical connection from a digital set-top converter or cable modem to a distribution hub. A reverse path can support multiple reverse data channels.

RF. Radio frequency.

RFC. Request for Comments. An IETF standard.

rms. Root mean square.

RPC. Remote procedure call. The capability of client software of invoking a function or procedure call on a remote server machine.

S

SAP. Secondary audio program. A second monophonic audio stream (typically in a second language) delivered on the right channel of a stereo broadcast.

scrambling. The alteration of the characteristics of a video, audio, or coded data stream to prevent unauthorized reception of the information in a clear form. This alteration is a specified process under the control of a conditional access system.

SCTE. Society of Cable Telecommunications Engineers.

SDH. Synchronous digital hierarchy.

SDTV. Standard definition television This term is used to signify a *digital* television system in which the quality is approximately equivalent to that of NTSC. This equivalent quality can be achieved from pictures sourced at the 4:2:2 level of ITU-R Recommendation 601 and subjected to processing as part of the bit rate compression. The results should be such that when judged across a representative sample of program material, subjective equivalence with NTSC is achieved. Also called standard digital television.

shared media access control (MAC). A technique for sharing transmission bandwidth in a shared media.

SMPTE. Society of Motion Picture and Television Engineers.

SNMP. Simple Network Management Protocol. An IETF standard protocol for the remote management of equipment over TCP/IP networks.

solicited application. An application that is downloaded by the network at the request of the client application.

S/PDIF. Sony/Philips Digital Interface. A digital interface for transmission of AC-3 audio in compressed digital form.

splicing. The concatenation performed on the system level or two different elementary streams. It is understood that the resulting stream must conform totally to the Digital Television Standard.

SS7. Signaling system 7.

SSL. Secure sockets layer.

system clock reference (SCR). A timestamp in the program stream from which decoder timing is derived.

T

TCP. Transmission Control Protocol. The transport layer (layer 4) of the OSI Internet Protocol, providing reliable transmission of data.

TDMA. Time division multiple access.

TFTP. Trivial file transfer protocol.

ticker. An application that displays data (such as sports scores) on top of another application or analog channel.

U

UDP. User datagram protocol.

V

VBI. Vertical blanking interval. The unused lines in each field of a television signal, seen as a thick band when the television picture rolls over. Some of these lines can be used for teletext and captioning, or might contain specialized data.

VBR. Variable bit rate. Transmission of data at a variable data rate. Most frequently used in conjunction with VBR encoding of MPEG-2 data.

VOD. Video-on-demand. An application through which the customer can rent a video that can fast forward, rewind, and pause. The video is delivered by a media server.

VSB-8. Vestigial sideband modulation with 8 discrete amplitude levels.

INDEX

Numerics

A

B

C

D

E

F

G

H

I

J

K

L

M

N

O

P

Q

R

S

T

U

V

W

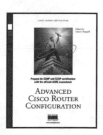

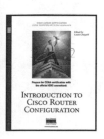

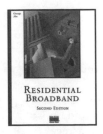

CISCO SYSTEMS

Cisco Press

ciscopress.com

Committed to being your long-term learning resource while you grow as a Cisco Networking Professional

Help Cisco Press **stay connected** to the issues and challenges you face on a daily basis by registering your product and filling out our brief survey. Complete and mail this form, or better yet ...

Register online and enter to win a FREE book!

Jump to **www.ciscopress.com/register** and register your product online. Each complete entry will be eligible for our monthly drawing to win a FREE book of the winner's choice from the Cisco Press library.

May we contact you via e-mail with information about **new releases, special promotions**, and **customer benefits**?

❒ Yes ❒ No

E-mail address ______________________

Name ______________________

Address ______________________

City ______________ State/Province ______________

Country ______________ Zip/Post code ______________

Where did you buy this product?

- ❒ Bookstore
- ❒ Online retailer
- ❒ Mail order
- ❒ Computer store/Electronics store
- ❒ Direct from Cisco Press
- ❒ Class/Seminar
- ❒ Direct from Cisco Systems
- ❒ Office supply store
- ❒ Discount store
- ❒ Other ______________________

When did you buy this product? __________ **Month** __________ **Year**

What price did you pay for this product?

❒ Full retail price ❒ Discounted price ❒ Gift

Was this purchase reimbursed as a company expense?

❒ Yes ❒ No

How did you learn about this product?

- ❒ Friend
- ❒ Cisco Press catalog
- ❒ Other catalog
- ❒ School
- ❒ Store personnel
- ❒ Postcard in the mail
- ❒ Magazine ad
- ❒ Professional organization
- ❒ In-store ad
- ❒ Saw it on the shelf
- ❒ Article or review
- ❒ Used other products
- ❒ cisco.com
- ❒ ciscopress.com
- ❒ Other ______________________

What will this product be used for?

- ❒ Business use
- ❒ Certification training
- ❒ School/Education
- ❒ Professional development/Career growth
- ❒ Other ______________________

How many years have you been employed in a computer-related industry?

❒ less than 2 years ❒ 2–5 years ❒ more than 5 years

Have you purchased a Cisco Press product before?

❒ Yes ❒ No

CISCO SYSTEMS

Cisco Press

ciscopress.com

How many computer technology books do you own?

❒ 1 ❒ 2–7 ❒ more than 7

Which best describes your job function? (check all that apply)

❒ Corporate Management ❒ Systems Engineering ❒ IS Management ❒ Cisco Networking Academy Program Instuctor
❒ Network Design ❒ Network Support ❒ Webmaster
❒ Marketing/Sales ❒ Consultant ❒ Student
❒ Professor/Teacher ❒ Other ______________________________

Do you hold any computer certifications? (check all that apply)

❒ MCSE ❒ CCNA ❒ CCDA
❒ CCNP ❒ CCDP ❒ CCIE ❒ Other ____________

Are you currently pursuing a certification? (check all that apply)

❒ MCSE ❒ CCNA ❒ CCDA
❒ CCNP ❒ CCDP ❒ CCIE ❒ Other ____________

On what topics would you like to see more coverage?

____

____

Do you have any additional comments or suggestions?

____

____

Thank you for completing this survey and registration. Please fold here, seal, and mail to Cisco Press.

OpenCable Architecture (1-57870-135-x)

Cisco Press
Customer Registration—CP0500227
P.O. Box #781046
Indianapolis, IN 46278-8046

Cisco Press
201 West 103rd Street
Indianapolis, IN 46290
ciscopress.com

Place
Stamp
Here